MAS
WCU
8/12

D0948243

Believe
Obey
Fight

TRACY H. KOON

Believe

Obey

Fight

Political Socialization

of Youth in Fascist Italy,

1922–1943

University of North Carolina Press

Chapel Hill and London

© 1985 The University of North Carolina Press

All rights reserved

Manufactured in the United States of America

Library of Congress Cataloging in Publication Data

Koon, Tracy H., 1945–

  Believe, obey, fight.

  Bibliography: p.

  Includes index.

    1. Fascism—Italy—History. 2. Italy—Politics
and government—1922–1945. 3. Fascism and youth—
Italy. 4. Youth—Italy—Political activity. I. Title.

DG571.K66 1985   945.091   84-28002

ISBN 0-8078-1652-3

To my mother and to

the memory of my father

The first step in liquidating a people . . . is to erase its memory. Destroy its books, its culture, its history. Then have somebody write new books, manufacture a new culture, invent a new history. Before long the nation will begin to forget what it is and what it was.

Totalitarianism is not only hell, but also the dream of paradise— the age-old dream of a world where everybody would live in harmony, united by a single common will and faith, without secrets from one another. . . . If totalitarianism did not exploit these archetypes, which are deep inside us all . . . it could never attract so many people, especially during the early phases of its existence. Once the dream of paradise starts to turn into reality, however, here and there people begin to crop up who stand in its way, and so rulers of paradise must build a little gulag on the side of Eden. In the course of time this gulag grows ever bigger and more perfect, while the adjoining paradise gets ever smaller and poorer.

> —Milan Kundera,
> *The Book of Laughter and Forgetting*

CONTENTS

TABLES

Many people helped and humored me during the research and writing of this book. Professor Renzo De Felice at the University of Rome provided valuable suggestions, and the staff members at the Archivo Centrale dello Stato in Rome—especially its former director, Costanzo Casucci, and Dottoressa Carrucci and Dottore Mario Missori—were unfailingly helpful and generous with their time. My thanks also to the librarians and archivists at the Biblioteca di Storia Moderna e Contemporanea, the Biblioteca Nazionale Centrale, and the Biblioteca Alessandrina at the University of Rome for their advice and their diligence in ferreting out critical source materials. My work at Stanford University was made easier by the staff of the Hoover Institution, who were patient with my innumerable requests and always ready to join in the search for an elusive book or journal.

Without the financial support I received at various stages this work could not have been completed. Grants from the Committee for Research in International Affairs and the Weter Fund at Stanford provided support in the early stages. Summer grants from the University of Virginia in 1979 and 1980 and a generous grant in 1982 from the Fondazione Luigi Einaudi, awarded by its director, Mario Einaudi, made it possible for me to take time off from teaching during the summers to complete the manuscript.

Many friends and colleagues both in the United States and in Italy have given me insightful critical comments and much support. Gian Giacomo Migone of the University of Turin provided me with valuable contacts in the Italian academic community and infectious enthusiasm for this project when I most needed it. Special thanks to my former academic adviser, Wayne S. Vucinich, who has always given freely of his time and energy. His encouragement and his humanity have for years been a source of joy and strength. I am especially grateful to my colleagues at the University of Virginia—particularly to Hans Schmitt and Enno Kraehe and to the chairman of the department, Alexander Sedgwick—for their interest and counsel. Cindy Aron's collegial support and friendship also helped to make my years in Charlottesville rewarding and enjoyable ones. The members of the departmental secretarial staff patiently typed several drafts of these chapters. Many thanks especially to Kathleen Miller and Ella Wood for their countless hours at the word xiv

———

Acknowl-
edgments

processor. Ella and Lottie McCauley helped enormously in the last stages of this project by explaining the mysteries of that machine to a particularly inept student. Finally, my gratitude to Robert, who was always there when I needed him, and whose faith and love smoothed over many rough spots.

S ince Plato sought to investigate the ways in which the values of citizenship could be instilled in the young, political thinkers have realized that the experiences of children play a vital role in the future of any nation. All political systems tend to perpetuate their structures and cultures through time; all rely to one degree or another on the mechanism of political socialization to accomplish that goal.

Political socialization is the process through which the young acquire attitudes, values, and beliefs about their political system or the way they absorb a certain political orientation from their environment. The study of political socialization is the study of cultural transmission in a given society. The goal of political socialization is to channel the behavior of the young into politically and socially acceptable forms, to make them into functioning members of the society in which they live.

The study of political socialization is one means of analyzing the phenomenon of political change or stability, for it is through the socialization process that the political culture can be altered or preserved, transformed or maintained. All societies undertake the political socialization of their young, but in this century—under the impact of two world wars, an ideological clash between East and West, and unprecedented technological advancements that have extended the control of the media over the masses—this effort has taken on new and sometimes alarming overtones. Political socialization in societies with totalitarian systems differs in tone and intensity from the process in pluralistic systems.

Totalitarian or one-party systems adopt a whole array of primary and secondary agents in the socialization process. Foremost among the primary agents is the family and, as an extension of early familial relationships, the encouragement of imitation among the young of adult leader roles. As the child's ideas become more abstract and take on cognitive substance, the secondary agents of socialization become more influential. First among those secondary agents is the school system, a crucially important tool in the political education of children. The formal instruction imparted in totalitarian states is characterized by a great degree of "manifest political socialization," the inclusion of an explicitly political content in the school curricula. There is a greater degree of uniformity and coercion in such systems than is present in pluralist societies.

The expressly political content of the formal school curricula is supplemented by the tenets of state-run youth groups and by a wide array of state-sponsored propaganda aimed at the young. The groups attempt to

reinforce a sense of belonging with badges of social acceptance: slogans, rituals, and uniforms are the external signs of community. The
goal is a collective identity, total immersion in a new group that is
bolstered by continual condemnation of the enemy, the unholy "them" as
opposed to the "us." Refusal to belong produces crisis, the necessity of
asserting diversity and separateness when all the pressures on the child
are pushing in the direction of sameness and togetherness.

For the Italian Fascist regime, youth was a central and essential
concern. Fascism was portrayed as a movement of the young, the daring,
the audacious. Italy under fascism would fulfill its glorious destiny as a
youthful and virile nation struggling against the decadent and fossilized
remnants of the old Europe for its rightful heritage. The word "youth"
occurs ad nauseam in Fascist propaganda; the choice of "Giovinezza" as
the Fascist anthem points up the fact that the mystique of youth was one
of the key myths of the movement.

The young were courted more assiduously than any other social group
in Fascist Italy. They were the regime's best hope for the future; they had
to be molded for their roles as future defenders of the faith and high
priests of the new political cult. The political socialization of youth was,
therefore, a fundamental prerequisite for the continuation of the regime:
Fascist leaders hoped that the indoctrination of youth would create a new
political culture and produce stability and continuity.

This study deals with the various tools used by the Italian Fascist
regime to socialize its young people.[1] Once the March on Rome changed
the political structure in Italy, the leaders of the regime made a deliberate
effort to change the political culture by manipulating the agencies of
propaganda and socialization. The regime also controlled the instruments of coercion, but force alone could not produce consensus or
stability. In a variety of ways the regime made a direct attempt at
political education, a self-conscious effort to shape the political values
of the young by structuring their social environment from their early
years.

Unlike many other one-party states, the Fascist regime made no concerted attempt to alter the family structure or to control early childhood
experiences within the family ambience, except indirectly by enrolling
as many parents as possible in Fascist mass organizations, such as the
Opera Nazionale Dopolavoro. The authoritarian and patriarchal structure of the Italian family, however, did not really challenge a political
system based on the myth of the leader as infallible father figure. The
real focus of the socialization process in Italy was the attempt to control
the secondary agents of socialization: the party, the educational establishment, the youth groups, and all the modes of political communication.[2]

This study of Fascist socialization can be divided into three main components: an investigation of the themes of youth-oriented propaganda, a detailed examination of the apparatus of socialization, and an evaluation of the success of the youth program.

The first theme involves an examination of the linguistic style of the Mussolinian political message and the myths manipulated by the Duce's propaganda machine. These myths were transfused into the school curricula, the youth group manuals, and the mass media. Fascism was defined as the agent of national salvation; propagandists mounted a political struggle against a whole host of internal and external enemies. The organization of consensus and the repression of dissent were two sides of the same coin, both designed as instruments of social control.

Incessant agitprop made use of a whole series of key myths that were repeated endlessly: fascism as continuing revolution, social justice, the glories of ancient Rome, the cleansing function of war and violence, the religious spirit of the new political creed, the omniscience of the leader. The regime called for sacrifices; it promised glorious achievements. The schools, the youth groups, and the media made a combined effort to keep youthful enthusiasm at a fever pitch through rituals that appealed to the simplest, and often the most violent, human emotions. Agitprop attempted to galvanize the energies of the young and to direct them into socially productive channels: the "battle of grain," the demographic campaign, and later, war.

More long-term conditioning attempted to integrate the young totally into the "new Fascist climate." In the most intimate sense, this intellectual and moral indoctrination sought to alienate the young: to deprive them of their own identity and to root in them a new identity with the leader or the group. The "new Fascist man," said Mussolini, had a religious view of life: he was motivated by unquestioning faith and lived by certain revealed truths. In order to mass-produce this new breed, however, the regime had first to eliminate all critical faculties and doubts and replace individual personal judgment with unreal stereotypes and pat answers.

The second theme—the apparatus of socialization—requires an examination of the institutions established by the Fascist regime to promote consensus among the young. This part of the study begins with an overview of the pre-Fascist educational system, the 1923 reform of education under Mussolini's first minister of public instruction, Giovanni Gentile, and the "retouchings" of that reform by subsequent ministers. This investigation of the educational system also looks at the process of *fascistizzazione* in the schools after Gentile: the regimentation of teachers, the militarization of education, and the politicization of the school curricula and textbooks. Youth groups were also a crucially important element in the socialization apparatus. This study traces the development of these groups from the earliest days to the establishment of the Gioventù Italiana del Littorio (GIL) in 1937, concentrating on the status of females in those groups and on the premilitary, sports, and welfare activities of the early youth organizations, the Opera Nazionale Balilla (ONB) and the Fasci Giovanili. The Catholic church challenged the regime's attempt to exert totalitarian control over the young, and this clash between church and state—especially over the issue of the Catholic Action groups—provides another leitmotif. The tempo of Fascist socialization intensified after the proclamation of empire. Understanding the regime's youth-oriented initiatives in the "new imperial climate" involves an evaluation of the work and impact of Giuseppe Bottai at the Ministry of National Education, the 1937 reorganization of the youth groups, the use of political manuals and the radio for indoctrination, and the character of Bottai's 1939 Carta della Scuola, or School Charter. This study also looks at the uneasy relationship between the school and the GIL and provides statistical data on the regime's youth groups according to gender, age, time, and region.

The regime devoted a great deal of time and attention to the university students who were to be its future ruling class. Rhetoric about "going to the people" aside, these students enjoyed a privileged position in the Fascist system. The development of the Fascist university groups, the Gruppi Universitari Fascisti (GUF), and the party's leadership schools for young members of the intelligentsia was, therefore, a vital part of the regime's socialization process. The party's official policy of *largo ai giovani* produced the much-debated annual competitions known as the Littoriali and the GUF press. Intended as a showcase for bright young Fascists, the Littoriali introduced some young people to a new world of dissent and, eventually, to antifascism. The editors of and contributors to the GUF newspapers were allowed a degree of free expression—within certain defined limits—not granted to other publications. Many of these papers followed the party line; some did not and were, in fact, used by anti-Fascist groups for their own propaganda. These two stories are a fascinating part of the whole history of the regime and its young people.

The study of themes and institutions answers some important questions: what children and young people in Fascist Italy learned and how they learned it. But there is a third, and more elusive, theme: How successful was the regime's socialization program? When and why did dissent or active opposition develop among many Italian young people?

The youth responded in a variety of ways to Fascist propaganda: active participation in and support for the system, some form of political careerism, total noninvolvement or apolitical behavior, active or passive deviance from Fascist orthodoxy, or active or passive opposition to the regime. No matter what the individual response—and these responses should really be described as a continuum rather than in the neat categories indicated—there were two principal personal variables affecting behavior, the individual's propensity for involvement and his or her degree of acceptance or belief in the system.

The political evolution of the young in Fascist Italy can be roughly periodized. These divisions are generalizations that can be used to characterize the overall relationship between the regime and the youth, but individual and regional factors (as will be evident from the statistical tables and autobiographical accounts below) influenced the passage from one stage to another. In general, however, these four stages of evolution can be suggested:

1. *The period of struggle to install the movement as regime*: The degree of political involvement among the youth is higher than normal, and the population is strongly oriented for or against the nascent movement. This stage is characteristic of Italian fascism in the *squadrista* period until the resolution of the Matteotti crisis in 1925.

2. *Consolidation of the movement into regime and emergence of the first generations socialized under the new order*: The propensity for political involvement is lower, and the regime, instead of producing a dynamic elite, recruits bureaucrats and young people motivated not by political faith but by personal ambition. This period of consolidation lasts from 1925 until the early 1930s, when the regime begins its military adventures.

3. *Reawakening of the movement and efforts to recreate its original élan in order to mobilize the energies of the young*: Politically involved young people tend toward some form of deviance. This is the so-called *problema dei giovani* that becomes widespread by the early 1930s.

4. *General realization among the youth that the regime has not lived up to its promises and cannot be changed from within*: The minority of young people with a high propensity for political involvement gravitate toward total rejection of or active opposition to the system. This descending portion of the parabola begins in many with the Spanish civil war, the end of the Starace era, and the passage of the racial laws, and it picks up steam with the German alliance and the outbreak of World War II.[3]

The Fascist regime did manage for a time to produce broad, albeit superficial, consensus among many Italian young people. But a caveat should be noted here. Research materials on the subject of youth and fascism present a clear class bias. Most of the PNF (Partito Nazionale Fascista) documents in the archives, the literary descriptions of the period, and the abundant autobiographical and memoiristic accounts record the impressions and experiences of a fairly restricted stratum of the youth—usually the urban middle or upper middle class, who were actively interested in politics—and tell us relatively little about much of the working class or rural youth. This bias reflects the regime's own interests, however, for despite its rhetoric, it never devoted as much time and attention to the lower class and rural young people as it did to those who were considered their social superiors.

Painted with broad strokes, the political evolution of the young during the Fascist period appears as a parabola with ascending and descending curves determined by the personal reactions and qualities of the young (internal factors) and by fluctuations in the direction of the regime over time (external factors). The final sections of this study investigate the various factors that contributed to plotting the points on this curve. Fascism was simply a given for many young people reared in the new political climate; this view of fascism-as-normality was reinforced by what one historian of the period called the "conspiracy of silence" by the old ruling classes and the church.[4] Acceptance was conditioned as well by the ever-present specter of economic ruin and by the desire among many highly motivated young people to make a mark in the professions. Fascist propaganda also attracted many of the young by appealing to their idealism and by encouraging them to believe that they had a real role to play in the future. Fascism was portrayed as a living thing, capable of changing and of being changed by the young. It was billed as a permanent revolution, not the past but the future, which would be based on a new social justice. Many were attracted by this mirage and by the prospect of being involved in the construction of that new society. Disillusionment came at different times and for different reasons. The slow-dawning realization that fascism *did not have to exist* is the common theme of much of the autobiographical testimony of the period. The title of Ruggero Zangrandi's "contribution to the history of a generation" describes the experiences of many young people who made the "long voyage through fascism" to the other side.[5]

In some sense Fascist mythmaking sowed the seeds of its own failure. The incessant and hammering propaganda, the repetitiveness and sterility of official culture, produced boredom and cynicism in many. Words were not enough to paper over the increasingly yawning cracks in the Fascist structure, or to temper social contrasts or disguise mounting failures. The divergence between observable fact and familiar rhetoric created at a certain point in many a cognitive dissonance: the more often the myths were repeated, the less credible they became. The sense of incongruity among the young grew as the subjective orientation toward the system instilled by the socialization process received less and less validation from their actual experience of the world.

The Fascist regime was never able to rid itself of this basic contradiction between rhetoric and reality. The *problema dei giovani* that came to the fore when the young finally became disillusioned with the never-realized promises plagued the regime until the day it was pushed out of existence. This deep-seated disaffection among many young people contributed not a little to the rather anticlimactic events of 25 July 1943.

Believe

Obey

Fight

CHAPTER ONE

![]

"The Kingdom of the Word"

In mass societies, myth takes the place of history.
—*William Bosenbrook*

Italian fascism was heir to a variegated political and cultural legacy, an intellectual product of the crisis of the 1890s. In its revolt against positivism, fascism echoed Friedrich Nietzsche and Henri Bergson. It emphasized spirit over matter, faith against reason, action over thought. Like the Futurists, the Fascists praised the purifying effects of war and dynamism and condemned pacifism and neutralism. For the Fascists, as for F. T. Marinetti and the Futurists, the future of Italy lay with the "young, the strong, and the living."[1] Like Gabriele D'Annunzio, Benito Mussolini had a vision of politics that glorified adventure and struggle, the sexual imagery of domination and virility, the religious rhetoric of sacrifice and duty, and, above all, the role of the man of action who could control the mass and mold it to his own design. Fascism replaced economic man with heroic man, decried the decadence and corruption of liberal and parliamentary systems, and exalted the cult of the elite, of force, and of youth. Against the fragmentation and anomie of modern mass society, it placed the harmony, belonging, and identity of the national community. Rejecting the rotting and defeatist *Italietta* of the past, it promised a glorious Italy in the future.

Fascism did have roots deep in the intellectual developments of the late nineteenth and early twentieth centuries. But it was less a coherent ideology than a cry of pain—or a war cry. It did not have an oracle like Marx, Lenin, or Mao, nor did it possess a body of sacred, written truths against which ideas and behavior could definitively be measured as orthodox or heretical. The titular theorists of the regime, Giovanni Gentile and Alfredo Rocco, both tried to provide such an ideological base ex post facto. But the theories of the ethical state or corporativism, though much in evidence in the regime's official propaganda, were never really the guides of political action in Fascist Italy.

Mussolini's real uniqueness lay not in the depth of his political analysis nor in the originality of his thought but in his conception of the political process as the art of political communication. No matter which side one takes in the hoary debate about fascism as ideology or how one traces its intellectual debts, fascism did have a doctrine, an essentially action-related set of ideas that were used to elicit a certain response from the masses, to pull certain emotional and intellectual strings. Mussolini's greatest talent—perhaps his only genuine talent—was his ability to manufacture and communicate myths and slogans that captured the popular imagination. Fascism made widespread use of the media and the educational system to push a whole series of myths that were, by virtue of repetition and familiarity, more real to many Italians than the philosophical musings of Gentile or Rocco or even the universally quoted, quasi-inspired articles on fascism by Mussolini himself. In these myths is the essence of fascism as it was presented to the Italian people: they tell us what the regime's leaders wanted the Italians to believe and what they wanted them to become. Fascism promised that it would transform Italy; many took that promise seriously. In order to understand how Italians (and in this context young Italians) saw fascism, we must pay more attention to its rhetorical elements, for rhetoric was an absolutely crucial part of what fascism was and why it was successful—at least for a time. Rhetoric, said Franco Venturi, "is the reduction to the absurd of all the ideological currents that had given rise to fascism. . . . The . . . regime was the kingdom of the word. Or better . . . of the loudspeaker."[2]

The Political Myth, Elites, and the Leader

Benito Mussolini's views on human nature and man in society show an intellectual kinship with the ideas of two French thinkers, Gustave Le Bon and Georges Sorel, and with contemporary studies of political elites by Vilfredo Pareto, Gaetano Mosca, and Robert Michels. All were interested in the historic function of the determined minority and in the relationship between belief systems and the political process.[3]

Mussolini readily acknowledged his intellectual debt to Gustave Le Bon (1841–1931), author of an influential study on the psychology of the crowd, *Psychologie des foules*, first published in 1895.[4] According to Le Bon, the art of politics had to be based on the irrationalism and conservative nature of mass man. Any successful political leader had to know how to harness and control the instinctual side of human nature. Le Bon emphasized the fundamental role played by belief in history. That faith might be an illusion, but its force in history was for Le Bon undeniable: "All great historical facts are the . . . direct or indirect consequences of strong impressions produced on the crowd."[5]

Le Bon suggested ways to turn the irrationalism of the mass into a positive social force and to counter the chaos it produced. The crowd could be tamed by the use of "magic": the creation of a myth that would have such powerful appeal that it could produce the national consensus the leaders—"*les grands meneurs des foules*," as Le Bon called them—were seeking. Their role was to create faith by striking the imagination of the crowd repeatedly with images, words, and slogans to produce feelings and beliefs that bolstered the position of the leader and his movement. To these "creators of illusions" the crowd, "a servile flock incapable of doing without a master," erected temples and altars. Gathered in a crowd they lost all force of will and turned instinctively to the man possessing those qualities of decision and charisma they themselves lacked. For Le Bon the mainspring of all authority was the personal prestige of the leader, which allowed him to exert a "magnetic fascination" on all those around him.[6]

In his talks with the German journalist Emil Ludwig, Mussolini elaborated on his notions of social psychology and political mythmaking in terms that were very reminiscent of Le Bon. "The mass," he said, "is a flock of sheep until it is organized. . . . The mass loves a strong man. The mass is a woman!"[7]

Like Le Bon, Georges Sorel (1847–1922) was interested in questions of social psychology: How do men in groups behave? What is the relationship between the individual and the collective consciousness? Sorel's ties to Italy went back to 1895, when he first began publishing in Italian journals.[8] *Reflections on Violence* appeared in Italy in 1906, and Sorel's work was much discussed and debated, especially among Italian Socialists, who often took exception to his heterodox views on Marxism. Mussolini did not know Sorel personally, but he was familiar with his work and referred to it in several articles. Though Sorel's influence in Italy had declined by the immediate postwar period, Mussolini did acknowledge his debt to Sorel in his 1932 article on fascism in the *Enciclopedia Italiana*, at least in part to give his own movement intellectual respectability.

Sorel criticized the determinism of the Marxist view and called for a moral and psychological reinterpretation of Marxism, which he saw not as a science but as "social poetry."[9] For Sorel, social change was not the automatic consequence of economic or material factors but involved questions of psychology: what moves men to social action? Emphasizing the role of heroic violence in the class struggle, Sorel claimed that the proletarian revolution would be led by an elite minority and based on an absolute moral rejection of any compromise or concession with the bourgeois order. Galvanized by the political myth—for Sorel the general strike—the masses would be shaken out of their inertia and moved to action. The political myth, then, aimed at arousing sentiments and not analysis.[10] The manipulation of the revolutionary myth led believers to see themselves as an army fighting for their apocalyptic vision of the future. Social action was thus the visible expression of the psychological reality of the myth, an image capable of fostering feeling and social cohesion. A political philosophy based on such a myth was not a logical or rational program but an incitement, a spur to action and loyalty.

Sorel was contemptuous of the corrupting influence of parliamentary democracy and fascinated with the role of syndicates and representation by economic category. He also came to see the power of the national myth. By 1910 Italian nationalists such as Enrico Corradini were speaking of national syndicalism: a reconciliation of economic syndicalism and political nationalism. Corradini translated the Socialist rhetoric of class struggle from a horizontal proletarian solidarity across national boundaries to a vertical solidarity among classes of the same nation. Public enthusiasm for the Libyan war of 1911–12 testified to the political value of the national myth. Many Socialists, including Mussolini, remained opposed to the Italian involvement in the Libyan war, but the currents of revolutionary syndicalism and nationalism forged a new, and potent, political combination in Italy. Mussolini's realization of the political potential of the mass-mobilizing national myth helps to explain his "conversion" of 1914.[11]

A trio of social scientists—Pareto, Mosca, and Michels—also influenced Mussolini's notion of the political process. All three of these thinkers helped to foster a general antidemocratic outlook by emphasizing the minority over the majority, the few over the many. All criticized what they saw as the reductionist fallacy of historical materialism and emphasized the role of belief systems in the social sciences while downplaying the causal relationship between economic factors and all other social phenomena. For Pareto, individual or group decisions were governed by "derivations" or "residues"; Mosca insisted on the importance of "political formulae"; Michels termed them "fictions."

In his *Les systèmes socialistes*, published in 1902, Vilfredo Pareto (1848–1923) called the Socialist apocalypse a mirage. The Marxist view of class struggle, he said, would produce not a true people's democracy but the rule of another "political class," an elite behind the proletariat ready to reap the benefits of working-class actions for their own individual or class interests. In this and other works—most notably his *Trattato di sociologia generale* (1915), translated as *The Mind and Society: A Treatise on General Sociology*—Pareto argued that there was no scientific foundation for the sovereign rights of the majority and struck at the roots of both socialism and democracy by proclaiming that government "by the people" was always a facade for the control of the state by an oligarchy, mere rhetoric masking domination of the disorganized majority by the organized minority. These elites vindicated their power through an appeal to the masses based on emotion: "Human actions," according to Pareto, "have their origin not in logical reasoning but in sentiments."[12]

This notion was also advanced by Gaetano Mosca (1858–1941) in *The Ruling Class* (*Elementi di scienza politica*), published in 1896. Mosca maintained that the organized minority always held and justified power by the use of "political formulae," energizing myths that were functional—they produced consensus—and not rational. Robert Michels (1876–1936), much influenced by Max Weber's notion of charismatic power and by Mosca, argued in *Political Parties* (1911) what he termed the "iron law of oligarchy" and emphasized the sociopsychological aspects of political behavior: the susceptibility of the mass to the appeal of a charismatic leader, the innate conservatism of the masses, and their resistance to social change.

For all of them, myths served to legitimize the claims of the political class or the elite that was the real center of social control over the majority. As legitimizing fictions, the myths organized human emotions for social action; they mobilized the mass on the side of the elite in its struggle for power and justified its hold on power. Myths allowed a dynamic minority to lead and control a passive majority by playing on the suggestibility of the mass and its general psychological predisposition to arrange itself in hierarchical order and to conform.

Alfredo Rocco explained that fascism rejected the theory of popular sovereignty, proclaiming that the "great mass of citizens is not a suitable advocate of social interests," because the capacity to subordinate private interests to the good of the whole "is a very rare gift and the privilege of a chosen few."[13] The "people" were replaced by the "few elect," quantity by quality, democracy by aristocracy. In Fascist theory, therefore, each individual was an integral part of the whole; there was no real distinction between public and private spheres, for the organic view of society synthesized the interests of the individual, society, and the state. The ruling class existed to remind the individual of his or her relationship to this organic community, because only the party leaders had a true consciousness of the destiny of the nation. Hence the rise of the single party as a pedagogical and ethical imperative: the needs of the society and those of the party were one and the same. Fascism thus rejected the principle of equality as a "soft" Judaeo-Christian ideal out of keeping with the new virile spirit of creative inequality. Society was divided into superiors and inferiors: believers and nonbelievers, leaders and led, men and women. The extreme form of Fascist elitism was the emphasis on the role of the leader, the one man who incarnated the aspirations and desires of the community. The many became the few; the few became the one.

Language and Myth: The Mussolinian Model

When Mussolini was asked in 1922 to write a collection of essays on the war, he declined. "Today in Italy," he said, "is not the time for history. Nothing is yet concluded. It is the time for myths. Everything is yet to be done. Only the myth can give strength and energy to a people about to hammer out its own destiny."[14] Communicated as they were in a variety of forms and a vast array of propaganda, these myths were one of the principal instruments used by the regime to create, organize, and maintain consensus. To understand the appeal of the regime, we must understand how fascism presented itself to the young, what images of fascism were presented in the regime's educational system and textbooks, youth organizations, and youth-directed media. The political myths were the appearance rather than the substance of fascism, what the regime said it was rather than what it was in reality. Without understanding how the regime spoke to the young, we cannot really understand that the development of dissent or antifascism among them was not merely a change of political views but for many a deep internal struggle for liberation from an illusion once accepted as real. "Inculcated from infancy and insistently repeated," these myths were "offered as an answer to youthful aspirations and hopes . . . to their desire for progress and liberty."[15]

Mussolini found his myth in a form of nationalism heavily overlaid with Socialist rhetorical flourishes. He had inherited an anarchistic/ Blanquist brand of socialism from his father, and often spoke in Marxist idiom after his final break with organized socialism. But his Marxist culture was superficial and secondhand and his ideas of revolution indeterminate and indefinite, based less on an objective analysis of the structure of society than on an instinctive recognition of the political value of action and violence and the emotional appeal of Socialist rhetoric.

World War I dramatized for Mussolini the power of the national myth and the weakness of working-class solidarity; if the notion of class unity would not inspire sacrifice in the multitude, men would fight and die for king and country. After Mussolini's break with socialism, his new orientation was symbolized in the name of his newspaper: *Lotta di classe* became *Il Popolo d'Italia*. In November 1914, in his first editorial for the new paper, Mussolini wrote, "It is certain that the nation represents a stage in human progress that has not yet been transcended. . . . The sentiment of nationality exists, it cannot be denied!"[16]

Fascist rhetoric was a mélange of socialism and nationalism: socialism stripped of its antinational, international, and pacifist overtones and inspired instead with love of country and militarism. In October 1922, just a few days before the March on Rome, the future Duce announced: "We have created our own myth. . . . Our myth is the nation . . . the greatness of the nation!"[17]

Fascist myths had two essential functions, positive and negative. The early myths were often negative. They aimed at turning the masses against internal and external enemies defined as politically dangerous or antinational: the red assassins, corrupt liberals, bourgeois defeatists, plutocratic Europe. A whole series of positive myths served to inculcate in the mass the new Fascist virtues of sacrifice, loyalty, and faith and to convince them that fascism was indeed building a new world. In both senses, the myth tended to portray fascism as the agent of Italian salvation.[18]

Rhetoric and the communication of political myths were not mere window dressing in Fascist Italy but an essential function of the regime. Denis Mack Smith has claimed that Mussolini devoted more time to publicity than to policy.[19] It might rather be said that in Fascist Italy, under the watchful eye of the Duce, publicity became policy. Mussolini, polemical journalist par excellence, was well aware of the power of the word. He was convinced that the masses would accept almost anything provided the appeal were clothed in the proper rhetorical garb. For Mussolini language had a magical power. "And why do I insist on proclaiming that that October was historically a revolution?" he asked on one occasion. "Because words have their own tremendous magic."[20]

Mussolini was a consummate propagandist, actor, and stage manager. His political style reflected his thought processes, which were less intellectual than instinctual. In politics he relied on his own understanding of group psychology and his intuition—what he often referred to as his "animal instinct"—rather than on strict adherence to ideology and logic. He was influenced by many other thinkers, but his approach to politics was based not on principles, at best useful nails on which to hang a particular policy, but rather on an intuitive grasp of what he perceived as the psychological needs of the mass.

Mussolini's insistence on the importance of myths and words was closely related to his conception of politics as gesture or theater and his belief in the political value of histrionics. Here he was influenced by D'Annunzio and the Futurists. D'Annunzio had a keen sense of the role of style and self-dramatization in politics. His departure for the war at the age of fifty-two, his daring flights, and his dramatic Fiume adventure were examples of gesture as politics. Futurist "evenings" were really a kind of political psychodrama, theatrical spectacles full of dramatic invocations, noise, sometimes general fisticuffs, and a prodigious waste of vegetables. Histrionic, too, were Mussolini's 1904 threat to God to strike him dead; his plane rides, car races, horse jumps, duels, and violin playing; and his poses: legs spread apart, chest thrust out bellicosely, jaw tensed. His speeches were dramatic spectacles: great rivers of fiery rhetoric alternating with long, pregnant pauses.

Mussolini's long experience as a political journalist and his preoccupation with the word affected his style of administration. He spent an inordinate amount of his time each day tending his public image and that of his regime: poring over foreign and domestic newspapers, writing articles, checking on the circulation figures for the PNF press, and composing the daily *veline* or instructions to the press that regulated in minute detail what did or did not appear in Italian papers and, just as important, how it should all be said.[21]

Mussolini's rhetorical and oratorical style developed during his career as a Socialist journalist. His style fitted his character: aggressive, polemical, and contentious. He spoke as he wrote, always conscious of how his words could be translated into banner headlines or apodictic slogans. His characteristic use of language and his style of political communication did not change much from his early days as a Socialist. In 1914 he said: "The great masses called to found a new kingdom do not need so much to know as to believe. . . . The Socialist revolution is not a mental schema or a calculation but, above all, an act of faith."[22] The use of the words "kingdom," "revolution," and "faith" is not coincidental.

Words and phrases were shorn of their semantic content and used as evocations, to conjure up feelings and images. The whole process was a kind of psychocultural conditioning based on irrational messages that sought to depersonalize individuals and reassert their identity with the community and the group, to identify them with some transcendent reality—nation, fatherland, state, empire. Mussolini was a master of what he called the action word. The goal was not to communicate rationally but to make the mass act, to persuade or dissuade, to incite, to move. The supreme moment in this communion was the leader's use of rhetorical questions to the multitude (a D'Annunzian device), which established an immediate contact with the crowd and associated the individual with the communal enterprise. The regime also adopted techniques of nonverbal communication. Fascist myths were presented in a whole series of elaborate rituals and ceremonies, oceanic meetings, uniforms, salutes, and flags, the goal being not dispassionate reflection but belonging and identity. These functions were liturgical and military; they stressed the view of fascism as a new religion on the march, an image of an Italy no longer in chaos but arrayed in imposing and orderly ranks and marching off in the service of a new cause, a new cult.

Mussolini's own characteristic use of language had a normative influence. The regime's propaganda machine sought to impose a certain linguistic style and use of particular oratorical and rhetorical models as an army of journalists and spokesmen took care to imitate the Mussolinian message. To investigate the Fascist use of political myth is thus to investigate the manipulation of a linguistic system, a system of political image making that was one of the regime's most powerful means for the organization of consensus and the imposition of cultural and political conformity.

Mussolini's oft-quoted utterances were used in Italian schools as models of expression, so that a generation of Italians was familiarized with the acceptable Mussolinian style and the ethos of his movement. The

standard grammar used in Italian secondary schools after 1934 included
Mussolini's inimitable (but often imitated) phrases alongside those of
such other great Italian authors as Dante, Petrarch, Machiavelli, and
Manzoni.[23] For the edification and illumination of the masses, collections of his sayings were published (note the religious allusion) as the
Breviario mussoliniano, a kind of Fascist version of Chairman Mao's
little red book.

As there was an official Fascist style of greeting, dressing, walking,
eating (sparingly), and even furniture, there was also a Fascist style of
writing and speaking and thinking: the Mussolinian model. His linguistic style made frequent use of rhythmic and tonal variations, hyperbole,
imagery, metaphor, and alliterative and onomatopoeic expressions chosen for their sound and evocative power. Official Fascist style emphasized conciseness and vigor of expression, as contrasted with democratic and liberal prolixity. Myths were conveyed in aphorisms, lapidary
phrases, and punchy slogans that became a continuing and hammering
presence on the walls of offices, factories, barracks, party headquarters,
and railroad stations; on the radio; and in textbooks, cartoon strips, and
newspaper headlines.[24]

Mussolinian, and hence official, propaganda used a vocabulary taken
from the barracks and the church that emphasized the regime's view of
politics as a religious mobilization in a great national struggle. Military
expressions portrayed Fascist Italy as a new army on the march in the
service of a rejuvenated nation. Words such as "struggle," "courage,"
"heroism," "intransigence," "cowardice," "death," "glory," "discipline,"
"war," and "order of the day" were commonly used to conjure up images
of strength and implacable (another favorite) force. Fascist will was
herculean, potent, granite, tenacious, made of steel. Fascism was not
only an army but also a cult. A religious lexicon hammered home this
message repeatedly, using words like "martyr," "sacrifice," "rite,"
"altar," "redemption," "communion," "mission," "commandment," and
"hierarchy." Fascism was a "sacred" or "holy" struggle; war the "supreme sacrifice"; service of the nation a "divine commandment."

The regime's attempt to impose a linguistic model produced a policy
of linguistic autarky or cultural chauvinism designed not only to root out
offensive foreign expressions from the language but also (after Gentile
left the Ministry of Public Instruction) to prevent the use of dialect in
the schools and the media. Foreign expressions were seen as signs of
unacceptable cultural deference.[25] Perhaps the most-publicized aspect
of the Fascist attempt to purify the Italian language of foreign influences
was Achille Starace's "anti-*lei*" campaign to prohibit the use of the third
person singular, which he saw as a clear sign of bourgeois snobbism and
a remnant of foreign invasions. The true Fascist used the second person
singular, *tu*, or the second person plural, *voi*. Dialects were, in the view

of the policy makers, holdovers from an inglorious past. As the fulfillment of the promise of the Risorgimento, fascism had united Italy; it had completed D'Azeglio's task of "making Italians." Hence all regionalism and particularism belonged not to the Fascist future but to the decadent and discarded liberal past.

Fascist myths were an amalgam of traditional and revolutionary themes, of nationalist and Fascist rhetoric. National themes emphasizing the past, tradition, and stability coexisted with those that portrayed fascism as revolution, dynamism, struggle, and a rupture with the sad past. Despite the regime's totalitarian pretensions, Fascist Italy was a dyarchy. The role of the king as a symbol of national unity and as a guarantor of national tradition and continuity was a crucial part of Fascist propaganda, a clear recognition of the monarchichal sentiments of the country and of the army, which, after all, took an oath of loyalty to the king and not (as did the militia) to the Duce. The importance attached to national emblems was very evident in iconography, where national and Fascist symbols regularly appeared side by side. To instill the message of fascism as liberator of the nation in chains, the two sets of symbols were linked inextricably in the popular mind: the muscular arm of a black-shirted *squadrista* held aloft the national flag; the *fasces* were superimposed over the tricolor or the Savoyard coat of arms.[26]

The Mussolini Myth: The Leader and the Nation

The kernel of Fascist mythology as presented to Italians was the identification between regime, symbolized by the *capo*, and the nation. Fascist propaganda unrelentingly hammered home the equations: love of country equaled faith in fascism, party equaled nation, fatherland equaled regime, Mussolini equaled Italy.

The deification of the leader did not take place overnight, but along with the consolidation of the regime went the transformation of Mussolini the Fascist into Mussolini the leader of fascism, from party leader to national and international strong man. In 1921 Mussolini had warned his followers: "Cure yourselves of me." The same man, speaking from the same podium in 1932, said: "You must be proud to live in the times of Mussolini."[27]

During the first years of the regime, the Fascist propaganda machine was aided by the widespread recognition and respect Mussolini seemed to enjoy abroad and by the apparent lack of real alternatives at home. Mussolini took great pains to cultivate good relations with all foreign journalists in Rome by granting hundreds of interviews and audiences with visiting writers. The effort paid handsome dividends as a steady stream of laudatory articles and books spread the general feeling among Italians that their nation was finally getting the treatment it deserved and that Italy was at last in the vanguard of European political and social events.

Legions of foreign correspondents returned from Italy and wrote the old saws about Mussolini making the trains run on time, about the tireless leader who never slept (or at least never turned off the lights in his office) or the fearless savior who had rescued Italy from the "Bolshevists, brigands, and Black Handers."[28] These tributes were given great play in the Fascist press. In 1923 Lord Curzon's characterization of Mussolini as a "man of marvellous energy and iron fist" was published in the *Popolo d'Italia* as the "eulogy of Lord Curzon."[29]

Mussolini was omnipresent. By the time the international situation began to degenerate and criticism arose from many quarters, Italians had grown used to seeing his familiar jutting-jawed face glaring down at them in every public place. But as people began to see the cracks in the facade of fascism more clearly, some of them clung to the legend of the Duce with even greater tenacity. Renzo De Felice claimed that Mussolini's personal prestige developed in almost *inverse* proportion to the prestige of the party, and that as the Fascist experiment began to show its "limits and its negative aspects, these people clutched on to faith, to hope in the [only] man . . . able to understand the true aspirations of the country, to set himself up as the arbiter and mediator of conflicts and internal contrasts and to impose his own will on all."[30] This was not accidental but a reflection of the essence of the Fascist regime. By the late 1920s the PNF had been shorn of its effective role in politics, and its energies, as Giuseppe Bottai commented, were "directed toward crystallizing the power held by the Duce."[31]

The Fascist regime was based on a compromise with the established elites and power structures—the church, the monarchy, big capital and landowners, and the army. Mussolini's essential function, then, was to serve as a mediator, and this role entailed clipping the wings of the more radical Fascists and reducing the PNF to the passive role of a chorus applauding policies decided on high. Mussolini did not dismantle the machinery of the state; indeed, after the famous circular of 5 January 1927, the real representatives of government policy in the provinces were not PNF officials but the state prefects under the control of the Ministry of the Interior.[32] Leaders of the PNF might grumble that the Duce was betraying the principles of the Fascist revolution, as did *ras* like Roberto Farinacci, but the institutions of the Fascist regime sanctified Mussolini's choice: a "totalitarian" system that proclaimed itself a revolution but safeguarded the interests of privileged groups and suppressed opposition to the growing power of the leader. Cohesion and consensus were thus organized around the "cult of the Duce" and not around the ideals of the Fascist movement. Opposition was defined as anti-Fascist and antinational.

Discipline and obedience were the highest virtues of the new Italian and the loyal party follower. The Mussolinian vision of the totalitarian state demanded the bureaucratization and devitalization of the party. But without an effective political party, the promise of creating a new ruling class was an illusion. The future of the regime was tied increasingly to the life of Mussolini and the effectiveness of his cult and myth.[33]

In its appeal to the patriotic and conservative bourgeoisie, the regime played on the people's need for security and order and stressed those moderate aspects of fascism that would guarantee harmony. Many bourgeois Fascists viewed the extremist *ras* with suspicion, but they could sympathize with the old nationalists and with Mussolini, a strong man in an era that demanded decisive action. He had saved Italy from the menace of social upheaval and had made it respected in the world. Without him the edifice of fascism would collapse and Italy would be plunged once again into chaos. Faced with Mussolini's successes, the negative and sometimes worrisome aspects of the regime passed into secondary importance for many. Faith in Mussolini did not always mean belief in fascism, but the extremism or corruption of many of the party hierarchs could be blamed on their betrayal of the Mussolinian vision. As the years passed the cult of the Duce became "the fulcrum of the regime, its permanent plebiscitary element."[34]

The hold of the Mussolini myth on the youth of Italy—and the very real distinction they often made between the regime and the vision of the Duce—is evident in some of the Fascist university group newspapers, where the shibboleths about the infallible Duce multiplied even as the university students criticized the PNF and its other leading lights. Their criticisms were based on what they saw as "pure fascism," which was not being realized under the regime. The Fascist state, they sometimes claimed, was not a true reflection of Fascist ideals because the revolutionary will of Mussolini was being hindered by corrupt hierarchs too tied to the bourgeois past. Some of these young men went to the war still convinced that they could return as heralds of a new fascism, a second wave that would sweep away the old conservative and reactionary forces still inside the regime and thus realize the promises of Mussolini. The war was for many, however, crucial evidence that the evils they criticized were not *in* the system but *of* the system. The detachment of the young from the regime must be seen at least in part as a liberation from the myth of the infallible leader. Ugoberto Alfassio Grimaldi, an early believer turned anti-Fascist, commented on the almost physical bond between Mussolini and the young: "Mussolini . . . was for all of us born in the Fascist climate an exceptional personality at whose altar . . . we burned at least a bit of our youth. We never saw him as just any ordinary mortal . . . [but as] a man infinitely higher than the others. . . . Of the various dogmas with which we had to break to get out from under fascism, that of the infallibility of the Duce was certainly the most resistant."[35]

Mussolini himself assiduously fostered and nurtured this myth of his own superhumanity. His reminiscences were rarely completely false but were fantastic embroideries on the more staid realities; they emphasized his paternal love for his people, his incredible strength, his valor, and his total incorruptibility.

The Duce was portrayed as vastly above ordinary mortals but tied to his people by loyalty and a true concern for their welfare: he had come from them, he was one of them, he was infinitely above them. So that the masses could identify with their leader, Fascist propaganda exploited his humble origins; the poor house of his birth at Predappio became a popular shrine for Italian pilgrims. The deprivations of his early years and his period of "exile" in Switzerland provided grist for his propaganda mill by identifying him as a man of the people and an enemy of the rich. Gallons of ink and reams of paper were used to retell Mussolini's own tales of his pecuniary disinterest: "In politics I never gained a penny. I detest those who live like parasites sucking away at the edges of the social struggle. I hate men who grow rich in politics."[36] Mussolini was in truth no sybarite, and for twenty years Italians had this drummed into their heads in story after story about his abstemious character and the extreme moderation of his personal habits.

Some of the most typical and frequently printed photographs of the Duce emphasized this communion and concern with the masses: photos of him listening with a concerned expression to an old woman, surrounded by adoring little children, in work clothes among the farmers, or brandishing a torch among factory workers. One of the recurrent images was the annual photograph of Mussolini surrounded by the "prolific mothers" being decorated by the leader for their contributions to the vitality of the fatherland. The Duce—or rather the DUCE—was thus presented as a son of the people and as a father figure, an ever-present source of consolation who heard the prayers and problems of his flock.

The regime's propaganda images were conveyed in a series of mythic and heroic episodes. One biographer claimed, for example, that in the hour of Mussolini's birth an eagle was struck by a bolt of lightning at Schoenbrunn, the residence of the Hapsburgs. The moral of the tale was clear: this prodigious child would by his interventionist campaign bring the end of the Dual Monarchy. In a pamphlet for the Libyan youth group, Mussolini's success was attributed to the fact that the famous ring of Solomon that had been lost for millennia had reappeared mysteriously, and by divine will, in Mussolini's hands.[37] Many of these tales emphasized the Duce's physical courage and virility. Young Italians heard again and again of his suffering and bravery in the war, and stories emphasized the fascination he exerted over his men: "I had an effect on my soldiers that seemed to be almost mystical. The boys saw me as the avenger of our wronged Italy. . . . I could not remain unmoved when I knew that their last thoughts were of 'our native land and the Duce.' "[38] Margherita Sarfatti's hagiographic biography claimed that during the war Mussolini received so many wounds (forty-two) that he seemed like "San Sebastian, his flesh pierced as if with arrows."[39] In his autobiography Mussolini claimed that although the wounds inflicted "indescribable pain," "I underwent practically all of my operations without the aid of an anesthetic."[40] The same man who, contemporaries reported, was physically ill at the sight of a syringe, had nightmares about the smell of ether, and was afraid of shadows and solitude proved his courage in duels—the difference being that one was a public demonstration of bravery, the other a private admission of weakness. There is in all of this Mussolinian exhibitionism, one is tempted to surmise, a compensation for real feelings of inadequacy and insecurity, a psychic need to prove in public that he was someone who in private he feared he was not.[41]

For public consumption, Mussolini was the symbol of Fascist strength and virility, a man who disdained physical danger and who was capable of meeting any challenge with sangfroid. He was a brave soldier and an accomplished athlete. Italians were treated to innumerable images of him swimming (still with his granite jaw out of the water), riding horseback, fencing, piloting rickety planes, riding motorcycles with dashing goggles and scarves. The press was expressly forbidden to mention dancing, though he was often photographed playing the violin—the one unmanly and bourgeois, the other an expression of deep cultural interests.

The emphasis on his physical virility and courage was closely tied to those aspects of the myth that pointed to his apparently perpetual youth. No mention of any illness was ever permitted in the Italian press, and papers were forbidden to mention his age or his grandchildren. In his diary for 31 May 1941 Galeazzo Ciano emphasized the Duce's determination to preserve his youthful image: "I learn from Bottai," said Ciano, "that the Duce is exasperated by the publication . . . of a motto by some Greek philosopher: . . . 'No greater misfortune can befall a country than to be governed by an *old* tyrant.' "[42] His closest associates were well aware of Mussolini's obsession with youth, which they saw as the explanation for his relationship with the much younger Claretta Petacci. Giuseppe Bottai wrote in his diary: "I sometimes think what this Leader would be if he had, among the many other kinds of courage which no one denies, [the courage] to mature with dignity and serenity."[43]

By 1931, when the super-Fascist Achille Starace took over as secretary of the PNF, the ritualization of the charisma of the Duce had become a full-time business and hagiography the order of the day. The Fascist press referred to him (or rather to Him) as the "magnificent" Duce, the "sublime" Duce, and even the "divine" Duce. Debates over what adjectives to use to describe his animal magnetism were legion, and hundreds of books and pamphlets were published analyzing the deep religious and philosophical significance of his thought or the historical imprint of his personality. One that recalled Thomas à Kempis's *Imitation of Christ* was entitled *Imitazione di Mussolini*. A series of books by Paolo Orano portrayed Mussolini as the apotheosis of Italian genius. Tracts, speeches, and articles compared him to Saint Francis or to Jesus himself. One was especially succinct: "Mussolini is God and Italy is the Promised Land."[44] In 1930 Ottavio Dinale, one of Mussolini's earliest collaborators and a man much smitten with the myth of the leader, wrote: "He was called Benito Mussolini but he was instead Alexander the Great and Caesar, Socrates and Plato, Virgil and Lucretius, Horace and Tacitus, Kant and Nietzsche, Marx and Sorel, Machiavelli and Napoleon, Garibaldi and the Unknown Soldier."[45]

As a leader Mussolini possessed semidivine characteristics, and the protection of the Almighty went with him. After an attempted assassination the *Giornale d'Italia* published the headline: "Insane attempt on the life of Mussolini. God has saved Italy."[46] All the initiatives of the regime also had divine blessing. One widely circulated postcard during the anti-League campaign of 1935 depicted the gathering of gold for the cause as overseen by Jesus, who would grant the nation success for the "Holiness of the Cause."[47] Mussolini himself was sometimes portrayed as having qualities beyond the natural. An article in a Tripoli newspaper claimed that the visit of the Duce to the colony brought the beneficial rains the Arab population had long desired.[48]

Mussolini quite consciously played many roles. He was variously the cold Machiavellian, the hot-blooded romantic who wrote verse and played the violin, the steely-eyed Renaissance *condottiere* with a will of iron, the determined Leninist revolutionary leader, the Nietzschean superman, the clairvoyant statesman, or the new saint of Italy. Mussolini was not a man given to soberness in politics or to the dreariness of routine administration. It was easier to cure the ills of society with words and slogans than with hard work and careful planning. But to make people forget the reality of lost liberty, the show had to be perpetually flamboyant and exciting. He was keenly aware that myths were of more value to him and to his movement than the truth, and so the regime's propaganda machine constructed a false and increasingly distorted image of a leader that "became the kernel . . . round which the fascist movement was built." In return for the surrender of their liberties to the godlike leader, Mussolini "would transform the nature of the Italians and make them mighty and irresistible."[49] "I cannot help thinking," said the art critic Ugo Ojetti, "how much his face must ache at night when he retires."[50] The technique was not sophisticated, but for a time many were willing to sacrifice their liberty in return for the perpetually new and startling spectacle of his rule and his promises for a bright and secure future.

After the Ethiopian war Mussolini was always greeted with the ritual invocation "Hail to the Duce, Founder of Empire!" His success in that war convinced him of his own infallibility and increased his detachment from the reality around him. Giuseppe Bastianini, who served as undersecretary of foreign affairs from 1936 to 1939, noted in his memoirs: "He is sure of himself and of his star; all others must, after that historic proof, grant him infallibility in every eventuality now and forever."[51] This belief in the political validity of his own intuition, faith, and will translated into a belief in his mission, an ever-deeper conviction that he had been called to a Caesarean vocation. His interest after the war was less in routine politics than in his own place in history.

Mussolini had always been naturally diffident toward others. He had few close friends and trusted almost no one except his brother Arnaldo, whose death in 1931 exaggerated the Duce's tendency to close himself off from those around him. But after the Ethiopian war and the proclamation of empire, he became still more Olympian in his detachment from even his closest advisers and much less accessible to the foreign press. In August 1936, after a meeting with Mussolini, Bottai noted in his diary: "Not the man but the statue stood before me."[52] He eventually became addicted to the myth he had created for others; perhaps even in his own mind he was the *Princeps Juventutis*, the perpetually young and virile prince whose destiny was inextricably linked to that of Italy.

After the Ethiopian war Mussolini withdrew increasingly from the day-to-day administration of the state; real business was conducted by a phalanx of undersecretaries who competed for the time and attention of their ever more distant leader—and by Galeazzo Ciano, who seemed in these years the most likely candidate to succeed Mussolini, though the Duce himself refused to discuss the topic of succession. His advisers served one key function: to bolster his own image of himself. He did not want to hear anything that contradicted his perception of reality or denied his mission. As a result, he was more and more protected from unpleasant truths and from words of dissent or pessimism.

Roberto Cantalupo, just returned from a long absence in Spain, met with Mussolini in August 1936. He found "a very different man than I had left four years before." The Duce "spoke from on high, with an 'official' voice and cadence . . . words enunciated as if there were a great public to receive them." Cantalupo noted Mussolini's great distance. "He addressed me using the *voi*, detached, as if it were impossible for him to return to this earth: he let fall a few words with extreme caution, like they were rare pearls that might vanish on contact with the air."[53]

But those weaknesses were hidden from the public, and Mussolini's image did strike responsive chords among the young. Giorgio Pini, a youthful admirer of Mussolini and from 1936 to 1943 editor of *Popolo d'Italia*, was drawn to the future Duce during the interventionist campaign. He remembered Mussolini's first editorial in his new paper in November 1914 as "the first true political initiation" for him and for thousands of other young Italians who identified Mussolini with rebellion against the "denials and renunciations" of a corrupt parliamentary system. Mussolini, Pini felt, spoke to a whole generation of combatants and asked them to join the "march toward liberty and power for Italy in the world"—a continuation of the wartime struggle that "identified the affirmation of our personalities and of our liberty with the affirmation of a strong and free Fatherland." Fascism, concluded Pini, was in this sense "the perfect meeting of a man and a generation."[54]

Fascism and the "Third Rome"

Memories of the imperial greatness of Rome—the myth of *romanità*—had been a potent political theme during the nineteenth century, but Mussolini was truly intoxicated by the heady fumes of past glories. His collected works are sprinkled with references to the Roman myth. "Rome is our jumping-off point and our point of reference," he said in 1922; "it is our symbol, our myth." Fascism would be the fulfillment of history, the third Rome: "After the Rome of the Caesars, after that of the Popes, there is today a Rome, Fascist Rome, that once again commands the admiration of the world."[55] In his autobiography Mussolini exclaimed: "I am desperately Italian! I believe in the function of Latinity!"[56]

The "function" of this Roman myth was clear: it served to legitimize the regime by identifying the glories of the past with the Fascist present and its promises for the future. The myth of Rome acted as an instrument of integration, linking the idea of the collective interest of the nation to the representation of fascism as a new civilization and a new primacy for the Italians. Fascism was thus rooted in the most ancient and sublime part of the history of the peninsula. The Roman myth was the "will to power and empire" and a justification for Fascist foreign policy: the *pax romana*, imperial expansion, and claims to *mare nostrum*. The obsession with the idea of Rome and the empire was at the very core of the domestic propaganda and rhetoric of fascism and one of the fundamental elements of official Fascist culture and political education. It had great appeal to wide segments of the populace and especially to the young.[57]

Mussolini's infatuation with things Roman was the central and pivotal point in his view of politics as spectacle; his preoccupation with the Roman myth reached epic proportions during Starace's tenure as party secretary. Current events became historic events and thus were placed in the grand process of evolution of which all Italians and Fascists had to feel themselves a part: Fascist Italy had a "historic responsibility," Mussolini's speeches were "historic moments," fascism was living a "historic struggle." On 9 May 1936 Mussolini proclaimed his new empire by saluting "after fifteen centuries the reappearance of the Empire on the fateful hills of Rome."[58]

Roman symbols and images abounded in Fascist iconography. The *fasces*, symbol of unity and strength, the she-wolf that had suckled Romulus and Remus, and the Roman eagle were ever-present. The PNF insisted on the adoption of the virile Roman straight-armed salute in place of the degenerate, effeminate (and germ-ridden) bourgeois handshake. The *passo romano*, suspiciously akin to the German goosestep, became the obligatory marching step of the Italian troops. Official Fascist architecture imitated modified Roman classical models and left Italy sprinkled with forums and triumphal arches. Permanent monuments to the regime's Roman obsession are still evident in railroad stations, post offices, and public buildings all over Italy. The Mussolini Forum on the banks of the Tiber still includes a marble stadium decorated with huge, nude male figures that can almost be seen to strain in emulation of their classical models. The focal point of the complex is the famous obelisk dedicated to Mussolini and inscribed with the Latin DUX. The Fascists, like the Romans, built roads; indeed, many of Italy's major highways were constructed during the *ventennio*. Many major archaeological projects involved excavations of Roman forums and the other Roman ruins in and around Rome. In 1925 the regime established the Institute for Roman Studies and built the *Augusteo*, a marble monument to the first Roman emperor, next to the old imperial burial grounds.

One of the most ambitious exhibitions staged by the regime was the Mostra Augustea della Romanità, which opened in 1937 after years of planning to celebrate the two-thousandth anniversary of the birth of Augustus. It began with exhibits on early Rome and ended, fittingly enough, with a section on "Fascismo e Romanità." Over the entrance Mussolini's words were emblazoned: "Italians, you must ensure that the glories of the past are surpassed by the glories of the future." During the closing ceremonies Mussolini was presented with an eagle, a sign that the imperial tradition had passed to the third Rome.[59]

From their earliest days in school and in their youth groups, the young were subjected more than any other sector of the populace to frequent doses of the Roman myth. Children were organized into paramilitary formations bearing Roman names—cohorts, *centurie*, legions, and so on—and were presented with an array of emblems, uniforms, and banners that harkened back to Roman images and themes. Very young children were reminded of the historical burden they carried on their shoulders when they joined the Fascist groups and became sons and daughters of the she-wolf, *figli e figlie della lupa*. The Gioventù Italiana del Littorio took its name from the ubiquitous lictor rods, as did the annual competitions for the university students, the Littoriali. The rite of initiation into Fascist youth groups took place each year on 21 April, the birthday of Rome, which replaced the old celebration of May Day. In state textbooks and training manuals the connection between the Roman past and the Fascist future was drawn without hesitation, and children were repeatedly and insistently barraged with stirring justifications of the claims to *mare nostrum* and promises to liberate *Italia irredenta*. Along with their lessons children heard all about the spiritual and moral primacy of the Roman stock and Italy's need for a "place in the sun" worthy of its great and glorious past.

In 1935 the minister of national education, Cesare Maria De Vecchi, wrote that Fascist education must be inspired by *romanità*. The example of the valor and military discipline of the Romans had to be ever-present for young Italians, he emphasized, "in the idea-force of imperialism, expansion, of unity and civilization." The destiny of Rome, he claimed, was a "perennially imperial destiny. Rome is alive . . . with all its wisdom, with all its power, in the heart of the Italian school and culture."[60] In a training book for ten-year-old boys the Roman myth was sold in even more emotional terms: "If you listen carefully . . . you may still hear the terrible tread of the Roman legions. . . . Caesar has come to life again in the Duce; he rides at the head of numberless cohorts, treading down all cowardice and all impurities to reestablish the culture and the new might of Rome. Step into the ranks of his army and be the best soldiers."[61]

War, Violence, and Action in Fascist Mythology

In their emphasis on the beauty of war and the cleansing social and political effects of struggle and violence, the Fascists sounded very much like the Futurists, who had also proclaimed war the "only hygiene of the world." Instead of being viewed as an abnormality or a tragic necessity, war for the Fascists became life's great test, the supreme manifestation of virtue and virility.

Even as a Socialist, Mussolini's use of language was replete with military allusions. Once he broke with the Socialist party he often reviled his former comrades for their pacifism and cowardice.[62] "War alone," he said, "brings up to its highest tension all human energy and puts the stamp of nobility upon those peoples who have the courage to meet it."[63] War was the supreme test of manhood, a necessary rite of passage. "A man who scrupulously avoids war will be anything but a man," said Mussolini in March 1945, "because only battle completes a man."[64]

The mystique of action and violence was tied in closely with the regime's mystique of youth. In a book of readings for the young, Arnaldo Mussolini reminded the new generations: "You must accept all responsibilities, understand all acts of heroism, feel as young Italians and Fascists the masculine poetry of adventure and danger."[65] In the first issue of *Popolo d'Italia*, Benito Mussolini addressed his call to the young: "It is to you, the youth of Italy . . . that I address my cry of greeting . . . a fearful and fascinating word: war." More than all the textbooks and learned words, war was the education necessary for the young: "Words are beautiful things but muskets, machine guns, ships, airplanes, and cannon are still more beautiful."[66]

The early movement appealed to the elite of the trenches, to what Mussolini called the "*trincerocrazia*," and played continually on the heroism of the Great War in "histories" that were really Fascist martyrologies and mythologies. Mussolini understood the psychological trauma of Caporetto and the rallying power of the myth of the revolutionary war and the nation in arms. He called for power to the combatants, the most noble and authentic part of the nation, who would bring a new society. "Italy," he said in 1917, "is composed of two great parties: those who have been [in war] and those who have not." The workers who returned from the trenches to the factories and fields of Italy would realize, he promised, "the synthesis of the antithesis class-nation."[67]

The very name of the movement, Fasci Italiani di Combattimento, conjured up romanticized images of the heroism of the trenches and the camaraderie of the war. For the young this credo was translated into Mussolinian slogans in textbooks and training manuals: "The creed of the Fascist is heroism, that of the bourgeois, egoism." "He who is not ready to die for his faith is not worthy of professing it." "We are against the comfortable life." Mussolini boasted, "We are becoming and will ever more become . . . a military nation. Because we do not fear the word, I will add: militarist. To complete: warlike. That is, endowed in an ever higher degree with the virtues of obedience, sacrifice, and dedication to the fatherland."[68]

The first Fascist *squadristi* were postwar replicas of the *arditi*, the daredevil Italian shock troops of the Great War. The groups had been established after the rout at Caporetto in October 1917, and they served first as commandos during the resistance on the Piave. The *arditi* wore black shirts, carried grenades and daggers, and wore fezzes on their shaved heads; their units, known as the "company of death" or the "black flames," had the skull and crossbones as their emblem. They had been trained for a life of violence, and many had difficulty adjusting to the quiet at war's end. In November 1918 Mario Carli founded a national organization, the Associazione fra gli Arditi d'Italia, which by mid-1919 had enrolled some twenty thousand young men. Many of the former *arditi* joined in D'Annunzio's expedition to Fiume. The Federazione Nazionale dei Legionari Fiumani, which the poet-adventurer established in January 1921, merged with the nascent Fascist movement later that year.[69] Realizing their potential importance to his movement, Mussolini appealed quite consciously to these elite troops. At the end of the war he told them: "You represent the admirable, warlike youth of Italy. The flash of your knives and the roar of your grenades will wreak justice on all the wretches who want to hinder the advance of a greater Italy! We shall defend her together."[70]

The *arditismo* of the war became the *squadrismo* of the first Fascist gangs; the new heroes became cult figures, and their motto, *Me ne frego*—"I don't give a damn"—found ready echo in many young men who, though perhaps not entirely clear what the movement stood for, were drawn to the uniforms, the jackboots, and the comradeship of the squads. The question later was how to harmonize the irrational activism that gave the movement its early spirit with the demands of fascism as regime. Many of the *ras* were in their twenties when the movement came to power, and some had been *arditi*. In their eagerness to realize the activist ideals of the movement they often came into head-on collision with such older nationalists as Rocco and Luigi Federzoni, whose tendency toward bureaucratization and compromise was anathema to them. Many of the early struggles involved in the stabilization and consolidation of the regime must be seen as attempts by Fascist hierarchs—in the first place Mussolini himself—to tame the activism of the squads but at the same time to retain their vitality and fervor as part of the revolutionary image of fascism.

The novelist Elio Vittorini made this violent aspect of fascism the subject of one of his most famous novels, *The Red Carnation*. The novel is a rather simple story of a group of young boys growing up during the Matteotti crisis; it was written in Florence between 1933 and 1935 and published in installments in the Florentine review *Solaria*. Publication of the third installment, however, provoked sequestration of the journal, and Vittorini later rewrote the book so that it would pass the censors. The regime, by then the standard-bearer of legality and order, objected to Vittorini's obvious suggestion that many of the young men in his novel were attracted to the Fascist movement because of its violent aspects, "the bloody and noisily arrogant side which, to our eyes as boys, was also the liveliest side." In its post-Fascist version, however, *The Red Carnation* presented a very clear picture of sixteen-year-old Alessio, who often dwelt on his need "to affirm himself, to enter into adult life." To do this he felt he needed to kill someone, or at least to spill blood, just as fascism had killed Matteotti. As Vittorini explained in the introduction to his novel: "To their eyes, which see that other political parties do not kill, fascism is strength, and as strength it is life, and as life it is revolutionary."[71]

All this emphasis on virility and heroism was played up in clearly sexual terms in the media. The dashing and irresistible Duce appeared in a succession of fast cars, airplanes, and motorcycles; his torso became familiar to all Italians as he was photographed bare-chested skiing, running on the beach, or reaping grain. His animal magnetism over the female of all species was dramatized in a series of famous photographs showing him subduing a lioness. Others showed women holding up their babies for his kiss or nubile girls strewing flowers in his path. In his martial poses he was usually shown sitting straight-backed on his powerful white charger. He was most frequently described as magnetic, virile, vital, willful, dominant, and energetic; his eyes were scintillating, flashing, blazing, smoldering, sparkling, like thunderbolts.

Mussolini's own attitude toward women was resolutely traditional. Despite some early relationships with women in revolutionary parties, he lived the double standard. He was a violent and sometimes sadistic womanizer with little regard for his casual partners; at the same time, however, he demanded total devotion and fidelity from his wife. Stories of his supposed sexual prowess circulated widely in the foreign press; it was said that women waited in line outside his office for a moment of his favors, that he took servants on the stairs in the Palazzo Venezia. Interestingly enough, apart from Mussolini's opposition to speculation in print about his relationship with Donna Rachele or his extramarital affair with Claretta Petacci, the regime did not make a concerted attempt to scotch such gossip.[72]

The Fascists' emphasis on the mystique of virility and potency had its counterpart for women; the rhetoric here was traditional with a vengeance, though designed to serve "revolutionary" aims. Though the 1919 program of the Fasci had called for female suffrage, Mussolini later changed his mind. In 1925 he said that "the concession of the vote to women is not a question of democracy" and would serve nothing, "because if the woman loves her husband, she votes for him and his party; if she does not love him, she has already voted against him."[73] Sidestepping the question about inferiority or superiority, Mussolini admitted in his talks with Ludwig only that women were "different."

When the page proofs of the book returned, Mussolini edited the sentence "Women should be passive" to read "The woman must obey" and continued: She is "analytic and not synthetic. . . . My view of the role of women in the state is opposed to feminism. Naturally she does not have to be a slave; but if I gave her the right to vote, she would deride me. In our state she simply does not count."[74]

The regime tried to encourage papers to print articles favoring motherhood, for, as the oft-repeated slogan said, "Maternity is to a woman what war is to a man."[75] In the *veline* to the press in 1933, papers were forbidden to publish pictures of women with dogs (child substitutes and evidence of foreign corruption), wasp-waisted women (clearly unsuited for frequent motherhood and probably syphilitic), or any thin women (dieting rendered women sterile and sick). Such women were seen as typical products of the decadent Western societies and had to be totally eliminated from the new Fascist climate. Whatever stimulated eroticism or portrayed females as women and not as mothers was to be outlawed. There were to be no pictures of women in skimpy bathing suits or short skirts in Fascist papers. There were to be no advertisements for cures for sexual dysfunctions or venereal disease, since fascism had presumably eliminated both.[76] The ideal woman was ample-bosomed, wide-hipped, and rosy-cheeked; she looked, in fact, a great deal like Donna Rachele Mussolini. Mussolini's feelings about the role played by women in public life and the relationship between women and men in marriage sounded much like those of Xenophon, who once asked, "Is there anyone with whom you hold fewer discussions than your wife?" In one interview in the late 1920s Mussolini said to a female journalist: "Women are the tender, gentle influence that represents a pleasant parenthesis in a man's life, the influence that often helps a man to forget his trials and his fatigue, but that leaves no lasting trace. . . . Women are a charming pastime, when a man has time to pass . . . but they should never be taken seriously, for they themselves are rarely serious. . . . My wife and my family are my dearest possessions, but so greatly do I treasure them that I keep them apart from my day."[77]

Mussolini's conviction that the vitality of the nation was tied to the birth rate, and his concern about growing unemployment, led him in the 1920s to inaugurate the demographic campaign and pass laws limiting female participation in the work force. In 1927 women's salaries were reduced to half of those of men in the Fascist syndicates; they were excluded (because of intellectual weakness) from teaching letters and philosophy in the classical *licei*. To discourage useless higher education, women were not permitted after 1928 to be directors of middle schools, and female students were required to pay double fees in secondary schools and universities. Despite this concerted effort, the proportion of female students at the universities actually increased from about 10 percent in 1922 to some 16 percent in 1936. After 1933 women were not allowed to compete in examinations for jobs in state administration. By 1938 legislation had reduced the number of jobs in public employment for women to 10 percent of the total. Women, the regime emphasized, should have roles that were complementary to those of men and not competitive. "Woman's place," said Mussolini in the tradition of many before and after him, "in the present as in the past, is in the home."[78] Though there was a temporary decline of women in the labor force during the 1930s, by 1940 wartime mobilization had checked the effects of the earlier quotas.

Mussolini's demographic campaign was part and parcel of his ruralization drive, because in his view urban settings decreased the disposition to procreate. Feminism, too, came in for its share of the blame for the falling birth rate. The emancipation of women was defined as counterrevolutionary, as it brought with it late marriage, easy divorce, independence, and abortion, all of which ate away at the foundations of the family and led to the decline and the eventual death of nations. Other leading Fascists shared Mussolini's concern about the falling birth rate; Rocco said that the greatest threat of feminism was that it "supported voluntary limitation on reproduction." Because "numbers constitute the ultimate strength of the race," feminism was anti-Fascist.[79] Just as workers, for the good of the nation, had to accept controlled wages and capitalists had to sacrifice profits for the development of a sound autarkic economy, so, too, women were commanded to increase and multiply.

Religion and Ritual in Fascist Mythology

One of the most powerful fictions of the PNF was the consistent identification of fascism as religion. In this context the party, which took on a chiliastic and apocalyptic character, was seen as a religious order: a sacred institution with its own high priests, its own liturgy, and its own body of inviolable truths. If the myths were static, ritual was an active linking of the mass with the traditions and the ideals of fascism and Italy. Fascist rhetoric appealed to the young by disparaging the materialism and egoism of the Left and the liberals and by proclaiming its own brand of political idealism and mysticism.

Reviling the neutralist Socialists in 1915, Mussolini said: "You have corrupted socialism: it was 'mysticism' and you have made it 'politics.'" Fascism, he said, "is an idea, a passion, a faith, an apostolate." Castigating the spineless governments of pre-Fascist Italy, he claimed that he had been forced "to carry the cross of power." Fascists, he maintained, "are inspired with a religious sense of duty." The PNF is "not only a party, it is a regime; it is not only a regime but a faith; it is not only a faith, but a religion."[80]

As in any other religion, ritual and symbol served to bind believers to the cult. Like a secular religion, fascism expressed its truths and myths through ceremonial and liturgical forms that brought the people into the worship of the nation. Ritual thus became a concrete expression of the national will; it transformed politics into a drama, one in which the people themselves were called to play their part. The role of the regime was to speak to the conservative nature of the mass and to build upon traditions familiar to them by using ritual to create, in turn, new traditions that would capture and hold the people. "Every revolution," Mussolini said, "creates new forms, new myths, and new rites."[81]

Symbols were thus the visible renderings of the national myths, and the party had an impressive array of them: remembrance parks, sacred flames, holy trees, flags, banners, uniforms, songs, and badges. Here the military and religious merged: the nation under the leadership of the party was an army organized in a military fashion in the service of the new secular cult. The mammoth displays arranged down to the most minute detail, the huge public buildings and monuments emblazoned with the *fasces*, served to illustrate the order, discipline, and hierarchy that were supposed to be the glory of the new society. They served as a link to the past, a fixed point in the chaos of the modern world. The "oceanic" meetings and public rituals demanded of the mass that they become not mere spectators but actors in the national drama of renovation. "The ceremonial," said Erik Erikson, "permits a group to behave in a symbolically ornamental way so that it seems to present an ordered universe; each particle achieves an identity by its mere interdependence with all others."[82] With the people united in the common observance of ceremony and ritual, old divisions of class were to be transcended in the new spirit of community. The atomized ones would become the one, the unity.

Like all religions, fascism had its heroes and saints. Commemorations of Fascist martyrs were among the most frequent celebrations staged by the regime. Each youth group took the name of one of the fallen heroes of the early movement, and each group meeting opened with the ritual calling of the roll. The names of the martyrs were greeted with "Present! Present! To us. *Eia, eia, alalà!*" Each group also had its own prayer and its own "ten commandments." Youth groups and school classes made pilgrimages to the sacred shrines of fascism: to the Duce's birthplace, to his former office at the *Popolo d'Italia*, to the Tomb of the Unknown Soldier. Fascists did not forget their dead, not only because they were worthy of being remembered for their own sakes but also because they served as an example to the masses and most especially to the young, who were taught to emulate their brave deeds in defense of fascism and the fatherland.

Uniformed children were marched out on all national and party holidays, and these became increasingly numerous and elaborate as the years passed. The new Fascist calendar, which added the notation *Era Fascista* and counted the years from the March on Rome, was in this sense not merely an affectation but an illustration of the Fascist conception of time and history, which would replace the Christian observances of the past. In the schools ritual and liturgy were built into the daily routine. The days began with the raising of the tricolor and prayers and songs for the regime and its leader; they ended in the same manner. Mussolini's portrait graced every Italian classroom. Classes were regularly interrupted for the performance of other cultic rites—an interference lamented by many educators and teachers. The regime even appropriated the traditional celebration of the Epiphany by establishing the *Befana fascista*, when PNF leaders passed out gifts to the needy children of the area.

As political style fascism demanded a direct link between the leader and the people, a sweeping away of the mediating institutions of democratic governments. Parliamentary systems reduced the individual to a cipher, a number in an electoral victory. The secular religion would provide at least the illusion of participation, the political cement between leader and led. This bond between the one and the many was enhanced by Mussolini's many orchestrated speeches, which were not expositions of ideology but liturgical functions and mass rites of national veneration. Mussolini knew the power of his voice, and the appeal he made was based not on content but on form: on the setting and on the sense of togetherness he aimed at arousing in listeners in squares all over Italy. For the moment the huge throngs were united in the ritual incantation "Hail to the Duce." In the almost continual round of brilliant displays, colors flew, bands played, and arms were raised in the Fascist salute. In the large cities these command performances were on a grander scale than elsewhere, and the ranks of the local Fascists were swelled by hundreds brought in from the provinces for the day. They stood beneath the windows of the Duce's office or at the Tomb of the Unknown Soldier; they listened to the shouts of the crowd; and, so the party planners hoped, they felt the greatness of their leader and their country.[83]

Presenting his new government to the Chamber on 16 November 1922, Mussolini said: "I insist that the revolution has its rights. . . . I am here to defend and enforce in the highest degree the Blackshirts' revolution, and to inject it into the history of the nation as a force for development, progress, and equilibrium."[84] Mussolini had always called himself a revolutionary leader, first as an advocate of the proletarian revolution, then as a leader of the national revolutionary war of 1915–18, and finally as leader of the revolutionary struggle of 1919–22.

"The Kingdom of the Word"

Fascism proclaimed itself a revolution: it would produce both a new Italy and a new Italian, a political and economic revolution that would sweep away injustice and class struggle and effect a spiritual and moral revolution in the character of the Italians. It was portrayed not as a reaction against Marxism but as a revolutionary alternative to Marxism that would achieve social harmony and productivity in the context of national self-assertion. Fascism was the third way, a rejection of the materialism and egoism of socialism and liberalism that would through the corporate state recognize the needs of the individual but harmonize them with the needs of the community. Fascism would be a true Socialist regime serving national purposes, designed not to destroy the capitalist system but to make it work for the good of all under the overarching control of the state, a syndicalism inspired not by pacifism and internationalism but by love of country and national solidarity. In this way fascism could reject socialism but promise social justice and reform— social change within the law instead of the anarchy and chaos of the leftists. In posters and propaganda tracts the regime played on this as the fundamental distinction between the Socialist revolution and the Fascist revolution. Leftist revolution would produce destruction, chaos, desolation, strikes, and poverty. The Fascist images were quite different: flowering and fertile fields, happy and productive workers, stabilization of the *lira*, order, and trains running on time.[85]

In all of these revolutionary endeavors youth was to play a key role. If the regime's militaristic rhetoric appealed to the youthful thirst for glory and adventure, the myth of the Fascist revolution, the "new order" that fascism would bring to Italy and to Europe, appealed to the idealism and the social conscience of the young.

Mussolini seemed to have little faith in the older generations, but in his autobiography he exclaimed: "I have trust in young people. Their spiritual and material life is led by quick attentive minds and by ardent hearts."[86] The March on Rome was presented as a revolutionary seizure of power that had begun the process of renewal in Italian society, a renewal in which the youth had a special role to play. The rhetoric of the regime seemed to promise construction, building, and a zest for the future—all of this tied to the dynamic image of the leader who offered to the young a way to channel their spirit of rebellion into politically productive outlets. The countless images of Mussolini in the fields and factories seemed to give credence to his promise that in ten years Italy would be unrecognizable.

Under fascism Italy was to be viewed no longer as a land of spaghetti-eating and mandolin-strumming romantics but as a land of sobriety, hard work, and seriousness of purpose. The party and the Duce had revolutionized Italy, and all was working according to his will. To maintain this image, the press office forbade the mention of any internal conflicts. Newspapers could not carry stories of crimes of passion, suicides, or obituaries, which were not in the Fascist style. Nor did Italians read stories of epidemics, natural calamities, or even bad weather. The new Italian would be physically and mentally hard and fit, lean and sinewy and ready for combat. "I have no pity for the fat," Mussolini was quoted as saying. "If you eat too much you steal from the Fatherland," read another propaganda poster.[87]

The showiest celebration of the Fascist revolution was the Mostra della Rivoluzione, which opened on 28 October 1932 to commemorate the tenth anniversary of the March on Rome. The myth of the "continuing revolution" to the contrary, this exhibition made it quite clear that the revolution was in the past, enshrined within the walls of the great hall on Via Nazionale in Rome. The exhibition dated the beginning of the "years of anguish" from 1914 and the interventionist struggle; it was in essence a martyrology, for the exhibits, in addition to memorabilia from the Duce's early years, included the bloody rags and uniforms of the early Fascist saints. The last room, the "sacrarium" or the shrine of the martyrs, was a votive chapel dedicated to those who had fallen during the revolutionary struggle.[88]

Millions of visitors over the years came to see this exhibit; the regime provided reduced fares for soldiers and members of Fascist youth groups and adult organizations. To emphasize the unity of the people with the revolution, the guard included people from all walks of life: soldiers, militiamen, peasants, workers, intellectuals, students. But the exhibit was a celebration and sanctification of the past, not a promise for the future. The exhibit, like the revolution, came more and more to be symbolized, as Dino Alfieri emphasized in an official communiqué, in "the will of the Leader, in whom all the mysterious forces of the race converge." The entire exposition had been "prepared and organized in such a way that one feels the personality of the Duce always present."[89]

The themes of the Mostra della Rivoluzione were very symbolic. It enshrined all the political myths of fascism: (the revolution of the spirit and social justice to be accomplished by the mobilization of the mass in a great national undertaking under the inspired leadership of a new party and a charismatic leader. For a time these myths had great appeal. But all the rhetoric could not change reality. Words, even words supported by the mechanism of social control and repression, were not enough to hold up a world constructed only on promises. The Fascist regime under Benito Mussolini had no real determination to realize its promises of renewal and reform. As the years passed the chasm between the ideal and the real, between myth and practice, only widened. However much the leaders talked about revolution, the reality of life in Fascist Italy belied their promises. The theme of the revolution of youth was contradicted by the continuation in power of the old leadership cadres. The myths of Fascist national grandeur and strength were gainsaid by the regime's failure to prepare for war, and the myths of glory and *romanità* by defeats and the increasing subordination of Italy to Nazi Germany. The myth of the continuing revolution and social justice contrasted with the real functioning of the corporate state and fascism's compromises with the privileged classes. And perhaps most important, the myth of the infallible Duce clashed with his own increasing identification with Hitlerian fanaticism, with anti-Semitism and aggression. If Mussolini had once been associated with construction and the uniqueness of the Italian spirit, he came more and more to be identified with destruction and subservience to his stronger ally to the north.

Fascism promised to rally the people in a great national revival. In fact the regime was predicated on depoliticization of the masses, whose participation in the political process was reduced to ritual cries of support for policies decided on high, to orchestrated demonstrations of faith in the Duce. The dynamism of the early movement was reduced to a few formulas, repeated incessantly. The ideals of creativity and activism were transformed into the dead weight of dogma. Slogans about renewal and construction were reduced to the immobility of the catechism. The tone became ever more exalted as the years passed, the ideas ever more barren. The great revolution was in the end reduced to the cult of one man, the study of Fascist "mysticism:" "The font, the only font of our mysticism . . . is Mussolini, exclusively Mussolini. This is our fixed point . . . fascism for us mystics is Mussolini, only and exclusively Mussolini."[90]

For the youth this contrast between revolutionary rhetoric and reality had especially important consequences. Giuseppe Bottai insisted that to avoid paralysis and decay, the PNF had to allow the young to assume real power in the Fascist party. They should be free, he warned, to rethink fascism and to make their own contributions to keep the regime in tune with the needs of a changing world. In 1929 he asked: "Is the Revolution therefore completed? Is nothing left but to accept the closed cycle of its history as it exists in the institutions, laws, the concretized regime?"[91] Bottai refused to believe that the revolution did not have a future, and many young people, too, clung tenaciously to the belief that, appearances to the contrary, the real battle for a new society was still ahead.

Fascism promised that it would build upon the spirit of rebellion and the youthful activism that had brought it to power, that it would provide real outlets for their spirit of criticism, their desire to create, to reform. In a special edition of *Popolo d'Italia* in 1932, Arturo Marpicati, then vice-secretary of the PNF, claimed that the "Fascist state considers . . . the educational mission as fundamental among its functions, and it has assumed this mission with ardor. To the youth it entrusts the duty of perpetuating the faith and continuing the work of fascism."[92] The regime promised to fulfill its motto of *largo ai giovani*—"make way for the young"—but proceeded to erect an educational system and youth organizations that aimed at suppressing all evidence of intellectual independence and courage and at producing blind believers armed with a catechism of Fascist responses. In this sense the Fascist revolution for the young was best summarized with the motto "Believe, Obey, Fight" or, perhaps more to the point, "Mussolini is always right."

CHAPTER TWO

"The Most Fascist Reform"

The Government demands that the school be inspired by the ideals of fascism . . . it demands that the school at all levels and in all its instruction train Italian youth to understand fascism, to ennoble itself through fascism, and to live in the historic climate created by the Fascist revolution.
—Benito Mussolini, 1925

ith these words Benito Mussolini outlined the goals of Fascist educational policy.[1] In Fascist society certain mystically derived abstract goals and imperatives were to take precedence over all individual and group interests and over all social relations. In theory fascism was to be based not only on the subordination of the individual to the state but also on the subordination of all human associations and all traditional institutions created to meet the social needs of man. The attempt to control these traditional institutions was one of the chief means of socializing individuals in the Fascist state. One of the most important of these traditional institutions was the school. Though the PNF came to power without any clearly articulated educational theories, attempts to tailor the school system to the needs of the new government began very early and continued until the fall of the regime.

Any study of educational reform and school policy in Fascist Italy must begin with a discussion of the role played by Giovanni Gentile and the neo-idealist educational reformers. Gentile's 1923 reform was the foundation upon which later ministers of education constructed the complex superstructure of school and party organizations aimed at socializing Italian youth. Gentile's personal and intellectual relationship to fascism is something of a conundrum. He was often put on display by the regime as its intellectual-in-residence, and many of his ideas on the state and the leader struck responsive chords among the Fascist hierarchs. But almost as soon as it became law, Gentile's reform was dissected by those who found it "lacking in true Fascist spirit"—much to the chagrin of Gentile and his followers. Gentile produced the philosophical and intellectual underpinnings of an authoritarian and elitist educational system; later Fascist ministers added large doses of militarism and extreme nationalism, seasoned it all with generous portions of Latin-spiced *Fuehrerprinzip*, and produced what they hoped would be the perfect socialization tool for the formation of the "new Fascist man" and the new Fascist ruling class.

The Gentile reform itself was not a revolutionary departure from pre-Fascist developments in education but rather a reflection of ideas current in pedagogical circles for decades.[2] The Fascist regime did introduce some significant institutional changes in Italian education: by 1943 the system was much more centralized and more directly controlled by the state; some new types of schools had been established to broaden the educational base (with varying results); religion had entered the classroom, and the Catholic church was playing a key role in educational affairs. But the really important changes in the Italian school system under fascism—the basis for the regime's claims that it had effected a revolution in education—were changes not so much in structure or administration as in spirit.

This new spirit was militaristic and nationalistic; it was based on Gentilian notions of the ethical state and national community stretched to their most extreme limits by men without his sensitivity to the social function of culture and the importance of individual creativity, and without his tolerance of diverse opinions. In this new view of things, the school was seen not as a vehicle for cultural enrichment and the formation of a socially responsible ruling elite but as an agency of indoctrination buttressing a personal dictatorship. The school was to be not a place of communion between teacher and student united in the process of discovery but a tool that, together with the regime's youth organizations, was to form the Fascist citizen-soldier.

The development of Fascist educational policy can be divided into three periods. The first begins with the Gentile reform of 1923 and the reaction to this key educational legislation until 1929. In that year the Ministry of Public Instruction became the Ministry of National Education, a change substantial as well as rhetorical. The second period stretches from 1929 to about 1939 and may be termed the period of "fascistization" (*fascistizzazione*) in the schools: increasing influence of the regime in academic affairs, competition between schools and youth groups for the time and attention of the students, conflicts with the Catholic church over educational policy, and the series of counter-reforms or "retouchings" (*ritocchi*) that all but made the Gentile reform a dead letter. The third and final phase begins with the introduction of Bottai's Carta della Scuola—in the view of some the "only true Fascist reform of the school"—and ends with the fall of the regime itself.[3]

In 1859 Count Camillo Cavour appointed the Milanese reformer Count Gabrio Casati minister of public instruction. The Casati law, promulgated on 13 November 1859 (Royal Decree no. 3725), was one of the Piedmontese statesman's most enduring legacies to united Italy. The Casati reforms remained substantially unchanged for sixty years; Gentile's school reforms modified the institutional structure of the 1859 law but did not radically alter its essential outline or spirit. One historian of Italian education has referred to the Casati law as the "Magna Carta of the Italian school."[4]

The Casati law was very much a reflection of the political and social biases of its authors and of the northern Italian context in which it originated. Its 379 articles were inspired by the principle of administrative centralization from secondary schools to the universities, and by a rigid separation between humanistic and technical education—the latter considerd a *brutta copia* of the former—and between elementary and higher education. The Casati law created a national system of public schools, and in this sense the framers were responding to the needs of the labor market in a newly industrializing society. But the reform, though it did introduce a limited scholastic obligation and provide the rudiments of the three Rs and vocational training for the masses, was most concerned with the education of the Italian ruling elites and the preservation of the social division of labor so dear to the hearts of its right-wing liberal authors.

According to the law, elementary schools were divided into two courses, each lasting two years. Each commune was responsible for the establishment of at least one lower course for each sex where there were at least fifty students of school age. The lion's share of state funds for education was funneled into the secondary schools and universities; primary instruction was to be paid for by local communes, many of which simply could not shoulder the financial burden or were run by local notables who considered the alphabet a dangerous weapon in the hands of the lower classes. In many rural and underdeveloped areas, this pattern meant that local children, if they attended school at all, received only two years of education, not enough to prevent a lapse back into illiteracy when they left school. Schools were most often lacking in precisely those areas where they were most needed, where parents did not have the money to send children to private institutions or hire private tutors. Where they were set up, they were usually without even the most basic equipment and staffed by teachers who were often forced to take second jobs to make ends meet. At the dawn of the unitary state about one-third of all Italian communes were still without any elementary schools.[5] The Casati law did little to solve the social or economic problems of either students (no provisions were made, for example, for students who spoke only dialect) or teachers in a society in which education was still seen by many as destructive of Christian morality and as a challenge to the traditional social order based on *patria potestas*.[6]

The secondary system under the Casati law was more complex, as befitted its more privileged status. At the crown of this system were the classical *ginnasio* and *liceo*, where the most fortunate students were provided with a literary and humanistic education that allowed them access to all university faculties. Children could be enrolled in these schools only after completing a four-year elementary course and after passing an examination. The law also provided for eighteen three-year normal schools to train teachers, as well as technical schools and institutes for those students who planned careers in industrial, trade, or agricultural management. Admission to these schools was regulated as in the classical schools, and after 1860 the physics and mathematics section of the *istituto tecnico* did allow admission to the science faculties of the universities.

The university was the apex of the Casati system. Permanent professors were appointed by the king for life, and only the main subjects in each faculty were taught by such professors. These state-financed universities awarded one degree, the *laurea dottorale*, after completion of course work and public defense of the thesis.

The Casati system was highly centralized in its administrative structure: the educational administration was composed of the minister, the *consiglio superiore*, and three general inspectors, one for each level of instruction. The *consiglio superiore* was composed of twenty-one members, all appointed on royal nomination after recommendation by the minister. Each university was directed by a rector, who was nominated by the king from among the permanent professors and was responsible to the central government. The secondary and elementary schools in each province were under the control of provincial directors (*provveditori agli studi*) nominated by the king after consultation with the minister.[7]

The Casati law provided for religious instruction in the schools. At the elementary level religion was to be taught in both the lower and upper courses; in the secondary schools the religious and moral education of the students was entrusted to a "spiritual director" appointed for each school by the minister. At the university the teaching of religion was confined to the faculties of theology, but these were closed in 1873. The spiritual directors also disappeared very soon from the secondary schools, and religious training in the primary grades became voluntary, the decision resting with local authorities and families. In practice, it ceased to be taught in many communes, especially in urban areas, a development that only increased the disaffection of many Catholics from the liberal state. Those children who did receive formal religious in-

struction often did so by making special arrangements to study in the
parish church or to attend private schools run by religious orders.[8]

The educational system established by the Casati law enshrined the social and political interests of a ruling class convinced that the people were too immature for self-government and that order and control had to be imposed on the mass by their social betters. The leaders of the Destra Storica, in power until 1876, followed policies that mirrored their lack of interest in elementary education and technical instruction and their desire—by no means confined to Italy—to use secondary education as a social filter to preserve the homogeneity and privileges of their own elite.

The advent of the Left in 1876 gradually brought some changes, though hardly dramatic ones: a renewed interest in technical and professional instruction, an increase in teachers' and professors' salaries, election of some administrators to the *consiglio superiore*, and state provisions against competition from private schools. But if the Left showed more concern with popular education, it still shared the same fundamental political orientation: primary education was aimed at forming not politically responsible citizens but obedient workers who would leave the government to those capable of governing for themselves and for others. However, the whole complex of social, political, and economic developments in Italy produced by the broadening of suffrage and the irruption of new social groups vying for an expansion of their own power and influence could not be totally ignored by the leaders of the Left. Members of the ruling class itself came to realize the advantages of literacy among the workers; a parliamentary inquiry in 1876 by Leopoldo Franchetti and Sidney Sonnino into conditions in Sicily ended by encouraging the state and the *latifondisti* to provide elementary education for workers, an education designed both to raise their human dignity and to make their work more productive. A law on compulsory school attendance to the age of nine was passed under Minister of Public Instruction Michele Coppino in 1877. The law remained a dead letter, however, because of the continued poverty of many families, who needed their children in the fields, and because of the lack of interest of many communal authorities.[9]

The most important educational legislation between the Casati law and the Gentile reform concerned elementary education. The 1904 Orlando reform provided for an increase in teachers' salaries to be borne partially by the state, established obligatory instruction to the age of twelve, and set up a two-year postelementary school called the *scuola popolare* for those students who failed to pass the examination that would allow them to continue on to secondary studies. In fact, the schools were established in very few communes, and then usually in large urban centers.

An official inquiry into the state of elementary education in Italy in 1908–12 produced a thoroughgoing condemnation of the system. One of the results of this investigation was the 1911 Daneo-Credaro reform that attempted to increase state control in educational affairs and to take the financial burden off the communes by transferring expenses to the ministry and budgeting significant new sums for a school building program. It also encouraged the development of local assistance organizations, called *patronati scolastici*, that had first been set up in 1879 as voluntary groups to provide for the moral and material welfare of poor children. Through the *patronati*, local elementary school students were given books, clothes, and often meals; in rural areas classrooms were fitted out with necessary school furniture and libraries as well. By law every commune was to establish a *patronato*, and in 1911 these groups were given the status of public agencies subsidiary to the ministerial organization in all communes.[10] The Fascist government recognized the political potential of these local organizations and in 1930 put them under the control of the Opera Nazionale Balilla (ONB).

The Casati reforms did succeed in raising the level of literacy in Italy, though results were by no means dramatic. The rate of illiteracy for those six years of age and over was some 75 percent in 1861; by 1871 it had decreased to about 69 percent; and by 1901 the figure for Italy as a whole was about 49 percent. However, the "southern question" weighed heavily in these averages. The rate of illiteracy in the south and the islands ranged between 89 percent and 86 percent in 1861 and was still about 70 percent by 1901. In that year Piedmont's illiteracy rate was only 17.7 percent, but the corresponding figure for Calabria was 78.8 percent.[11]

Figures on school attendance tell much the same story because in most rural areas, especially in the south, children stayed in school only two years. The 1907 figures on school enrollment are enlightening: of the total number of students enrolled in the first six years of school, 42 percent were in grade one; 28.5 percent in grade two; 20.2 percent in grade three; grades four through six accounted for 6 percent, 2.6 percent, and 0.6 percent respectively. Even those figures, dismal as they seem, are misleading, for by all accounts not more than half of those students enrolled at the beginning of the academic year (when the census was taken) remained enrolled the entire year.[12]

The reforms undertaken in liberal Italy before World War I did not alter the fundamentally bourgeois and elitist character of the educational system. The system aimed at making elementary education widely available to the lower classes and at conquering illiteracy, but also at preserving the secondary school and the university as bourgeois monopolies. Only the classical high schools allowed access to all faculties of the university; all other schools—technical, vocational, or normal schools

—were in a sense dead ends. As commonly viewed by the Italian liberals, the school was an instrument of "containment and attenuation of social tensions," not a vehicle for providing equal educational opportunity for all.[13]

The problems of the Casati system were only too evident by the turn of the century. Royal investigations and numerous debates on educational policy and school reform among educators and politicians did bring the issues into the public forum, but did not bear fruit in any overall reform of the existing system and structure. Teachers' organizations that emerged during the early years of the new century often took the lead in these debates. An organization for elementary school teachers, the Unione Magistrale Nazionale, was established in 1901 and chaired by Luigi Credaro; in 1902 secondary teachers were organized into the Federazione Nazionale degli Insegnanti delle Scuole Medie (FNISM), a group led by Giuseppe Kirner and Gaetano Salvemini.[14]

The relationship between these teachers' organizations and the Socialists was indirect but important. Members of the Italian Socialist party had been leading proponents of democratic reform of the schools in the late nineteenth century and had played key roles in numerous parliamentary debates on compulsory school attendance and popular education, the battle against illiteracy, and the strengthening of technical and professional education. Many Socialists also took leading roles in these teachers' organizations, and over the years their leaders became active and rather effective lobbyists, bringing the concerns of the Left to the attention of the ministry and the central government. The groups did not succeed in radically altering the educational system in Italy, but their activities did win a certain degree of political and academic autonomy for the teachers and did bring professional and financial recognition to their members. Not coincidentally, these teachers' groups were dissolved very soon after the March on Rome.[15]

Conservative commentators on the plight of the school in these years addressed many of the same issues, though from a different point of view. Most worrisome to many on the Right was the perceived threat posed by the growing number of children from the lower middle class and the upper levels of the working class seeking access to secondary education and even to the universities. In the view of the defenders of the status quo, this influx threatened to upset the old system that aimed at retaining higher education for the few. Worrisome also was the overproduction of university *laureati* and the formation of an intellectual proletariat increasingly embittered and opposed to a liberal order in which its members had not found a place.[16]

The cultural and political choice made by these liberals can be summed up in the famous phrase *poche, ma buone*—"few schools, but good ones," fewer teachers, but better-prepared ones. Their debates and proposals for reform suggested not any profound change in the school system in Italy but a reinforcement of the existing classist system based on the Casati law. Behind the rhetoric lay a firm conviction that the task of the schools at the higher levels was not education for the many but cultural and intellectual preparation of the ruling class, and political and social containment of lower classes not prepared by either background or interests for public responsibility. In the words of Edward R. Tannenbaum: "In no other modern European country did a class of would-be mandarins cling so blindly to a fixed classical tradition as did the Italian 'intellectual bourgeoisie' during the liberal period."[17]

The years after the war were full of ferment in educational circles, but there was in all these debates an air of unreality. Educators hotly contested issues of philosophy and pedagogy—debates between positivists and neo-idealists, or between opponents and proponents of laicism—but in the process neglected to address the crying needs of an educational system that had not come to terms with the new demands of a democratic and industrial society. Nationalist educators saw the school system as responsible for many of the ills of Italian society; they decried the expansion of secondary education and blamed the leftist noninterventionist stance of many teachers for the failure of national unity and the lack of a truly cultured ruling class. At the tenth congress of the FNISM held in May 1919, Ernesto Codignola, a neo-idealist educator and intimate of Giovanni Gentile, vehemently castigated these teachers and charged that their anticlerical and antipatriotic ideas had prepared the ground for the Italian humiliation at Caporetto. There was a crisis in the school, he said, because "all spiritual life in it has been suffocated by a plebeian clientele, born not for studies but for the spade and for servile labors."[18]

In this overheated atmosphere Gentile, Codignola, and Giuseppe Lombardo-Radice broke off from the FNISM and founded the Fascio di Educazione Nazionale, which, despite similarities in name, had no connections with the Fasci di Combattimento founded that same year. Several members of this group, however, eventually did serve in Mussolini's first ministry of education.

Between 1919 and 1922 five men held the position of minister of public instruction, and none really managed to address the practical questions of school reform. The best known was Benedetto Croce, who was minister in Giovanni Giolitti's government from June 1920 until July 1921. Croce, though he often disagreed with Gentile on philosophy and politics, acknowledged his intellectual debt to Gentile on matters of educational theory and shared the neo-idealists' rejection of positivist educational notions and their view of the school as an instrument of social and political selection.[19] Not all of the neo-idealist educators remained loyal to fascism, but their writings on educational reform in

the pre-1922 period did call for a renewal of the school as a bulwark of 41
the national community. Their view of the benefits of the strong state
that would bring order out of the prevailing chaos also produced a "The
temporary working alliance between the neo-idealists and the new Most
regime. Fascist
Reform"

Giovanni Gentile and the PNF

Benito Mussolini's appointment of Giovanni Gentile as his first minister
of public instruction was motivated more by the demands of practical
politics than by any real ideological considerations. The two men had
never met before the appointment, and Mussolini was probably not
familiar with Gentile's philosophical and pedagogical writings.

The appointment made good political sense. Gentile's nomination
allowed the regime to portray itself as committed to broad reform and as
capable of taking swift and decisive action on an important—and much-
debated—public issue. From Mussolini's point of view, Gentile's acceptance would also attract important groups to the nascent regime. He had
great drawing power among nationalists because of his interventionist
ideas; he was very well known in pedagogical circles as a result of his
involvement in the struggle to raise educational standards. His appointment would provide the regime with respectability by convincing the
intellectual community that the PNF was not a party of head-bashers, a
tactical maneuver that "would assure the government of support from
noted intellectuals and make a breach in the world of high culture."[20]
Gentile was also favored by some church authorities because of his stand
on parity for private schools. Many conservatives favored Gentile's
appointment because his commitment to the formula *poche, ma buone*
would, by reducing the number of state-financed schools, relieve the
government of a monetary burden and stanch the flow of unacceptable
elements into the classical schools. The Duce's choice, therefore, was
largely political in motivation and, as Renzo De Felice noted, had "little
or nothing to do with the ideological and political substance of the
reform itself."[21] When the political climate changed and Mussolini consolidated his own authority, he did little to defend Gentile's handiwork
from the "counterreformation" set in motion by later Fascist ministers of
education.

If there was no strict ideological brotherhood between the neo-idealists around Gentile and the PNF, there were points of intellectual kinship. There was no formal working relationship between the Fascio di
Educazione Nazionale and the Fasci di Combattimento until just before
the March on Rome, when the Fascio became the Gruppo di Compe-
tenza per la Scuola, allied with the PNF. But even earlier the two groups

had some common ideas that could justify collaboration: strong feelings against socialism, a fervent nationalism, opposition to prevailing positivist currents, and a determination to transform the life of the nation. The alliance of 1922 was based on hopes for the future and the political realities of the present. It seemed a mutually beneficial arrangement in the beginning: the educators needed powerful friends who could help them realize their ideas; the Fascist regime needed ideas and a well-defined program. Members of the Fascio accepted a working partnership with the new government provided that Mussolini would allow them to reform the school along the lines indicated by their neo-idealist philosophy. It seemed initially that he would. On the other hand, Mussolini felt that he had found the support of a group determined to renew the life of the nation, a group whose ideas—though more elegantly and abstrusely expressed—were congenial with his own and whose aspirations for the future seemed quite similar. Mussolini judged that the program of the Fascio could be rapidly translated into deeds, and thus would give substance to his boasts that fascism was a revolution that would sweep away the chaos and indecision of the past. He was willing, at least until the consolidation of his own power in 1925–26, to give these men a relatively free hand.

This marriage of politics and philosophy produced some initial results, but in the long run basic incompatibility led to a rift. Many of the *intransigenti* in the PNF did not share Mussolini's view of the need for respectability and conservative support. These black-shirted spokesmen for a "revolutionary" squadrist spirit in fascism were suspicious of the intellectual community and convinced that a real revolution in education could not be effected by effete snobs tied to bourgeois and elitist conceptions of society and culture, but only by virile Fascist "new men" inspired by the military virtues of discipline and self-sacrifice. Nor were the educators entirely satisfied with the bargain they had made. Some members of the Fascio, such as Piero Gobetti, never supported the regime and left immediately after the alliance with the PNF. Lombardo-Radice, who served as director-general of elementary education, waited until the Matteotti crisis to sever his connections; Ernesto Codignola lasted until the Lateran Accords. Of the important neo-idealists, only Gentile himself remained loyal to Mussolini until the end, and it was loyalty for which he paid dearly both intellectually and personally.

Gentile served for a time as something of an intellectual figurehead for the regime. He had years of firsthand experience in the Italian school system, having been a student at the prestigious Scuola Normale Superiore in Pisa and later a teacher at *licei* in Campobasso and Naples. From 1906 he was professor of theoretical philosophy at the universities of Palermo and Naples; in 1917 he transferred to the University of Rome. For several years before their falling-out he collaborated with

Benedetto Croce on the review *La Critica*, and by 1922 he was one of
the peninsula's intellectual luminaries.[22] His literary talents were soon
put to use by the regime. Gentile was the author of the 1925 "Manifesto
of Fascist Intellectuals," and his 1925 work *Che cosa è il fascismo?* was
the basis for the first section—"Dottrina—idee fondamentali"—of the
famous article on fascism in the 1932 *Enciclopedia Italiana* published in
Mussolini's name.

After his stint at the ministry from 1922 to mid-1924, Gentile was
relegated to academic posts and had no further real influence on government policy. He did have an honorary position as a senator and member
of the Fascist Grand Council after 1922. From 1925 he was director of
the *Enciclopedia Italiana* and was involved in founding the Istituto
Nazionale Fascista di Cultura, the journal of which, *Educazione fascista*, he edited.[23] In the thirties he served as director of the Università
Bocconi in Milan and the Scuola Normale in Pisa.

In all of these posts, Gentile exhibited a tolerance and a willingness to
collaborate and exchange ideas with non-Fascists that enraged the PNF
intransigents—a practical openmindedness that clashed rather strikingly
with the laudatory nature of many of his writings on fascism. During his
tenure at the *Enciclopedia Italiana*, for example, Gentile was responsible for hiring experts in various fields; he aroused the ire of many of the
PNF by including on his staff signers of the 1925 manifesto of non-
Fascist intellectuals and non-Fascist—or even anti-Fascist—university
professors. In response to criticisms, Gentile argued that he could not
close himself away in a "stronghold of my comrades" by neglecting to
make use of all the "elements and all the energies Italy can offer to
construct this great national monument . . . this for me is fascism . . .
which can and must call upon all Italians—even those of the countermanifesto—for every national undertaking."[24] Unfortunately for Gentile
and for the nation this was a concept of fascism shared by few of his
"comrades" in the party leadership.

Gentile had doubts about the direction the regime took in the 1930s,
and on occasion he clashed bitterly with some of the more fanatical (and
according to Gentile unworthy) hierarchs in the PNF. But he remained
personally loyal to Mussolini, whom he saw, even after the fall of the
regime, as the incarnation of the new Italy. In 1943 Gentile had a
meeting with the Duce, who persuaded him to come out of retirement to
serve as president of the Italian Academy in the Republic of Salò. This
decision probably cost him his life. He was murdered in his car while
returning to his home in Florence on 15 April 1944.[25]

Gentile was appointed minister of public instruction just after the
March on Rome. The Gentile reform was referred to by Mussolini as *la
riforma fascistissima* or *la più fascista delle riforme*—a less than dramatic endorsement since it was also the first major reform undertaken by

the new Fascist government. Political rhetoric aside, however, the 1923 school reform was not a revolutionary fracture with the past. The text of the reform itself was a collaborative effort: Gentile wrote only the sections on the secondary schools and universities, and Lombardo-Radice composed the legislation on the elementary schools.

Though he had been a teacher himself, Mussolini's own interests were less oriented toward books and classrooms than toward the streets and the piazzas of Italy; he was more interested in newspapers and speakers' platforms than in blackboards and teachers' platforms. Among his early advisers there were no educators; the PNF did not routinely debate educational issues at its party congresses as did the Socialists or the Popolari. The party did make an attempt to organize young people before the March on Rome, but these attempts did not involve active participation in the life of the schools. Instead the PNF set up youth groups that served to divert the attention of the students from their scholastic duties and their education. The conflict between the schools and the regime's political organizations for youth, which was to plague the PNF throughout its history, was born here. Still, the principles of Fascist education were roughly laid out: the atmosphere was one of exaggerated patriotism and militarism.

The June 1919 program of the Fasci di Combattimento referred to education only in passing, as one of the problems that would be considered after the revolution. Affirming the preeminent role of force and "revolutionary war," the program averred, almost as an aside, "The other problems—bureaucracy, administration, judiciary, school system, colonies, etc.—we shall consider after we have created a new ruling class."[26] The subject was broached vaguely at the third party congress of the PNF held in Rome in November 1921. After a ritual promise to eradicate illiteracy and extend elementary education, the section on educational policy in the party platform pledged to "introduce a rigorously national character into the schools" and "rigid state control" over curricular and hiring decisions. For the middle schools and the universities the party proposed free operation "except for state control over programs and the spirit of instruction, and the state's duty to provide premilitary instruction for the purpose of training officers."[27] These were very crucial exceptions, as it turned out.

Idealism and Fascism

With Benedetto Croce, Giovanni Gentile was the principal spokesman for the neo-idealist current in twentieth-century Italian thought. The strain of authoritarianism and elitism that ran through Gentile's work became the dominant characteristic of the reform that bore his name. His successors reformed his reform by adding heavy doses of militarism and extravagant *romanità*, but they had not inherited his concern with the individual student or the intellectual development of the creative person- ality. Gentile saw the school as an instrument of moral indoctrination; later ministers used it as an instrument of political indoctrination with little or no regard for the individual character of the student or the sanctity of the conscience. Gentile did not shrink from the use of politi- cal propaganda, but he believed that the goal of education and propa- ganda was to create a true moral community based on genuine belief rather than superficial acquiescence. As the years passed, he realized that the Fascist regime had failed in this task and that the national consensus, if broad, was also superficial—motivated by opportunism and not faith.

The 1923 school reform reflected the philosophical and pedagogical concerns of the Italian neo-idealists. The relationship between the Gen- tilian wing of the neo-idealist school and fascism is an important one; these thinkers provided Mussolini with the theoretical justification for the notion of a hierarchically organized society in which all values were to find expression in the state.[28]

In Gentile's view, World War I had revealed the moral bankruptcy of the liberal state that had failed to respond to the crisis by creating a truly united nation. Though he adhered to the PNF only in 1923, Gentile saw fascism as the necessary precondition for the restoration and revitaliza- tion of Italy, the way to realize once and for all the promise of the Risorgimento: a national community that could transcend particular interests for the common good. In his view, Italy's weak international standing was due to a lack of moral and political education in the liberal state. The solution was the merging of the mass with the state: the creation of a strong state that would articulate and express the national will.

The basic assumption of Gentile's "actual idealism" was that only thought exists: mind was central to understanding the world, and reality was the activity of the mind trying to comprehend the world. Gentile echoed the Mazzinian dictum of *pensiero ed azione* in his contention that all human activities were really disguised or incomplete forms of thought; thought and action were, therefore, one. All individual minds were encompassed in the absolute mind; the reality of the individual was subsumed into the ever-present and eternal reality, the Spirit. All soci- eties, individuals, and nations had meaning only as expressions of the Spirit. According to Gentile, the individual man was free only if he recognized his necessary relationship with the whole of reality, the Spirit; he was, otherwise, a slave. Individual interests had to be sacrificed to the universal will. This was the basis for Gentile's theory of the "ethical state" and for his notion of the relationship between liberty and authority.[29]

Gentile postulated a basic identification between the individual and the nation. For him the state was a moral, religious, and social entity that had existed before its citizens and would survive them. He saw the state as the sum of the individual wills, the embodiment of the universal will—the vehicle through which universal law became positive law. The state was an ethical state because it allowed the realization of human values; the truly ethical state was the state that was based on a religious or spiritual conception of life and that satisfied the human need for self-realization by providing the fullest merging of the individual with the community. The person who put him- or herself outside this universal will as embodied in the state was outside the law.[30] Because universal values were identified with the state, the restoration of the authority of the state was a means of human liberation. In Gentile's view, however, liberty was to be understood not in the Enlightenment sense of individual freedom and rights but as "that which realizes itself in the universal spirit . . . the liberty organized in the state."[31] In a very real sense, therefore, liberty was synonymous with authority.

This Gentilian conception of man and society was used as the philosophical justification for the hierarchical and authoritarian system erected by the Fascists after 1922 and for their aspirations for a "totalitarian" society. Gentile himself was never totally comfortable with the endless parades, the nation-in-uniform, or the Special Tribunal; his ideas, however, were congenial to Mussolini—an elegant rationalization of his own personal power. But if Gentile's theory of the ethical state was based on the nation, it also stressed the importance of individual self-development, a concept that was quickly pushed to the background as the propaganda agencies of the new government began their drive to produce the "new Fascist man" whose critical faculties were to be sacrificed to the nation, now conceived of not as a true community of faith but as a political reality demanding total and blind obedience. Fascism was portrayed as the expression of the universal will, the supreme example of Gentile's ethical state. According to party propagandists, only in the Fascist state could true community be achieved; only in fascism could the individual realize his or her true potential, which was social and not individual. The means for building this Gentilian national community was the totalitarian state.

Particularly appealing to Mussolini was Gentile's notion that the universal will could be incarnated in certain extraordinary leaders who possessed the "privilege of genius."[32] Gentile referred to Mussolini as the "powerful *condottiere*" of whom Machiavelli had dreamed. In a 1923 letter to the Duce requesting party membership, he referred to

Mussolini as the incarnation of liberalism, but the "liberalism of liberty in the law and therefore in the strong state conceived of as an ethical reality."[33]

This personal belief in Mussolini's historic mission was the crux of Gentile's continued support of fascism. He could, and did, remain tied to the leader while recognizing the faults of his movement. The goal of politics under such a historic leader was to create a new citizen and a new nation. The ethical state was to be realized not only by promulgating new laws or by creating new institutions but above all by fostering a new spirit. To accomplish this goal, fascism had to make use of all the agencies of the state, most especially the schools. Fascism was not a dogma but a "continuing revolution of the spirit of the nation," and education had a crucial role to play in that revolution.[34]

The application of Gentilian notions to education consisted first of all in a rejection of the prevailing positivist trends in Italian pedagogy that emphasized the need for a lay school (an "agnostic" school, according to Gentile) and the development of scientific instruction. Most observers agree that the Italian school of the early twentieth century was little more than a diploma mill. The curriculum of the elementary schools was encyclopedic in content, and the teachers were bound by minute directions to a certain timetable that emphasized methods for dealing with facts, not children. In the view of the idealists, the positivists had stressed the intellectual aspects of education at the expense of the humane, aesthetic, and ethical aspects of human development.

Gentile and the idealist educators saw teaching as a spiritual moment in which the souls and minds of teacher and student met in communion. They decried the positivist separation between mind and reality that made of education a pseudoscience, a mechanical process of filling minds with facts and information. Rightly conceived, education should be a process of initiation into the life of the Spirit, a formative rather than an informative exchange that would stress the development not only of the intellect but also of the character. The task of the teacher was to bring the student into the sphere of his or her own thought and to allow the student to share in the life of the Spirit. The emphasis in the classroom was to change from "listen and repeat" to the more creative "observe, describe, and discuss." Ideally the teacher was to build upon the child's early experiences—religious upbringing, folklore of the region, the dialect spoken—and to provide opportunities for enriched experiences, keeping in mind the inner world and the emotional life of the child.[35]

The success of this type of education clearly depended on the ability of individual teachers who were, especially after the establishment of the Opera Nazionale Balilla in 1926, under heavy pressure to conform and whose teaching was more and more controlled by the use of state textbooks and circulars from ministerial inspectors demanding scrupulous adherence to the political directives of the regime. The theory of communion between teacher and student was crucial in the Gentilian system, but over the years it became an illusion, crushed by the weight of pat phrases and political propaganda. Much to the distress of sincere idealist educators it became "a pious wish, an alibi, a fraud."[36]

The idealists particularly stressed the importance of philosophy, religion, and art in the school curricula; in their view, these subjects illustrated the life of the Spirit as embodied in the life of the national community with greater clarity than did the sciences. In practice, their efforts perpetuated a distinction between vocational and classical education and deemphasized the technical and scientific education that the developing nation most needed. Gentile especially stressed religious education in the lower schools. In his view, the nation's spirit was expressed in part in its religious beliefs and practices; he saw religion as "one of the essential moments of the spirit."[37] Religious instruction at the elementary level was to consist mainly in relating the traditional religion of the people, including their myths and popular superstitions. Later, as critical faculties developed, the student would begin to study philosophy, which would supersede religion in the life of the mature citizen. Most Italian students, however, did not go on to secondary schools where they could pursue philosophical studies. Gentile was using religious instruction in a conservative way, favoring the stabilizing effect Roman Catholicism could have on the young by teaching obedience and respect for tradition and authority.

In the Gentilian scheme of things, the school could obviously not be indifferent to national concerns. Because true moral freedom was an inner sharing in the culture and traditional life of the nation, the school had to be inspired by true belief in the destiny and uniqueness of the nation—no longer a school of skeptics but a school of believers.[38]

Gentile distinguished between "general culture," which was the "spiritual life diffused in the national body," and "higher culture," which "is not, and does not have to be, for all." He called for an intellectual division of labor: "We all have need of shoes, but is it therefore necessary that we all be shoemakers?" The duty of the state in the realm of education was to "open the door to higher culture, but a narrow rather than a wider door, so that the crowd will not rush in." In Gentile's view, the secondary schools in Italy were overpopulated with unsuitable pupils; in 1914, he estimated, some four-fifths of the students in these schools were "dead weight" (*zavorra*) who should be moved out of secondary humanist education and into technical and professional schools more in line with their needs. "Secondary education," he maintained, "is by its nature aristocratic, made for the few and to be given to the few."[39] In essence, Gentile recapitulated a concept dear to the Italian ruling elite: the strict separation between the classes on the basis of "culture" that cut off not only the poor and manual workers but also all those who had bettered their economic situation but did not know Latin.

Gentile's views on the place of women in the school system had also been elaborated before 1922 and were written into law in 1923. For Gentile, females were inferior both physically and spiritually to males; he condemned feminism as an "egalitarian illusion, a false and ridiculous ideal of the woman-man." He believed that one of the serious problems in the educational system was the influx of female teachers into secondary schools and universities. Although women could be elementary school teachers "because of their obvious maternal qualities," they were to be discouraged from teaching at the upper levels, where teachers should possess "well-marked characteristics of virility." Women, claimed Gentile, did not possess the "originality of thought or that iron spiritual vigor" the new school demanded.[40]

The educational system had clear objectives in his view: to bolster traditional class stratification and to maintain traditional sex and social roles. These were the foundation stones upon which Gentile would attempt to construct a new educational structure for Italy, a structure that was in some very fundamental ways built according to specifications of another time and one that, though "built for the ages," was soon to undergo drastic remodeling.

The Gentile Reform

The Fascist government was given full powers in education by the law of 3 December 1922 (no. 1601). From February to December 1923 the school system was the object of a dozen royal decrees that are known collectively as the Gentile reform. The reform can be seen as an attempt to fulfill the Fascist objective of reestablishing "order, discipline, and hierarchy in society, in places of work, in all institutions."[41] To accomplish these goals, the reforms made a fundamental distinction between various levels of education: elementary education was to be available for all and to provide the basic tools of knowledge; secondary education was rigidly streamed, allowing access to higher studies for some and denying it to others; the universities were reserved for the very few whose culture, background, and interests permitted them to develop the life of the Spirit. The reform provided for obligatory school attendance to the age of fourteen, but this goal remained more a hope than a reality.[42] Passage from one level to the next was controlled by a series of examinations designed to weed out those unfit for higher educational pursuits. Curricula at the *ginnasi*, the *licei*, and the *istituti magistrali* were based on classical studies and thus culturally biased in favor of the more privileged students. The system was divided into the three levels already noted—elementary, secondary, and university—and the most important changes in the structure of the system occurred at the secondary level.

According to the Royal Decree of 1 October 1923 (no. 2185), the old *corso popolare* was suppressed, and elementary education was to last five years: three in the *grado inferiore* and two in the *grado superiore*. Schools were divided into rural and urban and, if numbers permitted, into schools for males and females. The reform perpetuated and accentuated the distinction between rural and urban society by providing that only those schools in important centers—*scuole classificate*—were to be instituted and maintained by the state for the full five years. The smaller localities often had no school beyond the third or fourth grades; the least-advantaged areas had only *scuole provvisorie* managed by private agencies with some totally inadequate state subsidies. A three-year pre-primary school was the first level of elementary education, for children from three to six years of age; this school, called the *scuola materna*, was neither obligatory nor free and simply did not exist in most of the poorer communities. Despite his later promises to "go to the people" and the PNF campaign to extol the virtues of rural folk, all this gibed well with Mussolini's basic view of the masses: "By now it has been demonstrated," he said in 1922, "that the masses as such cannot be protagonists of history," and so their education is not a "sine qua non of progress."[43]

Lower-level secondary education was provided in five types of schools in the Gentile reform. The greatest innovation, and perhaps the greatest failure, was the establishment of two new types of schools at the postprimary level aimed at those students who wanted to "complete" their elementary studies but did not (or could not) go on to upper-level secondary schools: the *corso integrativo di avviamento professionale* (supplementary courses for vocational training) and the *scuola complementare* (a kind of trade or junior high school). These schools were the only choices for those students who failed to pass secondary school entrance examinations at the age of eleven. The communes were not required by law to establish these schools, and in communes where they did not exist, children who failed their exams were required to repeat the last year of the school nearest to them (often the third grade in rural areas). The *scuola complementare* was supposed to replace the old *scuola tecnica*, which had been the most popular of all Italian schools among the lower bourgeoisie and the more socially mobile members of the working class. The 1923 reforms reduced this school to a post-primary school by depriving it of any outlet in the higher schools. The *scuola complementare* was a blind alley, a kind of dumping ground for those who were by attitudes, income, and tradition destined to remain, in Gentile's words, "modest citizens."[44]

These postprimary schools were closed off behind high walls by the curricula prescribed for them: Latin, which not only provided mental exercise but also strengthened national feeling, was taught in all schools that provided access to higher studies. The sciences were given short shrift, a reflection of the antipositivist outlook of the reformers but also a clear indication of Gentile's notion that education should serve "culture not economics."

The new teacher-training schools, the *istituti magistrali* that replaced the old *scuole normali*, were divided into a lower and an upper course and their number reduced. The schools did not teach pedagogy and did not provide practice teaching (teaching being a communion of spirits and not a skill to be learned). The curriculum, in keeping with Gentile's ideas about the function of secondary education, was classical.[45]

The reforms established a new institution called the *liceo scientifico* that replaced the old *liceo moderno*, established in 1911, which had emphasized the sciences and modern languages in place of classical studies. A student could enter this semivocational four-year school from any other secondary school, after passing four grades. An entrance examination was required, and the *diploma di maturità* awarded at the end of the course did give access to some science faculties at the universities.

The Royal Decree of 6 May 1923 set up still another secondary school: the three-year *liceo femminile*, a sort of finishing school for girls of good family, aimed at diverting them from the teacher-training schools. One study has styled this the most "gracious and absurd" creation of the Gentile reform. It certainly did reflect the reformers' refusal to consider female students as a part of the labor market along with males, and their conviction that females had neither the natural intellectual qualities nor the social function to make use of higher education. Studies at the *liceo femminile* were based on the education of "woman as woman": in place of Latin, Greek, and philosophy, students were taught singing, embroidery, dance, and "woman's work."[46]

Gentile left the *ginnasio classico* and the *liceo classico* almost intact. These schools, the aristocratic institutions for the intellectual elite, were undoubtedly the best organized and the most efficient in Italy, and they embodied a long cultural tradition. The program in both schools was rigidly classical; admission was regulated by a stiff entrance examination. The *diploma di maturità* awarded at the end of the program gave students carte blanche at the universities, where all faculties were open to them.

One of the major innovations of the Gentile reforms was the introduction of the *esame di Stato*, the state examination, required at the end of each three- or four-year course in order to allow students to pass from the lower to the higher levels of the secondary schools. Such a proposal had been presented to the Chamber by Croce in 1921, but it was put into effect only with the Royal Decree of 6 May 1923 (no. 1054). The goal of the *esame di Stato* was to assure parity between students from public and private schools and to expand private initiative and raise educational standards by introducing a *numerus clausus* in the state secondary schools.

Examination boards were composed of teachers from state secondary schools and universities, but the law also provided that each board had to include a representative from private schools. The *esame di Stato* did not provide total equality for private school students: the boards were still dominated by state teachers, and the private school representative was to be chosen by the minister. But it was in some very real sense a victory for private school interests because it recognized the diplomas awarded in private schools and altered the old system under which public school students could be examined by their own teachers.

One of the side effects of the state exams was better relations between students and teachers, who were no longer feared as awesome examiners but seen as allies in the students' attempt to pass the state tests. But the reform also had negative effects. It brought the state into every Italian classroom and had a deadening effect on the free exchange of ideas that Gentile had tried to encourage. Teachers and students became primarily concerned with covering the assigned material on the state syllabi; there was little or no room for the creativity and spontaneity the idealist reformers had stressed. The *esame di Stato* was also one very convenient way of controlling exactly what was taught in every classroom in Italy.[47] In addition, because few private interests besides the church were prepared to take the initiative in providing education, the introduction of the state examination increased the role played by the church and religious orders in Italian education.[48]

Private schools were thus permitted, and even encouraged, under the Gentile reform, but always under the strict control of the ministry. Such schools could be set up only with the permission of the minister and were open to inspection by ministerial *provveditori*. These precautions notwithstanding, however, Gentile's introduction of the *esame di Stato* earned him the enmity of some of the more anticlerical Fascists, who were highly suspicious of the enthusiasm with which Catholic interests greeted the reform.

Centralization of Education: Gentile's Administrative Reforms

The administrative provisions of the Gentile reforms were based on the Fascist principle of hierarchy in a system characterized by bureaucratic centralism. Administrators at all levels were political officials, charged not only with management duties but also with political oversight of teachers, professors, and students.[49]

The power of the minister was greater than ever before. He had the right, for example, to appoint special inspectors whose job it was to evaluate the schools and even individual teachers. The Royal Decree of 16 July 1923 (no. 1753) also turned back the clock by returning to certain features of the Casati system. The minister was to be responsible for proposing to the king the names of all twenty-one members of the *consiglio superiore*, the central advisory body of the ministry. Educational legislation in the liberal period had increased the number of these advisers to thirty-six, and had provided that both parliament and the university faculties should have a voice in these appointments. The same law abolished all consultative committees, thus eliminating most of the influence exerted by teachers and professors at the ministerial level.[50]

For administrative purposes, Italy was divided into nineteen regions, each one overseen by a *provveditore*, or supervisor of studies. These men were named by the minister and acted as local superintendents of education, sending out directives on pedagogical questions—and later on political questions as well—to teachers and principals in their regions. Most also published bulletins that teachers received regularly and came to regard as the voice of the state in their schools.

The entire system was hierarchical: as the power of the minister increased, so, too, did the powers of the principals and headmasters over teachers and students. The school *presidi* (principals) had to be male, and they were charged with the task of instilling the new spirit in their schools. In this task they were directly responsible to the *provveditori*, who were political appointees. These *provveditori* could dismiss *presidi* or teachers who did not show the proper qualities of discipline, respect, and enthusiasm for the party. The *preside-capo* was to be replaced, in Gentile's words, by the "*preside-duce*."[51] In the first few years the reorganization carried out by these supervisors was usually motivated by educational concerns; in the early years the phrases "political unreliability" or "un-Fascist behavior" did not often appear among the causes for dismissal. Political dismissals did occur in later years, and became more and more common as the rhythm of *fascistizzazione* was accelerated. Under the Gentile reform—indeed, after 1908—teachers were required to take an oath of allegiance to king and country; by 1928 they were also required to swear loyalty to the regime and the Fascist party.[52]

Gentile did not tamper to any great extent with the functioning of the universities. An intense spirit of local pride (and centuries of tradition in some cases) prevented him from decreasing their number, though this step had been recommended by others.[53] Gentile did devise a rather over-intricate system to suffocate financially some of the less robust and less prestigious universities and to bring the rest under stricter state control. According to the law of 30 September 1923 (no. 2102), universities were divided into three categories depending on their importance and the degree of state financing provided to them. Only category A schools were totally maintained by the state. However, the system was doomed from the start, and Gentile's successors saw to it that things were changed to the benefit of the state.

Gentile's penchant for hierarchy was evident in the internal reorganization of the universities. Professors lost the right to elect their rectors and deans, who were instead to be appointed by the king on the advice of the minister. The influence of these officials was notable because they made up the academic senate, which became more and more Fascist in composition as new appointments were made from the ranks of the PNF.[54]

Any autonomy left to the universities by Gentile was soon eroded and finally disappeared entirely under Cesare Maria De Vecchi, who came to the ministry in January 1935. De Vecchi did not share Gentile's respect for high culture and was, in fact, leery of all intellectuals, whom he suspected en masse of anti-Fascist leanings. The situation at the university level is illustrative of what happened throughout the school system. Gentile's reforms in the university were authoritarian in nature, and they did extend the power of the state. But Gentile's long experience as a professor and his basic regard for intellectual creativity prevented him from totally quashing academic autonomy. Later Fascist ministers were not so inclined and sought in a variety of ways to broaden the control of state and party over the universities.

Religious Education in the Gentile Reform

The Gentile reforms also abandoned the principle of laicism in elementary education by introducing religion as a compulsory subject—a return to the 1859 Casati law and a departure from policies adopted by liberal governments in Italy since the 1870s. Article 3 of the Royal Decree of 1 October 1923 (no. 2185) stipulated that "the teaching of Christian doctrine in accordance with the Catholic faith shall form the foundation and capstone of elementary education in all grades."[55] This provision was extended to the secondary schools in 1930, carrying out the terms of the Concordat with the church.[56]

Before the reforms, religion had been taught, upon request of the family, in hours not employed for regular instruction; after 1923 those parents who did not wish to have their children receive such instruction had to present a written request to school officials justifying their decision.[57] Teachers for these religion courses were to be appointed by the school council, but all such appointments were subject to the approval of local ecclesiastical authorities, who also had the right to make on-site visits during religion classes.[58]

The issue of religious instruction was a political hot potato. Gentile was not a clerical or a Catholic—indeed, he called himself a nonbeliever—but perhaps because of that fact he felt he could make concessions to the church that those suspected of clerical leanings could not make. As we have seen, for Gentile religious instruction did serve a very specific national and intellectual purpose: that of teaching discipline, respect for authority, and traditional values. It produced national cohesion because Roman Catholicism was "a peculiarly Italian institution" and a "store-house of national tradition."[59] Religion in the Gentile reforms was to become not only a powerful stabilizing force for the masses but also a powerful community bond.

Reactions and Ritocchi

Some of the provisions of the Gentile reform were dead letters from the beginning. Especially in the rural south, the requirement of compulsory school attendance was widely flouted or simply could not be implemented. According to the law, upper sections of the elementary schools were to be established only in major urban or rural centers. As a result, many children in more isolated areas had no access to school beyond the first three years, and for many those years were spent in one-room schools with one poorly trained teacher for all students. The Gentile reform did little to improve the existing primary school system in many rural or disadvantaged areas. A 1923 survey indicated that of some eighty-three thousand classrooms in Italy, over thirty-seven thousand were classified as "lacking" or "unfit"; in the south some 62 percent were so classified.[60] The slack was sometimes taken up by private agencies that set up schools in the less populous areas, but there were simply not enough of these agencies to go around. In 1928 the party stepped in directly and turned over management of the rural schools to the Opera Nazionale Balilla. It was an important step in the regime's attempt to "fascistize" the schools and to bring the new Fascist spirit into the hinterlands.

The corsi integrativi di avviamento professionale, always something of a white elephant, fared no better. They had been set up to keep children in school until they reached the age of fourteen, and in this matter they failed. In many communes they were never set up at all, and the money that should have been spent on them was channeled into more "productive" areas. These schools were eliminated in 1929. The attempt to provide some vocational training to the lower-class children suffered another setback with the failure of the *scuole complementari*, from which students stayed away in droves. For most students and their parents, these schools simply served no purpose because the children entering, no matter how gifted, were denied the possibility of continuing their studies. The defection of Italian children from these schools is a rather vivid demonstration that education was increasingly seen as a vehicle of upward social mobility.[61]

The *liceo femminile* was also a dismal failure. The privileged preferred to send their daughters to private schools instead of dead-end finishing schools, however elegant. In the Senate debates on the ministry budget in February 1925, one senator scathingly referred to these girls' schools as "miserable abortions"; the liberal Piero Gobetti dismissed them as "servants' schools."[62] In the academic year of 1926–27 these *licei* had an enrollment of only 113 students and, mercifully, they disappeared the following year.

Reactions to the reform were not long in coming. It was praised by many conservatives who shared Gentile's view of education and by many Catholic spokesmen pleased by the introduction of religious instruction and the new status of private schools. Croce maintained that the reform was not really Fascist but a reflection of developments in education much debated "when fascism had not yet appeared in the distance." He predicted that it would be the "beginning of a true regeneration of the school . . . aimed at the reinvigoration of thought . . . and of Italian culture."[63]

There were also many critics, however. The Accademia dei Lincei began a debate on the reform in September 1923; members were especially concerned about the neglect of science in the school curricula. Debates in both houses were vigorous, but the Chamber, reduced in numbers by the Aventine secession, accepted it more easily than did the Senate, where non-Fascists attacked it for a variety of reasons in debates in February and March 1925. Among other things, senators deplored state control over the universities, ministerial nomination of professors, violations of academic freedom, and the extension of religious instruction.

The dissent came mainly from radical leftist and republican elements, though *La Stampa* in the spring of 1923 criticized the reform for its aristocratic spirit and its failure to provide sound technical and vocational instruction that would address the needs of the labor market in an industrializing society. The *Voce repubblicana* accused the reform of taking a "police-state turn"; it also deplored the reform's classist flavor and the dangerous increase in the power of the church.[64]

Piero Gobetti had at first been favorable to Gentile's thesis of *poche, ma buone*, but later he condemned the reform and rejected the nationalistic and authoritarian overtones of Gentilian thought. "The religion of actualism," said Gobetti, "is a little sect that has rejected the seriousness of Crocean teaching. Gentile has suggested to us an exhaustive definition of his teaching: the philosophy of Mussolini."[65] The Socialists of *Critica sociale* were especially vehement in their denunciation of the elitist character of the reform. Filippo Turati referred to it as the "cudgel applied to the school."[66] Antonio Gramsci later wrote that the Gentile reform was nothing but a rehash of the Casati law, though in a profoundly altered historical and cultural climate. He castigated Gentile for his "culpable abdication" of cultural hegemony in turning education over to the Catholics, and maintained that the reform sanctified a dangerous division of labor: the education of the masses was left in the hands of the church, but the state was to educate the bourgeoisie.[67]

In his own defense, Gentile claimed that the reform was not the fruit merely of his own lucubrations or personal convictions but the culmination of a long tradition of Italian pedagogical thought: "I have invented nothing," he said.[68] He saw the reform as the product of debate among many political groups, an expression of bourgeois ideas on the school as a state institution that, renovated and invigorated with a true spirit of national unity, could fulfill its task as the custodian and protector of a glorious cultural patrimony.

Gentile's reform looked not to the future but to the past; it was inspired by a view of the school's educational mission based on a nineteenth-century conception of the political and social order. There was a basic contradiction in the reform: between freedom, individual growth, and creativity, on the one hand, and the needs of an authoritarian state and its desire to produce political homogeneity, on the other. How was it possible within the context of the Gentilian system to harmonize the view of education as the formation of a free, creative personality with the view of education as political indoctrination?

Mussolini himself waffled on the issue. In his autobiography he praised the reform: "The problem of the school," he said, "has finally found its solution in the Gentile reform."[69] But the Duce's actions often belied his words. Gentile had served a purpose in 1922; by 1924 he had outlived his usefulness. In July 1924 he resigned, after having received a promise from Mussolini that the reform would not be attacked.

Gentile was replaced by Alessandro Casati. The new minister, a descendant of Gabrio Casati, was a liberal still very much tied to the idealist school and a friend of both Gentile's and Croce's. Casati promised not to abandon the reform but to proceed with its "gradual modification." But his tenure at the ministry was short-lived; on 5 January 1925, as the regime began its process of consolidation in the wake of the Matteotti affair, the ministerial portfolio passed to Pietro Fedele, whose hostility to Gentile's handiwork was no secret. Fedele remained in office until July 1928; his stint as minister was the beginning of the process of counterreformation and *fascistizzazione* of the school that accelerated in the late twenties and early thirties.[70]

After discussion of the ministry budget in February 1925, the Senate's order of the day, while recognizing the fundamental principles of the Gentile reforms, recommended that the government "undertake to bring to the reform those retouchings which experience have shown to be necessary."[71] This was the opening shot in an ongoing battle, with the school as contested terrain. With Gentile out of the public eye and Fedele at the ministry, many of Gentile's disillusioned collaborators also retired from the scene. The field was left to those who were overtly hostile to the former minister and his view of education. Gentile's reform was simply too bourgeois and too elitist in its approach to education and culture to be congenial to many of the new Fascist leaders, who were more comfortable in jackboots on a parade field than in a classroom. They set out to reform Gentile's reform in the interests of a state that defined its values not in terms of the national community of faith but increasingly in terms of militarism and imperialism. A 1932 article entitled "Educazione virile" summed up this new view of the truly Fascist school. The school, the author claimed, had the duty of educating Italians to realize that "in decisive moments of life for a people, war is the great testing ground of virtues and of all possibilities for the future . . . for war we must always be spiritually prepared as for an event that always was and always will be."[72]

Mussolini, embroiled in the Matteotti affair when Gentile left office in 1924, was after that time no longer much interested in strictly academic questions, if indeed he had ever been. With the "clarification" of 1925 and the erection of the institutional mechanism of the new state, the basic differences in their conceptions of education came to the fore. For Gentile it was important to educate students; for Mussolini the objective was to indoctrinate subjects. By 1931 Gentile's work had been totally repudiated by Mussolini, who referred to the school reform as "an error due to the times and to the *forma mentis* of the then minister."[73]

In the end, the counterreformation of the school system—or the process generally termed *fascistizzazione* by the regime's leaders—radically altered this "most Fascist reform." Gentile had wanted to reduce the domination of the textbook in the classroom, to do away with rote memory work, and to "bring the tang of actual life, and the problems of conduct, into the schools."[74] The reform was condemned to sterility as the idealist conception of education based on the individual student clashed with the tendencies of a government that stressed regimentation of the group. The spontaneity and initiative that had been the outstanding characteristics of the Gentile reform (at least on paper) were replaced by a stifling uniformity in classrooms all over Italy. From Gentile's departure until the mid-1930s, the regime used increasingly repressive measures to abolish any vestiges of academic freedom and to bring the schools into line with its policies of militarism and extreme nationalism. Guido De Ruggiero, himself minister of public instruction for a short while in the Bonomi government of 1944–45, maintained that the Gentile reform as first proposed was very un-Fascist and was from the beginning subject to a process of "slow and continued erosion that gradually caused it to assume the form of fascism . . . with authoritarian methods and distortion of the educational processes . . . thus making it a tool in the hands of the government."[75]

Gentile watched the progressive disfigurement of his reform with growing alarm during the 1920s. In the 1925 Senate debates, he had compared himself to Saint Sebastian, surrounded by criticism and recriminations on all sides. In a letter to Giuseppe Bottai in March 1925 he said: "Betrayed? Yes, the word is hard, but it is the only correct word."[76] In 1927 he wrote to Mussolini complaining that the PNF was sabotaging his reform through the "constant, minute, arbitrary, and irresponsible interference of party authorities in the administration of the school . . . on the pretext of fascistization—which in reality too often means a way to favor the worst Fascists."[77]

Gentile's bitterness and disillusionment were shared by many of his collaborators, who had had high hopes for the proposed alliance between the neo-idealists and the PNF. Giuseppe Lombardo-Radice defended the reform in the journal *Educazione nazionale*. Ernesto Codignola wrote shortly before the Senate debates of March 1925: "Fascism has the merit of having faced the reform of the school immediately but also the fault of having abandoned it to its fate—or what is worse, to its adversaries—as soon as it was born."[78] In 1928 Codignola wrote in *La nuova scuola*: "He who has the illusion of imparting political education with parades, demonstrations, with the continual distraction of pupils and teachers from their daily tasks, and, worse still, by police-state inquisition into the secrets of conscience . . . has nothing to do with fascism."[79]

By 1928, however, parades and demonstrations were the order of the day, and the Gentile reform was a relic of the past. Gentile himself ended up in a no-win situation: vilified by anti-Fascists for his association with the regime but rejected and deprived of real influence by party leaders who felt he was not one of them.

The second stage of the process had begun: the period of *fascistizzazione* that eventually produced Giuseppe Bottai's Carta della Scuola in 1939.

CHAPTER THREE

The New Spirit in the Schools

The entire nation has become . . . a great school. . . . Italy has found her Teacher.

—Armando Carlini

Benito Mussolini appointed Giovanni Gentile as minister of public instruction and defended his reform of the school as revolutionary and Fascist for some very specific reasons. As noted, the Gentile reform was the first important reform undertaken by the Fascist government, and Mussolini hoped that it would prove that the regime could take decisive action on an important national issue and make use of the intellectual community in the process of national renewal. In his effort to resolve the long-standing conflict with the Catholic church, Mussolini also saw Gentile's reform as laying down the basis for cooperation with the Vatican. The minister's desire to cut down on the number of state schools further served the regime's purposes in the beginning by decreasing the expenses of the ministry, thereby contributing to economic stabilization.

Gentile's reform and the cultural vision that inspired it were less and less congenial to the spirit of the new regime as it developed in the twenties. Gentile and his idealist disciples had attempted in their reforms to construct society according to their own vision: a rigidly stratified society run by an elite of humanist intellectuals. In Gentile's view, freedom of teaching and the needs of the state were not incompatible. He claimed that his reforms would both encourage the creative intellectual process and serve the new national government.

The idealists who shared this vision were, however, a distinct minority. Gentile's reform was attacked by many in the Fascist movement for its lack of attention to physical education and its neglect of technical and vocational training. Many critics maintained that there was too much high-flown theory and too little of real practical value in the philosopher's handiwork.[1] In parliamentary debates some deputies criticized the reform as too abstract and intellectual; others claimed that it allowed too much freedom for private schools; still others charged that Gentile's system was classist and aristocratic. Several speakers accused the minister of living in the clouds.[2]

Though he had at first defended Gentile, as we have seen, Mussolini eventually encouraged the reform of the reform. By the mid-twenties the Duce's own political concerns had changed, and the new direction demanded new men and new initiatives. The idealists began a losing battle to preserve the spirit and the letter of Gentile's reform after his departure from the ministry, in July 1924.

The date is significant. The order of the day after the resolution of the Matteotti crisis was *fascistizzazione*: on 3 January 1925 Mussolini at last put the indecision of the past months behind him and began to lay the foundation upon which he and his party faithful would build the "totalitarian" edifice of the Fascist state. Fascistization of the schools did not take place in a vacuum: attempts to infuse the new Fascist spirit into Italy's educational institutions were part and parcel of the attempt to fascistize the entire political, social, and economic life of Italy that was characteristic of the period after 1925.

In his speech on 3 January 1925 Mussolini shook off the temporary paralysis of the Matteotti affair and promised, "The situation will be clarified in every field."[3] Clarification came in a series of decrees over the next few years. In late 1925 a decree on the prerogatives of the head of government endowed Mussolini with full executive powers (though he was still subject to removal by the king), gave him the right to initiate all discussion on legislation in the Chamber, and freed him from responsibility to parliament.[4] Several attempts on the Duce's life in 1926 provided the political justification for a rash of repressive "exceptional decrees" during late 1926 and 1927 that suppressed all non-Fascist parties and syndicates, established the use of *confino* or enforced residence for offenses against the state, and set up the Special Tribunal for the Defense of the State to try political crimes.[5] Reform of the electoral laws in 1928 provided for the use of a single list (nominated by members of the Fascist syndicates and chosen by the Grand Council) that voters accepted or rejected in toto. Such plebiscites were the only shred of political participation left to Italians.[6] In late December 1928 the law defining the powers of the Fascist Grand Council entrusted this party organ with responsibility for nomination of the head of government and the cabinet, and with advisory powers on matters such as succession to the throne and the prerogatives of the crown.[7]

Changes in the party leadership during this period also contributed to the forward motion of fascistization—and to the PNF's loss of real influence over the regime's political direction. On 30 March 1926 the Fascist Grand Council accepted the "resignation" of Roberto Farinacci, the explosive *ras* of Cremona who had served as PNF secretary since February 1925, presiding over the consolidation of the regime in the wake of the Matteotti crisis.[8] Farinacci was replaced by a man who was in almost every way his temperamental and political opposite. Augusto Turati has been called "the Duce's closest collaborator" and the best secretary of the PNF.[9] An enthusiastic interventionist, Turati had served during the war but had joined the Brescia *fascio* relatively late, toward the end of 1920. He was a faithful executor of the Mussolinian vision, an organizer with a taste for administration every bit as keen as Farinacci's love of adventure and violence. Farinacci had envisioned an elitist, oligarchic party based on the power and vitality of the *squadristi* and opposed to the "transformation of the state" by compromise with existing powers. His removal from office signaled Mussolini's desire to rid himself of the troublesome Fascist *intransigenti* and the ebbing of the Fascist "second wave."[10]

Turati aimed at making the PNF a loyal instrument of the Fascist regime. His goal was to liberate the party from independent-minded provincial leaders and the pockets of personal power around the *ras*. The PNF, in his view, was to be an "instrument of the will of the state."[11] For Turati the quality of members counted more than quantity; in January 1927 enrollments in the PNF were closed except for new recruits from the youth groups.[12] Reforms of the party statute in 1926 and 1929 accentuated its hierarchical character.[13] Under Turati the process that would be continued by his successors began: the suppression of the PNF's real power to effect policy, but the broadening of its sphere of administrative and bureaucratic competence over the auxiliary mass organizations of the regime.

This was a goal shared by Turati's short-lived successor, Giovanni Giuriati, who served as PNF secretary from October 1930 to December 1931.[14] Giuriati's goal was to bring the PNF under the total control of the Duce: to increase its technical and administrative functions but to strip it of real political autonomy. Giuriati continued the policy of closed enrollments; during his fourteen-month tenure some 120,000 PNF members were purged.[15]

Storau

If Augusto Turati and Giovanni Giuriati wanted to fascistize Italy, their successor, Achille Starace, wanted to put the nation in uniform. Starace served as party secretary from December 1931 to November 1939—longer than any other man. He was a true zealot, a *diciannovista* who had been elected vice-secretary of the PNF in 1921 and had commanded the Fascist legions from the Veneto during the March on Rome. Starace was a humorless and imperious man, most at home in jackboots and a black shirt presiding over one of the innumerable parades and demonstrations that became standard fare during his stewardship. He dreamed that Italy would become a great military power, and to this end everything in sight—language, dress, leisure-time activities, and even paunchy party functionaries—had to be fascistized. Under Starace the regime reached its maturity. By the end of the twenties the course had been charted, the key choices made, and the most characteristic institutions set up.

By 1929 the new direction in education was manifest. In that year the Ministry of Public Instruction became the Ministry of National Education. The school's traditional goal of *istruzione* was supplanted by the Fascist goal of *educazione*: the indoctrination and political formation of the young. The change was an expression of Mussolini's desire to introduce new elements into the school, elements that would make education into something bolder, more virile, more disciplined—more Fascist, in a word.[16]

Fascistization took many different forms: an increase in the blatantly political content of school curricula and the introduction of state textbooks; ever-tighter control and subordination of teachers to make them faithful servants of the state and eliminate academic freedom; more rigid centralization of the school administration to bring all academic personnel under the close supervision of the ministry; the use of the school as an agency of military regimentation; and the establishment of paramilitary party youth groups that would complement the political work of the schools. With the establishment of the ONB in 1926, military instruction and participation in PNF ceremonies and rituals became an integral part of the students' school life. As the years passed a kind of tug-of-war developed between those teachers who did not want the school to lose its true function of forming critical minds and those who stressed political education. The relationship between the schools and the PNF youth groups mirrored in microcosm the conflicts between the state and the party on matters of education. Following Mussolini's dictum *Libro e moschetto, fascista perfetto*, the schools and the youth groups together were to form the perfect Fascist: "warlike and studious."[17]

Outward manifestations of the government's desire to deck the school out in Fascist garb came very early. These early attempts, however, were sporadic, and the results varied greatly from province to province. In November 1922 Gentile ordered the establishment of "remembrance parks" dedicated to the local war dead in each town. These parks were the special concern of the school children, who were to keep them tidy and stand guard, dressed in their group uniforms, on days of Fascist or national celebrations. Letters from the minister to all *provveditori* in January 1923 ordered that Fascist songs and the Roman salute be included in daily flag ceremonies at the schools.[18] Each classroom was also to be dedicated to one of the martyrs of the Fascist revolution.[19] Herman Finer, who observed the Italian classroom in these years at close range, said succinctly: "Every school has been converted to a subbranch of the Fascist Party."[20]

Believe, One of the main lines of attack in the government's campaign to
Obey, fascistize the school was the drive to control and organize the teachers.
Fight Despite (or perhaps because of) his own experience in the schools,
Mussolini was suspicious of teachers who could easily "awaken doubts
and play politics" by the timely use of an allusion or an opinion from the
lectern. The teacher, he said, "has a political office and must be a
Fascist."[21] Teachers in the Fascist state were, in the words of another
commentator, to be "apostles and priests."[22] Agnosticism had no place
in the realm of the intellectuals any more than it did in the political
sphere; culture under fascism had to be Fascist culture—meaning culture
serving the needs of the regime.[23]

There was sufficient early opposition among teachers and professors
to worry the leadership. In July 1924, for example, a demonstration
at the University of Florence protesting the government's role in the
Matteotti murder resulted in six arrests. Involved in the demonstration
was the historian Gaetano Salvemini, whose active ties with the opposition journal *Non mollare* later led to his arrest. Salvemini's fate provoked another demonstration in Florence and publication of a manifesto
of support signed by several thousand, among them the literary critic
Giuseppe Antonio Borgese and Giuseppe Lombardo-Radice. Borgese
himself later left Italy for the United States, after he lost his position at
the University of Milan for refusing to sign the loyalty oath.[24] These and
other examples of unrest in the intellectual community resulted in the
passage of a law on 24 December 1925 providing for the forcible retirement of any public employee who demonstrated views "incompatible
with the general political aims of the government." Salvemini, one of the
most distinguished of the early *fuorusciti*, left Italy for Paris in 1925 and
later went to Harvard.[25]

Other university professors and teachers also served in the early years
as rallying points of anti-Fascist sentiment. Francesco Ruffini, professor
of church law at the University of Turin, was a popular lecturer until his
refusal to take the loyalty oath also forced his resignation.[26] The *licei*
produced other examples of intellectuals who would not be exploited as
political pillars of the regime. In November 1926 Umberto Cosmo was
removed from his position at the Liceo Massimo d'Azeglio in Turin
because of his refusal to conform. On that occasion he wrote to Minister
Fedele: "My thought as a teacher and as a writer has always been
inspired by the purest springs of the Christian religion and the Italian
Risorgimento. . . . Your Excellency gives me fifteen days to justify
myself. I thank you, but I confess that I do not see what I have to excuse
myself for." In 1929 Cosmo sent a letter of solidarity to Croce after his

speech against the Lateran Accords; he was shortly thereafter shipped off to *confino* on the island of Lipari.[27]

One of the most effective means of shaping a loyal teaching cadre was simply to eliminate all those teachers who did not conform. The December 1925 law on public employees allowed the regime to carry out a purge of the teaching corps that was apparently accomplished on quite a large scale.[28] After February 1929 elementary and secondary school teachers were required to take an oath of loyalty to the regime—one way of offsetting the apparent gains made by the church that same month in education.[29] Political merits were considered routinely in salary and promotion decisions, and as Mussolini's demographic campaign gained momentum, teachers were often given bonuses for marrying or producing offspring. In 1933 membership in the PNF became a prerequisite for employment in the state administration, including the schools.[30] This law did provide that those who were already employed were not bound to request membership, but the regulation was applied so rigidly that by the mid-thirties the civil servants who "did not have a party card could be counted on one's fingers."[31]

The regime also exerted pressure on teachers, especially primary school teachers, to participate as group leaders and officers in the PNF's youth organizations. By the late 1920s teachers who expected to be promoted had to devote considerable time and energy to these activities. The aim was identification of the school and regime: fascistization of the academic institutions by blurring the lines between the school and the party. In rural areas, where the schools were run directly by the ONB, it became increasingly rare to find elementary school teachers who did not also serve as officers of the youth groups. This was less true in urban areas, but even there the party made an all-out effort to see that as many teachers as possible became identified with the regime's youth program.

As party members, teachers were obliged to attend the meetings of the local *fascio*, march in parades wearing the black shirt, and come to class wearing the PNF insignia. By 1926 the Roman salute was imposed on all state employees. After 1934 every elementary school teacher was also required to wear the uniform of the PNF or the Fascist militia during school hours to impress upon the student that he or she was no longer a teacher but an "officer, educator, commandant of his students . . . who prepares them in and out of school for service to the Fascist Fatherland."[32] Failure to discharge any of these obligations with the proper dedication and enthusiasm meant withdrawal of the party card and unemployment.

The intellectual and cultural pretensions of the regime and Mussolini's own suspicions of academics combined to make the party's fascistization drive in the universities something of a carrot-and-stick affair.

The government constantly tried to bring non-Fascist intellectuals into its political orbit by tempting them with subsidies, awards, and positions of beribboned honor—in the Italian Academy, for example. This attempt to penetrate the world of high culture was never very successful. The *Enciclopedia Italiana* project, to take one case, could not get off the ground using only those intellectuals faithful to the regime. In the end—and Gentile was the key force here—the project included the contributions of many scholars and scientists who were decidedly non-Fascist or even anti-Fascist: men such as Attilio Momigliano, Antonio Banfi, Federico Chabod, Piero Calamandrei, Rodolfo Mondolfo, Enrico Fermi, and Gaetano De Sanctis, among others.

Attempts to fascistize the universities continued during the early 1930s. In March 1930 the Grand Council decreed that all faculty deans and university rectors should be chosen from among those professors enrolled for at least five years in the PNF.[33] A circular from Starace in October 1933 required the presence of a *fiduciario* or party trustee at all university lectures. Later all rectors and deans were ordered to wear the black shirt with their academic garb for solemn university ceremonies.[34]

In August 1931 all university professors were required to sign the following oath: "I swear to be loyal to the King, to his royal successors, to the Fascist Regime, to observe loyally the Constitution and the other laws of the State, to exercise the profession of teacher and to carry out all academic duties with the aim of training upright and hardworking citizens who are devoted to the fatherland and to the Fascist Regime. I swear that I neither belong to nor shall belong to associations or parties whose activities do not harmonize with the duties of my profession."[35] Recalcitrant professors were subject to unsubtle pressure from university rectors for several months, and in December Pope Pius XI threw the weight of the church into the balance by approving the oath for Catholics provided they make a mental reservation that it would not conflict with their duties to God or the church.[36]

On 20 December 1931 the names of those men refusing to take the oath were published: only 11 or 12 out of some 1,250 refused to bow, though two others did retire from their positions rather than swear the oath and one apparently continued to teach without signing. Those who would not capitulate were dismissed from their positions.[37] Clearly many of those who did sign were motivated more by practical considerations than by faith. Many saw refusal to sign as a futile gesture and, following the counsel of Croce, accepted the oath in order to avoid abandoning the universities and the students to the servile Fascists. There were probably few committed Fascists among the university professors, but there were also few instances of open political resistance, especially as the regime tightened its control during the 1930s.

As protests reached Rome from professional organizations in Europe

and America, the Fascist loyalty oath became something of an international cause célèbre. The issue was used rather effectively outside Italy
by anti-Fascists as proof of Fascist repression. But inside Italy the almost
total adhesion of the intellectuals was flaunted as a victory by the
regime, and zealous Fascist university students organized demonstrations against uncooperative professors. Perhaps the most lasting impression on other professors was made by the beating of nonjuror Bortolo
Negrisoli, a surgeon at the University of Bologna, who was severely
injured in January 1932 by a gang of young zealots. A newspaper
editorial in December 1932 indicated, however, that even with the oath
the climate did not change as fast as the regime wanted. "It is time,"
warned the editorial, "to be done with scientific and academic individualism which are signs only of professional pride. Under the Fascist
regime even the universities, like every other institution of the state,
must be an *instrumentum regni*."[38]

The PNF and the Teacher Associations

Compelled to become party members and oath takers, the majority of
teachers in Italy were also corralled into "professional" organizations by
the PNF. Teachers' associations and congresses had been a regular feature of Italian academic life for decades, but under fascism they became
mere window dressing, organizations whose job it was to issue periodic
statements parroting the party line and to hold meetings to rubber-stamp
the latest declarations of the ministry.

Pre-Fascist teachers' organizations had won for teachers the right to
be consulted on educational policy. Because most were under the control
of Socialist and democratic elements, however, they were viewed with
great suspicion by the nationalists and conservatives. Gentile was especially concerned lest these organizations stymie the application of his
reforms. He pointedly refused to meet with the representatives of the old
associations, and the Gentile reform provided that members of the teachers' groups be eliminated from all consultative committees in the ministry. Teachers, he said, were to respect ministerial directives as "a sacred
thing, with military devotion, with ready, absolute, and unconditional
obedience."[39]

The regime made various attempts to organize the teachers before it
found the right formula in 1931. The Associazione Nazionale Insegnanti
Fascisti (ANIF), headed by Acuzio Sacconi, specifically refused membership to any teachers in Catholic or democratic organizations. Pressure to join was heavy, and by 1927 the ANIF had already achieved
impressive enrollments. In 1931 all teachers' organizations were merged
into the Associazione Fascista della Scuola (AFS).[40] The group was

divided into five sections corresponding to the various levels and types of schools. It published two journals—*La Scuola fascista* and *La Cultura fascista*—and held annual meetings in Rome featuring little discussion of pedagogical problems but heady doses of political propaganda. In November 1932 the AFS came under the direct control of the PNF, as did all other associations of public employees. Membership in the AFS was voluntary until 1937, but refusal to join was considered tantamount to open opposition to the regime. Not surprisingly, enrollment increased rapidly.[41]

In 1933 Starace shackled teachers ever more closely to the party by ordering that all members of the AFS also be active in the National Fascist Institute of Culture, later renamed the Istituto Nazionale di Cultura Fascista (INCF).[42] The idea of a uniquely Fascist culture had been suggested by the Gentile manifesto of 1925; Mussolini inaugurated the organization on the Capitoline Hill in December of that year. By 1941 the INCF had branches in all major Italian towns and on all university campuses. Its enrollment reached almost two hundred thousand that same year, though the majority of this number were teachers who had joined at the "suggestion" of their superiors.[43]

The INCF was clearly a device to keep the teachers politically aligned with the PNF. The organization concentrated on promoting Fascist studies at home and abroad by organizing public lectures, publishing books and pamphlets, and establishing libraries. The group also published a journal, *Civiltà fascista*. The involvement of schoolteachers and university professors as lecturers for the INCF was another example of the conscious blurring of lines between the educational function of the school and the political function of the party.

De Vecchi at the Ministry of National Education

Despite all the regime's attempts to adapt the Italian school to the new Fascist climate, there were many in the party who felt that the question of the school was still an open one. In April 1935 an editorial in *Critica fascista* charged that the schools still wavered between "the old and the new, between institutions and dispositions imposed by the regime and the spirit which remains what it was."[44]

Mussolini realized that the results had been less than satisfactory and, indeed, had already taken steps to try to solve the problem. In the past all of the ministers of education had come from the ranks of upper-level teachers or from the *fiancheggiatori*. Fascistization of the school shifted into high gear with the disastrous appointment of Cesare Maria De Vecchi—Count of Val Cismon by virtue of Fascist merit—as the minister of national education in January 1935. De Vecchi, who served in this

capacity until November 1936, had been a *quadrumvir* during the March
on Rome and was a life member of the Fascist Grand Council, a senator
since 1924, and Italy's first ambassador to the Holy See in 1929. He was
a staunch Catholic and monarchist, a rude and dull-witted reactionary
completely closed to culture but firmly convinced that it was his duty to
subdue the unfaithful denizens of all educational institutions by demanding complete loyalty and obedience to the regime. De Vecchi seemed
like the perfect man to bring the new martial and virile Fascist imperial
style into the schools. He proposed to correct the lack of discipline in
education by carrying out what he termed a "complete reclamation of the
school."[45] In practice this meant the elimination of any shred of autonomy in administration or freedom of teaching in the classroom, and
the imposition of rigid centralization aimed at the complete identification of the interests of the party and those of the ministry, schools, and
youth groups.[46]

Gentile's administrative reforms had also reinforced the hierarchical
and pyramidal character of educational institutions, but most of his
efforts had been devoted to tightening academic standards and closing
off the higher levels of the system to the unfit. He had reduced the
number of state schools by about 10 percent, limited the number of
students in each class to thirty-five, and left some schools in places with
fewer than a hundred thousand inhabitants in the control of the munici-
palities. None of this sat well with the Fascists, who were determined to
monopolize the educational process. Later reforms of Gentile's reform
removed limitations on class size, increased the number of state schools,
and brought under the control of the state hundreds of previously private
schools. Under Fedele in 1928, all professional and technical institutes
were removed from the jurisdiction of the Ministry of National Economy
and put under the control of the Ministry of National Education.[47] By
January 1935 all public elementary schools had been brought under the
direct control of the central government.[48]

Other administrative reforms undertaken by De Vecchi altered the
grievance procedure in the schools by investing the minister with full
disciplinary authority and reorganized the *consiglio superiore*. After De
Vecchi this group consisted of thirty-five members, all nominated directly by the minister, who could accept or ignore their suggestions.
Later provisions also gave the minister complete control over all school
curricula, class programs, and schedules. De Vecchi boasted that he
knew what subjects were being taught in classrooms all over Italy at any
hour of the day. Such devotion to regimentation was of course diametri-
cally opposed to Gentile's insistence on the need for spontaneity in the
classroom.

De Vecchi also struck at the administrative authority of the *provveditori*, who had had responsibility under the Gentile reforms for a wide

range of educational decisions in their own regions. To ensure central control, their office once again became a provincial one, and their duties were severely circumscribed. In fact, the *provveditori* became vassals of the minister, who operated very much like an absolute monarch.

De Vecchi left his personal stamp most clearly on the universities, which he suspected of harboring anti-Fascist elements. In November 1935 he won full authority over university curricula; the law stipulated that although individual professors might petition for changes, the minister was not bound to grant such requests unless the needs of national culture were judged to require it. The minister also became the final arbiter in matters of hiring: he was to approve all appointments made by the various university departments and could even make appointments on his own initiative or transfer professors or teachers at his pleasure.

De Vecchi also did away with Gentile's over-intricate classification of universities, which smacked to him of diffusion of authority. A June 1935 law empowered the minister to control, suppress, or create universities.[49] In De Vecchi's system, all universities were to be controlled and maintained by the state. By law not more than one state-supported university could exist in any city; this meant that separate institutes (of engineering, architecture, or agriculture, for example) became departments of the local university, a process that resulted in even more control by the central government.

In November 1936 De Vecchi was replaced by Giuseppe Bottai, who held the ministerial portfolio until February 1943. Both men were ready for a change of scene: Bottai was then governor of Rome, and De Vecchi asked to be sent to Rhodes as governor of the Aegean Islands.[50]

His departure was greeted with great relief in educational circles. Both his programs and his manner had elicited widespread opposition from teachers and administrators. Gentile, among many others, could not abide him. In 1935 he had written to Codignola: "I begin to worry about the new minister who is in good faith but an ass and a fanatic with a hard head."[51] Police reports commented that teachers dismissed him as unintelligent, unmannered, arrogant, overbearing, and a megalomaniac. Still others wrote that teachers referred to him as "a pig," "Tsar of Russia," or "Caligula," and complained that he had staffed the ministry with totally servile and incompetent bootlickers. One police informant reported that De Vecchi had ordered a thousand copies of his own portrait for the schools.[52] A letter from Rome closed with the comment: "Everyone here agrees that for the people of the Aegean, the quiet life is over."[53]

Curriculum revisions of one sort or another were introduced almost every year after the Gentile reform. By the 1930s the curricula at all levels, but especially in the elementary schools, reflected the increasing chauvinism and militarism of PNF policies.

The basic subjects taught in the primary schools remained the same, but Fascist propaganda was ladled over all in generous measure. Professional journals and ministerial directives for teachers emphasized that fascism could, and should, be introduced into all school subjects. "All Italian educational life," a 1938 conference report stressed, "must have one focus: MUSSOLINI."[54]

The link between fascism and religion was to be consistently underlined. For every religious maxim there was a parallel Fascist maxim: children should be taught that they owed absolute loyalty to fascism just as they owed blind obedience to God; mysteries of the faith should not be discussed or debated, nor should the truths of fascism; just as the church had its martyrs, so, too, did fascism.[55]

The arts were also to be pressed into the Fascist mold: children were to be taught singing so they could raise their voices in praise of the regime (or so the young boys could go into battle with a song on their lips), and art was to fan the students' national pride. Instead of the "cold letters of the alphabet," teachers were urged to have their students trace out the most incisive and stirring phrases of the Duce, patriotic mottoes, and memorable Fascist proclamations. Italian-language instruction usually began with the repetition of certain key words in grade one (words such as "Benito," "Duce," *fascismo,* or *re*) and progressed in the later grades to compositions on Mussolini's speeches or celebrations of the regime.[56]

Even arithmetic and the physical sciences could be instrumental in forming a Fascist conscience in the young. Beginning with the introduction of numbers (the first lesson recommended the basic equation of one God equals one Duce) and into more complex calculations, the problems aimed at showing the remarkable industrial and commercial progress being made in Fascist Italy and the blessings enjoyed by the Italians as a result of the regime's policies. Studies in the physical sciences were to "illustrate the theories of Galileo and Marconi with remarks designed to emphasize the primacy and excellence of the Italian genius."[57]

Children began to study history in the third grade; it was the subject most deeply influenced by Fascist propaganda in the primary schools. Teachers were urged to make the new imperial spirit of Italy the chief focal point of their lessons in order that all Italian children might feel the pride of being "born . . . on this soil bathed by so much blood, sanctified by so many martyrs, made powerful by His great genius."[58]

Secondary school material was more technical and specialized and did not lend itself as easily to a general infiltration of Fascist notions. In addition, the need to prepare students for state examinations and professional careers made wholesale changes in the curricula unfeasible. In these more advanced schools certain subjects were singled out—especially classical studies—and in these classes the students received concentrated exposure to the world according to fascism.

Historical studies served primarily to construct the myth of the divine civilizing mission of Italy throughout history: Italy was portrayed as the cradle of civilization (the contributions of the Greeks were minimized or overlooked entirely) and the conqueror of the Western world. Ancient history was Roman history, meaning military history and studies of heroic figures such as Caesar and Augustus. The Risorgimento was portrayed as a prelude to the glories of the Fascist epoch.

The reading lists and the examination material for the secondary schools reflected the regime's policy of cultural autarky. Selections of reading matter presented obvious difficulties, and usually offensive names (of well-known anti-Fascists such as Croce, or later of Jewish authors) were simply crossed off and selections from more congenial writers added. Curriculum revisions under De Vecchi, for example, excised readings by such authors as John Stuart Mill, Henrik Ibsen, Leo Tolstoy, and Victor Hugo to make room for selections by Alfredo Oriani, D'Annunzio, and Mussolini. Italo Balbo's account of his Atlantic crossing also became standard fare in the *liceo*. In response to objections from the church, writings by Rousseau, Kant, Hegel, Leibniz, Bruno, Schopenhauer, and Gioberti were eliminated from courses in philosophy. After 1936 Mussolini's *Dottrina del fascismo* was required in all secondary schools as the apex of studies in philosophy and history.[59]

In 1930, following the accords with the Vatican, the compulsory religion classes introduced in the elementary schools by the Gentile reforms were extended to the secondary schools of the kingdom. Religious studies accounted for only one hour each week, but the courses were taught by priests instead of by lay teachers as in the primary grades.[60] In the beginning there was no examination in religion, but the student's performance was recorded on the teacher's progress reports. Under De Vecchi, however, proficiency in religion courses became a requisite for promotion to the higher grades.

Between 1929 and 1931 two new courses, both of them entirely Fascist in content, were also introduced into the secondary school curricula: corporative law and Fascist culture. The corporative law courses, based on the Labor Charter, emphasized Fascist doctrine, the structure of the PNF and the Fascist state, and the ordering of the corporate system.[61] These courses served primarily as vehicles for attacks against liberal economic and political theory. The very real problems of corporativism were naturally never discussed. Undoubtedly, many teachers required to teach the lessons never attached much importance to them, but these Fascist courses on political and social theory were often the only treatment of such topics that most students ever heard in their school careers.

The precise nature of the new courses in Fascist culture is more difficult to define. In 1931 they were added to many secondary school programs in geography and history, even in the technical and vocational training schools. These courses never had any great importance; they were little more than a mishmash of Fascist platitudes and repetitions of material the students heard often in their other lessons. In November 1936 De Vecchi extended Fascist culture lessons to the elementary schools, beginning in the third grade.[62]

The regime introduced in the universities some subjects that were totally or predominantly Fascist in character, though on the whole university curricula were less influenced by PNF propaganda than those of the lower schools. Fascists had long been using university lecterns as soapboxes, but the influence of the party was also evident in some regular courses. Corporate economy was taught in much the same vein as in the secondary schools; at the university, however, it was a required subject in law, commerce, and economics. History and geography were also deeply influenced by the Fascist world view. The courses stressed Roman imperialism (and downplayed Renaissance individualism) and emphasized the Risorgimento, the Italian national mission, and the corruption of the liberal state. Agrarian economy was taught as a "manifestation of the rural spirit of fascism."[63]

The regime established political science as a separate discipline and department in the Italian universities. Before the March on Rome, the only school of political science in Italy had been the Istituto Cesare Alfieri, set up in Florence in 1888. The first Fascist school of political science was organized at the University of Rome in March 1924 to train the regime's future managers. Other schools were set up that same year in Pavia and Padua, but many of the more zealous Fascists were unhappy with the tenor of instruction. In 1925 the Rome department included Alfredo Rocco, Gioacchino Volpe, and Gaetano Mosca, but there were also others less congenial to the regime: Antonio Salandra gave courses in administrative law, Vittorio Emanuele Orlando taught constitutional law, and Antonio De Viti De Marco lectured on finance. The last two were forced to leave teaching after they refused to sign the loyalty oath. A 1925 editorial in the aggressive Gruppi Universitari Fascisti (GUF) journal *La Rivolta ideale* in Rome denounced the "demoliberal mentality" of the "mummies" of the Rome faculty and called for a thorough housecleaning.[64]

In response to this and other complaints, the regime inaugurated the faculty of political science in Perugia during the academic year 1927–28.

The four-year program of the school, first headed by the syndicalist Sergio Panunzio (later rector of the University of Perugia), relied heavily on the theories of Pareto and Mosca; its staff included both Paolo Orano and Robert Michels. Students chose from a wide variety of courses, but all were required to take exams in the history and doctrine of fascism, Fascist legislation, corporate law, and colonial policy. The school was a bastion of orthodoxy. Enrollments in this and other political science schools increased rapidly over the years because many young men believed (wrongly, as it turned out in most cases) that the training promised good prospects for employment in the government.[65]

The school curricula were also deeply infected by the spirit of militarism, especially after the Ethiopian war. In order to produce the new Italian citizen-soldier, the regime introduced courses on military culture into the secondary schools and the universities in 1934–35.[66]

The courses, taught by army officers, were required for certificates or diplomas and began in the third year of the *ginnasio* (or the equivalent in other types of schools). The program was divided into three levels. The first concentrated on basic military organization, map reading, and the history of the Great War. The second (in the first and second years of the *liceo*) emphasized the role of the military in the Fascist state and the relationship between the military and the political life of the nation. At the highest level (reserved for those students in the first two years of the university or *istituto superiore*), students were treated to speculation on more metaphysical points, such as the philosophy and theory of war.

Curriculum changes also affected female students, but in a decidedly different way. In 1938–39 the ministry introduced special courses for girls in infant hygiene and child care parallel to the military culture courses in secondary schools.[67] Such lessons were never extended to the universities, perhaps because the leaders of the PNF assumed that any woman who chose to pursue her education that far had no natural inclinations toward motherhood.

Introduction of the Libro Unico

In 1929 the regime introduced state textbooks in all public and private elementary schools. This state text, or *libro unico*, was a trump card in the regime's program to fascistize the schools and socialize the young—a truly mass medium that reached virtually all children educated in Italy between 1930 and 1943.

Since 1923 school textbooks had been chosen by provincial or regional committees under the direction of the *provveditori*, and lists of those texts approved for use in the schools had been published annually by the ministry. The work of the committees was slowed down by the

sheer volume of material presented for inspection; in the first year 2,491
textbooks were inspected and only 338 (less than 15 percent) were
approved. Until 1927 the judgments of these committees seem to have
been based on sound pedagogical concerns; in that year, however, the
party appointed an overseer from the ONB to sit on all book review
committees.[68]

The law requiring the adoption of the state texts passed under Minister
Giuseppe Belluzzo in January 1929.[69] One scholar of the period has
referred to the adoption of the *libro unico* as "the most drastic step in the
field of education taken by Fascism after the foundation of the ONB."[70]
The move did speed up the tempo of fascistization in the schools and
silence once and for all Gentile's call for freedom of teaching.

The regime established a ministerial commission to direct and coordinate the compilation of the necessary texts. This commission chose
authors in all fields, though it was the duty of the minister to see that all
books approved were "pedagogically sound and imbued with the true
Fascist spirit." Mussolini was extremely interested in the publication of
these texts and became personally involved in the choice of authors. The
first texts were presented to him by Minister Balbino Giuliano on 21
April 1930, 2,684 years to the day after the founding of Rome.[71]

Publication of the texts was an enormous undertaking. In the first year
they were used in the school (1930–31), the state arranged for the
printing of 5,445,000 books. Primers and religion texts were provided
for the first two grades and combined texts on history, geography, arithmetic, and science for the last three grades. The church was actively
involved in the selection of the religion texts, because all such material
had to be approved by an ecclesiastical committee.

A similar monopoly was never imposed on the secondary schools,
though texts used in these institutions were subject to censorship and
some were withdrawn. In theory the minister had always had veto power
over all books adopted in the secondary schools; in practice the decisions
had usually been left to a council of teachers in each school. By the mid-
thirties this state of affairs had begun to worry some of the more radical
advocates of total fascistization, but no concrete steps were taken until
the passage of the Carta della Scuola in 1939. Article 27 of this charter
required prior approval from the ministry before printing all secondary
school texts, but the outbreak of the war made realization of Bottai's
grand plan impossible.[72]

A Sample of State Textbooks for the Elementary Schools

An examination of some of the state textbooks sheds considerable light
on the fascistization program in the elementary schools. The textbooks

examined here were used in grades one through five in all Italian schools from 1938 to 1944 (these last edited by the Allied Commission). Studies of such school texts for earlier periods indicate that the tone and content of the volumes were substantially the same as in the later years. The law on the *libro unico* had stipulated that the books should be revised every three years, but the first real revisions came after 1935 to keep the books in tune with the regime's imperial and racial policies. As Fascist policy evolved, pages were added to the texts, most frequently in the readers and in history and geography sections. The material chosen here is representative of the reading matter presented to schoolchildren in classrooms all over Italy in these years, and should serve to highlight the main propaganda interests of the regime and the view of politics and society inculcated in Italian youngsters from their earliest days in school.[73]

In general, the books were of good quality technically, profusely illustrated and enlivened with an eye-catching use of color. The distinctly Fascist content of the books increased after the first-year primer, which concentrated on phonics. In the higher grades the nationalistic and militaristic tenor of the stories and lessons was striking. In addition to the compulsory Fascist themes, most of the books also stressed the simple virtues; elementary notions of hygiene and nature were included in all the books, though emphasized especially in the texts destined for the rural schools, which had separate books after 1938. Even in the sections not dealing directly with religion, there was a considerable amount of Catholic influence: stories about religious holidays, lives of the saints, and simple stories and prayers about Jesus and the Virgin Mary.

The children reading these state textbooks were to be left with one overriding impression: the world revolves around Italy, and Italy, in turn, revolves around Benito Mussolini and the Fascist party. Flags and symbols of the fatherland abounded. Cheek by jowl with these national or royal symbols were those of the PNF. In these texts there was no distinction made between patriotism and fascism; service to fascism was portrayed as a patriotic duty. The presence of both king and Duce in these textbooks served also to stress the unity and community that fascism had supposedly realized in Italy.

The genius and goodness of Mussolini were praised in a litany that became a grotesque exaltation of the Duce as a wise father come up from poverty and misery to guide the fortunes of all Italians. Veneration of this benevolent leader was religious in tone: he was portrayed as omnipotent and omniscient (knowing, for example, what a small boy wanted for his birthday and sending it to him personally). Stories compared him to the saints and told tales of children who became better for having visited his sacred birthplace or for having glimpsed him as he spoke from the balcony in Piazza Venezia. Another recurrent theme was that of the Duce as indomitable war hero; the Great War, it would seem, was fought at his bidding and under his direction. In the pages of these school books, the Duce was brave and felt no pain; around him flocked the most shining flowers of Italian youth, the heroes of the Fascist revolution whose often gory tales were also told and retold.

Later on the children began to read about the glories of his (or rather His) regime. They saw color pictures of rosy-cheeked men, women, and children all dressed in their PNF uniforms; they learned about the orderly and clean new cities that the genius of the Duce had created where once there had been only swamps. Fascism, the texts reiterated in simple terms, had produced social justice for all, and the old distinctions of rich and poor had disappeared. Mussolini became something of a magician who, having proclaimed the policy of autarky, then produced wool (or *lanital*, as it was called) out of ordinary milk, and waving fields of grain from the poor earth of Italy.

The regime's demographic campaign appeared in countless subtle and not so subtle ways in the pages of these texts: in most of the families in the readers there were many children, little girls were given dolls to prepare them for their job as (very young and very frequent) mothers, and stories ended with traditional formulas such as "God bless you and give you male children." The result of this boom in procreation was, naturally, overpopulation, which just as naturally was to be solved by expansion and colonization in the underpopulated and undercivilized areas of the world.

Another key theme was that of Fascist militarism and the new power of Italy. In these books all the young children ardently desired one thing above all: to put on their uniforms and march around with play rifles in preparation for the day when they could become real soldiers in the army of the Duce. They were fascinated by the strength and power of the young black shirts and mesmerized by tales of the heroism and derring-do of the Fascist legions in Ethiopia, Spain, and Albania. They learned to repeat the war cries of their big brothers and marched around town shouting, *Bombe a mano, carezze di pugnal!* ("Grenades and caresses from the dagger!"). Nationalism became chauvinism in these texts, especially in the frequent discussions of the African war. The Abyssinians were presented as bloodthirsty barbarians; their emperor was portrayed as a corrupt and ferocious slave-trader. The highlight of such stories was the bravery of the Italians, who responded to the perfidious British and French by rallying around their Duce in iron-willed opposition to sanctions. All of this is easy enough to ridicule, but it was the standard—in many cases the only—intellectual fare for millions of Italian children.

Religion lessons for the first and second grades were included in the readers; in the upper three grades there was a separate section on religion in the combined texts. In the later grades the material devoted to religion usually constituted about 20 percent of the textbook. Often the religious pictures and lessons seem out of place, juxtaposed as they are with stories and songs aimed at filling the child's mind with militarism and violence. "In the minds of the children," wrote Herman Finer, "Christ and Mussolini are brothers who speak the same language and hold positions of equal importance in the scheme of the universe, perhaps with Mussolini a little in the lead, since he is, after all, a living being and Christ is somewhere behind the clouds."[74]

The first-grade primer included in this sample was used for two years (1942 and 1943) in Italian schools.[75] Studies in phonics accounted for almost one-third of its content, but the regime intruded here as well. The letter *F*, for example, was illustrated with a picture of the *fasces*; the first word to be pronounced after learning the vowels was *eia*, a Fascist war cry. But the amount of material devoted exclusively to Fascist topics in the 1942 text was under 20 percent, considerably less than in the upper grades. Stories and poems about nature, by contrast, accounted for almost one-third of this first-grade reader, a much higher proportion than in books for the later grades. Many of the illustrations in the book, however, were of children dressed in their PNF uniforms, and the cover depicted two black-shirted youngsters surrounded by flags and a cannon.

The identification of regime and country was made abundantly clear to first-graders in a life story of the Duce told by Grandmother, who ended her tale: "He loved his Fatherland ever more and wanted to make it stronger and more powerful than all the other lands. All good Italians love him and repeat his blessed name." One young boy told his brother: "Believe, obey, fight: that is the command of the DUCE. Never forget it if you want to be a true soldier of the Fatherland." The stories were accompanied by designs showing the children surrounded by Italian and Fascist banners.[76]

The amount of material devoted to Fascist and patriotic subjects increased in the second-grade schoolbooks. In the 1938 reader and religion text, *L'italiano nuovo*, almost three-quarters of the stories and poems contained oblique or direct references to the regime and its achievements. In the 1942 book for the urban schools this type of material accounted for almost 60 percent of the total. Interestingly enough, in the 1942 volume for the rural schools the patriotic/Fascist stories were only a little over one-third of the total, but the amount of material dealing with nature accounted for over 40 percent. Stories about war and the military made up almost 20 percent of the second-grade text in the urban areas; less than 10 percent of the rural text was devoted to such stories. There was, in addition, a definite bias in the 1942 rural text supporting Fascist populism: frequent emphasis on the goodness of rural folk and the sanctity of the land, and continual references to the dirt and chaos of the city.[77]

From the first page of the 1938 second-grade textbook to the last there was hardly a page from which fascism was absent. Two families formed the core of the story: one the family of engineer Frattini, a former *squadrista*, and the other the family of Grandfather Gianni, farmer and stalwart Fascist. Grandfather's son Fausto returned blind from the war but never lamented his fate. He had only one regret: that he could no longer see the formidable black shirts arrayed in their impressive ranks. When Grandfather felt poorly, he called his family to his side to remind them of his last wish: to be buried in his black shirt. The book was illustrated only in black (for the *squadristi* shirts and banners that appeared so often) and in the national colors. The children on the cover and in the illustrations were also dressed in their youth group uniforms.

A story called "The Yes of the Deafmute" painted Mussolini as a thaumaturge with supernatural inspiration. Immersed in the crowd cheering the Duce on the day the empire was proclaimed, little Giuliano wanted more than anything else to be able to shout a reply to the leader's questions. In the end, his eyes brimming with tears, he miraculously overcame his affliction and shouted his answer: "Yes! Du-ce! Du-ce!" The story concluded: "A star is watching from the heavens. It is the eye of God."[78]

Many stories dealt with the regime's public works projects. One, entitled "Reclamation and the Battle of Grain," introduced children to the robust farmer Sandro, tilling the soil that just a few years earlier had been "unhealthy and unproductive swamps." This was when Italy was "poor and not respected and her sons, forced to search for bread in foreign lands, were like orphans." But, the story concluded, those days are gone and "the earth laughs and gives bread and joy to those who work it."[79] In another story, called "My House Is Small but My Faith Is Great," Grandfather Andrea told his grandchildren that he got his new house from the regime, and remembered back only twenty years "when beasts and men had to live together."[80]

On the cover of the 1942 second-grade text for the urban schools there was the ever-present *figlio della lupa* writing "WIN" on the walls. The text, not surprisingly, given the date of publication, was decidedly militaristic and racist in tone. One especially distasteful story was "The White Soul of Black John," about a missionary who came home from Africa with a native boy who, the priest explained, "is black outside but white inside . . . he loves Italy which has taught him to know the Lord. When he came to the missions he was little more than a beast: he went about nude and ate raw meat. Now he reads, writes, and wants to become a missionary like me to help his black brothers to find their white souls." The children were not convinced, and one asked if the little

African boy should be put in the laundry to make him clean again. This story was not removed from the 1944 version of the textbook.[81]

In the 1942 rural text, second-graders read the approved version of the Fascist revolution. Years ago, ran the story, Italy was a "beautiful and flowering garden," but in the garden there were a lot of wolves who wanted to destroy everything, "evil men who wanted to ruin the Fatherland." But then "to save everything one Man rose up and put himself at the head of an army of courageous men," who undertook a "glorious march during which the evildoers hid trembling with fear." Benito Mussolini, "the man who had defended the Fatherland so nobly, became Head of Government and DUCE OF ITALY."[82]

In the 1940 third-grade textbook used in urban schools almost three-quarters of the stories and poems related to Italy, the Duce, or the PNF. The cover carried out the familiar identification of fascism and fatherland: the title *Patria* was written on a background of Italian and Fascist banners. The tone was aggressively militaristic; the illustrations almost without exception were of uniformed men, women, and children.[83]

The long story called "23 March 1919," about the founding of the Fasci di Combattimento, was typical of the dramatic nature of much of the material in this book. Though the Socialists hated Mussolini, the story went, his men "pledged their loyalty to the 600,000 fallen for the greatness of Italy. And war, war without pity on the sad betrayers of the Fatherland. . . . How many fell? How many martyrs of Red barbarity? But heroes create heroes. For everyone that falls, there are one hundred who run to occupy his place. The squads become legions. The black stream, vigorous and cleansing, floods all the districts of Italy." A story about Mussolini's office at the *Popolo d'Italia* conjured up an equally striking image. In a room littered with the remnants of war—grenades, revolvers, flags of the *arditi*—sat a man: "The face of the Man is illuminated with the light of a superior intelligence and a great and passionate soul. . . . He sees the desolation of Italy. . . . He sees the Flag, bathed in blood of martyrs, trampled. No, no! Italy must be saved . . . at all costs. And he begins to write nervously. He etches words on the paper that seem to be made of fire, they burn so furiously. But they will do good. They are . . . words of warning to the Italians . . . to wake them to love for their outraged Mother."[84]

One of the favorite themes in these school texts was the African war ("the war Italy had been forced to fight") and the brave Italian response to the suffocating sanctions imposed by ungrateful ex-allies who "forgot that the World War had been won, above all, by Italy."[85] The 1938 text portrayed the war as being fought against the "ferocity of the *Ras*," who was a "true monster, blacker in his heart than in his face, who treated women and innocent children as his victims."[86]

The most popular of all the state textbooks for the fourth grade—one

used for many years—was written by Piero Bargellini, one of Italy's
best-known Catholic publicists, and illustrated by A. Della Torre. In the
1942 edition almost two-thirds of the fables, stories, and poems dealt
directly with fascism.[87]

The reader included several stories that expressed Fascist views toward women. One fable, entitled "Bertoldo and the Queen," began:
"The queen was rather ambitious. She wanted . . . to participate in
the king's council as the equal of men." The king responded to this
effrontery by sending Bertoldo to the queen with a small bird in a box,
with the order not to open the box until morning. Predictably, the queen
could not resist and the bird flew away. When the king received his wife
he said: "You want to come into the council, but you are not even capable
of keeping a secret for one night." Thus Italian children learned that
woman's place was in the home and not in the halls of state. The
Bargellini reader also contained a paean to the Duce called "Caesar and
Mussolini," in which nine-year-olds learned that Mussolini, like Caesar,
"has marched on Rome, not to sack it or punish it, but to liberate it from
incapable leaders. . . . He too has conquered the world. . . . He sees
. . . whole regions to be colonized; countries waiting for law; people
who want to work. He wants to see justice done, injustice set right; He
sees there are wounds to heal, sadness to console, treason to punish, and
heroism to exalt."[88]

The most popular fifth-grade reader was *Il Balilla Vittorio*, written by
Roberto Forges Davanzati, a former Nationalist who wove patriotism,
fascism, and Catholicism into an entertaining story about a young boy
named Vittorio Balestrieri and his ideal Fascist family. In the beginning
of the story Vittorio's father, a PNF secretary in Umbria, moved the
family to the bustling capital. Vittorio's school days in Rome and his
travels all over Italy provided a vehicle for propaganda about the regime
and its achievements.[89] Millions of ten- and eleven-year-olds read with
fascination about Vittorio's meeting with the Duce, his trip to the new
city of Sabaudia, his enthusiasm for the Ethiopian war, and his many
adventures in Rome. Vittorio's schoolteacher was an ex-combatant and a
fervent Fascist. All social classes were represented in the classroom, but
the book provided many opportunities for polemics against the bourgeois students (rich, overbearing, and usually from small families) and
praise for Fascist populism (the poor boy Meniconi from Trastevere was
one of seven children, and unfailingly protective of the weaker children
in the class).

In one particularly lyrical scene Vittorio went with his uncle to Assisi,
where he met a Franciscan monk whose monastery had been returned to
the order by the Duce. The story, originally written just before the
Concordat and published for the first time just after, emphasized the
close relationship between the state and the church. Comparing the

words of the Duce to the voice of God, the monk told Vittorio: "We Franciscans pray every day for the Duce's well-being which is, after all, the well-being of Italy."[90]

These state-approved readers were not the only textbooks deeply colored with Fascist propaganda; the combination volumes issued for the third to the fifth grades also contained frequent references to all aspects of Fascist history (or history according to fascism) and mythology. The Italian-language books spiced even the most prosaic grammar rules with fascism.[91] The study of mathematics, not quite as readily adapted to the propaganda needs of the regime, still showed Fascist influence. Third-graders learned their numbers by writing, "The Duce proclaimed the Empire after 174 days of economic siege by 52 states against Italy." Elementary calculations were taught using problems like this: "The glorious war in Africa lasted seven months. How many days is that?"[92]

Geography studies were a catchall for Fascist propaganda; they usually began with an outline of the Fascist government, praise for the regime's various reclamation projects, and discussions of sanctions. Italy's colonial mission also received concentrated attention in the geography sections. The new colonies of Italy were rich, fourth-graders learned, "but inhabitants were living in hovels and had a primitive life. There were slaves to liberate, children, men, and women to clothe; there were diseases to cure."[93] In the fifth-grade geography section, children read: "The Germans are tenacious and strong. . . . Today they form one solid and disciplined Nation that has need of living space." Concerning the Axis they learned: "Having identical political and economic interests, the Italians and Germans are indissolubly united in a common undertaking to give the world a just peace."[94] The 1942 fifth-grade geography textbook also parroted the regime's racial policies: "The white race is the most civilized, that is the most capable of great ideas; to this group the Italic race belongs."[95]

Voltaire once said that history is a series of accumulated imaginative inventions, and this definition certainly applies to the content of the state textbooks during the Fascist period. As taught in these school books, history was totally Italocentric, viewed in relation to the arrival of the man of providence and reduced to incomprehensibility because it ignored the role of other nations. History thus became a series of convenient myths directed toward a practical aim: producing consensus and enthusiasm for the regime among Italian schoolchildren. Separate sections on history in the mass-produced textbooks began with the third grade. The entire year's study was little more than an ode to the regime and a repetition of all the most commonly used Fascist myths. Mussolini was always portrayed as Italy's savior: "The deserters, traitors and cowards . . . sought to render vain the sacrifices of our 600,000 dead. . . . Our beautiful tricolor was reduced to a rag by sacrilegious hands . . .

while another flag, a red one symbolizing destruction, was waved and carried in triumph. . . . Then Benito Mussolini—the Man sent by God —determined to save the Fatherland from the Communist danger."[96]

The perfidy of the British and French, which had been a favorite propaganda myth of fascism since the Ethiopian war, was also blamed for the outbreak of the Second World War. After twenty years of trying to stifle the aspirations of the Italians, so the stories went, these ex-allies also tried to strangle the Germans, who, under the admirable leadership of Adolf Hitler, had set themselves to the task of reconstruction. But the selfish states, "who for some time had been used to bossing the whole world around," could not permit Germany to realize its rightful place in the world. After nine months of nonbelligerence the Italians joined in the conflict and, faithful to the orders of the Duce, "won everywhere: on land, on the sea, in the air." The conclusion of the chapter on World War II left the youngsters with food for thought: "The most luminous and complete victory will smile upon the forces of the Axis because their cause is just and holy." These words must have rung hollow by 1943 when Italian schoolchildren saw a much different reality all about them.[97]

Textbooks in the Secondary Schools

Although there were no *libri unici* for most of the courses taught in the secondary schools, the regime did publish various texts for use in the Fascist culture courses. These lessons actually began in the student's fifth year at school; they continued in the various types of secondary schools and in the postprimary *corsi integrativi* and the *scuole comple-mentari* to ensure that all students, regardless of social position, would have more than a nodding acquaintance with the basic tenets of the new political faith.

The books used in these courses were similar in content and approach to the state texts. Their general tone and level can be illustrated with reference to one volume used in the schools after 1928: *Ordinamento dello stato italiano fascista*, by Valerio Campogrande. The book, in essence a handbook on the organization of the Fascist state, began with the assertion that "in the Fascist state the duties of the individual have more importance than the rights of the individual." The ensuing discussion of the Fascist state as "ethical state" amounted to an identification of fascism with religion: "As there is only one official State religion which is the Catholic faith so, too, there must be only one political faith. . . . Religious dogmas are not to be discussed because they are the revealed truths of God. Fascist principles are not to be discussed because they have come from the mind of a Genius: BENITO MUSSOLINI."[98]

Vincenzo Biloni's *Cultura fascista*, a book used in the postprimary *scuole d'avviamento al lavoro*, was also liberally sprinkled with quotations from Mussolini and other PNF luminaries, poetic exhortations to love the richness and beauty of the Italian soil, and discussions on the "magnificent superiority" of the Italian race. A fairly frank discussion of the violence of the early Fascist *squadristi* (as well as their fondness for the *santo manganello* and castor oil) prompted this interjection justifying unfortunate means to achieve a just end: "Holy violence, necessary violence! . . . You must always remind yourselves that without this early violence fascism would not have triumphed and Italy would have been thrown into the abyss. One must be ready to use all means to bring about the triumph of one's own ideals."[99]

School Themes and Compositions

Children in Italian schools were reminded of the Duce and the PNF in countless other ways during school hours. A large portrait of Mussolini hung in every classroom, and dedication of this portrait was one of the most solemn events of the school year. All schoolchildren were provided with a "national notebook" for in-class assignments and homework, the cover of which was emblazoned with a smiling photo of the Duce and some of his most inflammatory phrases. The children prayed for the great man at the beginning of each lesson; they learned songs, hymns, and poems that sung his praises. Besides the state-approved *libro unico*, the regime distributed Giorgio Pini's hagiographic *Vita di Mussolini* gratis to all students, and sent out frequent memos to all teachers requiring them to read and explain in class long passages from the equally poetic version of the Duce's life by Margherita Sarfatti. In the colonial schools the cult of the Duce was also part of the students' daily routine. In Tunisia, for example, they learned the following prayer: "I believe in the supreme Duce, creator of the Black Shirts, and in Jesus Christ His only protector. Our Savior was conceived by a good teacher and a hard-working blacksmith. He was a valiant soldier. . . . He came down to Rome; on the third day he re-established the State. He rose to high office seated at the right hand of the Sovereign from whence He judged Bolshevism. I believe in the wisdom of the laws, the communion of citizens, the remission of sins, the resurrection of Italy, eternal strength. Amen."[100]

The personal diaries that Gentile had meant to be an expression of the experiences of each schoolchild and a record of his or her creative development were, as the fascistization process spread and took root, anything but spontaneous. A sample of themes and classwork done by students in the fourth and fifth grades from 1937 to 1941 provides clear evidence that much of what was written by the children was suggested, if not directly dictated, by their teachers. One group of diaries, for example, reported on a particular speech by the Duce and ended with the identical refrain that Italy "is courageous, tenacious, strong, and proud" and that the fatherland has "always fought and always won, and always will win."[101]

Compulsory class compositions and themes on required topics were supposed to have disappeared from the Italian classroom after the Gentile reforms, but such exercises were particularly well adapted to the needs of the regime. During the 1930s the assigned topics became more and more lyrical. The entire exercise, in fact, seems to have become a group effort aimed at producing pat phrases full of Fascist clichés. Perhaps the saddest exercise was the one given to the children in December 1940: "Write a letter to a soldier wishing him Merry Christmas and best wishes for the new year." One child wrote to his cousin fighting on the Greek-Albanian front, where the soldiers walked on cardboard shoes: "Food and arms are plentiful for you because the Fascist Government thinks of its soldiers. I am certain that in you, led as you are by such brave officers, the victory is already secure."[102]

In the secondary schools the amount of manifest political socialization in student compositions and assigned themes was just as great as in the elementary schools, but the topics assigned were more sophisticated and the responses even more poetic. The themes for admission to the lower secondary schools in the 1930s included: "Write an essay on the origins of *squadrismo* which . . . struggled against subversives and the renouncers of the Fatherland and with the March on Rome saved Italy from certain ruin."[103] In order to graduate from high school, students all had to take a final written examination on themes prepared by the ministry. Among the themes assigned during the 1930s was: "Of the numerous aspects of the Fascist revolution, the candidate should illustrate the one that has made the most vivid impression on his soul."[104]

Regardless of the specific topic assigned, it appears that many students felt compelled to inject some element of fascism. Whether they believed what they wrote or were pandering to official taste is difficult to say. But the majority of the themes produced were too similar to have sprung from heartfelt feelings of love or loyalty. It is likely that most of the students had a vague sympathy with the ideas being expressed (if for no other reason than that they had heard them for many years), and that they also realized that such expressions of enthusiasm were sometimes the quickest way to the head of the class.

Believe,   The regime's campaign to fascistize the Italian school eliminated the
Obey,   best aspects of the Gentile reform and exaggerated its authoritarian bent.
Fight   The introduction of the state textbooks, the enormous increase in the
power of the minister, the curriculum changes according to the preestab-
lished political needs of the regime, the cowing of professors and teachers with loyalty oaths and party requirements—all these things and many
others called for an immense outlay of financial and human resources.
The PNF never reaped the intended benefits of this expenditure because
the schools and teachers, though deeply affected by the philosophy and
practice of fascism, were never completely fascistized, nor did they
serve as the bulwark and stronghold of fascism as the regime's leaders
had hoped. In the end few students or teachers came to the defense of the
regime when it was threatened.

Even Fascist authors admitted ruefully that the regime had not been
totally successful in its socialization program in the schools. Ermanno
Amicucci, a Fascist publicist, expressed a common belief when he said:
"After twenty years of fascism, everyone agrees that we still lack the
Fascist educator—I mean the educator who is physically, morally, politically, and militarily a Fascist."[105] A steady stream of ministerial circulars calling for greater solidarity between the school and the regime—
between culture and politics—testified that the regime's initiatives were
not always received warmly in educational circles.

Some teachers undoubtedly supported the regime; many more bowed
to external pressure in prudent conformity; many were disillusioned and
discouraged. The most exaggerated aspects of the regime's fascistization
drive in the Staracian era very often produced not conviction or inspiration but resignation and disgust. In many cases the negative response can
be explained only, as Adrian Lyttelton said, by individual resistance to
the excesses of the regime—by some "inextinguishable residue of humanity and good sense."[106]

Fascistization was most successful in the elementary schools, the
most important socialization tool for preadolescent children. Primary
school teachers were key authority figures for younger children, who
usually believed what their teachers told them in the classroom. In
addition, especially during the frenzied period from the Ethiopian war to
World War II, elementary students were barraged with proregime propaganda in the mass media—particularly the radio—that served to reinforce all they heard in the classroom. Awareness of possible alternatives
to fascism most often began with the onset of adolescence. Many did not
seriously begin to question the policies of the regime, or dissent from
them, until they entered the universities. For those politically active
young people, the GUF often became centers of political heterodoxy.

Teachers at the elementary level responded with the greatest enthusiasm to the blandishments of the regime.[107] They did so for many reasons. Teachers in these schools were controlled more strictly by the
government than were teachers in the upper schools. What they taught
and how they taught it were the concerns of their direct superiors, who
interfered more in their classrooms than did administrators in the secondary schools and universities. The subject matter was more deeply
influenced by Fascist propaganda than were the more varied and technical subjects taught in the higher schools. The state textbooks required
in the primary grades guaranteed that heresy would be stamped out, at
least in formal lessons. The teachers in the primary schools were also on
the whole younger than other teachers; they were less often committed to
any pre-Fascist ideology and more likely to accept the regime's world
view. The resistance of the old humanistic spirit was stronger in the
secondary schools and the universities, because these schools were
largely in the hands of those formed in the liberal climate of the pre-
Fascist period. Fascism simply intruded more into the classrooms of the
elementary teachers, especially in the obligatory participation in the
activities of the PNF youth groups. These groups had an increasing
impact on the schools during the 1930s, particularly after the establishment of the party-controlled Gioventù Italiana del Littorio (GIL) in 1937
and the passage of Bottai's School Charter in 1939, which attempted to
integrate the youth groups and the schools into one harmonious tool of
Fascist socialization. By the outbreak of World War II it would have
been virtually impossible for most elementary school teachers not to
have been affected by fascism. Even if they were not convinced Fascists,
most had learned that silence was the only way to make the best of a
difficult situation. Even silence was not always permitted them, and so
the process of co-opting spread out and gradually included all those who
remained in their teaching positions.

The teachers who stayed in the schools were convinced Fascists who
exalted their political credo at every opportunity, or fearful but ineffec-
tual teachers who put up with the dictatorship in order to avoid making
waves, or men and women who were anti-Fascists in their hearts but had
to adapt themselves to the regime and hide their convictions from zealous superiors or colleagues. There were certainly cases of teachers who
did maintain an independent spirit, whose criticisms of the regime were
subtle and implicit. Few, however, were able to present a multifaceted
view of the world to students; few were role models of anti-Fascist
activism.[108] One critic of the schools in Fascist Italy claimed: "At a
distance of thirty years my judgment on my teachers, save a very few
exceptions, remains hard; from them almost no light came to us. . . . To
liberate ourselves by ourselves from the remnants of D'Annunzianism,
pseudo-patriotic nationalism . . . conformity, from the bigotry, from all

the squalid myths . . . cost us many errors, doubts, temptations to give in."[109]

At the university many shades of opinion were represented, but these opinions had to be guessed at because they were not openly expressed. Fascism was represented vocally in the departments of political science and law by a number of young recruits who had absorbed and accepted the totalitarian and imperialist myths. But there were many others who clearly bowed to the political pressure only because they wanted to be allowed to carry on their work. In return for their professional survival, they accepted a political modus vivendi with the regime. How was their silence to be interpreted by their students? Sometimes the students were aware of a professor's unspoken feelings; sometimes they interpreted silence as acceptance.

Mario Pomilio, critic and novelist, was born in 1921 and educated in the new political climate. Very early on, however, he began to realize that the mask of conformity around him was just that: a mask hiding deep-seated feelings of revulsion. Pomilio's haphazard attempts at rebellion in high school convinced him that the regime had weak spots that could be prodded. Speaking of the compulsory themes on fascism, Pomilio said: "They irritated me, especially because I did not know what to say except to put down some rhetorical phrases; more than once I turned in a blank page—with a bit of daring but, I have to admit, already sure of impunity because I had realized, with the intuition of the young, that many of my professors were not Fascists."[110]

Giuseppe Melis Bassu, born in Sardinia in 1921 and coeditor of the island's GUF newspaper *Intervento* during the war years, recalled his teachers more fondly: "I remember the teachers who . . . in the days of the regime when it could have truly cost them dearly, did not hesitate to bear witness for us, perhaps only with the silent examples of their lives, the evidence of their doubts."[111]

It is not possible to make a definitive judgment about all schools or the teachers as a class under fascism. The success enjoyed by the regime varied from school to school and from region to region. The human element was always present to disrupt even the most carefully laid plans. What is quite evident is that the schools under fascism were not able to educate children to critical reflection and freedom of choice. Many Fascists admitted that they had not succeeded in completely remaking teachers and schools, and they often saved their most vitriolic blasts for the professors. Behind the exterior of the black shirts and PNF insignia, there was much of the old tradition left in the schools. That so many emerged from these intended factories without having bowed to Fascist indoctrination indicates that the attempt to exercise totalitarian control over the schools and the young minds in them did not succeed as the regime's leaders had hoped.

During the 1930s, however, the idea that fascism had to enter the school through every available nook and cranny became educational policy. The drive to fascistize all classrooms and all students shifted into high gear as the decade progressed, and World War II accelerated the tempo of propaganda. Working side by side with the schools (though not always harmoniously) in the attempt to fascistize and socialize the young people of Italy were the various youth groups established and run by the PNF.

CHAPTER FOUR

The Regime's "Breeding Ground"

In would-be totalitarian systems, the political socialization of youth is essentially a problem of succession and continuity: the formation of a politically orthodox second generation that will keep the regime in power and carry out its political program. In traditional autocratic political systems, the ruling elite exercises negative control over the young. Its primary task is to free the educational process and the media from subversive ideas. Totalitarian systems, by contrast, attempt to exert both negative and positive control. They exorcise subversive notions, but once young minds have been purged of dangerous ideas, they attempt to substitute for those outmoded concepts the political tenets of the new faith. The ultimate goal is not only to stay in power but also to proselytize: to spread the word that will save the nation and safeguard the revolution.

To accomplish these goals in Fascist Italy, the schools and the educational system were gradually brought into line with the ideals of the new regime. But the schools alone could not guarantee that integral education of youth which the regime demanded. They did not, above all, provide the physical and military training that was so important in the Fascist scheme of things. The most specialized organs of Fascist socialization—the regime's "breeding ground"—were the youth groups that aimed at supplementing the academic propaganda of the schools with social, military, and sports activities liberally laced with ideological indoctrination. In this way, at least in theory, the PNF and the state—the youth groups and the educational system—would work together to produce the new Fascist citizen.

The PNF did not come to power with a well-defined youth policy. The development of the regime's youth groups was an attempt to resolve the sticky problems of party-state relations in Fascist society. The first stage of development extended from the founding of the earliest student groups in 1919 until the establishment of the ONB in 1926. The groups set up during this period depended on the PNF, but their status was often unclear because student leaders attempted to safeguard some shred of autonomy against increasing party demands for centralized control. The second stage of evolution began in April 1926 with the founding of the ONB; in 1929 this organization passed to the control of the Ministry of National Education. The ONB organized schoolboys (and girls after

1929) under the age of eighteen, providing them with leisure-time activities as well as sports and military training. There were no separate
groups for nonstudents (working-class and rural youth) until 1930, when
the PNF set up the Fasci Giovanili di Combattimento, which, unlike the
ONB, were directly controlled by the party. The rivalry between the
party-run Fasci and the state-controlled ONB was a source of friction
until 1937, when, after years of controversy and infighting among PNF
leaders, Mussolini tried to bring some order out of the prevailing chaos
with the establishment of the GIL. Until the fall of the regime the GIL
functioned as a unitary youth organization controlled directly by the
party, enrolling all Italian young people from the ages of six to twenty-
one.

From the Avanguardie Studentesche to the Opera Nazionale Balilla

The Fascist regime portrayed the revolution of 1922 as a victory of
ardent youth over the decadence and senility of the liberal bourgeois
state. Although the adherence of the young was never as complete as the
regime's publicists claimed, youthful enthusiasm and élan did play an
important role in the success of the early Fascist movement. A Fascist
martyrology published in 1925 claimed that over one-quarter of these
Fascist saints were students and that one-half were twenty years of age or
younger.[1] At the time of the Rome Congress of the PNF in November
1921, some 13 percent of the total membership of the *fasci* were secondary school or university students and over one-quarter of all the members
were under twenty-one years of age.[2]

Many students, especially university students, participated in the interventionist campaign of 1915, and a large number served in the armed
forces during the war—most of them, given the class composition of the
higher levels of Italian education, as officers.[3] Inspired by the powerful
slogans of national renewal and the heroism of the struggle, many
became deeply involved in antiliberal and anti-Socialist agitation once
the war ended. Many of those who had lived the great adventure of the
war opposed the Giolittian system, which they saw as, at best, dull, flat,
and mediocre and, at worst, a repudiation of the national sacrifice. Many
officers still under arms were given special concessions to resume their
university studies, and these officer-students often took leading roles in
the political struggles of the early postwar period in their universities.
What united these young men was not their specific political beliefs—
some were republicans and others monarchists, for example—but their
belief in an ethos of heroism, their ardent patriotism, and their feeling
that fascism was the only real hope for a rupture with the inglorious

world of their fathers.[4] "In 1919–20," said Italo Balbo, "I was one of the four million veterans of the trenches. [Could I leave the] struggle . . . to return to the nation of Giolitti who had sold out all our ideals? No. Better to deny everything, destroy everything, in order to renew everything from the foundation . . . a revolution at whatever cost!"[5]

Many of the earliest *fasci*, especially in the north, were founded by groups of students and veterans.[6] These *fasci* set up action squads that mounted armed attacks against the leftists. In the beginning the squads were a rather ragtag assortment of young men, prominent among whom were the Futurists and ex-*arditi*—who contributed their official song, "Giovinezza," to the movement—and local students. One of the first punitive actions, for example, was the burning of the *Avanti!* office in Milan in April 1919, a raid led by Ferruccio Vecchi, a founder of the national association of the *arditi*; the Futurist Filippo Tommaso Marinetti; and students from the Milan Politecnico.[7] Student agitation was intense during late 1919. Fascist and nationalist students engaged in pitched battles with leftists at some universities and secondary schools and led demonstrations against "antinational" professors. In Rome and Naples local students set up anti-Bolshevik groups to oppose unions and harass strikers.

The process of forming a national youth organization allied with the Fascist movement really began with the establishment of the Avanguardia Studentesca dei Fasci Italiani di Combattimento (Student Vanguard) in Milan on 20 January 1920.[8] Fired by Gabriele D'Annunzio's seizure of Fiume (in which many of them had participated), these students called for a rejuvenation of Italy based on the new aristocracy of youth. The local *fascio* supported this initiative and invited members to enroll in combat schools led by ex-*arditi* to learn "civic *arditismo*": to make them the shock troops of the revolution.[9]

The Milan *fascio* and the Avanguardia were closely tied: the executive committee of the Avanguardia included members from the central committee of the *fascio*, which also chose the general secretary of the Avanguardia, Luigi Freddi.[10] Students in other cities soon emulated the Milanese model, and the movement spread rapidly. By May 1920 thirty Avanguardie had been established, enrolling thirty-seven hundred members—or some 12 percent of the total enrollment of the *fasci*.[11] Beginning in December 1920 the Avanguardie had their own journal, *Giovinezza*, directed by the leaders of the Milanese group.

Members of the Avanguardie routinely took part in the punitive actions of the *squadristi* during the winter of 1920–21, a period of intense violence and great expansion for the Fascist movement. They also spearheaded the agitation against the educational policies of the government and led strikes against Croce's proposed institution of the *esame di Stato*, which they saw as a concession to clerical interests.[12] The leaders of the Avanguardie were outspokenly anticlerical; they believed that the Catholic youth groups were the primary obstacle to the expansion of fascism in the schools.

Members of the Avanguardie saw themselves as the defenders of the revolutionary line of 1919 and pointed to their contributions to the Fascist movement to justify their desire for autonomy and freedom of action. Neither stance was viewed with equanimity by Mussolini, who was by then engaged in a compromise with existing elites and anxious to justify his own claims to national power. In December 1921 the PNF transformed the youth organization into the Avanguardia Giovanile Fascista (AGF).[13] The group was still headquartered in Milan, under the leadership of a seven-member council headed by Freddi and Asvero Gravelli. This council was appointed by the central committee of the PNF. Each *fascio* was to set up a youth wing, enrolling young men between the ages of fifteen and eighteen. Each Avanguardia was divided into two quite separate sections, one for the students and one for rural youth and workers. The statute of the new organization, published in January 1922, clearly emphasized the group's subordination to the Fascist party.[14] If the earlier Avanguardie had been spontaneous groupings, the AGF was born by will of the PNF and was designed to serve its needs.

Party leaders soon became aware of the need to begin indoctrination and organization of the young at an even earlier age. On 15 June 1922 the PNF formed the national organization of the Balilla for boys from eight to fourteen years of age. These groups were put under the tutelage of the local Avanguardie, whose task it was to undertake the "most assiduous propaganda to spread the Fascist idea" and to ensure that these youngsters developed into "flowers of the faith."[15]

The first congress of the new youth organization, held just after the March on Rome, was a time of celebration and not political debate. Shortly before the meeting the PNF had made its intentions for the new group very clear by appointing Giuseppe Bastianini, former vice-secretary of the party, the new director of the youth groups. At the congress all requests for voting privileges in party councils and changes in the group's statute were firmly rebuffed; the congress "debates" amounted to little more than a ritual vote of approval for the party line.[16] The PNF had set out to transform a spirited and sometimes rebellious component of the early movement into a docile and obedient instrument of political indoctrination for the regime. The activism of the early youth vanguards had to be tamed and their energies directed toward support of the PNF.

Membership in the Avanguardie and the Balilla was never high in absolute terms, and the activities of the groups were modest after October 1922. Most of the early leaders of the Avanguardie had moved on to positions in the PNF, and many of the younger members were in the groups because they had a zealous father or brother. There was little money available and few trained leaders to take on responsibility for these new recruits. At the meeting of the Fascist Grand Council on 16 March 1924, however, the Avanguardie passed to the direct control of the PNF. The stage was set for the rapid development of the youth group movement.[17] The first step in this development came with the establishment of the ONB in April 1926.

The Opera Nazionale Balilla

The primary task of the ONB was to create "Fascists, Fascists without spot . . . Fascist soldiers" who would be "conservators of national values . . . [and] the secure military garrison of the new Italy."[18] Boys from eight to fourteen years of age became Balilla; those from fifteen to eighteen became Avanguardisti. The military flavor of the ONB was evident in its organization. The prime minister chose the central council and the president of the organization from the ranks of the Fascist militia. The ministries of war, the navy, and the air force also sent representatives to the council meetings. The groups themselves were organized along Roman military lines. Officers from the Milizia Volontaria per la Sicurezza Nazionale (MVSN) commanded the Avanguardisti; the Balilla were led by teachers, with preference given to those also members of the militia.[19] The hierarchical organization of the ONB paralleled that of the PNF: authority flowed downward from Mussolini to the central council and then to provincial and communal councils. The straight-armed Fascist salute was the obligatory sign of respect for superiors, and all members were required to wear their uniforms during group events and public ceremonies.

Given the problems with the Catholic church that surfaced after the establishment of the ONB, the provisions on religious instruction were especially important. According to the ONB statute, each cohort was to have its own chaplain, who would teach Catholic doctrine, ethics, and Bible studies and officiate at all religious ceremonies for group members. Often these chaplains were also members of the militia.[20] To oversee the chaplains, a religious inspector general also sat on the ONB council. The religion courses, seen by church authorities as supplements for the meager instruction given by lay teachers in the schools, were designed "to merge religious ardor with patriotic fervor."[21]

Renato Ricci was named president of the ONB. His appointment was in some ways symptomatic of the general difficulty the PNF encountered in filling ministerial and administrative positions: how to make good bureaucrats out of action-oriented *squadristi* or, in a broader context, how to tame talk of "continuing revolution" and find competent men to

oversee the ritualization of the Fascist movement as regime. Renato
Ricci was a young man of little distinction, known more for his "overbearing and violent" nature and his shady deals than for his expertise in
education or youth training.[22] He was hardly the most qualified candidate for the lofty position to which Mussolini appointed him, and contemporary reaction to Ricci was often unfavorable. He was accused, for
example, of corruption, of incurable ignorance, of sadism, and of in-
stability. On more than one occasion he was the subject of anonymous letters to the police and pungent, if not poetic, graffiti on public
buildings.[23]

But in some ways Ricci typified the "new Fascist man." Born in 1896
into a working-class family, he had volunteered for military service with
the *bersaglieri* in the spring of 1915. He returned from the war with two
bronze medals for valor. A Fascist since 1919, Ricci joined D'Annunzio's legions in Fiume and was active in the punitive raids of the
squadristi and in the politics of the *fascio* in his Tuscan hometown of
Carrara. He passed rapidly through the ranks of the militia and participated in the March on Rome. He was elected a deputy in 1924 and
served as vice-secretary of the PNF in 1925–26. Later that same year
Ricci's reputation as a zealot and his penchant for martial airs brought
him to the attention of the Duce and landed him a political plum:
presidency of the newly founded ONB. This unstable but loyal young
man was to be one of the key figures in the Fascist ruling elite until the
end. He served as undersecretary and then minister of corporations from
late 1937 until 1943, and later as head of the national guard in the
Republic of Salò. In some ways Ricci symbolized the worst aspects of
the Fascist regime. Certainly he represented its violent side struggling
for respectability. Perhaps the most ironic aspect of the situation is that
Ricci, who had held a position of authority in the regime's youth program for eleven years, was rejected in the 1940s as a possible minister of popular culture because he was a man of "little education and
breeding."[24]

Until 1939 membership in the PNF youth groups was voluntary,
contingent upon parental approval and party acceptance. In fact, however, the regime enticed the youngsters and their parents with a whole
range of political, economic, and social pressures.

The school was a particularly fertile ground for recruitment. The local
group leaders were usually schoolteachers enrolled in the Fascist teachers' association and entrusted with the special task of proselytizing
among their students. Those teachers who also joined the militia were
given pay raises as an added incentive to work for PNF interests. Youth
group membership for those young people who spent their days in
the classrooms of these especially zealous instructors could hardly be
termed voluntary. School principals were required to send regular mem-

bership reports, and low enrollments were viewed with a decided lack of enthusiasm in Rome.

Economic pressure also played a role. In 1928, for example, Minister Fedele ordered that competitions for all scholarships, prizes, and assistance programs be decided with preference given to ONB members.[25] In addition, the groups provided food, clothing, and school supplies to needy children and made cruises, excursions, and summer camps available to members at greatly reduced rates. In the ONB students could learn arts and crafts, sailing, aviation—a whole range of activities not offered by the schools. The ONB provided free libraries, and the local Casa di Balilla showed entertaining (and politically instructive) films to members. The youth groups also provided insurance and care to orphans and sickly children and vocational and professional training to interested young people.

Applications for membership in the ONB were sent home with the students; refusal to join had to be accompanied by a written explanation. Parents who did not allow their children to participate realized that the children would be subjected to discrimination at school and deprived of some real benefits. Those ONB members who distinguished themselves in group activities would get a head start on their careers; they were, for example, assured of preferential treatment when called up for military service. By the early thirties youth group membership was also required for state employment. Parents who were ambitious for their children could not overlook the long-term consequences of their refusal. In some cases the parents had to enroll their children because their own professional positions demanded it. Many attempted to counteract the indoctrination of the schools and the groups at home; some were undoubtedly successful, but social and peer pressure weighed on the side of the party. For many children, especially the younger ones, being a member of the ONB was just fun: members wore snappy uniforms, they sang catchy songs, they learned mysterious rituals and rites that fostered a sense of belonging and exclusivity. In addition, the varied sports and leisure-time activities provided the children with a ready-made social life. The education imparted in the schools and the activities of the ONB aimed at the child's renunciation of self and his acceptance of the collective life of the regime. Membership was not obligatory until 1939, but in practice social and political pressure pushed the children in the direction of conformity and not resistance, belonging and not separateness.[26]

The "Cult of the Cradle": PNF Youth Groups for Girls

The youth groups for girls played a distinctly minor role in the regime's scheme of things because the female of the species had a role of secondary importance in society at large. Fascist propaganda strummed the antifeminist chord, though the lyrics stressed the rhetoric of national interests and social harmony. Article after article condemned the horrors of feminism and modernism, the "insane passion that has seized all the women of Europe who want to imitate the American girls," the masculine and unnatural desires of the English suffragists, and the frivolity and worldliness of the French coquettes. The Italian woman, claimed Starace, "holds in such a definite and unalterable way to her happy femininity that there is no danger she will ever develop masculine tendencies or profess foolish egalitarian ambitions."[27] Sweetness and femininity could be preserved, however, only by separating the girls (as proximate occasions of sin) from the boys in ONB activities—a provision that allayed the suspicions of church leaders who looked with undisguised horror at coeducational sports and recreation.

For this reason the groups for girls and young women were not originally part of the ONB. Girls between eight and twelve were organized as the Piccole Italiane; those from thirteen to eighteen were called Giovani Italiane. Both of these groups were controlled directly by the Fasci Femminili, the women's wing of the PNF. In November 1929 all youth groups passed to the control of the Ministry of National Education; thereafter the groups for girls were organized in the same manner, though they were never the object of the same interest, as the Balilla and Avanguardisti groups for boys.[28]

Activities for the younger girls consisted of basic courses in first aid, rhythmic exercises, and group games; they also saw regime-approved films, heard simple lectures on fascism, went on outings, and attended music recitals. The activities of the Giovani Italiane were more varied, including light athletic competitions, excursions, and patriotic lectures on fascism and Italy's "past glories and heroism." The older members were also required to do some philanthropic work (as an extension of the female nurturing role, this was the special preserve of the Fasci Femminili), such as visiting the sick or aiding the poor. Evening and Sunday courses were provided in many areas; their aim, however, was not to "arouse silly illusions of knowledge" but to guide the students to become good housewives and mothers. The list of courses offered to the Giovani Italiane included child care, gardening, livestock breeding, flower arranging, hygiene, ironing, knitting, embroidery, first aid, typing and shorthand, tailoring, and midwifery.[29]

The excursions and sports activities provided for the girls were a far cry from the rough-and-tumble military games required of the boys. Instead of close-order drilling and war games, the younger girls danced around poles or played at something called the "doll drill," passing in review holding dolls "in the correct manner of a mother holding a baby."[30] If the Fascist educational system in general can be called an experiment in the mass production of citizen-soldiers, then the activities of these poorly financed groups for girls clearly had a eugenic purpose: mass production of prolific citizen-mothers.

The Citizen-Soldier: Premilitary and Sports Training in the ONB

"It is absurd," said Achille Starace, "to believe in the possibility of perpetual peace. . . . Fascist education must be education for battle. Fascism believes in sanctity and heroism."[31] The development of the ONB premilitary program pointed up the crucial importance attached by party leaders to military education—entrusted not to the armed forces but to the MVSN—and dramatized the sometimes uneasy relationship between PNF hierarchs and the regular army officer corps. These courses aimed at producing an officer corps that would act as a leaven for the regime within the armed forces. The leadership hoped that such a system, under the guidance of the zealous MVSN premilitary instructors, would gradually transform the officer caste into a loyal instrument of fascism.

The Fascist militia was first given control over the premilitary program in 1924; by 1930 premilitary instruction was obligatory for all Italian males over eighteen in preparation for military service at the age of twenty-one.[32] ONB membership and completion of the MVSN's premilitary course were also required for admission to the armed forces' academies and colleges.

The premilitary program was standardized only late in 1934. The male citizen's life from ages eighteen to fifty-five was divided into three phases: premilitary, military, and postmilitary. Premilitary training lasted three years; candidates who excelled in military discipline and political fervor went on for officer training. Those who refused to attend the courses received stiff penalties—up to six months in prison for habitual offenders. In 1934 there were over fifteen thousand MVSN officers teaching these courses to over four million males.[33]

Despite all the official hoopla, the program was never very popular among the young men it was supposed to inspire. Edward Tannenbaum claimed that premilitary courses, always tedious, were particularly so for Italians, whose "weak military tradition and strong dislike for routine discipline of any kind" militated against the success of the program. In his words, "Most eighteen to twenty-one-year-old males still preferred to . . . view themselves as lovers rather than fighters."[34] At the risk of perpetuating the stereotype of the Latin lover, it is true that there were widespread complaints about the program and that even the PNF's glamorous courses in aviation and glider flying could not attract enough students to fill their quotas. Starace railed throughout the thirties against this lack of enthusiasm.[35]

If the Fascist regime did not succeed in making the youth of Italy more military, it did succeed in making them more sports conscious than ever before. Sports training was an integral part of the PNF military training program; the chief goal of the ONB was physical education for military purposes. Sports became an industry in Fascist Italy. The sports programs for the youth groups tended to stress team sports and those that prepared young men for military service.

The regime also intended to use sports for patriotic purposes: to foster a sense of national pride. Sport, claimed a 1924 editorial in the *Popolo d'Italia*, was not an end in itself but a "national necessity for the prestige and progress of the race."[36] There was propaganda value to be reaped from victories in international competitions, and the government gave encouragement and subsidies to individual athletes who carried the flag to victory in such contests. Newspapers played up the Italian victories in the 1936 Berlin Olympics, and the press waxed eloquent on the career of world heavyweight boxing champion Primo Carnera (who was never to be shown on the canvas). In competition Italian teams wore party uniforms; athletes were ordered to offer the Fascist salute when opponents wanted to shake hands.

The stadia built by the regime also served national and political purposes: they were intended to impress visiting dignitaries and Italians with the efficiency and organization of the regime. The center for much of the sports activity and for most of the choreographic displays was the ambitious sports center constructed by the government near the Farnesina. The Mussolini Forum was among the most garish architectural projects conceived by the regime, but it was superbly equipped and appointed and served as a focal point and showpiece for the PNF sports propaganda.[37]

The regime attempted to control the development of sports on both national and local levels. After 1927 all provincial and local sports federations had to include representatives from the PNF. In 1925 Lando Ferretti was elected president of the Italian Olympic Committee (CONI) under pressure from the PNF. Ferretti, an early Fascist who had participated in the March on Rome, began in 1926 to replace directors of various Italian sports federations with men of proved political faith. Late that same year Turati put CONI under the direct control of the party. Sports would henceforth be under the shadow of the lictor.[38]

The regimented sports program of the ONB was also intended to serve totalitarian ends: the creation of disciplined mass man. The massive gymnastic displays of identically clad young men singing Fascist anthems and moving in harmony were planned as vivid demonstrations of the force, order, and unity fascism had brought to Italy. The press was replete with rhapsodic articles praising the virility and manly virtues of these young men whom fascism had turned into finely tempered fighting machines. And there awarding the medals was usually the Duce, the supreme exemplar of the Fascist sportsman, whose presence was almost a guarantee of victory. "From on high in the tribune of honor," gushed one article, "a Man nourished the vigor of the athletes and inspired them with a look of unquenchable victory: the Duce."[39]

The situation had been far from bright when the regime came to power. Physical education had been included in all school programs since the De Sanctis reforms of 1878; since 1909 physical education had been obligatory at all levels of the educational system. But equipment was scarce and teachers in the program—referred to by one Fascist commentator as the "Cinderellas of pedagogy"—were generally scorned, especially in the classical schools.[40] In March 1923 a new organization, the Ente Nazionale per l'Educazione Fisica (ENEF), was established to prepare physical education teachers and sports curricula.[41] But the ENEF was always underfinanced and understaffed, and in 1927 the ONB took over its functions. The regime also ordered the dissolution of all other sporting organizations not affiliated with the ONB. Rather than wait to be given the coup de grâce, the Catholic sports federations quietly disbanded.

Little by little, every activity even remotely associated with sport and physical training for youth was taken over by the ONB. Obligatory physical education was enforced in the schools at all levels, even in the private schools. For the younger children the program was really little more than organized play, but for the older students emphasis was placed on those activities that had a military purpose. In addition to exercise and team sports, older students also trained in fencing, boxing, and shooting; they ran obstacle courses and went on periodic twenty-kilometer marches. All physical education teachers were required to attend special training courses sponsored by the ONB and to be members of the PNF. Physical education courses were put on an academic par with all other subjects, and successful completion of the requirements was necessary for promotion each year.

This link between the PNF youth groups and the school was another factor encouraging enrollments in the regime's youth organizations. The playing fields constructed by the ONB were rarely on the school grounds, for example, but part of the local Casa di Balilla. Children who wanted to use the equipment and facilities after hours had to be enrolled in the ONB. Because all local and national sports events were sponsored by the ONB, anyone interested in more specialized training or competition was virtually forced to enroll in the groups.

To provide the PNF with a reservoir of highly trained physical education teachers, Mussolini inaugurated the Accademia Fascista di Educazione Fisica at the Farnesina in February 1928.[42] Students admitted to the program were required to pass a competitive examination that included an investigation of the moral and political background of the candidate and his family. In addition to courses in physical therapy and physiology, the three-year curriculum required a wide range of subjects relating to fascism: courses on Fascist legislation, social policy, and military strategy and tactics. The young teachers who graduated from the Farnesina—referred to variously as "among the most enthusiastic Fascists in the country" or as a "mass of fanatics"—were highly politicized technicians whose dedication to sport and to fascism was notable.[43] Nine-tenths of the graduates also became officers in the MVSN. In January 1932 the government set up a school in Orvieto to train female instructors, though on a much smaller scale. Here the emphasis was on child care, hygiene, and home economics instead of heavy physical training. The women graduates were, however, also deeply committed to the Fascist movement, and were leaders in the ONB.[44]

The PNF sports program for youth was an enormous undertaking. By 1938, for example, the GIL (heir to the ONB) employed 138,194 physical education instructors. Each year the PNF sponsored the Festa ginnastica for ONB members in the provinces, and in the mid-thirties these provincial trials drew over two million competitors annually. National competitions were held in almost every conceivable sport, with literally thousands of meets and events held each year all over Italy.[45] There was something for nearly anyone interested in sports in the PNF youth group programs, and, most important, the PNF sports program was literally the only game in town.

One of the ONB showcase events was the annual week-long training camp for Avanguardisti known as the Campo Dux, held beginning in 1929 in the late summer in the wooded area around the Mussolini Forum. The provincial ONB delegations paid the expenses of the young men attending the camps, and each year participants included thousands of Avanguardisti from all over Italy and from *fasci* abroad.[46]

Mussolini and other high party leaders were present for many of these group events, and delegations from friendly foreign nations with large fascist movements usually made appearances. The grand parade of the 1937 camp included 450 members of the Hitler Youth, for example; in 1938 representatives from other Fascist parties (including Oswald Mosley from the British Union of Fascists) shared the reviewing stand with Mussolini. These annual camps were given as much coverage in Italy as the Nuremberg rallies in Germany. They were always filmed by the Istituto L.U.C.E., and theaters all over Italy showed excerpts from the most inspiring events. During the late thirties films of the group rhythmic exercises, the flag swirling, and the military maneuvers were exported to foreign markets as well.[47]

The regime was eager to publicize its efforts to "go to the people" through the PNF's much-vaunted social welfare and public assistance programs. The ONB provided needy children with a range of social services, from summer camps and medical examinations to school lunches and supplies, books, scholarships, and accident and health insurance.

The camp program was one of the most popular of the projects. The camps were located in mountain or seaside settings all over Italy; they ranged from permanent "colonies" for long-term tubercular cures to summer and day camps for deprived or sickly youngsters. All these camps employed nurses and medical personnel, and most offered some type of physical therapy as well as medical examinations for children who did not receive such attention at home. All children enrolled in the ONB were eligible to attend these camps, but preference was given to those from poor families and to sons and daughters of war veterans or "martyrs of the Revolution."[48]

The camps were not luxurious, however, and the authorities were urged to avoid frills and extras that would be "antieducational and antisocial."[49] Every attempt was made to teach the children basic hygiene and to provide a strict regimen of healthy food, sun, and exercise that would benefit especially those children from "unsound" environments. These camps were inspected annually by the ONB, and the reports indicated that as late as 1938 the situation in many of them remained marginal.[50] But the camps were no doubt a boon for many lower-class children, and enrollments increased steadily over the years.

Fascism was a constant presence at these camps, even during hours of recreation and play. The children wore uniforms sporting PNF youth group insignia, and the rigidly planned schedules for each day always included time for stories and lectures on Fascist themes. The children were taught to salute king and Duce twice daily (using the Fascist straight-armed salute), they prayed for the martyrs of the PNF, and they practiced Fascist marching songs and war cries. Even physical exercises were designed to provide a forum for PNF propaganda. Camp directors were advised to schedule games and gymnastics that would give the teachers the opportunity to praise the achievements of the regime and "to speak of the prestige and power of Italy."[51]

Another aspect of the regime's assistance and social welfare policies was the ONB's management of Italy's rural schools, which gave the youth organization entrée into the realm of general education. The Gentile reform had delegated responsibility for these "nonclassified schools" (those with fewer than forty students) to local semiofficial agencies.

Table 4-1
ONB Camps, 1926–1942

Year	No. of Camps	No. of Children
1926[a]	107	60,000
1927[a]	410	80,000
1928[a]	434	84,000
1929[a]	571	103,000
1930[a]	680	110,000
1931	1,195	242,233
1932	1,621	332,519
1933	2,022	405,142
1934	2,492	506,536
1935	3,128	568,681
1936	3,821	690,756
1937	4,240	744,049
1938	4,357	772,000
1939	4,526	806,964
1940	3,592	623,518
1941	4,684	654,400
1942	5,805	940,615

Sources: PNF, *Foglio d'ordini*, 31 July 1926; Istituto Centrale di Statistica, *Annuario statistico italiano*, 1933–43.

[a]Figures before 1931 are approximate.

Many educators argued, however, that these rural schools required more and not less government assistance. In July 1928 the nonclassified and adult schools in Calabria and Sicily were turned over to the ONB. In September 1929 schools in Sardinia were included, and by 1935 all rural schools in the kingdom had come under ONB auspices.[52]

Depending on the social complexion of the particular area, the ONB took over the planning, staffing, and general organization of regular five-year elementary schools, of evening courses for adults and weekend courses for women, and of vocational training courses. The undertaking called for close cooperation between the party and the ministry, between local PNF representatives and local state bureaucrats. The results seem to have been generally satisfactory. Teachers in these rural schools were required to be PNF members and involved actively in the ONB; almost all students enrolled in these institutions were also enrolled ipso facto in the youth groups, a matter that helps to explain the impressive membership statistics in these schools. Table 4-2 indicates the development of the rural school program run by the ONB from 1928 until 1937, when the organization was suppressed.

Needy students in these rural areas and disadvantaged children all over Italy also benefited from the scholastic welfare program organized by the local *patronati scolastici*, which passed to the control of the ONB in 1930.[53] By 1937 *patronati* had been set up in almost all communes and provided a wide variety of assistance: school books and smocks, shoes, paper supplies, child-care centers, nursery schools, and, in some areas, school lunches. The *patronati* never succeeded in meeting all the needs of the poorer school children, but each year hundreds of thousands of young people who might otherwise have had to leave school did receive aid. The program was always more a charity than a real social assistance system—motivated more by political considerations than social or humanitarian ones. The poor were recipients of the largesse of the regime and, the prevailing attitude seemed to indicate, should be grateful for that assistance. Poor children who received free school lunches, for example, were required to begin their meal with a prayer of thanksgiving to the Duce and his regime. The regime's leaders clearly thought that there were political points to be made from the good work being done by the *patronati* among the always suspicious lower classes.

The ONB also provided national scholarships, awarded with much fanfare each year to one hundred deserving Avanguardisti and Balilla. The competition for these Benito Mussolini Scholarships was keen: students had to be recommended by the principals of their schools (recommendations were based on political as well as academic merit) and then had to compose a theme on an assigned topic. In 1929, for example, themes for the Avanguardisti included "The Duce: tender as a mother and strong as a diamond," "How we won the war," and "Italy must have a colonial spirit."[54]

In addition to this scholastic assistance, the ONB also managed an accident and health insurance program. The fund, named after the Duce's brother Arnaldo, paid compensation for sickness and death and also provided medical examinations, orthopedic apparatuses, medicines, physical therapy, and rehabilitation for needy members. For some boys and girls this was the only available medical care.[55]

The Fasci Giovanili di Combattimento

The various youth groups under the umbrella of the ONB organized and regimented young Italians from eight to eighteen years of age, at which

Table 4-2
Attendance at Rural Schools of the ONB, 1928–1937

Academic Year	No. of Schools[a]	No. of Students
1928–29	1,178	41,771
1929–30	1,457	55,542
1930–31	1,538	60,135
1931–32	1,508	60,646
1932–33	1,550	62,737
1933–34[b]	2,398	90,909
1934–35	2,015	71,460
1935–36[c]	7,894	244,898
1936–37	9,139	265,915

Sources: Istituto Centrale di Statistica, *Annuario statistico italiano*, 1931–38, and *Compendio statistico*, 1930–32.

[a]This number includes all types of courses offered in rural schools: elementary schools, evening classes for adults, weekend courses, *corsi complementari,* and *scuole di avviamento professionale* for technical and vocational training.

[b]By 1934 the ONB managed rural schools in Campania and Molise as well as the schools in Sicily, Calabria, and Sardinia.

[c]By the academic year 1935–36 rural schools in the northern provinces had also been added; hence the dramatic jump in enrollment.

time the males were to enter the ranks of the party and the militia.[56] Mussolini had always felt, however, that the years between eighteen and twenty-one were crucial ones, and that most eighteen-year-olds were simply too immature for PNF membership.

The decision to set up the Fasci Giovanili was made at a meeting of the Fascist Grand Council in October 1930. The new organization enrolled young men from eighteen to twenty-one years of age coming from the ranks of the Avanguardisti, and others not enrolled in the ONB who presented formal petitions. In theory the Fasci Giovanili were intended as the premier Fascist youth group: "the fertile breeding ground for the ranks and leadership of the National Fascist Party and the Fascist Militia."[57]

Members of the Fasci Giovanili were drawn from the same age group as the university students belonging to the Gruppi Universitari Fascisti (GUF); the distinction between the two organizations was, along broad lines, one of class. The members of the Fasci were generally enrolled in trade or vocational schools, or young workers. Most were from the urban proletariat or the rural areas that sent fewer students to the universities.

The regime's youth program had always been least successful among working-class and rural youth, and the Fasci were intended to bridge the class gap and to involve nonstudents over eighteen more deeply in party affairs.[58]

In November 1929 the ONB passed to the control of the ministry as a special undersecretariat under the direction of Renato Ricci. The Fasci Giovanili—with the official motto "Believe, Obey, Fight"—were put under the direct control of the PNF.[59] The job of commander went to Carlo Scorza, a Fascist of the first hour, *squadrista*, and organizer of the *fascio* in his Tuscan hometown of Lucca, who was perhaps best known for his role in the fatal beating of opposition leader Giovanni Amendola in 1926. Besides being a sorry commentary on the moral qualities of the Fascist hierarchy, however, Scorza's appointment also boded ill for future relations between the state bureaucracy and the PNF on questions of youth policy. Dissension began soon after he assumed his new position.[60]

The organization of the Fasci Giovanili paralleled the hierarchical structure of the PNF. The secretary of the party was commander general of the Fasci. In some ways the Young Fascists were the direct heirs of the Fascist action squads and the wartime *arditi*, though most of their activities were more wholesome. And the Fasci filled some real social needs. The cultural activities, theatrical and dramatic performances, sports events, and libraries of the Fasci widened the horizons of many of the less-advantaged young men and provided them with a range of activities they might never otherwise have been able to enjoy. *Gioventù fascista*, the expensively printed and profusely illustrated organ of the Fasci Giovanili, was sent free to all members, and it was a lively link to the life of the party. Besides weekly sections on politics, foreign affairs, and Fascist doctrine, the magazine ran frequent poetry, prose, and design competitions that provided national exposure and prize money to many young Italians. The price to be paid was political conformity. The primary goal of the Fasci was to produce not artists or thinkers but young men who would believe what they were told, obey their superiors, and fight when the needs of their country—or their party—demanded it.

The public celebration of the ideal relationship among the various PNF youth groups was the annual *Leva fascista*, or Fascist Levy. This elaborate ceremony took place on 21 April, the anniversary of the founding of Rome. It was patterned after the old Roman ritual in which young men donned the *toga virilis*, the symbol of their manhood and maturity. In the Fascist version of this highly stylized rite, young men and boys in towns all over Italy passed from one rung of the ladder to the next: a full-fledged member of the PNF gave a rifle to a selected young man representing the Giovani Fascisti and he took his place in the party ranks; the Giovane Fascista in turn gave an Avanguardista the blue

neckerchief of his new group; the new Avanguardista gave a little Balilla
the white shoulder ribbons of the young boys' group.[61]

The unity of purpose and the harmony expressed in this yearly ritual The
were more illusion than reality. The PNF's youth policy was character- Regime's
ized from the start by a lack of focus and administrative confusion. After "Breeding
1930 the Fascist youth groups were racked by internal dissension, rival- Ground"
ries, and infighting that shattered the apparent accord, laid bare some
rather violent personality clashes among party leaders, and revealed a
fundamental lack of agreement on the entire issue of youth socialization.
Even the intensity of the personal feuds could not camouflage the basic
problem: did ultimate authority for the youth program rest with the
traditional state educational bureaucracy or with the party? In 1937 the
jockeying for power and control produced a new institution: the Gioventù Italiana del Littorio (under the direct control of the PNF), which
was to be the unitary youth organization of the Fascist regime. This
began the third and final phase in the development of the Fascist youth
program.

Strains on the System: The Status of the PNF Youth Groups

The status of the ONB changed more than once in its short history. The
1926 decree establishing it had placed the new organization directly
under party control; in 1929, however, it was transferred to the jurisdiction of the Ministry of National Education—a move made to dramatize
the state's commitment to the socialization program. But the change was
more cosmetic than substantial. Renato Ricci remained at the head of the
ONB, and ties between the ONB and the PNF continued to be very
close. Ricci himself was a leading member of the party directorate, and
many other national and local leaders of the ONB were also members of
the party apparat. Ricci's dual role allowed him access to all planning
and policy-making sessions at the ministry, where he could act as the
spokesman for PNF interests against more traditional members of the
ministerial staff.[62]

The confusion between state and party functions in the ONB was not
unique to that organization. The entire Fascist system was characterized
quite intentionally by a kind of political double vision—referred to as
doppiezza, or "doubleness"—which meant that every state agency was
paralleled by a PNF organization with duplicate functions. There were,
in essence, two hierarchies with separate organs joined at the head:
Mussolini was head of government and Duce of fascism. The system
allowed the regime to present itself as having adopted a moderate
course, observing constitutional forms and guarantees. The dyarchy of
king and Duce was reflected all along the line. Parallel to the prefect

were, for example, the Fascist federal secretaries; alongside the regular army was the Fascist militia; next to the state courts was the Special Tribunal for the Defense of the State.

In the realm of youth policy, the working relationship between the state and the party was far from a smooth one. Many within the PNF pushed for a more active and complete fusion between the school and the ONB, and Mussolini was well aware of the need to establish a working relationship between the educational institutions and the party youth groups.

The youth organizations, at first mere complements to the schools, began increasingly after the late twenties, when the verb *fascistizzare* became the order of the day, to dominate the life of the schools and to sap the energies of students and teachers alike. Teachers lost precious classroom hours as students were excused for the endless round of parades, speeches, and ceremonies that were so characteristic of the PNF during the Starace era. The result was a further growth of tension between the ministry and the party.

The frictions already present were intensified by the establishment of the Fasci Giovanili; a complex set of personal battles and administrative rivalries came to light, finally getting so serious that Mussolini himself stepped in to resolve the problems. In part the difficulties arose over jealously guarded territory, but there were also real differences of opinion about the direction of the PNF youth groups and relations between the party and the schools.

Perhaps the bitterest clash began in the spring of 1931 when Renato Ricci and Carlo Scorza both protested bluntly to Mussolini against raids into their respective bailiwicks. Ricci had never been pleased that the Fasci Giovanili had been kept apart from the ONB; in his view, Scorza's groups simply had no reason to exist. He suggested instead that the ONB be expanded to include all boys and girls between six and twenty-one years of age. In Ricci's view, Scorza's claims that the ONB was too tied to the ministry were evidence of "willful ignorance." This was only the opening salvo in a running battle between the two men that lasted throughout the thirties.[63]

Scorza and Ricci were not the only PNF leaders at loggerheads on the question of youth. Achille Starace waged the most concerted campaign to increase the prerogatives of the PNF and its power over the young. His battle brought him into headlong confrontation with some of the most important party leaders during the thirties.

In 1935 De Vecchi, then minister of national education, recommended in strong terms that all activities relating to the spiritual and physical education of youth be centered in the schools.[64] Starace took his case directly to the Duce, vehemently reaffirming the "exquisitely revolutionary task" of the PNF. In a revealing conclusion, Starace blasted the "lazy bureaucratic bourgeoisie which, after thirteen years of the regime, has remained more or less what it was . . . [that is,] not Fascist historically or spiritually." The majority of state teachers, he allowed, were filled with nonrevolutionary ideas or, worse yet, were women too concerned with the trivialities of life to be good Fascists. Starace's tug-of-war with the ONB and the ministry continued for the next several years; in September 1937 he once again lost patience and turned to Mussolini for a hearing. This time his target was Ricci, whom Starace blamed for the problems plaguing the youth movement. The feud between the two had reached epic proportions by this time, and Starace ended his plea on a pessimistic note guaranteed to arouse the Duce: the PNF, he said, "is far behind in the political preparation of the young."[65]

The already murky waters were muddied still further in the thirties by other infighting. Giuseppe Bottai, who served as minister of national education from 1936 to 1943, was cordially hated by Starace, who suspected that Bottai's elegance and verbal dexterity masked an incipient antifascism. Starace also denounced Bottai as insensitive and incompetent for his prominstry stance on the youth question.[66] Ricci and Bottai also locked horns in the spring of 1937 on the question of the ONB, and police reports informed the Duce that Ricci was at odds with the minister over the latter's plan to structure the ONB as a special branch of his ministry.[67] All of these problems contributed to Mussolini's decision to set up the Gioventù Italiana del Littorio in October 1937.

Achille Starace and the Cult of the Duce

Though the organizational structure of the PNF seemed rigid on paper, in practice the lines of authority were never very clearly drawn, nor were administrative functions precisely delineated. After the consolidation of the regime in 1925–26, the local *ras* were gradually shorn of their influence, and the PNF was increasingly centralized. Local party leaders, for example, were no longer elected but appointed by the PNF secretary. Career men staffed the central party apparatus, which was organized along hierarchical lines with authority flowing downward from the secretary, who served at the pleasure of the Duce. The system discouraged initiative on the local level and enshrined as the highest virtues of the party member not creativity or innovation but obedience and conformity. The Fascist hierarchy was not an effective ruling elite but a collection of notables at the command of the Duce, without effective power to influence political choices. The party secretary kept his job as long as he kept Mussolini's confidence—meaning as long as he was not too powerful or too much his own man.

Achille Starace enjoyed the longest tenure as PNF secretary, from December 1931 to November 1939. He was perhaps the most unpopular personage in the Fascist pantheon during the *ventennio*. He was criticized and derided by non-Fascists, anti-Fascists, and Fascists alike, by young and old, by those inside and outside Italy.[68] One sympathetic Fascist said that his appointment "must be considered as fatal for the Fascist party, because on that day began the activities of the man who, with his great errors, was among the factors that contributed the most to the dissolution of the power of the regime."[69]

The "great errors" committed by Starace were not the errors of one man. The PNF did go through a period of crisis in the 1930s, and the fundamental choices made during that period contributed to the moral and political bankruptcy of the regime. But the ultimate responsibility for the crisis of the PNF lay not with Starace but with Mussolini, whose political conceptions Starace implemented. Starace was merely the most zealous and fanatical executor of a policy laid down by Mussolini himself.

Starace, born in 1889 near Lecce, served during the war as an officer in the *bersaglieri* and joined the Fascist movement in 1919. He took part in squadrist actions in the Trentino and Puglia before the March on Rome and commanded the Fascists of the Veneto during the seizure of power. He served periodically as a vice-secretary of the PNF until his nomination as party secretary.

By temperament Starace was a military man and not a politician; he was more comfortable with the certainties of the barracks than with the subtleties of the political process. Most important, he was fiercely, even blindly, loyal to Mussolini, who referred to the secretary as his "mastiff."[70] Starace was a pathetically servile flatterer who, so rumors reported, stood at attention even when speaking to the Duce on the telephone. In the end, Starace hung alongside the leader he had served so fanatically for so many years. Dedicated as they were to the service of the same cult, the two seem to have gotten on well—or at least as well as Mussolini got on with any of his subordinates. What problems they did have were related more to Starace's excess zeal than to any basic differences on policy.[71]

Following Mussolini's lead, Starace conceived of the party as something far different from the revolutionary elite envisioned by the Fascist *intransigenti*. Starace saw the PNF as a mass organization—what Farinacci scathingly referred to as an "athletic and leisure time organization"—not as a restricted elite of revolutionary leaders.[72] He reopened enrollments in the PNF for the tenth anniversary of the March on Rome.

From October 1932 to October 1933 membership jumped from 1,007,-231 to 1,415,407, an increase of over 40 percent.[73] Clearly many of these new recruits were motivated less by a burning belief in fascism than by an opportunistic desire for security and career advancement. The decision was a significant one for the future of the regime and symptomatic of Starace's whole approach. He concentrated on style and numbers, on exterior form and not on substance. He attempted to extend control over the mass organizations of the PNF, and in the thirties enrollments in all these organizations increased notably.

Starace attempted to reorganize the party to eliminate all those in positions of authority who were not prepared to emulate his inspiring example of discipline. He was interested not in encouraging new ideas but rather in enforcing a bureaucratic and military discipline that reduced real participation in the political life of the nation to the formal observance of his famous (or infamous) rituals. Politics under Starace became a series of mass celebrations that had as their goal the collective exaltation of the leader—with Starace as the regime's high priest. By the early 1930s the Duce was fascism; the motto emblazoned everywhere in Italy—"Mussolini is always right"—became a fitting encapsulation of a system that was less a political movement or an ideological reality than a political fetish, a Weberian routinization of the charisma and the "mystique" of the deity of fascism. Starace rewrote the PNF statute in 1932 and 1938, and that document sanctified the regime's political choice and direction.[74] The party was increasingly visible and audible but liquidated as a political force, incapable of taking real initiatives, and reduced to the role of choreographer for the cult of the infallible leader.

In his role as stage manager of the regime, Starace imposed on the Italian people a whole range of pettifogging regulations. His "reform of custom" elicited widespread criticism and—most dangerously for a regime with totalitarian aspirations—near universal derision and laughter. By 1933, for example, all official correspondence and party press had to include ritual reference to the Duce.[75] In May 1933 Starace published regulations for parades decreeing that all units should march nine to ten abreast to give the "illusion of mass," and that all cavalry should proceed at a trot or gallop to give the impression of life and enthusiasm.[76] Such examples could be multiplied, but the point is that such picayune directives occupied an inordinate amount of Starace's time and energy and brought ridicule on the regime and its secretary.

One of Starace's most irritating meddlings was his imposition of the so-called Fascist style in everything from clothing to language. Italians were forced to use *voi* in place of the "hypocritical and anti-Fascist" pronoun *lei*. Benedetto Croce, following the custom of his region, had always used *voi*, but he adopted *lei* for the duration. His was not an isolated case of resistance. The handshake was branded antinational and un-Roman, a sure sign of anti-Fascist sentiments. Starace also irritated many with his order that all civil employees were to wear uniforms while at work, and amused and bemused others with his introduction of the imperious ritual chant "Let us hail the Duce, founder of empire" at all public functions. In March 1933 he ordered that all federal secretaries learn how to ride horses and motorcycles. Perhaps the last straw for many was Starace's directive that party leaders put themselves through the paces in gymnastic trials. Many Italians snickered when treated to the unedifying spectacle of potbellied Fascists stuffed into tight gym clothes and floundering after Starace, bouncing on trampolines, or jumping through hoops of fire.[77]

As the decade progressed, Starace became more and more fanatical, more determined to put every man, woman, and child in Italy in uniform, and more convinced that the uniform made the "new Italian." During the same period PNF leaders (some say Mussolini himself) came up with the idea of setting aside each Saturday for the political education and military drilling of the population. The Fascist Grand Council voted the establishment of the *Sabato fascista*, or "Fascist Saturday," on 16 February 1935.[78] By law all state offices were to be closed on Saturday afternoons, and those hours were to be used for pre- and postmilitary training and for political, cultural, and sports activities by the various PNF groups. Exceptions were allowed in certain cases, but never for those under twenty-one. The law was quite clearly intended primarily for the young.

This rather comic *Sabato fascista* was a failure from the very beginning, killed more by obstinate passive resistance than by any show of active opposition. For most Italians Saturday became a day of rest, an "English" instead of a Fascist Saturday, as the press lamented. Starace frequently complained about the lack of cooperation, but all his laments and threats do not seem to have produced results.[79]

In some ways Starace served as a kind of lightning rod for the regime by drawing criticisms away from the Duce. He was so fanatical in his devotion to duty and so easily satirized that it was tempting to make him the butt of jokes, and to blame him for all the ills of the party. But those who seriously reflected on the situation realized that Starace was damaging the regime. Galeazzo Ciano noted in his diary in October 1938: "Starace is placing the country under a leaden cloak of personal and sectarian tyranny and it is here that we must look for the principal cause of the restlessness and lack of enthusiasm." In late December 1938 Ciano reported on a meeting with Giuseppe Bastianini, then undersecretary of foreign affairs, who painted a somber picture of the internal situation and "fulminated against the usual culprit, Starace."[80]

Starace was finally relieved of his duties in 1939, allegedly for having had a militiaman walk his dogs.[81] Mussolini praised Starace's long

service, but he had finally become convinced that the universal dislike
of Starace threatened to tarnish his own legend. Even loyal Fascists
breathed a collective sigh of relief. Starace, the culprit, had been removed, and things could, they hoped, get back on track.

But Achille Starace was merely a symptom of the malaise, not the
source of the problem. The high priest was removed, but the cult of the
Duce remained. Under Starace the gap between rhetoric and reality
became ever more apparent, but this was not the work of one man. If
Starace was the most available target, he was certainly not the only
celebrant of the cult. In a letter to Mussolini dated 11 July 1931 Carlo
Scorza mused over the failings of the youth movement and pointed out
that the young, deprived of the heady experiences of the war and revolution, needed a myth. "It is necessary," Scorza maintained, "to give a
Myth to the youth, because youth needs to believe blindly in something."
Predictably enough, Scorza found this energizing myth in Musso-
lini. "The Mussolini Myth," he rhapsodized, "equals LOYALTY-COUR-
AGE-THOUGHT-LIGHT-BEAUTY-HEROISM-ETERNITY."[82]

Provincial Reports on the ONB to 1937

During his tenure as party secretary, Starace undertook a vast and intense
effort to organize the young. But the results were not what the regime
had desired. Party statistics showed increasing enrollments in the youth
groups, but at the same time PNF leaders noted an alarming state of
mind among many in the second generation. During the thirties it became painfully clear to many Fascist leaders that myth and rhetoric could
not forever mask the growing detachment of many young people from
the life of the regime. This feeling of malaise became more distinct and
diffuse as the years passed, though it did not until very late in the history
of the regime develop into mass antifascism. But if the majority continued to be enrolled in the youth groups and to attend meetings, they did so
increasingly out of conformity; if most adapted to the external discipline
of the regime, for a growing number the participation was superficial,
based not on real belief but on opportunism or self-interest. Some
withdrew into apathy, some continued to hope for the social and moral
renewal the party had promised—but others adopted critical stances that
eventually brought them to active antifascism. The din of hundreds of
parades and rallies was not enough to keep many in the fold, nor did
massive enrollments and a sea of black shirts put to rest the nagging
suspicion among many Fascist leaders that, rhetoric to the contrary, all
was most definitely not well.

Evidence of the increasing alarm about the situation of the PNF youth
groups was included in the hundreds of monthly reports sent by the

provincial secretaries to Starace. The tone of most of the reports was predictably placating and, in the early years at least, generally gossipy. Few local PNF leaders were anxious to indulge in heavy self-criticism by laying bare the shortcomings of the movement in their provinces. But even given this natural reticence, some of the reports were alarmingly pessimistic about the state of the youth groups. This pessimism was not confined to a particular zone of Italy, nor was it more prevalent in the rural or urban areas. A few examples of such reports will suffice to indicate the general tenor of the criticisms.[83]

In a rather typical report dated November 1931 the provincial secretary of Turin warned: "Unfortunately instead of diminishing, the detachment between fascism and the youth sector seems to us to be growing. . . . [There] is an aversion to what fascism represents and a repulsion for the idea of coming closer and understanding what fascism really means."[84] Frequent reports of absenteeism from various party functions also made their way into these files. In 1932 the PNF secretary in Trent reported, for example, that "only a handful" of the Young Fascists came to the meetings.[85] Similar reports were sent in by the PNF officials in Milan in 1932 and Syracuse in 1934, though these were by no means the only such examples.[86] In 1936 the provincial secretary in Savona, reporting on recent ceremonies involving the youth groups, said: "The Fasci Giovanili were a joke from all points of view. . . . Discipline did not exist and I was forced to resort to . . . severe punishments to get them to show up at meetings."[87] In 1937 the secretary in Turin reported: "The Young Fascists are deserting the meetings. . . . Only the books are full of members, but the truth is that the young no longer go to the groups."[88]

In the south numerous reports mentioned the general lack of financial subsidies from the central office of the party and the administrative disorganization of the PNF groups. The November 1933 report from Matera, for example, described the state of the Fasci Giovanili as "extremely deficient . . . [there is] an absolute lack of organization and financial means."[89] In Syracuse the reports for May–June 1932 contained this notation: "The Fasci Giovanili exist only on paper. . . . The few demonstrations organized have been complete failures. . . . Out of 6,741 Young Fascists, fewer than 500 even have a uniform."[90] In March 1934 the provincial secretary in Reggio Calabria sent an especially damning report: "It is enough to see these young men march in the streets . . . to realize the indiscipline that reigns in the ranks. You do not see the young proud to wear the black shirt."[91]

All of this evidence served to buttress Starace's repeated claims that the young could be truly brought into the Fascist climate only if the PNF youth groups were reorganized and placed under the direct supervision and control of the party. Mussolini, finally convinced of the need for some thoroughgoing reforms in the socialization program that would put an end to the infighting and give the youth program new life, acceded to Starace's wishes. In October 1937 the regime brought its youth groups under the umbrella of the new unitary youth organization, the Gioventù Italiana del Littorio.

But these internal disputes and tensions were not the only obstacles the regime had to overcome. The PNF also had a potent external adversary in its drive to socialize Italian youth: the Catholic church. Relations between church and party on the issue of youth education were complicated and strained to the breaking point on occasion during the late 1920s and 1930s. The development of the conflict over "custody of the child," and the ultimate resolution of this vexed question, had important consequences for both regime and church—and for the future complexion of the Italian political scene.

CHAPTER FIVE

The Battle for Custody of the Child

The Catholic church was the most formidable obstacle to the regime's self-appointed mission to mold the "new Fascist man." The church's refusal after 1870 to recognize the legitimacy of the "sub-alpine usurper" was one of liberal Italy's perennial problems and the solution of that Roman Question one of Mussolini's chief legacies to Italy. The history of church-state relations during the Fascist period is one of substantial collaboration, punctuated by periodic confrontations and almost continual tension.[1] The highwater mark of church-state harmony came in 1929 with the signing of the Lateran Accords. Both sides realized the value of an agreement, and neither desired a total rupture. Both pursued a policy of caution, reluctant to stall negotiations before 1929 and eager to preserve the conciliation afterward. But this caution did not prevent verbal clashes and occasional physical violence. The Vatican initially condemned the PNF's use of force and questioned its loyalty to Catholic principles. In the late 1930s the regime's Nazi alliance and racial campaign aroused opposition among the church hierarchy and many individual Catholics. But the most serious and enduring tension arose over the question of education. For both sides control of the young was a guarantee for the future. Neither was prepared to abandon this contested terrain without a struggle.

Toward a Conciliation

The Italian leader who boasted of having resolved the Roman Question had from his earliest days been a vehement anticlerical and a self-proclaimed atheist. Mussolini was born in the Romagna, formerly part of the Papal States and a hotbed of revolt against ecclesiastical authority. Despite the example of his pious, churchgoing mother, Rosa Maltoni, Mussolini imbibed anticlerical and antireligious sentiments from his early environment and from his nonbeliever father, Alessandro.

One of Mussolini's earliest tirades was a speech delivered in March 1904 in Lausanne, a ringing denial of the existence of God and denunciation of the church. Religion, the young Mussolini thundered, "is a psychic malaise of the brain." In an anticlerical tract written during this early period, he dismissed Catholicism as a religion based on a "dozen ignorant vagabonds, the scum of the plebs of Palestine."[2]

His language was no more temperate once he returned from his Swiss wanderings. In 1906 he was charged with blasphemy in the classroom. In 1908 he wrote scurrilous attacks on the church for a radical paper and was dismissed from his teaching position under pressure from local clergy and conservatives. One of his particularly poetic pamphlets referred to priests as "black microbes who are as fatal to mankind as tuberculosis germs."[3] In 1909 Mussolini became editor of a Socialist paper in Trent, in the pages of which he distinguished himself for the virulence of his invective against the church and religion. During the same period he also wrote "Claudia Particella; or, The Cardinal's Mistress," which purported to be the story of a former bishop of Trent.[4] At the congress of the Socialist party in Forlì in 1910, he introduced an order of the day that declared all Catholic religious practices—including marriage, baptism, and burial—inconsistent with socialism and that provided for the expulsion from the party of observants.[5]

Mussolini's anticlerical vehemence did not tone down once he broke with the Socialist party. During the war the new editor of *Popolo d'Italia* frequently singled out the church as Italy's principal enemy because of its support of Catholic Austria. An especially violent series of articles published in September 1916 prompted an official condemnation by the archbishop of Milan and a public protest by Pope Benedict XV.[6]

The June 1919 program of the Fascist movement called for the "confiscation of all the properties belonging to religious congregations and abolition of all revenues of episcopal sees, which at present constitute an enormous burden on the nation while serving as a prerogative for a few privileged persons." In May 1920, at the second congress of the Fasci di Combattimento, Mussolini swallowed his earlier republicanism, but the program repeated the 1919 party planks on confiscation of religious properties.[7]

After the election of May 1921 Mussolini and thirty-four other Fascists sat in the Chamber of Deputies. Mussolini's first speech to the Chamber, on 21 June 1921, was a departure. Far from presenting himself as a blasphemous, anticlerical atheist, he took great pains to emphasize his respect for religious faith and especially for the Christian faith. He reminded his audience that "in the history of Fascism there are no invasions of churches" and claimed, "Fascism does not preach and does not practice anti-clericalism." Addressing the question of relations between church and state in Italy, he added: "I affirm here and now that today the Latin and imperial tradition of Rome is represented by Catholicism."[8]

Why the radical shift in views? What did this *volte face* say about future relations between the regime and the Vatican? Mussolini's "conversion" was not a religious revelation. No bolt of lightning or finger of God convinced him to mend his errant ways. His was a change of policy, not a change of heart. He became a "believer" in the social and political utility of the Catholic tradition in Italy. Mussolini's comments in the 1921 speech reflected his own fascination with the social function of *romanità*, as well as hardheaded political calculation. He realized that the grandeur of Rome was intimately bound up with the majesty and authority of the Vatican, that the prestige of Italy was inextricably tied to its unique position as home of the universal church. Mussolini came to see Catholicism not as a pietist creed of humility for the outcast and the downtrodden but as an enormously influential force that might be harnessed for his own ends. He realized that sharing the religion of his people (at least on the surface) would be a "special element of strength and consensus" for his regime.[9]

Mussolini had few illusions about the strength of his movement in 1921, and he came to accept that the power of the clergy and the church hierarchy was a force he could ill afford to tackle head on. But if he could not crush the influence of the church, he might be able to use it as an *instrumentum regni*. In short, he accepted the collaboration of the church after 1922 because he realized that he had more to gain from conciliation than from hostility. "All of Western history," he once admitted, "teaches us that when the state dedicates itself to a battle against religion, it is the state that will emerge defeated in the end."[10]

In charting a new course, Mussolini had to contend not only with the reactions of the Vatican but also with diverse opinions within the Fascist party leadership. Conservative former Nationalists welcomed the policy of conciliation; many anticlericals in the PNF opposed it. This tension within the party helps to explain the mercurial character of Fascist policy: an alternation of blandishments and threats, official protestations of respect for religion contrasted with violence against religious organizations. The relationship was never without tension. In periods of open conflict Mussolini's old anticlericalism, simmering just below the surface, boiled over. In periods of harmony the poisonous invective against the church ceased; the blasphemer turned pious and God-fearing.

The year 1922 also inaugurated the papacy of Pius XI, a man no less determined than Mussolini to solve the Roman Question. Achille Ratti, a Lombard of lower-bourgeois origins, was a shrewd and inflexible man, deeply patriotic and imbued with a love for Italy. Contemporary accounts noted his authoritarian personality and his determined anticommunism, fruit not only of his religious convictions but also of his service in the papal diplomatic service in postwar Poland. After his election as pope in early February 1922, his first act was to impart the papal blessing from the outside balcony of Saint Peter's—a tradition-breaking

gesture because all "prisoners of the Vatican" since 1870 had blessed the
crowds from inside the basilica.[11]

The church and the new government had many common attitudes that
help to explain the stance of the Vatican hierarchy toward the regime.
Fascism presented itself as an implacable foe of a whole range of modernist "heresies" against which the church had struggled; despite occasional protests about tactics, the church viewed the party's opposition to
socialism with special favor. For the church, the regime could serve as
the first line of defense against the possible proletarian conquest of
power and as the savior of those who upheld property, order, and the
nation against the forces of chaos and anarchy. Both stressed the need for
discipline and hierarchy. Both viewed the human as a social being who
needed to be guided, corrected, and limited. Both were suspicious of the
modern heresy of individualism and stressed submission to constituted
authority and an infallible leader. More pragmatic concerns also dictated
the church's policy of conciliation. If Mussolini saw religion as a valuable tool in his campaign to produce consensus for his regime and
greatness for the nation, the church also attempted to use fascism for its
own ends: the restoration of Catholic influence and power, or what
Catholic leaders referred to as the "Christianization" of Italy.

To achieve this restoration and penetration, Pius XI counted on Catholic Action and its vast network of groups for the laity. Significantly,
church and state came most directly into conflict over the status of
Catholic Action and its youth groups. The disagreement was less a
theological or ideological one than a confrontation over power: each side
protested to defend its own institutions, to guarantee its own position in
Italian society. For both, prospects for the future depended in large part
on training the young in the present.

Mussolini's claim that the PNF demanded a total monopoly of the
training of youth was the party's bid for continuity and permanence, its
insurance against possible decline and fall. But the church pressed its
rights in education no less forcefully, arguing that society could be
reclaimed only through reaffirmation of Catholic hegemony in education. Natural law gave the "right to teach and to educate" to the church,
"and after the church, and under its guidance, to the parents, and not to
the state."[12] The duty of the state was to offer the church and parents the
means to carry out their educational mission. Though both sides sought a
modus vivendi, on this issue neither was prepared to surrender without a
fight: "Two exclusivisms, one typically political-étatist and the other
religio-ecclesiastic, were contending for predominance over the lines of
development in civil society."[13]

A cycle of goodwill gestures and truculence—or on occasion open violence—characterized Mussolini's early relations with the church. Once in power, he lost no time in proclaiming his respect for religious values and his desire for an understanding with the Vatican. On 16 November 1922 he ended his first speech as prime minister with the invocation: "May God help me bring my arduous task to a victorious end!"[14] Vatican authorities were appropriately pleased by this metamorphosis of their old nemesis. *Civiltà cattolica* pointed to the speech as proof that the new leader wanted to detach himself from the "necropolis of official atheism."[15] The first meeting between Mussolini and the Vatican secretary of state, Cardinal Pietro Gasparri, took place shortly thereafter, on 23 January 1923.

In the early days actions matched verbal assurances. The return of the crucifix to the schools and other public buildings after November 1922, and the regime's tax exemptions and state subsidies for the clergy and appropriation of funds for churches damaged during the war, pleased ecclesiastical authorities. In December 1923 the new government also recognized some religious feasts as civil holidays. The regime's stance against divorce, its demographic campaign to raise births and ban the use of contraceptive devices, its battle against pornography and blasphemy, and its antimasonic laws all elicited positive responses from the Vatican, as did the prohibition against the building of a mosque in Rome and restrictions on the activities of Protestant missionaries. The Duce himself made personal gestures calculated to prove his good intentions. In April 1923 his children were baptized and confirmed, and on 29 December 1925 he sanctified his 1915 civil union with Rachele Guidi in a religious ceremony in Milan.[16]

The Vatican also had cause for joy in education. While church leaders were not always pleased with the philosophical and ideological stances of Giovanni Gentile, they were favorably impressed by certain provisions of his reform. *Civiltà cattolica* greeted the reintroduction of religious education in the elementary schools as a step in the right direction, if only a first step.[17] In the view of church leaders, Gentile's approval of the *esame di Stato* was also a move toward full recognition of confessional schools. The Vatican was lavish in its praise of the regime's decision in 1924 to accredit the recently founded Catholic University of the Sacred Heart in Milan, a school which under its rector, Father Agostino Gemelli, was to be one of the strongest links between church and state during the Fascist period.[18]

One of the major obstacles to church-state cooperation in this early period was the existence of the Catholic Popular party (PPI). Fascist leaders emphasized that the regime would respect and defend the position of the church in Italian society. In their view, therefore, the PPI had lost its function—indeed, it was a positive hindrance to a possible understanding with the Vatican. Although Mussolini accepted Popolari into his first cabinet, the relationship was always an uneasy one.

The Popular party congress in April 1923 gave Mussolini the pretext he needed to take action. At that meeting the rank and file split on the question of support for the regime. The Fascist press soon unleashed a campaign against PPI secretary Don Luigi Sturzo, referred to in an editorial in *Popolo d'Italia* as "an enemy."[19] This attack, coupled with the opposition of many Popolari to the Acerbo election law and the party's strong showing in the election of 1924, led to the removal of PPI ministers from the cabinet. Sturzo resigned as party secretary in July 1924 after editorials in the Catholic press hinted none too subtly that his continued presence was a source of embarrassment to the church. (He was replaced by Alcide De Gasperi.) In 1924 the pope forbade priests from belonging to political parties and ordered the total separation of Catholic Action and all its organizations from the PPI. That same year Sturzo emigrated to London.

After the right wing of the PPI split off and formed the proregime Centro Nazionale Italiano in August 1924, the rump of the PPI participated in the Aventine secession. The Catholic representatives returned to the Chamber in January 1926, but they were insulted and physically abused by PNF deputies. Mussolini made it clear that their continued presence in the government was contingent upon full acceptance of the Fascist revolution and silence on questions of PNF tactics. This demand the remaining PPI deputies could not meet. In November 1926 the government dissolved all non-Fascist political parties with a law that marked the end of organized Catholic political activity in Italy until 1942–43.[20]

Pius XI had never been comfortable with the idea of a Catholic democratic movement; he was convinced that the church had more to gain from cooperation with a stable government and a powerful leader than from party politics. When it became clear that the PPI was an obstacle to the long-awaited accord with the new government, the Vatican abandoned the Catholic party in return for a settlement of the Roman Question and recognition of Catholic Action.

The Battle over Catholic Action: Round One, to 1929

The abandonment of the Popular party coincided with, and in some respects was prompted by, a reform and strengthening of Catholic Action. The reorganization of the multi-faceted Catholic organization into one monolithic entity under strict papal control was one of Achille

Ratti's first priorities when he ascended the papal throne in February 1922.

Founded in 1863, Catholic Action was an international organization of the laity dedicated to the defense of Christian religious and ethical principles in modern "paganized" society. Pius XI defined the goal of Catholic Action as the collaboration of the laity in the hierarchical apostolate of the church. Its task of cultural, educational, and moral penetration aimed at extending the influence of Catholicism over the masses and the formation of leadership cadres in the Catholic movement. Though the leaders of the organization claimed it was above and outside politics, its activities had aroused anticlerical opposition in the early years of the twentieth century. After lifting the *non expedit*, for example, Pius X had routinely used the organization to instruct Catholic voters. Don Sturzo was president of the executive committee of Catholic Action after 1915, a link that helps to explain later suspicions that the association was a refuge for anti-Fascists. Despite Sturzo's repeated claims that the PPI had no connection to Catholic Action or the Vatican, Catholic Action members were usually supporters of the Catholic party, and many members of the PPI were also enrolled in Catholic Action.[21]

In the immediate postwar period the growth of the Popular party and Catholic trade union organizations diverted many Catholics away from the Catholic Action groups, a state of affairs that Pius XI—known as the "pope of Catholic Action"—viewed with alarm. Partly to allay the suspicions of the regime, the pontiff reorganized Catholic Action in 1923 in a series of reforms that accentuated the unitary character of the organization and reinforced its dependence on the church hierarchy.

After the 1923 reforms, Catholic Action consisted of four associations: groups for adult males, adult females, youth, and university students. Overall direction remained in the hands of a central committee composed of a president and four members, all appointed by the pope. Authority passed from this central committee down through diocesan and parish councils. Ecclesiastical authorities—bishops or parish priests —appointed the presidents of these local groups, and group members elected committee members. Officers in all organizations were laymen, but each group also had a chaplain nominated by church authorities.

Catholic Action was an impressively organized association, with its own journals and papers, its own social activities, and a wide network of local groups that appealed to Italian Catholics in both urban and rural areas. By 1929 Catholic Action in Italy had some 250 diocesan committees, 4,000 men's sections, and some 5,000 youth and university groups.[22]

Jealous of his mission to provide for the totalitarian education of the Italian populace, Mussolini viewed the popularity of Catholic Action groups with a jaundiced eye. The existence of an autonomous nationwide association outside the control of state and party clashed with his desire to control all public activities and mass organizations. At the insistence of the Vatican, the national directorate of Catholic Action after 1923 attempted to keep its distance from former PPI leaders, but this was often not possible at the local level, where former Popolari frequently served as group leaders. The organization provided an alternative for Italian Catholics, a meeting place where they could and did hear other voices besides the gospel according to fascism, where "enthusiasm for a regime they disliked was not compulsory."[23] Though they were not actively involved in anti-Fascist activity, the existence of these groups kept alive the possibility of an island of separateness in a sea of officially enforced conformity.[24]

Open attacks against church organizations punctuated the regime's policy of conciliation in the early years. Roberto Farinacci was in the forefront of Fascist opposition to Mussolini's attempts at pacification and compromise with the church. Farinacci's tenure in the PNF leadership was one of violence against Catholics, and most especially against the Catholic Action groups he wanted liquidated. Catholic Action leaders protested against Fascist violence as early as January 1923, but the antichurch campaign on the local level became more violent in 1924–25 during the Matteotti crisis and with the consolidation of the dictatorship. This escalation prompted protests from the *Osservatore romano* and even a letter from the pope to the minister of the interior. The attacks provoked a wave of general indignation and eventual action by Mussolini, who was himself none too pleased with the spontaneous activities of the squads. On 5 October 1925 the Grand Council dissolved the squadrist groups and ordered their members to enroll in the MVSN. Farinacci left office in March 1926, but the violence did not end there.

The first round in the dispute between the PNF and the Vatican over Catholic Action came on the question of the Esploratori Cattolici, the Catholic Boy Scouts.[25] The Esploratori were founded in 1916 on the model of Lord Baden-Powell's British groups. These uniformed "soldiers of Christ" were organized into paramilitary formations based on strict principles of discipline and hierarchy. In just ten years membership grew to almost a hundred thousand, with branches in over a thousand locations; such growth was bound to arouse the suspicions of Fascists, who viewed the movement as a highly successful rival. Despite Vatican assurances to the contrary, many PNF leaders were also convinced that the Esploratori danced to a tune piped by leaders of the dissolved PPI.

The establishment of the ONB in April 1926 aggravated the tension. Vatican officials had been alarmed by the activities of Fascist youth groups before 1926 because members had often been involved in attacks against church organizations. In 1925 the Holy Office condemned the so-called Balilla Catechism used in these early groups as a "blasphemous parody of the Christian catechism."[26] Despite assurances of official toleration, the Fascists went on the attack against the Catholic Scouts in September 1926. On 8 September an editorial in the fanatical *Il Tevere* termed the Catholic Scouts a "foreign movement perniciously deforming and adulterating the character of the Italian spirit," and labeled the groups "survivors of *popolarismo*." On 24 September the blast continued: "Scoutism with its varied attractions is a deadly menace to the Balilla. . . . Eighty-eight thousand children brought up to 'universal brotherhood'—we don't want that in Italy."[27]

Opposition to the Catholic organizations was not limited to words. In August 1926 Avanguardisti broke up meetings of the Esploratori, wrecked their meeting halls, and beat up members and, on several occasions, their clerical directors. No official action was taken against the young Fascists, though reprisals by Esploratori were immediately punished by local police authorities. In late August a national congress of the Catholic University Federation (FUCI) was disrupted by members of the Fascist university groups, and several Fucini were severely beaten. The pope retaliated swiftly, canceling an international conference of Catholic athletic and sports organizations that was to have been held in Rome in early September. The incident was covered in the *Osservatore romano* and in the foreign press, a public washing of dirty linen that outraged Fascist leaders.[28]

By the end of 1926 the situation seemed to have quieted, although Pius XI was under no illusion about the permanence of the truce. In early December the Vatican received the text of the proposed law on the organization of the ONB. Article 29 reserved to the ONB supervision over all organizations for the moral, physical, and spiritual education of youth; other articles forbade the creation of new groups and provided for the dissolution of the Esploratori in towns with fewer than ten thousand inhabitants.[29]

Vatican authorities immediately objected to these proposals and advised Mussolini that such actions would seriously imperil the delicate negotiations for a church-state rapprochement. Pius XI's Christmas message to the cardinals on 20 December reflected his concern about the widening of the dispute. He lamented the assassination attempt against the Duce that had occurred in late October, but went on to castigate the regime for its use of violence against its own citizens and to warn of dire consequences for the party if it could not control its members at a local level.[30] Mussolini stood firm. He could not afford to lose face with the anticlerical wing of his own party, nor could he encourage the church to dictate his policy on education. In the first week of January 1927 negotiations between the Vatican and the Italian state were suspended.

The raison d'être of the Catholic groups was called into question after the publication of the ONB law in January 1927. Article 26 provided for religious teaching and Catholic chaplains in all ONB units.[31] Chaplains provided a course of religious instruction that consisted of twenty half-hour lessons during the year. Monsignor Angelo Bartolomasi, the inspector general of the ONB chaplains, pressed frequently after 1927 for a more rigorous religious education program. For the time being, however, PNF leaders used the law to justify their contention that the Catholic groups were superfluous.[32]

The Royal Decree of 9 January 1927 (no. 5) addressed the question of the Esploratori directly. Article 2 forbade the establishment of new groups promoting the "physical, moral, and spiritual education of youth" in communes with fewer than twenty thousand inhabitants (except for county seats); article 3 ordered the dissolution of groups already existing in such communes. In addition, this latter article provided that in the larger cities the groups could continue to function only if their banners sported the party and ONB symbols to show their solidarity. Article 4 stipulated that these provisions did not apply to groups having primarily religious functions, a device to placate church leaders, who feared the repercussions of this legislation on other Catholic Action youth groups. The framers of the law clearly hoped that the ONB groups would overwhelm the Catholic Esploratori in the larger towns. Party leaders were also well aware that the Catholic organizations were deeply rooted in the rural areas, where only drastic measures could reduce their influence. In these areas, therefore, the groups had to be banned completely.

Pius met the challenge head on. In a lengthy letter to Cardinal Gasparri on 24 January 1927—published the next day in the Jesuit organ *Civiltà cattolica*—the pope denied that the state had any power to dissolve church organizations and lamented the teaching in the ONB of a doctrine that "we have reason to fear is founded . . . on a conception of the state . . . that does not conform to Catholic doctrine." Claiming that "right has ceded to force," the pope took the initiative: he dissolved the Esploratori groups affected by the PNF legislation and detached the remaining groups from Catholic Action in order to protect that organization's other youth groups from a similar fate. Once again caution on a specific issue was dictated by a general concern over the future of the church-state accord. Negotiations between Vatican officials and the government resumed in late February 1927.[33]

The issue was far from resolved, however, and the government did not relax its vigilance. In March the regime ordered prefects to provide membership lists for all Catholic groups in their areas and to make regular reports on the activities of those groups.[34] Police reports from all over Italy testify that all Catholic organizations were under constant surveillance during this period. In 1927 police agents noted increasingly frequent confrontations between Catholic and Fascist youth. In October twenty-six serious incidents were reported in the north in which members of ONB groups attacked and destroyed Scout meeting places, beat up members and priests of those groups, or distributed leaflets with the legend "Death to the Esploratori."[35] Members of the FUCI were also singled out for special treatment at the hands of overzealous members of local GUF chapters. In April 1928 the government renewed the order for close surveillance.[36]

The increasing violence did not go unremarked by the Vatican. In an address to the Gioventù Cattolica Italiana on 4 March 1928, the pope deplored the "veritable war, more or less secret," being waged against the Catholic institutions so "dear to the heart of the common Father of the faithful."[37]

New Fascist measures against the Catholic groups were not long in coming. At a meeting of the Council of Ministers on 28 March 1928, Mussolini declared that the progress of the ONB made toleration of other youth organizations a thing of the past and warned that "it has become necessary to alter the law according to the intransigent Fascist style."[38] In April 1928 a government order directed all prefects to dissolve within thirty days all youth organizations not related to the ONB that were engaged in promoting "instruction, preparation for professions, arts or crafts, or the physical, moral, or spiritual welfare of the young."[39]

The order seemed to sound the death knell for all Catholic youth groups. The reaction of the pope was immediate and bitter: Pius ordered a halt in negotiations with the Italian government on 17 April. Father Pietro Tacchi-Venturi, who had once described himself as a "good Jesuit and a good Fascist"—and a man who enjoyed the confidence of Mussolini as intermediary during the negotiations—exchanged a series of letters in April with the Duce and other PNF representatives stressing the pontiff's deep concern and making only vaguely veiled threats of dire consequences for the regime if the impasse should lead to a complete rupture. Such a break would be, he said, "the prelude to the final collapse of the regime."[40]

This pressure and the realization that tension between the sides was once again escalating into violent confrontations, along with the Duce's own desire to take credit for an impressive resolution of the long church-state conflict, led Mussolini to back down from his initially "intransigent" stance. An "interpretative" circular that finally went out over his signature on 14 May 1928 clarified the issue: only those "semimilitary" organizations in direct opposition to the ONB were to be disbanded. This decision struck at the remaining branches of the Catholic Scouts but left the Catholic organizations of a prevalently religious nature—especially the organs of Catholic Action—unmolested.[41] The final demise of the Scouts did not cause a ripple; the remaining groups dissolved themselves on 6 May 1928.

In a letter dated 16 May, Tacchi-Venturi conveyed the pope's "great pleasure" at the clarification and his fervent hope that the settlement would be only the prelude to resolution of a "much more serious question that has troubled church-state relations for over half a century." On 25 May negotiations between the Vatican and the government resumed.[42]

The passing of the Catholic Scouts did not end the regime's fears about the influence of the church over Italian youth. In the period between the dissolution of the groups in May 1928 and the signature of the Lateran Accords in February 1929, all Catholic Action groups were still under constant surveillance. Quarterly reports to the Ministry of the Interior contained details about meetings, speeches, and excerpts from purloined mail gathered by police agents who had infiltrated Catholic groups. The regime was especially concerned to know whether the groups served as propaganda centers for ex-Popolari, and police informers reported just such activity in the traditionally Catholic areas of the Veneto. Here operatives also observed a general attitude of resistance among the clergy and intense efforts to attract students and rural elements away from the PNF youth groups.[43]

A circular to all prefects in December 1928 requested information on all Catholic youth group activities and biographical information on group leaders. The majority of the provinces reported no especially alarming news, but responses from cities in the Veneto, Piedmont, and Lombardy and from Rome noted intensified recruitment to draw the young away from the PNF groups and an intense propaganda campaign among students and teachers in the secondary schools and universities.[44]

Problems over what Mussolini termed the "scoutist parenthesis" held up negotiations on the all-important conciliation between the Vatican and the Italian state for one year. Neither side emerged from the clash totally victorious. Mussolini had tried to flex his political muscle by dissolving all Catholic groups that competed with his own youth groups. In the end, he accepted half a loaf: dissolution of the Catholic Scouts but tacit recognition of other Catholic Action associations for the young. The pope was comforted by the progressive desecularization of the ONB groups after 1927. He was willing to give ground on the issue of the Catholic Scouts in the hope of preserving the status of his pet organization, Catholic Action. In this he was disappointed, however, for within two years the regime was also challenging the integrity of that organization. For the time being both sides retreated and devoted their energies to the final settlement of the Roman Question.

Believe,   On 11 February 1929 years of delicate negotiations ended with the
Obey,   signing of the Lateran Accords: a treaty, a financial convention, and a
Fight   concordat. The Italian state recognized the state of Vatican City under
the sovereignty of the pope, and the Holy See recognized the kingdom of
Italy.

Some of the terms of the Concordat, however, caused serious problems. In effect the document repudiated the laic tradition of the Risorgimento by giving the church wide powers in important spheres of Italian
life, including education. Article 35 emphasized the juridical parity of
Catholic schools by guaranteeing the right of students in those schools to
take the *esame di Stato* under the same conditions as students in state
schools. It stated: "Italy considers the teaching of Christian doctrine,
according to the form handed down by Catholic tradition, as the foundation and capstone of public education." Religion, already taught in the
elementary schools, was also to be taught at the secondary level by
priests using church-approved textbooks.[45] Pius's determination to protect Catholic Action bore fruit in article 43, which recognized Catholic
Action but emphasized its apolitical nature. The same article also pro-
hibited ecclesiastics from participating in the activities of any political
party.

Mussolini was not pleased with article 43, the most debated in the
Concordat and the one that had caused the greatest difficulties during
the long negotiations. Significantly, the wording of the article had not
changed in drafts of the agreement over the years—testimony to the
pope's steadfastness on the question. Mussolini agreed to sign the article
because it was the sine qua non of the entire settlement. In return for the
guarantee of Catholic Action, the pope had once again repudiated the
Catholic party and had, at least officially, severely circumscribed the
permissible activities of Catholic Action groups. The seeds for future
conflict were sown.

In an audience with professors and students from the Catholic University in Milan shortly after the signing of the accords, Pius praised both
Mussolini and the settlement in words widely quoted in Italy and abroad:
"The times called for a man such as he whom Providence has ordained
that We should meet. . . . It is with profound satisfaction that We express the belief that We have given God to Italy and Italy to God."[46]
Mussolini received a kind of moral recognition that the pope's predeces-
sors had always denied to liberal governments. On 13 March 1929 the
central committee of Catholic Action passed a resolution calling for a
yes vote in the coming elections. For the PNF the accords seemed to
have borne fruit.[47]

The conciliation came as a surprise to Italians, though the general reaction was favorable and the settlement undoubtedly redounded to the credit of the regime. The newly elected Chamber ratified the agreement by an overwhelming vote. Only six senators voted against the accords. The only voice of open dissent in the Senate was that of Benedetto Croce.[48] Some Catholics, however, were not resigned; some were offended by the eulogy of a dictator they still regarded as a violent and irreligious ruffian. However, for most Catholics—and certainly for the Vatican—the accords were a kind of insurance, a legal recognition of the political and social influence of the church in Italian life.

Though gratified by paeans in the press, the "Man of Providence," as Fascist propagandists hastened to christen him, still had to contend with the anticlerical wing of his own party. In his four-hour speech on the conciliation delivered to the Chamber of Deputies on 13 May 1929, Mussolini took pains to reaffirm the laic character of the state and to reassure any doubting Thomases that the Concordat did not modify the totalitarian nature of fascism. In the process he offended the pope and touched off another controversy. Responding to a senator who proposed the formula "free and sovereign church, free and sovereign state," Mussolini replied: "In the state the church is not sovereign and not even free. . . . The Fascist state categorically reaffirms its ethical character. It is Catholic, but it is Fascist—indeed, it is exclusively, essentially Fascist." In tones recalling his youthful anticlerical diatribes, Mussolini continued: "We have not revived the temporal power of the popes, we have buried it." On the subject of education, the Duce maintained that the conciliation should not be seen as a capitulation to the church. He claimed, for example, that on article 36 he had firmly rejected the Vatican proposal to require religious instruction in the universities and concluded: "In this we are intractable! Education must belong to us."[49]

The pope read Mussolini's speech on the morning of 14 May and replied later that same day during an audience with visiting pilgrims of the Jesuit College of Mondragone. His comments were a stinging indictment of Mussolini's contention that children belonged to the state. Attacking the Fascist leader's declaration that education should instill a spirit of conquest, the pope said: "We cannot admit that in its educational activities the state shall try to raise up conquerors or encourage conquests. . . . But perhaps what was meant . . . was education for the conquest of truth, in which case We are perfectly in agreement."[50]

In a shorter and more restrained speech presenting the accords to the Senate on 25 May, Mussolini drew a distinction between *istruzione* and *educazione*. The latter, he claimed, was the total formation of mind and character and was the preserve of the state: "What, then, is the education that we claim in a totalitarian manner? The education of the citizen to which we will finally give a name because hypocrisy is repugnant to us: education for war."[51]

For several weeks the press rang out with harsh statements and rebuttals on both sides. In response to Mussolini's Senate address, Pius wrote a long letter to Cardinal Gasparri. The papal letter, a detailed refutation of the Duce's claims, was published in *Osservatore romano* on 6 June. It was the last salvo in this particular stage of the war. Mussolini, irritated but shrewd enough to realize that he had little to gain from prolonging the dispute, drove to the Vatican the next day for ratification of the accords. All went according to plan: the ceremony was correct if not exactly cordial. The first telegram was sent that day from the Vatican to King Victor Emmanuel III.

Open conflict had ended, but the positions taken by the two sides clearly indicated the possibility of future clashes. The Fascist regime intended to absorb the residual forces of the Catholic movement and use them as far as possible for its own ends. The church intended to preserve its own organizations and carry out a policy that would protect the gains ratified in the Concordat and extend the influence of the church in Italian life. The resolutions of the problems over the Catholic Scouts and over the interpretation of the Lateran Accords were only the first skirmishes in the wider war between church and regime on the question of education and youth. The next battle came over the status of the youth groups of Catholic Action.

The Battle over Catholic Action: Round Two, 1931

Two years after the signing of the Lateran Accords the regime launched its second offensive against Catholic Action. The existence and autonomy of the organization was recognized in the Concordat. A legal formula, however, did not guarantee mutual understanding, and in some ways article 43 increased the possibility of conflict. The church prized Catholic Action as a legally recognized instrument for Catholic penetration into Italian society and the transformation of Italy into an ever more confessional state. Determined to control all mass organizations, the Fascist regime saw Catholic Action as a serious threat to its own integrity and educational mission. Mussolini had not managed to destroy Catholic Action in 1929. Indeed, the organization seemed to be flourishing.

The PNF leaders viewed the activities of Catholic Action with growing alarm. They again accused the organization of harboring ex-Popolari and of carrying out social programs that competed with the regime's syndical and welfare agencies. They directed their wrath especially against the Catholic youth groups—the Gioventù Cattolica—and against the university groups—the Federazione Universitaria Cattolica Italiana (FUCI)—and the professional sections of that organization established in 1926. No doubt some of their fears were well founded. But the accusations that filled the Fascist press were a smokescreen for the party's deeper concern: "The so-called war against the 'political activities' of the Catholic Action was but another round in the struggle for custody of the child."[52]

The conflict over the FUCI was especially bitter. Both sides tenaciously defended their university groups. For both church and state, control of the intellectual elite represented the best hope for the future.

The first Catholic university groups were established in 1874. The nationwide organization of the FUCI, designed "to train a Catholic ruling class," came in 1896. Fucini were early targets of squadrist violence because of their opposition to actual idealism and certain aspects of the Gentile reform—and because of their close association with members of the Popular party. The FUCI was reorganized in 1925 by Pope Pius XI, who, in his eagerness for a church-state agreement, attempted to bring the organization under the strict control of the hierarchy. The old leadership was jettisoned. Monsignor Luigi Piastrelli, whose "modernist" past and sympathy for the PPI aroused the suspicions of both the PNF and the Vatican, "resigned" as ecclesiastical assistant in 1925. Igino Righetti served as president of FUCI until 1934, and Piastrelli's former post was held by Monsignor Giovanni Battista Montini, son of a PPI deputy and the future Pope Paul VI, from 1925 to 1933. The reorganization also provided that officers of FUCI would be appointed by the pope, not elected by group members, a reform that did not sit well with Fucini, who had long guarded the independence and autonomy of their organization. During the Fascist period the FUCI continued to be an active center of independent thought and culture, thanks largely to the efforts of the Righetti-Montini leadership and the activities of FUCI's journal *Studium*. In 1932 a group for Catholic graduates, the Movimento Laureati, was founded to continue the FUCI activities outside the universities. In 1933 the Movimento took over editorial responsibilities for *Studium*. The existence of a "Catholic cyst within the Italian body politic" alarmed the Fascists and certainly contributed to the violence of 1931 aimed at excising that irritating presence.[53]

Contrasts between the FUCI and GUF continued after the signing of the accords. Just after the conciliation, *Libro e moschetto*, organ of the Milanese GUF, published an article entitled "Can Fascist Youth and Catholic Youth Collaborate?" The article urged cooperation in common activities and none too subtly hinted that continued protestations of autonomy by the FUCI would put the very existence of that group in jeopardy. Cooperation for the Gufini in this case apparently meant the quiet suicide of the Catholic groups.[54]

In September 1929 the Bologna GUF ran in its journal *Vita nova* an article by Julius Evola that opened with a provocative, and for Evola rhetorical, question: "Is a Catholic education compatible with a Fascist education?" Can there, he wondered, be any real convergence between Christian values such as "evangelical equality, peace, the exaltation of the weak, of the disinherited, praise of humility and charity," and the "Roman and virile values of courage, valor, aristocracy, wisdom, and power" on which Fascist education was based?[55]

On 31 December 1929, in response to these and other truculent statements by PNF leaders, Pius XI published the encyclical *Divini illius magistri*, again underlining the church's views on education. The papal message criticized the regime's youth groups for their excessive emphasis on militarism and violence and denounced their attempt to monopolize the time and energies of the young. The pope also spoke out against coeducation and public gymnastic displays for girls, labeling them "contrary to the very instincts of human nature."[56]

Thanks to the explicit recognition of Catholic Action in the Lateran Accords, these groups, and especially the Gioventù Cattolica Italiana, seemed to have a new lease on life. Fascist leaders calculated on the eve of the 1931 crisis that Catholic Action had about one million members and that its daily press reached some hundred thousand readers.[57] The government responded to these alarming statistics by stepping up observation of the Catholic groups and by taking repressive measures—sequestration of Catholic papers, intimidation of local group leaders and members. This action, in turn, prompted protests by bishops, cardinals, and Vatican officials.

Quarterly police reports sent to Rome testified to the regime's concern about the popularity of the Catholic youth groups and, by extension, its own failure to attract all the youth into PNF groups. These same reports illustrated that the regime's fears, especially in areas where the Catholic movement was deeply entrenched, were not without foundation.

Surveillance reports for January–March 1929—just before and just after the conciliation—noted a decrease in overt antiregime agitation, even in the Catholic strongholds in the Veneto. But by the spring of 1929 this temporary trend reversed, and reports once again commented on increased activity among Catholic groups. Between July and September 1929 agents with increasing frequency pointed out the hostility of the local clergy and successful efforts by the leaders of Gioventù Cattolica to attract the young. Once again the center of activity was the Veneto, but reports from cities with large Slav populations (Gorizia and Pola), cities in central Italy (Pistoia and Reggio Emilia), and the islands (Messina) also sounded the alarm about the spreading "Catholic virus."[58]

From October to December 1929 agents also noted stepped-up activity in Piedmont, and during the same period an informant in Padua warned: "The activity of the Catholic organizations is still intense and directed principally at making converts among the young." The same refrain was repeated in many other cities in northern Italy.[59]

secretary during this period also made reference to increased activity and growing membership in the Catholic youth groups. A 1930 report from Vicenza—the city most consistently mentioned as a hotbed of Catholic opposition—said: "On the pretext of religion, the Catholic organizations carry out work denigrating and damaging to the regime. They are spreading rapidly and have great influence."[60]

After months of sparring, *Il Lavoro fascista* finally launched the attack against Catholic Action in March 1931. Editorials objected to the establishment of sections for workers in Catholic Action, charging that these were but "camouflaged syndicates" and accusing the organization of welcoming members who could "no longer conceal their antifascism" and were openly hatching plots to supplant the regime by using Catholic Action to "take the place of the defunct Popular party." Once the opening salvo was fired, the anti–Catholic Action campaign spread rapidly in the Fascist press.[61]

The offensive was orchestrated by two leading Fascists: Giovanni Giuriati and Carlo Scorza. Giuriati, who had been appointed PNF secretary in October 1930, agitated throughout the spring of 1931 for strong measures against Catholic Action. A vituperative article by Scorza in the pages of *Gioventù fascista* on 12 April 1931, entitled "Odiare i nemici" ("Hate the Enemies"), served to fan the fires. In March and April Mussolini canceled FUCI congresses planned for Pavia and Ferrara, claiming that they would have aggravated tensions.[62]

In a meeting with the papal nuncio on 8 April, Cesare De Vecchi, then Italian ambassador to the Vatican, conveyed Mussolini's "requests": moderation of the Catholic press, vigilant attention to ensure the apolitical nature of Catholic Action, and the exile of all former Popolari from the Vatican, beginning with De Gasperi. The pope refused and the battle heated up—a battle Pius chose to fight in person and Mussolini fought using emissaries and mouthpieces in the Fascist press.

In an intemperate speech in Milan on 19 April, Giuriati pulled no punches: the Fascist state was a totalitarian state, Catholic groups should not and could not exist. The pope answered this and other outbursts in an unusual letter sent on 26 April to Ildefonso Cardinal Schuster, archbishop of Milan, and made public by *Osservatore romano*. Pius came very close to openly condemning fascism for corrupting the youth by instilling in them "hate and irreverence, making the practices of their religious duties difficult or impossible" because of demands for their presence at youth group functions. He restated in forceful language the church's educational mission and warned that Fascists had only one duty as Catholics: to obey the church and its leader.[63]

The papal letter produced violent reactions in the Fascist press in the following days. Mussolini himself was surprised and angered by the pope's audacity. But neither side wanted to press matters too far. Pius, realizing that Catholic Action was protected by the Concordat so long as the regime had no open cause for intervention, continued to stress its apolitical nature. Mussolini, though he permitted and even encouraged these "spontaneous" diatribes in the Fascist press, clearly did not want the situation to degenerate into an open war that would only damage the image of his regime abroad and encourage the intransigents in his own party. But he did want to dissolve Catholic Action or, if that proved impossible, to circumscribe its activity as proof to his followers that he was still firmly in control. On 28 May he sent a coded message to all prefects urging them to avoid any incidents that would "offend the religious sentiments of the people."[64] For a few days calm prevailed. But between 21 and 24 May the Fascist papers *Tribuna* and *Il Lavoro fascista* published a series of "exposés" that purported to prove the subversive goals of the leadership of Catholic Action, charges that were rebutted in *Osservatore romano*.

Violence erupted. Offices and meeting halls of the Catholic Action groups—especially those of the FUCI and the Gioventù Cattolica—were broken into and sacked by GUF members. Igino Righetti, dogged by police agents, finally took refuge in Vatican City. The FUCI headquarters in Rome was put under round-the-clock surveillance and its files ransacked for incriminating evidence. The Rome office of the *Civiltà cattolica* was invaded; members of the Catholic youth groups were beaten, books burned, statues broken, religious ceremonies disturbed even in churches, and parodies of Catholic rites staged. In the streets processions of young neo-*squadristi* chalked offending slogans on walls and shouted "Death to the traitor Ratti!" "Down with FUCI!" "Down with the pope!" and "Death to Catholic Action!" Carlo Scorza was once again leading the troops. He concluded a rabble-rousing speech in Parma: "Do you know who are the real enemies of fascism? Those stinking Catholics!" The mob took the hint and devastated the local FUCI headquarters.[65]

Prodded by Giuriati and other anticlerical Fascists, Mussolini took steps to put an end to the confusion. On 29 May 1931 he ordered prefects to dissolve all youth groups not affiliated with the PNF, and to close their headquarters and confiscate their records as evidence.[66]

Rather surprisingly, given the drastic nature of the action, new violence did not erupt after the Duce's decision. Church leaders did not remain silent, however. The pope publicly protested during two ceremonies at the Vatican; telegrams from prefects all over Italy reported that in carrying out the order they encountered vociferous protests from clergy and bishops and a general feeling that the confrontation could well lead to a final break.[67] The prefect in Turin commented that the initiative "has exasperated the clergy mightily and they have thrown themselves into the work of sabotage." Frequent reports of antiregime lectures by religion teachers in the schools and sermons against "the new persecutions" served only to exacerbate the already tense situation.[68]

On 3 June Mussolini presided at a meeting of the national directorate of the PNF in Rome. The leadership approved an order of the day laying responsibility for the conflict at the feet of the pope and claiming to have documentary evidence of the subversive activities of Catholic Action. While paying lip service to their respect for the Catholic religion and its leader, the authors of the message ended with a declaration of the regime's firm resolve not to "tolerate that antifascism . . . shall receive refuge or protection under any banner old or new."[69]

The pope's reply came on 5 July with the publication of *Non abbiamo bisogno*, an encyclical on Catholic Action dated 29 June. To avoid confiscation of the papal message, about which the police had been tipped off, Pius sent copies of it to Paris with Monsignor Francis Spellman of New York. The text was published in newspapers abroad before Italians could read it in *Osservatore romano*, which went on sale five hours early that day to confound the authorities. Written in uncommonly strong and forthright Italian, instead of Latin, to give impact and urgency to the pontiff's words, the letter was divided into two sections. The first part of the message was a slashing indictment of the regime's "false and unjust accusations" against Catholic Action and a condemnation of the "real and true persecution" against the church in the "hostile party press." In the view of the pope the regime's concern with Catholic Action was really only a smokescreen for its attempt to "tear away from Catholic Action and so from the church, the young—*all* the young." In the second part Pius went on to reaffirm the church's "universal and divine mandate to educate children" and to assail the regime's efforts "to monopolize the young . . . for the sole and exclusive benefit of a party and of a regime based on an ideology that clearly resolves itself into a veritable pagan worship of the state."[70]

Pius declared unlawful the loyalty oath required of all youth group members, an oath to a "revolution that seduces the young from the church and from Jesus Christ and teaches them hatred, violence, and irreverence"; he rejected it as "an act of religion surely out of place on the membership cards of a political party." For those who had to take the oath of allegiance merely for the sake of their careers, the pontiff urged a mental reservation that they would do nothing contrary to the laws of God or the church.[71]

On 9 July the party responded. A circular from the national directorate to all provincial secretaries declared that membership in Catholic Action groups was incompatible with membership in PNF organizations.[72] The official press was whipped into action to support the leadership. The organ of the PNF in Sicily and Calabria, for example, published an editorial on 12 July that threatened: "We want to demonstrate the depth of our blind devotion: if the Duce ordered us to shoot all the bishops we would not hesitate an instant." Mussolini also permitted publication of a violently anticlerical book entitled *Svaticanamento* ("Devaticanization"), which railed against the "treason of Achille Ratti, renegade Italian who . . . attempted to form a coalition of all anti-Fascists in the world." When the climate later changed, the book was sequestered.[73]

Reaction in Catholic papers abroad to the Fascist attacks against the Church was hostile. The French Catholic paper *La Croix* on 14 July 1931 defended the pope's encyclical as the "defense of human dignity against *raison d'état*." A London paper, the *Tablet*, condemned the acts of "Fascismo's bullies" and decried the regime's apparent efforts to "secure all Italy and all Italians for the totalitarian and omnivorous State."[74]

On 14 July party leaders met and approved a statement of "vibrant indignation" against the offensive accusations of the pope, dwelling particularly on his remarks on the Fascist oath. The pope's message they termed "an appeal to the foreigner," and they warned of the "alliance forming between the Vatican and masonry today united in common hostility to the Fascist State."[75]

Resolution of the Conflict: September 1931

Charges and countercharges rang out in the press for another month, but both sides realized that little was to be gained by continued aggravation of an already tense situation—indeed, that both stood to lose in a dispute that threatened to wreck the conciliation of 1929. Discreet negotiations for a resolution of the conflict began on 25 July, and once again Father Tacchi-Venturi acted as the pope's intermediary. After eleven meetings the negotiators reached a tenuous truce on 2 September 1931.

According to the September accords, Catholic Action was once again recognized by the government, but in an "essentially diocesan" form. Its lay and clerical leaders were to be chosen by bishops rather than elected by members, and all those belonging to "parties hostile to the regime" were to be excluded. Catholic Action was expressly forbidden to concern itself in any way with politics; its syndical and professional groups were to be dissolved. The youth organizations of Catholic Action were allowed to have membership cards and badges of their own but were not permitted to display any banners or flags other than the national tricolor at meetings. These groups were also forbidden to sponsor any sports or athletic events or political activities. In essence they were to become religious discussion groups. In January 1932 ecclesiastical authorities drew up a new statute for Catholic Action conforming to this agreement. For its part, the regime lifted its ban on simultaneous membership in

PNF and Catholic Action groups.[76] Mussolini further attempted to smooth ruffled feathers by removing the two PNF leaders who had been in the vanguard of the anti–Catholic Action crusade: Scorza and Giuriati lost their respective positions as GUF and party secretaries in December 1931.[77]

The 1931 controversy over Catholic Action was buried in an avalanche of decorations. On 9 January 1932 Pius XI bestowed papal decorations on Benito Mussolini and King Victor Emmanuel III. On 3 March Eugenio Cardinal Pacelli (later Pope Pius XII), Cardinal Gasparri, and Father Tacchi-Venturi all received the coveted Collar of the Annunciation, the highest decoration of the Italian state. On 11 February 1932, the third anniversary of the Lateran Accords, Mussolini appeared at the Vatican for a much-ballyhooed private audience with the pontiff and a moment of prayerful repose at the tomb of Saint Peter.[78]

The crisis over Catholic Action thus ended on a conciliatory note. The pope and the Catholic press contended that the essential purposes of Catholic Action had been preserved. Not everyone agreed. From Paris, Luigi Sturzo referred to the September accords as "the complete triumph of the Fascist state over the church."[79] Hyperbole aside, it is difficult to escape the conclusion that, at least in the short run, the church had suffered a notable defeat.

In order to salvage Catholic Action, the pope had agreed to proscribe precisely those activities that were most appealing to many young people. Catholic Action had been confined to the sacristies. Its reorganization on a diocesan level made it easier for party and state to keep the groups under a close watch and even to control their activities. With the purging of the remaining ex-Popolari, many of the most politicized and capable elements were eliminated.

Pius also dropped his objections to the loyalty oath imposed on children. That issue, which had figured so prominently in his encyclical, was not even mentioned in the September agreement—an omission that seemed to give Vatican blessing to the PNF groups. Catholics could in good conscience belong to both Catholic Action and PNF groups; chaplains could, and often did, carry out their role as ONB officers without divided loyalties. The reality of the September settlement in this sense was symbolized in macabre "Fascist masses." At the 1938 Campo Dux celebration, for example, the mass began with the singing of "Giovinezza" and a prayer for Mussolini. The PNF secretary served as chief altar boy. At the elevation of the host, the fifteen thousand young men present drew their bayonets and pointed them to the sky. The ceremony ended with a prayer for the Duce and the singing of Fascist anthems.

The years between 1931 and 1938 were generally cordial ones in church-state relations. Given the apparent harmony, it was increasingly difficult until the late 1930s for Catholics to perceive the real differences between Christian and Fascist world views. The mutual desire to preserve gains already won produced a "marriage of interests" that, although it did not guarantee absolute peace, did prevent further serious problems until 1938. The church supervised religious instruction in the state schools, provided chaplains for ONB units, carried on its own educational mission in parochial schools, and ran Catholic Action groups protected by the law.

The high point of church support for the regime came in the mid-thirties with the Ethiopian war and the Spanish civil war. While the reaction of churchmen to the African campaign was by no means unanimously positive, examples of clerical support were given great play in the Fascist press and no doubt exerted a powerful influence over many Catholics. Bishops were photographed blessing departing troops and their colors, contributing gold for the Fascist cause, and saluting local PNF hierarchs with outstretched arms. Father Messineo, Jesuit editor of *Civiltà cattolica*, portrayed the conflict as the "restoration of the true faith" against "religious errors, superstition, slavery, and ignorance" and vindicated Italy's need for "living space."[80] In a sermon in the Duomo on 28 October 1935, Cardinal Schuster of Milan exalted the "valorous armies . . . that open the doors of Ethiopia to the Catholic faith and the civilization of Rome." A few days after the occupation of Addis Ababa, the pope celebrated the Fascist victory as the "triumph of a great and good people." Less than a year later came the Spanish civil war. Again clergy blessed departing troops, and much of the Catholic press portrayed the war as a defense of the "rights and honor of God and religion" against the heathen red emissaries of Moscow.[81]

Despite these official obeisances, however, tension between the church and the regime did not totally disappear. Close surveillance of Catholic youth groups continued. Under instructions from the Ministry of the Interior, prefects received monthly reports on all the activities and the membership of local Catholic Action groups.

The reports were sometimes alarming. In February 1932 the informer in Padua observed that "under the pretext of religion, active anti-Fascist propaganda that is damaging and denigrating to the Regime is being undertaken by the Catholic student organizations." Politics in these groups, the agent continued, is "always spoken of in the anti-Fascist sense of the word."[82] Police reports from Milan and other cities often repeated the refrain that the local Catholic groups were "gathering places for all those who profess anti-Fascist ideas."[83]

By 1935 the tone of the reports became even more worrisome. In July

the PNF federal secretary in Pistoia reported that attempts to penetrate the local population were met with "passive resistance from the Catholic organizations, particularly on the part of the young." In June 1935 the report from Trent warned: "The teachers are almost always in the hands of the priests who are their absolute masters. . . . In some schools priests still teach, and they stupefy the little ones with religion to the detriment of . . . patriotic teaching."[84]

Aside from continued worries about the Gioventù Cattolica, the regime and the church did not come into direct conflict during the thirties on issues involving education. Official Vatican reaction to the passage of the School Charter in 1939 was restrained, partly because the reform was enacted only five days after the death of Pius XI and two weeks before Eugenio Pacelli's election as Pope Pius XII. Giuseppe Bottai, then minister of national education and author of the Carta della Scuola, was received at the Vatican by the new pope and had a long conference with the new Vatican secretary of state—both acts seen as official approval of his reform. Reaction in the provinces, however, was not always so favorable. Police informers observed that some of the local clergy opposed obligatory enrollment in PNF youth groups; an agent commented in May 1939 that the clergy in Brescia also opposed the School Charter because of its "neglect of religious teaching." The agent in Venice noted criticism of the new *scuole materne* that took children at an "early age away from the priests and the nuns." Reports from both Rome and Padua echoed these criticisms and commented that the local clergy condemned the reform as an example of Fascist "exclusivism" and predicted an impending clash between church and state.[85]

The first wide chinks in the armor of externally correct relations between church and state came in the late 1930s, dictated not by new school reforms but by the logic of the Rome-Berlin Axis. Any dreams of an alliance of Catholic states died with the Nazi annexation of Catholic Austria, and Italy's capitulation to Nazi-inspired racial laws testified to the increasingly subordinate position of the Fascist regime in that "brutal friendship."[86]

Official Catholic response was not monochromatic, but even some of the most supportive members of the hierarchy (notably, Cardinal Schuster) opposed the new legislation. Pius XI made a clear distinction between ideological and biological anti-Semitism—the latter objectionable because it denied the sanctity of the human soul. The church also opposed laws forbidding marriage between "Aryans" and Jews, claiming that they were a violation of article 34 of the Concordat, which recognized canon law on marriage questions. The pontiff publicly taunted Mussolini for having imitated Nazi Germany—an obviously well-founded charge that elicited harsh reaction from the dictator, understandably sensitive, and a barrage of abusive articles by the old *squadrista* Farinacci in the pages of *Il Regime fascista*.[87]

The Fascist government's pro-Nazi policy and its adoption of Nazi anti-Semitism led to troubled times between the Vatican and the regime in the late 1930s, although once again these troubles did not result in a total rupture between church and state. Despite official Vatican caution, however, Mussolini's new course did alienate many individual Catholics; in ever-greater numbers, they began to turn away from fascism and its leader.

Catholic University Groups and the Regime after 1931

The fate of the FUCI and the Movimento Laureati is of special significance because these groups were the fertile soil in which Italy's Christian Democratic party took root, and the training ground for some of postwar Italy's most prominent Catholic political leaders. In the heat of party struggles after World War II, and in an effort to spruce up the anti-Fascist credentials of the Democrazia Cristiana (DC), Catholic spokesmen often pointed to the activities of these groups as proof of the antiregime stance of Catholics during the *ventennio*. Some of the influential leaders of the postwar DC had indeed been leaders of FUCI. In May 1939 Aldo Moro, a recent graduate of the University of Bari, became president of the FUCI. When he left for the war in February 1942, his position was taken by Giulio Andreotti, who had been editor of the federation's newsletter, *Azione fucina*. Guido Gonella, Mario Scelba, and Emilio Colombo were all FUCI members; Stefano Jacini and Alcide De Gasperi both wrote articles for *Studium*.[88] But the careers of a few do not tell the entire story.

It is impossible to make valid generalizations about all Fucini and their views of the Fascist regime. The regime did attempt to control the federation and to restrict and depoliticize its activities. The Vatican also sought to keep the groups safe within the bounds of its conciliatory policy. To some extent, both were successful. But many of these groups, in however halting a fashion, remained autonomous reference points contrasting with the logic of an authoritarian/totalitarian state.

For some members the conflict of 1931 was a watershed. One FUCI leader wrote: "1931 was an illuminating time because it made it clear that you could not collaborate with fascism because of its stance of intolerance and violence."[89] After 1931, however, it was virtually impossible for Fucini not to be members of GUF chapters (Moro, for example, was enrolled in both groups). The events of the 1930s served to convince many Fucini that their hope that the regime could be "Catholicized" was an illusion.[90] The passing of that illusion brought many into the ranks of the active anti-Fascist opposition during the Resistance.

The FUCI groups were watched very attentively after 1931 by police informers who managed to infiltrate meetings and congresses. Despite the September accords, the FUCI maintained a certain autonomy by holding assemblies and conferences that provided a national network of contacts for members. Reports from provincial party leaders and police agents seemed to vindicate Fascist fears that the FUCI was not merely a parish organization dedicated to pious works. A 1937 letter by a Milan party informer, for example, warned that the FUCI and the Movimento Laureati were determined to train a new Catholic ruling class and to establish the bases for a Catholic syndical and corporative movement.[91] In the Catholic stronghold of Treviso, the prefect reported in 1935 that the Catholic university group was "the fulcrum of a vast, tenacious, and hidden political action that . . . is bent on forming the cadres that will educate new recruits for every eventuality."[92]

PNF leaders were especially worried about FUCI initiatives among the workers, and they viewed with alarm the charitable work of the groups that seemed to threaten the Fascist monopoly on social welfare agencies. In March 1934 agents of the MVSN reported that the Catholic group at the University of Palermo was actively involved in providing financial aid and lodgings to needy students, hoping in this way to "keep them tied to the FUCI."[93] In February 1934 the GUF secretary in Viterbo warned that although the majority of FUCI members were enrolled in the GUF, they accepted "GUF membership cards only because they think it is necessary for their professional lives."[94] In November 1942 the prefect of Padua sent an especially revealing report that concluded: "The young university students enrolled in the FUCI are all anti-Fascists. . . . they have a mentality all their own: they say they love the nation and the king . . . but they are not Fascists."[95]

This observation is very close to the mark. By the late 1930s, and increasingly during the war years, many of the articulate and politically aware members of the FUCI and the Movimento Laureati did have a "mentality all their own." Many managed to keep alive a critical spirit in the face of official attempts to enforce conformity and consensus. But before the final crisis of the regime that spirit should really be characterized not as anti-Fascist but as non-Fascist. Most of the Fucini did not take an active role in anti-Fascist agitation before the fall of the regime; their posture was one of prudence and watchful waiting. The only significant anti-Fascist Catholic group before the war was the small Milanese Movimento Guelfo led by Piero Malvestiti, most of whose leaders were arrested in the early 1930s.[96] However, in growing numbers young Catholics did begin to make a clear distinction between love of country and loyalty to the Fascist regime. The antifascism of many Fucini was based on their own growing awareness of the true nature of fascism, a recognition that it could never be reconciled with their Catholic beliefs. Fascism failed with these young Catholics because of its own internal contradictions, not because of external agitation and propaganda by

Catholic anti-Fascist leaders. Opposition to the regime for many began as a cultural and moral repugnance—what Giorgio Amendola referred to as a "clubby cultural antifascism"—that matured in the late thirties into a rebellion against the regime's connection with "pagan" Nazi Germany, with its racialism and frantic militarism.[97] In this sense the war was a catalyst. It laid bare the internal failings of fascism, the absolute bankruptcy of the regime. With the war many Fucini began actively to plan for the *dopo fascismo*. The first meetings of the groups that formed the Democrazia Cristiana took place in August 1942, and the movement gained momentum in 1943. After the fall of the regime there emerged a new democratic, political antifascism among Catholics that matured during the common struggle of Catholic groups and the Italian Left during the Resistance.

In the end, therefore, the dispute over Catholic Action gained the regime very little. Mussolini had succeeded in limiting the activities of Catholic youth groups, but he was never able to strike a fatal blow against Catholic Action, which, despite harassment, continued to grow in influence. The regime's apparent success in the battle for "custody of the child" in 1931 was only a temporary victory. The church proved to be as tenacious a competitor as Mussolini had always feared.

Both sides paid a price for the 1929 conciliation. Intransigent Fascist rhetoric notwithstanding, the regime had, however grudgingly, been forced to accept the church's role in education and socialization. The Lateran Accords guaranteed the presence of the church in the Italian schools and in Fascist youth groups. The existence of Catholic youth groups over the years provided an alternative to Fascist conformity. On the other hand, the church abandoned some of its Catholic Action activities to save the Concordat, which assured it a privileged position in Italian society. The most serious dispute between the regime and the church, in 1931, never led to an open break. The pope charted a cautious course, willing to concede tactical victories in his overall strategy to preserve the gains of the conciliation. Fascism never succeeded in totally co-opting the church, but the church, in the years after 1929, was never a rallying point of organized antifascism. The pope did keep Catholic Action groups alive, however, and these groups provided a network of contacts and a gathering place for the growing numbers of disaffected young Catholics, as well as the organizational structure from which the postwar Catholic movement emerged.

Mussolini and his regime passed from the scene. The largest and most influential party in Italy today is still the Democrazia Cristiana. Born out of the anti-Fascist struggle and led by many trained in Catholic Action groups, the party still protects the gains made by Pius XI in 1929. Perhaps that is the main lesson of the church-state struggle during the Fascist period.

■■■■■

The "New Imperial Climate"

T he Ethiopian war and the events that followed in its wake marked a turning point in the history of Italian fascism and an important stage in the regime's attempt to indoctrinate and organize Italian youth. The schools, the youth groups, and the youth-oriented media were all deeply affected by the "new imperial climate" and by the increasingly militaristic and pro-Nazi tenor of Italian policy in the last half of the 1930s.

Cesare Maria De Vecchi's departure from the Ministry of National Education in 1936 brought to that office one of the most fascinating and controversial of all Fascist leaders. Giuseppe Bottai held the ministerial portfolio for six years and three months, longer than any man since 1848. Bottai was involved in some way with all the key developments in education and socialization during this period. But his singular view of fascism and of the role of youth in the new Fascist state contrasted in many ways with the vision of the monolithic state that inspired Mussolini and such Fascist leaders as Starace. A study of the Fascist socialization program in its imperial phase must, therefore, begin with a discussion of Bottai's ideas and his appeal to Italian youth.

Giuseppe Bottai and Revisionist Fascism

Evaluations of Giuseppe Bottai's character and career run the gamut; no one, however, denies his importance in the history of the regime.[1] Bottai has been called the "most Fascist of all the Fascists," but he was often accused by his detractors of providing aid and comfort to anti-Fascists. He has been judged the "best man in the regime" for his good faith and sincerity, but also dismissed as a political opportunist interested chiefly in carving out his own power base to guarantee his influence in post-Mussolini Italy.[2]

Bottai was one of the most cultured of the young Fascist leaders and one of the most complex. He was the only intellectual who consistently held important political posts during the *ventennio*, but he was always suspect—especially to the *intransigenti*—because of his unorthodox ideas and political ambitions. He was never appointed, could never have been appointed, party secretary, the one position that might have provided him with an opportunity to realize "his fascism." His career after the March on Rome was a constant clash between his belief in the possibility of a true Italian revolution and the reality of Mussolinian fascism. He was attracted to Mussolini in his youth but was one of the few who later spoke openly of fascism without the infallible leader. He was never really comfortable with the "fascism of the billy club" or with the enforced conformity and repression of dissent characteristic of the regime, but he continued until very late to be a faithful executor of its policies. Like many others he admitted too late that the evils were not *in* the system but, as the saying then went, *of* the system.

Like many others in his generation, Bottai came to fascism by way of interventionism, futurism, and *arditismo*. Like many others, he saw fascism as an original solution to the problems of the modern world: it would pull Italy out of the chronic crises of the liberal/democratic system without pushing it into socialism. It could and would strengthen the authority of the state without denying the principle of freedom.

Bottai was born in Rome in 1895, the son of bourgeois republican parents who instilled in him an awareness of the contrast between mediocre *Italietta* and the dreams of Mazzini and Garibaldi. Bottai was increasingly drawn to the heroic nationalism of Corradini and D'Annunzio, to the imperialistic, anti-Socialist, and antidemocratic nationalism that replaced class struggle with an epic struggle between nations. War seemed to promise the heroism lacking in Italian life, and Bottai volunteered for service in early 1915, before Italy entered the war. He was sent to the front in August 1915 and saw action at Caporetto. He joined the *arditi*—the "Fiamme Nere"—was wounded, and returned to civilian life with the rank of lieutenant and several medals to begin his search for something that could satisfy his desire for action in peacetime.

When he returned to Rome, Bottai was intrigued by the Futurist movement and attracted by Marinetti's promise that the youth would make a new Italy. For a time futurism seemed to fulfill his urge for action and his poetic bent, but the studied excesses and eccentricities of Marinetti's group soon clashed with his basic rationality and practicality. Though he continued to write for Futurist journals such as *Roma futurista*, Bottai broke with the group in the summer of 1920, when Marinetti's increasing distance from the new Fascist movement became clear.

Although he was one of the founders of the Roman *fascio* in 1919 and a participant in punitive expeditions, Bottai was never a typical *squadrista*. He did, however, share the *squadristi*'s rejection of the past and their hopes for the future. Bottai's own future was decided in April 1919, after his first meeting with Benito Mussolini.[3] Elected to the Chamber of Deputies, Bottai—like Dino Grandi and Roberto Farinacci—was disqualified in 1921 because he had not reached the prescribed age of thirty. He was reelected in 1924. After the March on Rome, during which he commanded Fascist squads from Lazio, Bottai settled down to work for the realization of Fascist revolutionary promises in the new regime.

In 1926, at the age of thirty, he was appointed undersecretary to Mussolini at the Ministry of Corporations; in that capacity he was one of the architects of the 1927·Labor Charter. Bottai served as minister of corporations from October 1929 until July 1932, when Mussolini once again assumed control of the portfolio. His later duties as president of the National Fascist Institute of Social Security (1932–35) and as governor of Rome gave him little access to real political power, so he was pleased when Mussolini moved him to the Ministry of National Education in November 1936, where he continued to serve until February 1943.

Bottai supported the Grandi resolution during the last Grand Council meeting in July 1943 and was arrested in August by order of Pietro Badoglio. After his release from prison under the terms of the September armistice, Bottai went to North Africa, where he joined the Foreign Legion. He served in France and Germany during the last year of the war and in North Africa from 1945 to 1947. He was condemned to death in absentia by the Verona tribunal and, after liberation in 1945, to life imprisonment by the High Court of Justice. In 1948, taking advantage of government amnesty, Bottai returned to Rome; he lived there until his death in January 1959.

Elegantly dressed and soft-spoken, Bottai was in many ways a contrast to the rude *squadristi* he criticized so often. Their view of fascism, he maintained, could not have been more different from "his way of being Fascist." Against those who stressed the dogmatic and quasi-religious aspects of a fascism based on mysticism and blind faith, Bottai emphasized the need for clashes of opinion and debate. Against those who sought to isolate the Italian experience from the European tradition, Bottai sought links with the past and present outside the peninsula. Against those who stressed the rural and populist *strapaese* vision of fascism, Bottai argued that fascism had to be an urban and modernizing phenomenon. Against the provincial *ras* of *squadrismo*, he called for a new political aristocracy of intellectuals, a political elite of technocrats and managers.

Bottai saw fascism as part and parcel of the twentieth-century rejection of the chronic inefficiencies and corruption of the liberal democratic state in favor of a strong executive, but he also had a deep sense of the uniqueness of the Italian experiment. For Bottai fascism was a rupture with the immediate and inglorious Italian past, but he was also convinced that its strength lay in its fundamental harmony with the values of the Western political and philosophical tradition, its ability to realize the true democracy envisioned in the principles of 1789.[4]

For Bottai the revolution was not an accomplished fact but always in progress. "We do not have power because we made the revolution," he said, "but . . . because we have to make the revolution."[5] He hoped that fascism would be a new Italian rebirth and a new greatness, not a police state or a bureaucratic apparatus of administration. Against the *intransigenti*, Bottai argued for internal democracy and normalization. Fascism would realize a new relationship between the masses and the government: the true unity promised but never realized by the liberal state. The party was to have a hierarchical structure, governed by a new elite class that would encourage mass participation.

In Bottai's view only a changing of the guard could protect and perpetuate the revolution. The "old fascism" of 1919–22 had been appropriate to a period of struggle and action: fascism as militia with its typical representative the *squadrista*, not a political man but a soldier. But the old guard did not, in his view, have the qualities of reflection necessary for the new responsibilities of fascism as a regime. They were bound to the movement by courage and instinct, not by intellectual conviction. True revolution was not synonymous with violence: revolution was a problem of ideas, not force. In the early days fascism had needed fighters; after 1922 it needed "doctors and builders."[6] The party, he argued, had to live by its brain and not its muscle: "with intelligence, with conscience, with faith."[7]

For Bottai, the two central concerns of fascism after the March on Rome were the need to form a new ruling elite and the need to create a new state. The two were inextricably linked. Only a new technocratic ruling class free from outmoded notions of liberalism and socialism—and free also from the taint of violence and illegality—could conceive of and create a new state and compete with the old liberal caste.

The youth had a crucial role to play in Bottai's fascism. The young, he said, came to the party "not only to think, but with the will to rethink everything from the beginning."[8] They offered the independence of thought, dynamism, and energy that would protect the regime from sclerosis and decay. Only they could "enliven the dead corners" and serve as the circulating lifeblood of the regime.[9] The fascism of the young would be the fascism of the future, or there would be no future for fascism. The task of the regime was therefore not indoctrination but stimulation; the party should be not a Prussian barracks but rather a forum for change.[10] All of these ideas became common themes in *Critica fascista*, especially in the years after 1930.

It was in his vision of the role of the young that Bottai's ideas contrasted most clearly with those of the Duce. For Bottai, fascism had begun with Mussolini but it most certainly did not end there. In his view, one of Mussolini's most important tasks was to provide for the succession by preparing a new class of leaders who could carry the revolution into the future. Mussolini's vision was radically different: a monolithic society in which all forces were coordinated by the will of one. For Mussolini there was one fascism, the one defined by him for all and for all time. Instead of a new, dynamic ruling class, Mussolini wanted docile executors of his orders and blind obedience. Fascism was his creature, his orthodoxy; the notion of fascism as process and evolution was—as was the question of succession—anathema. Bottai's influence and popularity with the young were therefore causes for suspicion and resentment on the part of the Duce, who referred scathingly to the youth as "Bottai's brood."[11]

When he spoke of the young, Bottai meant above all the students and most especially the university students, who found in him "a friend, a supporter . . . the representative of the most open and democratic tendencies within fascism."[12] But this was their perception only to a certain point. When many young people realized the futility of working within fascism for change, they had also to free themselves of their fascination with Bottai. In the words of one university student of the period, Bottai was for many young people "a myth that for some time nourished our hopes . . . [he] was for some of us a great illusion, and then a great disappointment."[13]

Bottai's journals provided an alternative to the obtuse Staracian conformity of the thirties. Many young people received their first exposure to journalism in Bottai's reviews, which often addressed the problems of the second generation of fascism. *Critica fascista*, designed as a review of the intelligentsia and above all of the young, first appeared on 15 June 1923. Bottai wanted it to be a reference point for a loyal Fascist opposition, a forum for the constant revision of thought and practice that fascism required. In his view the mindless conformity of the party press served only to kill initiative. Bottai argued prophetically that to outlaw criticism would produce the opposite of the desired effect: it would, especially among the young, serve to open the way to fatal deviations and defection among those who should have been the regime's staunchest supporters and its best hope.[14]

Many well-known personalities in the Italian cultural arena contributed to Bottai's second journal, *Primato*, which has been called the "most vital cultural experiment" undertaken during the Fascist period.[15] Its first issue appeared on 1 March 1940 and its last on 15 July 1943; publication was suspended by the fall of the regime just ten days later. In its pages Bottai and other contributors called for the reintegration of Italian culture with the world beyond the Alps and criticized the sterility of official culture based on propaganda and autarky.

Neither of Bottai's reviews had any influence on or response among the Italian masses. Despite his notions about mass participation, Bottai was an intellectual speaking to other intellectuals, an elitist who never really understood the situation of those living under the Fascist system.

He believed in fascism as political theory, and he believed that fascism, albeit his own version, could create a new state. But he never resolved the inherent contradictions in his own ideas. How could he reconcile his belief in open debate with his belief in authority and hierarchy? How could he really reconcile fascism with freedom? Bottai proposed a revisionist fascism that, given the realities of power in the Mussolinian state, had no possibility of realization. He was the "most Fascist of all the Fascists" only if we define fascism as something very different from what it was in Mussolini's Italy.

Confusion reigned at the Ministry of National Education when Bottai took over in 1936. A welter of laws, decrees, ordinances, and ministerial circulars—all "retouchings" to the Gentile reform—had not solved the basic problems of the educational system, nor had they eliminated the competition between the schools and the youth groups—between professional educators and political leaders—on the issue of education.

Bottai's tenure at the ministry was characterized by a whole series of major and minor reforms with these problems in mind. The rural schools, administered since 1928 by the ONB, were taken over by the newly founded Royal Commission on Rural Schools under the direct control of the ministry. By the academic year 1940–41 such schools numbered over eight thousand, enrolling over one-quarter million students.[16] In June 1938 the ENIM (Ente Nazionale per l'Istruzione Media) was established with the goal of unifying methods and standards in the private middle and secondary schools of the realm. Through the ENIM the ministry directly supervised all administration and teaching; accreditation by the ENIM placed the private schools on an equal footing with the state schools and provided a mechanism for pedagogical and political control.[17]

The most important developments that occurred during Bottai's long term at the ministry were the establishment of the Gioventù Italiana del Littorio in 1937, the increasing use of the radio as an instructional and propaganda tool in the schools, the approval of the Fascist School Charter—the Carta della Scuola—in 1939, and the application of anti-Semitic laws in the schools.

Gioventù Italiana del Littorio

Even before he assumed his post at the ministry, Bottai had called for the fusion of school and youth groups as unitary instruments of education and political preparation of the young. Well aware of the past conflicts between party and state, Bottai proposed to increase the control of his ministry over the youth program. This attempt brought him into conflict with other PNF leaders, especially Starace.

The GIL was established in October 1937.[18] This step was supposed to provide the youth movement in Italy with a unified structure and direction by combining the ONB, formerly under the control of the ministry, with the Fasci Giovanili, which had been under the auspices of the PNF. The new group—with its motto "Believe, Obey, Fight"—was to be under the direct control of the PNF secretary, who was to serve as its commander general in the kingdom and the empire. This was clearly an attempt to lay to rest the old problems of clashing ministerial and party authority, though not in the manner proposed by Bottai.

The GIL enrolled young Italians of both sexes from six to twenty-one years of age, divided into several groups:

Males	Ages	Females	Ages
Giovani Fascisti	18–21	Giovani Fasciste	18–21
Avanguardisti moschettieri	15–17	Giovani Italiane	15–17
Avanguardisti	13–14	Piccole Italiane	8–14
Balilla moschettieri	11–12	*Males and Females*	
Balilla	8–10	Figli e Figlie della Lupa	6–7

Every member of the GIL was required to take the following oath: "In the name of God and Italy I swear that I will execute the orders of the DUCE and serve with all my strength and, if necessary, with my blood the Cause of the Fascist Revolution."

The military character of the GIL was emphasized in the profuse use of military titles and in its hierarchical structure: the commander general, two vice-commander generals, and the chief and vice-chief of the general staff headed the national organization. Parallel posts existed in the group's provincial and communal organization, where the local secretaries of the PNF took over management of the GIL. There were comparable ranks for young women, though, as in the ONB, these groups were never given the same attention or funding as those for males.

Foremost among the tasks of the GIL was the physical, sports, and premilitary preparation of the young, including physical education in the elementary and secondary schools and in the youth groups. Physical education had been a part of group activities for years, but in the "new imperial climate" this training became even more military in tone. The most important task of the GIL was military preparation per se. This began for the boys at the age of eight and continued until they began their formal premilitary training at the age of eighteen. The early years of training aimed at developing the national military spirit in the young, who learned to use rifles, machine guns, tanks, and other modern weapons. The most advanced part of the military instruction came with the premilitary courses.

In February 1938 the regime decided to entrust the entire premilitary program to the GIL, taking that function away from the MVSN, which had run the courses since 1934. In reality little was changed, because the militia officers involved in the premilitary program remained on the job and all GIL premilitary teachers were required to be members of the MVSN.[19]

If the military instruction given to the Balilla and Avanguardisti was often a haphazard affair, depending on local conditions and levels of enthusiasm, these formal premilitary courses were quite a different matter. They became almost as compulsory as military service and, as the years went by, took up more and more time on the weekends for six to eight months each year. By 1938 there were over 7,000 premilitary centers in Italy, with a total enrollment of approximately 700,000 young men. In 1939 some 38,000 GIL instructors taught classes to almost 800,000 students.[20] Numbers, however, do not tell the whole story. If most young men put in an appearance at these courses, they did so very often in order to avoid sanctions and with a marked lack of fervor that did not go unnoticed. One typical report from the provinces in 1940 noted, for example, that the participants were totally "unprepared and lacking in enthusiasm" and that they came "only because they were threatened with disciplinary action."[21]

The schools of the GIL existed to provide the cadres of zealous instructors required for the group's ambitious training programs. The most important of these were the Fascist academies at the Foro Mussolini in Rome and at Orvieto, which were granted university status in 1939. The GIL institutions also included an academy where young men mastered the "traditional and very Italian art of fencing," an academy of music to train military band and choral instructors, and several naval colleges and a school of aeronautics. The women's school at Orvieto had a more limited curriculum, stressing those subjects "appropriate to the woman and her specific social function . . . [as] future mother and companion of man."[22]

Students were admitted to these elite training academies on the basis of their moral conduct and political merits. Preference went to sons and daughters of ex-combatants, and by the late 1930s only "Aryans" were admitted. In these schools the dream of a totally Fascist education seems to have been realized. But the kind of zealotry that inspired these young men and women was simply not characteristic of the majority of Italian young people, nor was the intensely politicized content of their studies geared to producing the new ruling class of which Bottai dreamed.[23]

The GIL also attempted to entice children of rural and working-class families through assistance programs and vocational training. After 1939 the GIL managed the *patronati scolastici* and a national scholarship competition. In Rome GIL schools also trained young women as children's nurses, nursery school teachers, and mothers' helpers; the curriculum combined courses in home economics, hygiene, and agriculture with political training and lectures on Fascist culture.[24]

The most extensive effort at political socialization undertaken by the GIL was the yearly program of Fascist culture courses organized in each provincial command. In 1939 there were over 24,500 courses attended by over four million members. Having successfully completed these training sessions, the older teenagers then took part in the Ludi Juveniles, originated in 1934 by the Duce's two sons, Bruno and Vittorio, at their schools in Rome. The idea caught on and in later years students between sixteen and twenty-one competed in provincial and national trials in various cultural, artistic, and sports events. Each entrant was also required to write a theme on some aspect of Fascist culture assigned by the jury.[25] In 1941, for example, each female competitor wrote on the role of women on the home front: "To work in silence and in humility to be worthy of our soldiers who are preparing the victory of the Fatherland on all fronts with their valor and their sacrifice."[26] The Ludi were quite popular because they offered an opportunity to travel and, for the politically ambitious, the chance to make a name in the Fascist movement. In 1939 almost two million young men and women participated in the competitions.

In 1940 the GIL also broadened cultural relations with the Hitler Youth, beginning a series of international meetings called the Ponte Culturale Weimar-Firenze. At these sessions youth representatives from Fascist movements all over the world met to discuss issues and problems of common interest and to compete for prizes in literary and artistic fields. The themes assigned were indicative of the policy alignment of the regime: "*Romanità* and Germanism," "The new order," and "Goethe and Italy," among others. These meetings, as well as frequent sports competitions between the German and Italian youth groups, continued until 1943.[27]

Local GIL offices also set up libraries for their members: by 1939 there were some four thousand libraries housing almost seven hundred thousand volumes, including, in each library, the complete works of Benito and Arnaldo Mussolini.[28] Films and radio also came into widespread use in the 1930s. Projectors and viewing rooms were available in many of the more affluent GIL headquarters, and in 1938–39 the groups started offering prizes for propaganda and documentary films for children. In 1941 the organization also began publication of a new journal, called *Cinegil*, to encourage the dissemination of war-related productions for youth. The propaganda and media arm of the GIL continued to offer regular programs for children on the weekends, and "Radio GIL" also provided broadcasts for the schools. In addition to the official biweekly organ of GIL, each age group also had its own party-subsidized magazine distributed both in the schools and at the GIL headquarters. All of these journals were intended to form the political conscience of the young by "diffusion of the major accomplishments of the regime . . . celebrations of Italian genius and valor . . . and the virtues of the race and *romanità*."[29]

GIL Training Manuals and Handbooks

To complement the world view presented in the state-approved textbooks, the GIL also published training manuals and handbooks for use in the political preparation courses. The most famous book used in both the ONB and the GIL was *Il primo libro del fascista*, which went through numerous editions and was also adopted in the schools for the Fascist culture courses. The authorities in Rome urged the federal secretaries to ensure the widest possible circulation of this volume; in 1941 alone over half a million copies were sent to local groups. The book was simplistic in style and content, written in the form of a catechism with questions and answers on the history and achievements of fascism. The objective of the 1940 edition was succinctly stated: "to realize the imperial greatness of the Italian people."[30]

A series of definitions served to direct the young along the politically approved track. The Duce was the "renewer of society" and the "founder of empire" who led the "greatest colonial war that history records." Democracy was based "on the game of artificial parliamentary majorities," but fascism was "the will to bring order and power . . . a place in the sun and a new empire."[31]

The GIL manual for the training of the squad leaders, the *capo centurie*, contained a section of rules of conduct that were not much different from those found in any Boy Scout handbook. The boys were told to keep clean, to avoid bad companions, to be courteous, not to spit on the floor or put their feet on the furniture, to help the weak, and never to gamble, smoke, or drink. The good *capo centuria* was urged to demonstrate on all occasions "the intimate conviction and solid preparation that underlies his political faith." The manuals often combined the antibourgeois rhetoric of the regime with some very bourgeois admonitions. The *capo centuria* was instructed to "show fraternal affection for compatriots, even for the poor, uneducated people who work for a living. Every Italian shares (even if he wears coarse clothing) in the treasures of a great culture."[32] An earlier manual still in use in the late thirties reminded the good young Fascist to respect old age and the "sacred mission of maternity." The manual advised: "Do not deride the fallen woman who wants to redeem herself but give her fraternal aid, always thinking of your mother."[33]

The manuals for females were much the same as those for the males:

the same self-serving view of history, the same respect for authority and traditional sex roles, and, above all, the same heavy doses of the Mussolini myth. The Duce was "the greatest and kindest man on earth," a man "sent by God" who had, quite simply, "resolved all the problems that have troubled mankind for centuries."[34]

Rabid anticommunism was also very much in evidence in these youth group manuals. The Piccole Italiane learned that the twentieth century was a struggle between civilized Rome and barbaric Moscow.[35] In a volume for the Avanguardisti, Caporetto was blamed on subversive propaganda "nourished by Russian gold." After the war the reds were "masses drunk with hatred" who stopped trains, raped nuns, murdered priests, and committed unheard-of horrors: "Shreds of flesh were scattered here and there, heads were severed from trunks, eyes burned out with pokers." There was apparently no social ill that could not be laid in some way at the feet of the Bolsheviks. Cocaine, the manual contended, had been imported as part of a red plot to undermine the moral fiber of the nation. In 1923 the Fascist regime had stopped the trade in drugs and closed all dance halls, thus saving the honor of Italian women who had been "hurling themselves into the vortex of obscene exotic dances under the influence of the terrible drug."[36]

During the late thirties racist stories and anti-British and anti-French tirades also became common in these handbooks. A GIL manual published the day Germany invaded Poland debunked the idea of a Latin sisterhood between Italy and France and decried the monopoly of the Suez Canal by a "few dirty French and English capitalists." Another story in the book accused the French of bringing opium, morphine, obscenity, and all types of sexual perversions into Italy and compared the virile imperial life of the Italians with the way of life of the British—a "people of hotelkeepers" dedicated only to their bedroom slippers and easy chairs.[37]

Racism, especially racial anti-Semitism, was the topic of the *Secondo libro del fascista*, used in Italian elementary and secondary schools and youth groups. The book categorized races according to physical and moral characteristics and posited the existence of an "Aryan primacy" that linked "Greece, Rome, the Renaissance, and fascism" and justified Italian claims to domination in the Mediterranean. The discussion ended with a shrill warning against the Jews, who were condemned as "exalters of dandyism, cultism, licentiousness, free love, feminism, deriders of the family and children." The handbook also trotted out all the familiar saws about the anti-Fascist Judaic alliance led by "Guideo Roosevelt," pusher of liberalism, communism, anarchy, and other dread diseases of the body politic, and included gory tales of the red regime in Spain that massacred nuns and committed "sacrileges on the Cross of the Redeemer."[38]

The regime's leaders consciously sought to strike responsive chords of religiosity in the Italian populace through a constant identification of religion and fascism that sometimes reached grotesque proportions. PNF literature for children was full of prayers, invocations, and religious stories, many of them about the "Italian Savior" who was the main protagonist in all these youth group books. This "Balilla Creed" aroused Vatican officials and was denounced by the pope as sacrilegious: "I believe in Rome the Eternal, the mother of my country, and in Italy her eldest Daughter . . . who descended to the grave and was raised from the dead in the 19th century; who ascended into heaven in her glory in 1918 and 1922; who is seated on the right hand of her mother Rome. . . . I believe in the genius of Mussolini, in our Holy Father Fascism, in the communion of its martyrs, in the conversion of Italians and in the resurrection of the Empire."[39]

Various versions of the Fascist Ten Commandments had to be memorized and recited at group meetings. One of the most famous was composed by PNF secretary Giovanni Giuriati in 1931: "The Decalogue of the Giovane Fascista." A later version of this decalogue was in keeping with the martial spirit of the mid- and late-thirties:

1. Know that the Fascist, and in particular the soldier, must never believe in perpetual peace.
2. Days of imprisonment are always deserved.
3. The Nation is also served as a sentinel over a can of gas.
4. A companion must be a brother first because he lives with you and secondly because he thinks like you.
5. The rifle and cartridge belt and the rest are confided to you not to be ruined in leisure but to be preserved for war.
6. Do not ever say "The Government will pay" because it is you who pays; and the Government is that which you have willed and for which you have put on a uniform.
7. Discipline is the soul of armies; without it, there are no soldiers but only confusion and defeat.
8. Mussolini is always right!
9. For a volunteer there are no extenuating circumstances when he is disobedient.
10. One thing must be dear to you above all else: the life of the DUCE.[40]

The Radio

In comparison with the other large nations of the West, Italy developed the radio as an effective medium of mass communications relatively late. The early 1920s saw the real takeoff of radio broadcasting in the United States, Great Britain, Germany, and France, which already had major transmitters, regular transmissions, and a growing listening pub- lic. In contrast, Italian radio in the early twenties was still very much in a precommercial stage.[41] Development of the radio in Italy was hampered by a severely restricted audience, by competition from technically ad- vanced foreign industries, and by the indifference or outright skepticism of many in the Fascist hierarchy—foremost among them Mussolini, who showed little early interest in its political potential.

The progress in radio technology being made abroad served to high-light the notable gap between foreign developments and the state of the art in Italy. By 1924 the United States had some 1,000 stations, and in Germany over 100 factories were producing radio equipment. Even in the smaller countries and in the Soviet Union radio services were being consolidated and the quality of programming was improving. As indi-cated in Table 6-1, the availability of radio lagged far behind in Italy. In 1927, when Italy had just over 40,000 radio subscribers, Germany had just under 2 million and England over 2.5 million. BBC profits in that year were equal in one month to twice the annual profits of the Italian radio network. In 1931, when Italy had less than 0.25 million subscrib-ers, Germany had almost 4 million and England almost 4.5 million. In 1928 the Soviet Union had some 50 radio stations but Italy had only 5.[42]

There were also clear regional variations in the overall picture, as indicated in Table 6-2. The market in Italy was still limited to a few privileged areas and classes, and rural Italy remained for a long time largely beyond the reach of the new medium, owing both to the lack of radio transmitters and to the prohibitive cost of radio sets. A good four-tube radio sold for between 2,500 and 3,500 *lire* in the mid-twenties (in addition to the cost of taxes and licenses), when the average per capita income was still only 3,498 *lire* per year.[43]

The early organization of radio communications in Italy was tied to the relationship between the Marconi interests—SISERT (Società Ita-liana Servizi Radiotelegrafici e Radiotelefonici)—and the Ministry of Communications, headed after early 1924 by Costanzo Ciano, who played a key role in the development of the new medium.[44] If he did not totally grasp the propaganda potential of the radio in these early days, as most Fascist leaders did not, Ciano was enthusiastic about its use in Fascist celebrations and commemorations. But he had first to convince Mussolini, always an advocate of the printed word, who felt that the radio was unreliable and that it separated him from direct contact with the masses.

Mussolini's first experience with the new medium was hardly an auspicious one. Ciano managed to persuade the Duce to allow one of his speeches to be broadcast in March 1924. The broadcast was a fiasco and

Table 6-1

Radio Subscribers in Italy, 1926–1942

Year	No.	% of Total Population	Year	No.	% of Total Population
1924	2,000[a]		1934	438,733	1.05
1925	10,000[a]		1935	535,971	1.28
1926	26,865		1936	682,656	1.61
1927	40,788	0.10	1937	822,871	1.94
1928	61,458	0.15	1938	997,295	2.33
1929	99,146	0.25	1939	1,169,939	2.70
1930	176,332	0.43	1940	1,375,205	3.14
1931	240,824	0.59	1941	1,638,317	3.71
1932	303,273	0.74	1942	1,827,950	4.10
1933	396,690	0.79			

Sources: A. Papa, *Storia politica della radio,* 1:15, 25–26, 33, 52, 94, 96, 2:5–6, 27, 36, 114; Ente Italiano Audizioni Radiofoniche, *Attività dell' Eiar nell' esercizio 1939,* p. 9. Statistics compiled by other sources vary slightly: cf. Monticone, *Fascismo al microfono,* pp. 43, 181; and Monteleone, *Radio italiana,* p. 85.

[a]Statistics before 1926 are estimates.

had to be ingloriously interrupted as soon as Mussolini began to speak; he did not try again for over a year. His first successful radio speech came on 28 October 1925, during the celebrations for the third anniversary of the March on Rome in Milan. That experience was more to his liking, and he began to use the radio regularly by the early 1930s. Given the continued lack of popularly priced equipment, however, the rule was still "collective listening": groups gathered in public squares to share the experience. Gradually the radio became an important feature of the Italian propaganda effort, ensuring one of the most indispensable supports of the mass regime, the omnipresence of the leader.[45]

The government extended its control over the radio in fits and starts. In August 1924 the various groups then in existence, including the Marconi group as the major financial interest, were combined to form the Unione Radiofonica Italiana (URI). Its president was Enrico Marchesi and its vice-president Luigi Solari, Marconi's main representative in Italy. After a brief period of experimentation, the URI transmitted its inaugural program on 6 October 1924.[46]

By the terms of the agreement, the state conceded to the URI the exclusive right for all radio broadcasting in Italy for six years, and the URI guaranteed the government two hours of broadcast time each day and special transmissions during state emergencies. In addition, the

Table 6-2
Radio Subscribers by Region as a Percentage of All Subscribers, 1928–1941

Year	North	Central	South	Islands
1928	65.5	16.8	16.1	1.6
1929	74.6	14.0	9.7	1.7
1930	70.2	16.7	10.5	2.6
1931	68.0	17.1	10.7	4.2
1932	65.6	18.8	11.2	4.4
1933	64.9	19.2	11.4	4.5
1934	64.1	19.5	11.8	4.6
1936	62.6	19.7	12.6	5.1
1937	61.7	19.7	13.2	5.4
1938	60.6	19.8	13.6	6.0
1939	59.7	20.2	13.8	6.3
1940	59.2	20.6	13.7	6.5
1941	58.9	20.7	13.7	6.7

Source: A. Papa, *Storia politica della radio*, 1:71–72, 102–3, 2:26–27, 36–37, 116.

agreement stipulated that the government could exercise censorship power over all radio programming and appoint certain members of the URI directorate. The only approved source of news for the URI's broadcasts was the semiofficial Agenzia Stefani, under the control of Mussolini's faithful follower Manlio Morgagni. In 1926 the URI was allowed to extend its news coverage to include excerpts from *Il Popolo d'Italia*, a step that, while providing some variety, was hardly a giant one toward freedom of expression.[47]

In an attempt to rationalize administration and programming, URI was reorganized in November 1927 as the Ente Italiano per le Audizioni Radiofoniche (EIAR). The governing directorate remained the same, with the addition of Arnaldo Mussolini as a vice-president. The directors of the EIAR received a twenty-five-year monopoly and guarantee of profits, although the political authorities retained control of program content through a "high committee for radio inspection." Despite these provisions, however, the real control exerted in the late twenties was still relatively slight. The first inspection committee, for example, included several important Fascists, but in general its membership was chosen more for technical expertise than for political merits.[48]

The early programs of the URI and EIAR were characterized more by a patriotic-nationalist flavor than by transparent political propaganda.

As late as the early 1930s musical programs still accounted for over half of the hours broadcast, and despite a preference for Italian composers, there was no discrimination against foreign music. Regular sports programs began in 1926 and soon gained an enthusiastic following.[49]

Fascism was not absent from these early programs, however. Many stressed the blessings brought to Italy by Mussolini and his government. The radio was increasingly used to broadcast commemorations of the great moments of fascism, and PNF luminaries became familiar radio personalities. In 1930 Mussolini inaugurated the program "Condottieri e maestri," which recounted the lives of great Italians past and present—thus making a clear identification between the historic glories of the nation and the new achievements of the regime.[50] Regular religious programming began in 1930, and though such programs were not openly Fascist in inspiration, they were designed to support the regime's line of cultural patriotism and to underline the unique position of Italy as the home of world Catholicism. The Vatican began its own broadcasts in 1930.

Another programming innovation came in 1929 with the inauguration of "Giornale Radio," which, greatly expanded in later years, became the linchpin of the regime's political programming. In 1933 the EIAR began an evening program of political commentary called "Cronache del Regime." Its key speaker was Roberto Forges Davanzati, the author of *Il Balilla Vittorio*, who was the best-known radio personality in Italy until his death in May 1936. Along with the broadcasts for the schools, these programs were in the 1930s the key elements in the regime's effort to adapt the radio as a tool of mass consensus.[51]

In 1925 the Milan station broadcast the first program especially for children, the "Cantuccio dei bambini" directed by Elisabetta Oddone. The program was not political in content but consisted of contests, music, and fairy tales. Programs for children soon became a staple. Timed to coincide with the establishment of the ONB in April 1926, Radio Roma began transmission of a daily program for adolescents called "Il Giornale radiofonico del fanciullo," created and produced by Cesare Ferri. The program combined songs, fables, and lectures on hygiene with tales of adventure about Mussolini and other Italian heroes. So impressed was the Duce that he gave the go-ahead for another children's program called "Bambinopoli" on the new Naples station in 1926. Ferri remained one of the foremost personalities in children's radio programming; his two characters Nonno and Zia Radio greatly appealed to younger children, as did Ettore Margadonna's Mago Blu on the Milan station. The regime gave special encouragement to these children's programs, and they very soon gathered a faithful audience of young listeners. In the 1930s all the transmissions for children were merged into one, the "Camerata dei Balilla."[52]

Exploitation of the political potential of the radio was a slow and uncertain process in Fascist Italy. Just as the political and economic structure of the regime evolved over time, so, too did the instruments adopted for the organization of consensus. The consolidation of the regime's political control after 1925 affected all forms of mass communication, but in the twenties more attention was devoted to the press and the cinema than to the radio. Between 1929 and 1936, however, the radio clearly began to be used as an instrument of mass socialization. The causes of this evolution are primarily two: during this period the regime attempted to develop the institutional structures to disseminate and organize propaganda, and the propaganda machine had a cause to champion: the Ethiopian war.

Control of mass communications during the early Fascist period rested with the Press Office of the Council of Ministers, managed until December 1931 by Lando Ferretti and then by Gaetano Polverelli. In the early 1930s there was still no effective central agency to articulate cultural policy and coordinate the mass media, but that situation began to change after Galeazzo Ciano took over the Press Office in August 1933. The period from 1933 to 1936, which saw Hitler's rise to power and the crusade for empire, was a crucial one in the development of Fascist cultural and propaganda institutions.

The Nazi example provided Italian leaders with a model of efficient organization. Ciano, much impressed by visits with Joseph Goebbels and by observations of the Reichministerium for propaganda, was eager to apply those lessons in Italy. In September 1934 the Press Office was abolished and its place taken by the Under-Secretariat for Press and Propaganda, a move that marked the real beginning of the regime's attempt to centralize its institutions of cultural control. The press was still the major organ of consensus, but the addition of the term "propaganda" in the title of the new agency also indicated a new direction. In June 1935 the Under-Secretariat was elevated to the Ministry of Press and Propaganda, with authority to manage not only the press but also the cinema, tourism, the theater, and the radio. The Ethiopian war presented the regime with a cause around which to rally public opinion and to galvanize national energies. In May 1937 the Ministry of Popular Culture was created—with its own radio office and direct responsibility for the EIAR—to bring the new imperial message to the masses.[53]

Obviously the radio could never become a mass medium until it reached a mass audience. As part of its rural and demographic campaigns, the regime introduced radio programs for agricultural communities in 1926, but they were never very successful in reaching the public they were intended to instruct—in part because of the dearth of radio receivers in rural areas and in part because of the middle-class cultural bias of the programming itself. The first concerted effort to bring the radio to the masses came in June 1933 with the establishment of the Ente Radio Rurale (ERR). The plan was to supply rural elementary schools with radios that would be used for educational programming during the day for the youth and agricultural programs geared to the farmers in the evenings.

The ERR was nominally under the jurisdiction of the Ministry of Communications, but its activities were watched with a jealous eye by the minister of national education, Francesco Ercole, who intended to preserve and extend his own authority for scholastic programming. This desire did not sit well with Starace, and in November 1934 Mussolini transferred the ERR to the direct control of the PNF secretary.[54] The move had a predictable effect: the political content of the rural programming increased markedly and propaganda programs became a staple in Italian schools.

As indicated in Table 6-3, the diffusion of the radio in the rural elementary schools progressed slowly and unevenly. Even by the end of the 1930s only one-half to one-third of the classrooms in rural elementary schools were equipped with radios, far below the enthusiastic projections of the ERR directors.[55] Part of the problem was still the cost of radio sets. After the first free distributions in the mid-thirties, local schools were supposed to buy their own equipment, but they were simply unable to do so in many rural areas. The program got a much-needed boost in the spring of 1937 when a new, inexpensive radio set, the Balilla radio, became widely available. Arrangements were made through the ERR for schools to pay for the equipment on the installment plan.[56]

Though the ostensible purpose of the ERR was to bring the rural masses into contact with the national life, party leaders were most interested in the use of the radio for the political formation of the young. The first experimental broadcasts for the schools came in February 1933, when some thirty-five thousand students in Milan were treated to a program of patriotic music. In April 1933 the Milan and Turin stations covered ceremonies celebrating the birth of Rome. The first regular classroom broadcasts coincided with the opening of the school year in 1934. The programs, which opened with the Fascist and national anthems and speeches by PNF notables, usually dealt with history (or at least a dramatized manipulation of history), religion, or current events. In all of them Mussolini loomed large. One of the first school programs, for example, was a dramatic piece entitled "The Duce and the Children," an exaltation of the paternal love of Mussolini for the youth of Italy in which, as the program notes stated, all the children agreed in their "enthusiastic gratitude to the Duce for his many works of kindness and goodness."[57] Religious programs usually dealt with the lives of great Italian saints. In addition to propagandistic programs, the radio sched-

Table 6-3
Number of Radios in Elementary Schools, 1934–1943

Year	No. of Classrooms with Radios
1934	2,718
1935	7,045
1936	9,676
1937	13,632
1938	23,945
1939	34,107
1940	59,232
1943	68,925

Sources: Figures from Ministero dell'Educazione Nazionale, *Ufficio per la radiofonia scolastica*, p. 21; Monteleone, *Fascismo al microfono*, p. 92; A. Papa, *Storia politica della radio*, 1:138–39, 2:54, 111; Mazzatosta, *Regime fascista*, p. 173; Cannistraro, *Fabbrica del consenso*, p. 240.
Note: If the radio sets available to party organizations in rural areas are included, the numbers amount to something over 4,000 for 1934 and over 40,000 for 1938.

ules also included sessions on academic subjects prepared by professional educators and children's authors. Some non-Fascist content was also introduced into the dramatic scenes in the form of fables and cartoon characters; Mickey Mouse was a favorite in the schools in 1934–35.

Such frivolous entertainments were increasingly unacceptable in the second half of the decade, however. Radio became an essential part of the spectacle of the Ethiopian war and was used, like all the media, to fire up public opinion and create a climate of siege. The weekly radio magazine promised in September 1935 that the programs for the schools would "have a new direction, one more in keeping with the atmosphere of martial virility that fascism has introduced." In 1935–36 almost half of the broadcasts treated topics relating to colonial and military affairs, inspired by the "triumphalism of the nation guided by the genius of Mussolini."[58] Especially frequent were dramatizations of soldiers leaving for the front, visits to military barracks, and interviews with Fascist troops. Between 1936 and 1939 the hero was much in vogue; the adventures of the intrepid legionnaires in Spain battling "the red terror" became regular classroom fare in these years, for example.[59]

Racism and anti-Semitism were also woven into these school programs after 1938. One program broadcast for the middle schools in January 1940 by Roberto Farinacci was an especially poisonous presentation of Fascist theory on racial inequality. All men, claimed Farinacci, do not have the same soul, and hence "men and races do not enjoy—nor can nor must enjoy—the same rights." For centuries, he maintained, the Catholic church had protected the Aryan race in Europe from contamination by Jews, but the French Revolution, "proclaiming with ignorant fanaticism the equality of all men," had opened a Pandora's box of troubles. The present war he portrayed as a "Jewish war that Israel fights. . . . But we are certain that the Rome of Mussolini will win once again over Jewish Jerusalem."[60]

Giuseppe Bottai was an ardent proponent of scholastic programming and was interested in extending such broadcasts to the middle and secondary schools. The twice-weekly programs for older students, which began during the academic year 1937–38, included everything from musical interludes and history lessons to political conversations and current events, much of this a repetition of the lectures already presented in GIL meetings. The regime never really devoted great care or resources to these programs for the older students, and many secondary schools were never equipped with radios at all.

The more sophisticated children of the urban secondary schools were often offended by the intellectual poverty and the low technical quality of these transmissions—a fact admitted even in ministerial reports. Marcella Olschki, a student in an urban *liceo* in 1938–39, recalled in an amusing article that the programs were produced in "such an infantile and stupid manner that they well-deserved to be called clownish." She remembered one especially hilarious broadcast dramatizing a meeting between a lovely gossamer-clad lady called Autarky and a poor street cleaner, the former teaching the latter how to contribute to the glory of the fatherland by salvaging toothpaste tubes and coffee grounds for recycling. "For us," Olschki said, "these programs were nothing but a confused jumble of music chosen by chance, little scenes of obscure meaning, and profuse Fascist propaganda lavished over all with the coarse measure used by the authorities of the day."[61]

Radio programming never became an integral part of the university curriculum. The ERR established the Università Radiofonica in 1938, but it was used primarily for Italian-language courses for foreigners. The GUF, however, did play a role in the diffusion of the radio. In 1934 a radio section was set up in every GUF, and in the same year the regime added radio competitions to the Littoriali. The EIAR also provided equipment and technical advice to students at the larger universities, such as Turin and Milan, to help them produce their own programs. Under PNF guidance the GUF also set up schools to train broadcasters, writers, and technicians. Several of the universities had their own radio stations, where the students gained valuable experience in the new medium.[62]

Scholastic programming had a renaissance during the war, in number of hours broadcast if not in quality. Bottai, who believed that the radio would "sustain the faith and courage" of the children and their families, inaugurated a special program called "Radio scuola" that was supposed to be a complement to the school lessons. During the long suspension of school in the winter of 1942–43, it also served as a substitute for classroom lessons.[63]

The war did not really produce any creative innovations in radio programming, though the authorities introduced some new special services. For the armed forces the regime began transmission of "Radio del combattente," characterized by a continued exaltation of Fascist myths that must have rung increasingly hollow for the frontline soldiers. In January 1941 "Radio GIL" began broadcasts on weekend evenings of heavy-handed war propaganda: interviews with soldiers, martial songs, and war news. Perhaps the most important new program in the elementary school schedule was one called "Radiogiornale Balilla," a relentlessly triumphalistic news program. Students in the middle schools heard "Moschettieri, a noi," consisting of news comments that aimed at "patriotic edification."[64]

On balance the results of the regime's radio campaign were less than impressive. Certainly Mussolini's dream of a radio for every school fell far short of realization. The most creative period seems to have been in the mid-thirties, before the expansionist fever and the grosser aspects of Starace's "reform of custom" had begun to infiltrate all school broadcasts.

The school broadcasts were most successful among the younger students and in rural areas. The radio was undoubtedly a boon for many of the less-prepared teachers, and the use of music and dramatic scenes provided the color and excitement lacking in many lessons. The radio also attempted to produce cultural homogeneity by introducing many children to correct, if hyperbolic, Italian. For these children the school broadcasts were a very real link with an Italy outside their small communities—and with the voice of the regime as well. At the elementary level the academic programs were often produced by noted educational experts, many of them non-Fascists attracted by the pedagogical possibilities of the new medium. The ERR also sponsored annual contests for original radio scripts, though as the years passed these were judged more for their political than for their intellectual content.

The judgments of the older students were more damning. The political propaganda in these programs seems often to have had quite the opposite effect from that intended, and the academic programs were usually mere repetitions of classroom lessons that added little or nothing to the students' knowledge. These programs were introduced, of course, during the last years of Starace's tenure as PNF secretary, when the "long-winded rhetoric, the sergeant-major style, the narrow and superficial mentality, the infantile love of command—all the characteristics of *Staracismo* . . . permeated the content of the programs to the point of making them the faithful mirror of the very worst in Fascist custom."[65]

The Fascist School Charter

Giuseppe Bottai was a theorist of revisionist fascism, but he was also an ambitious politician eager to increase his own power and influence and to avoid political isolation. He was not personally drawn to the imperialist myths of a fascism based on military might and subservience to the infallible "founder of empire," nor was he a proponent of brotherhood with brown shirts. But he was astute enough to sense the political possibilities of the winds blowing in the late 1930s. The Fascist School Charter was the expression of Bottai's belief in the need to create a technically and intellectually prepared ruling class and his appraisal of the economic needs of Italian society, but it was also an attempt to bring the schools into line with "totalitarian" and expansionist fascism. Despite its egalitarian rhetoric, the School Charter was inspired by the principle of hierarchy, in relations both between the sexes and between classes.[66]

In Bottai's view, Gentile's reform did not correspond to the new economic reality of the nation because it had been conceived of strictly to suit a liberal, bourgeois society. Seventeen years had passed since the reform, said Bottai, and "it is evident that to a regime so transformed, to a regime so alive, to a regime so eager for the future, we must give a new school."[67]

Gentile's reform had failed to stem the flow of students going on to higher education. The Bottai reform was inspired by the need to restructure the relationship between the Italian school and the labor market, to establish a congruence between the kinds of schools and their curricula, on the one hand, and the regime's perception of the economic and productive needs of the state and society, on the other. Despite claims that the reform was animated by a desire to "go to the people," it aimed at freezing social classes. The essence of the reform was social immobility presented as social progress.

Bottai argued that before the 1930s the educational system had been geared to an economic reality in which agriculture was the principal productive reality. Since the Giolittian age, however, the working class in Italy had grown by some one million, the great majority of these people concentrated in new metallurgical, chemical, electrical, and textile industries, all of which needed semiskilled and skilled workers. The Italian economy required a new school to respond to the needs of a new economy and a new urban population. With its emphasis on humanistic education and its neglect of technical and vocational instruction, the Gentile reform had, in Bottai's view, produced a growing number of unemployed and unemployable *laureati* and *diplomati* who were a drain on a market unable to absorb them. The new Italian reality, he argued, demanded "many laborers but few doctors."[68] The Fascist school should not "offer, even involuntarily, an incentive to the young to change their own social position." It should not "nourish illusory ambitions" by offering "crumbs of culture" or "a flight from manual labor as the price of social elevation."[69]

Bottai presented the Carta della Scuola to the Grand Council on 19 January 1939. The School Charter, like the charters on labor and race that served as models, was not a detailed piece of legislation but rather a statement of broad principles. Its twenty-nine declarations aimed at creating a new and truly Fascist school based on study, physical training, and manual labor. The charter envisioned education as a collaboration among the family, the school, and the youth groups—what Bottai called "scholastic service," to which all citizens were bound until the age of twenty-one.[70] Membership in youth groups was obligatory. From birth the child was a citizen-soldier whose job it was to render national service until such time as he was called into active service in the armed forces.

The main organizational innovations of the School Charter came in the primary and lower middle schools. All children began their education at the age of four for two years of nursery school, and then passed on to a three-year elementary school program and a two-year labor school (*scuola del lavoro*). The labor school, compulsory for all from nine to eleven years of age, was designed to produce social cohesion by instilling a consciousness of the "high human dignity" of manual labor. From the age of eleven the choices were three, but they were determined by the background of the students and corresponded to the divisions between urban and rural communities.

The three-year *scuola artigiana* was really a postprimary school designed for "workmen not students" from eleven to fourteen years of age. The artisan schools, to be set up in elementary schools in the rural areas and small towns, were really a kind of scholastic ghetto; they provided no outlet to higher education, and students in them were instructed by elementary school teachers. For students in urban areas and larger cities, the charter set up the three-year *scuola professionale* and the two-year *scuola tecnica*, which aimed at preparing skilled workers for the great "industrial, commercial, and agricultural enterprises." Neither school offered Latin or classical studies, though they awarded diplomas and students were taught by secondary school personnel. The divisions evident in these provisions were further underlined in 1939 when the ministry began to publish separate texts for the rural and urban elementary schools.

The School Charter also introduced the much-debated *scuola media unica*—combining the lower course of the *ginnasi*, the *istituti magistrali*, and the technical institutes—which provided the same education from ages eleven to fourteen for all those students who intended to pursue higher studies. The *scuola media*, set up by law only in July 1940 and styled as a "real school for students and scholars," was highly selective and accessible only through an admissions examination. Based on a classical curriculum, the *scuola media* required study of Latin, "the means for moral and mental training." This was the only school that allowed access to the upper reaches of the educational system—the five-year *liceo classico*, *liceo scientifico*, and *istituto magistrale* and the technical-commercial institutes, all of which allowed students entry into the universities—as well as to the programs of the professional and art institutes, which did not provide such access.

The School Charter aimed at separating students not only according to social conditions but also according to gender. Church authorities were favorably impressed by the promise to alter the system of coeducational instruction. According to declaration 22, the "destination and social mission of women, which are quite distinct in Fascist life, have as their foundation different and special educational institutes." In his speech to the Senate on the ministry budget in May 1939, Bottai said succinctly: "The woman is always mother."[71] The charter set up special schools for females—the three-year *istituto femminile* and the two-year *istituto magistrale femminile*—with the goal of preparing them "spiritually for home management and for teaching in the nursery schools." De Vecchi had closed the number of teaching posts for women in the secondary schools, and Bottai continued this practice. In addition, the law setting up the *scuola media* expressly forbade the appointment of female *presidi* in these schools.[72]

Bottai's School Charter was supposed to realize the ideal of a "school of life," and to that end it emphasized work as a social duty. Reflecting the influence of the Nazi *Arbeitsdienst*, the charter set aside a place for manual labor in the curricula of all schools, from the elementary to the universities. The Fascist press gave the idea a great deal of attention. "At last," exulted one editor, "we have a school where the gentlemen will learn to dirty their hands."[73] In fact, very few educators seemed to understand how Bottai's ideas were supposed to be translated into peda-gogical practice, and the work program remained largely in the experimental stage through lack of both equipment and trained personnel.[74]

The School Charter elicited diverse reactions in political and academic circles. The Fascist press soon produced a wave of laudatory books and articles, former ministers of education hurried to praise the man of the hour, and Bottai's faithful attempted to demonstrate that the charter totally superseded the Gentile reform. Gentile himself claimed that the Carta della Scuola was not a counterreform but a continuation of his own work, stressing its retention of the selective function of the *liceo classico* with a humanistic program.[75]

Reaction among teachers ran the gamut, but reports from police and local party authorities indicated that many were confused or downright hostile to Bottai's grand plan. "No one has been able to understand anything [about the charter]," claimed one report, "and everyone understands less and less as the minister tries to clarify his real mystery on the radio."[76] Some opposed the charter as unrealizable given the lack of material means available; others criticized its stance on women.[77] Some teachers felt that the charter neglected the needs of the poor and that it did not, rhetoric aside, serve the cause of social justice. Many seemed to feel that after the initial brouhaha it would become a dead letter, killed by the almost total hostility and lack of support among the teachers. Other reports referred to it as the *scuola della carta* ("the paper school"), and one called it a "hole in the water."[78] Some reported criticism among Catholics of the "atheistic" orientation of the reform and its lack of religious spirit. Many church authorities were worried by the overtly racist and militaristic spirit of the new reform, but other religious leaders praised the new schools for females and the promised end of coeducation. Several agents reported opposition to the charter because of its political orientation, which "is putting Italy clearly on the road of subordination to Nazi Germany." Another letter noted that Roman teachers criticized the regime's attempt to educate the "new youth in the service of the state and not as spiritually independent individuals." A report on the general climate of opinion at the University of Rome claimed that the academic personnel were unalterably opposed to the "political fanaticism that is ruining the university" and proving to all that "fascism is afraid of its shadow."[79]

Despite the chorus of praise in the press, the regime had a difficult time convincing many that the reform had really produced anything revolutionary. The most durable of the reform's provisions—the distinction between the *scuola media unica* and the *scuola professionale*—lasted until 1962, but many of the other provisions remained in the realm of abstract principle, practical realization hampered by the skepticism and hostility of the academic community, by the lack of adequate means for implementation, and by the pressures of war. School vacations stretched out to two months during the winter to save fuel, and a lack of manpower and raw materials curtailed building. In April 1943 Italian schools closed in anticipation of the Allied invasion. Bottai's new scholastic structure, which had never really had a chance to settle onto its foundations, began to fall to pieces.

Prior to the introduction of anti-Semitic legislation, the Italian Jews represented a very small but fairly well-assimilated minority. Early in the history of the Fascist movement, Mussolini frequently disclaimed any anti-Semitic tendencies: "Anti-Semitism does not exist in Italy. The Italian Jews have always behaved well as citizens, and as soldiers they have fought courageously. They occupy high posts in the universities, in the army, the banks."[80] Though small, the number of Jews in the PNF increased steadily in the early and mid-thirties.[81] Mussolini often expressed his distaste for Hitler's racial tirades, and in 1933 he sent a message to the German leader urging him to moderate his anti-Jewish campaign.[82]

Mussolini's belief in an international Jewish opposition to the Ethiopian war, the perceived necessity of drawing color lines after the conquest of empire, and the logic of the alliance between Italy and Nazi Germany all contributed to ending this policy of official toleration.[83] Publication of the "Manifesto of Racist Scientists" in July 1938 marked the beginning of the overt campaign against the Jews in Italy. This ten-point document, affirming the existence of races and the necessity of a biologically defined concept of race, posited the existence of a pure Italic race from which the Jews were excluded.[84]

The effect of this anti-Semitic campaign on the schools was far-reaching. Before 1938 Jewish children had attended state schools (though they had been exempt from religious instruction), and the various Jewish communities had also run their own schools with the same rights as other private institutions. Jews had taught at all levels of the state school system, with a large number of university professors being Jewish. Books by Jewish authors had regularly been used as textbooks in the schools.

Bottai's own feelings on the subject are far from clear, but his active support for the racial laws probably had political motivations. Among Bottai's friends and collaborators at *Critica fascista* there were many Jews, and persistent rumors circulated that he was half Jewish, on his mother's side. These factors, plus the widespread suspicion among many in the PNF hierarchy about his political loyalties, may have influenced his decision on this occasion to demonstrate his unimpeachable orthodoxy.[85]

Bottai claimed that the racial legislation in the schools served a national purpose. Race was less a biological than a cultural concept; the Jews had to be separated because they had a different culture and civilization, one irreconcilable with the Italian nation. The racial laws were "neither a persecution nor a mortification." They were motivated by a belief not in inequality but in the necessity of separation—a kind of

Fascist "separate but equal"—which denied that Jews could be good Italians: "The Jews will have, in the ambit of the state, their schools; the Italians will have theirs., This is all."[86]

Bottai lost no time in applying the new legislation. On 6 August he sent out memos to all school authorities recommending the widest possible circulation of Telesio Interlandi's new anti-Semitic journal *La Difesa della razza*. Shortly thereafter he distributed a list of forbidden books by Jewish authors that were to be expunged from school reading lists and established a committee, the Committee for Library Reclamation, to weed out such offensive tomes. Some local school authorities printed their own lists of *librorum prohibitorum*, and the ministerial circulars and scholastic press for teachers regularly strummed the new anti-Semitic chord.[87]

Formal application of the regime's policy began with the passage in September 1938 of the "Provisions for the Defense of the Race in Fascist Schools."[88] In essence this law, and the other anti-Semitic statutes on the schools passed in the fall of 1938, aimed at the elimination of all "Jewish influence" from the state schools and the cultural life of Italy. All Jewish teachers and assistants were to be dismissed, no Jews were to be hired in those positions, and no Jewish children were to be permitted to attend state schools, though Jewish university students were to be allowed to finish their degrees. Jewish students were also denied admission even to private schools attended by "Aryan" students, though students professing Catholicism were allowed to attend Catholic schools. Special state elementary schools could be established where there were at least ten Jewish children, and Jewish communities were given permission to open their own schools, provided that they conformed to the regulations of the ENIM. Jewish scholars were denied admission to any academic associations for science or letters, and no texts by Jewish authors were to be used in any Italian school. Jewish children from the private schools were to be allowed to take the *esame di Stato* for the *maturità*, but in segregated sections so as not to "contaminate Aryans with their physical presence."[89]

No specific curriculum changes were made immediately in the primary and secondary schools as a result of the new laws, though a barrage of circulars from PNF and ministry officials reminded teachers and students that they had to become race-conscious, that they should have no "false pity" for the plight of the Jews but rather a loyal concern for the purity of their race. By 1939 the new racist jargon began to infect the state textbooks and PNF training manuals for the youth groups.

The universities, however, were to play a key role in the regime's racist crusade. PNF circulars called for the establishment of a "chair of racism" at all Italian universities, and material of an anti-Semitic or racist cast was introduced into all courses in anthropology and demography. Some totally new subjects were added to the curriculum in September 1938: racial demography, racial anthropometry, racial statistics, something called the "Biology of the Human Races," and a course entitled "Development of Population and Racial Politics."[90]

The youth groups were directly involved in this anti-Semitic campaign. Jewish children were naturally not allowed to belong to the GIL or the GUF and thus were deprived of physical education and sports facilities. Starace was eager to tap the brainpower and creativity of the GUF members in the racial campaign. In September 1938 he established at every GUF headquarters an office of demography and race and ordered that the GUF papers take an active role in disseminating anti-Semitic material. Some of these journals were in the forefront of the crusade against the Jews. At the Littoriali of 1939 Gufini competed to produce the best "monograph of a racial character."[91]

Aside from the obvious spiritual and intellectual perversion wreaked by the anti-Semitic legislation, the schools suffered in other ways from the regime's policies. About two hundred professors and teachers lost their jobs. One out of ten professors at the universities was Jewish, and losses were especially damaging in medicine, mathematics, law, and physics. Perhaps the best-known scholar to leave Italy at this time was the Nobel Prize–winning physicist Enrico Fermi, who, though not Jewish, could not tolerate the harassment of his colleagues and his wife. Official records indicated that some 5,600 Jewish students were barred from Italian schools: 200 university students, about 1,000 secondary students, and about 4,400 at the elementary level.[92] The ban on "Zionist" books was felt most keenly in the secondary schools, where many of the most widely used and most popular textbooks in several fields (literature, geometry, geography, law) were withdrawn and no suitable substitutes found. The anti-Semitic laws thus had a negative effect on the educational experience not only of Jewish students but of all students in Italian schools—and, because of the disgust and opposition the laws provoked in many, on the history of fascism as well.

The School and the GIL

The School Charter identified the school and the GIL as "one single instrument of Fascist education," but making that identification in practice was difficult. Party publicists inundated the country with articles and books on the subject, and PNF leaders made a concerted effort to do away with the old debilitating competition between the two institutions. Soon after the founding of the GIL, the PNF established a liaison committee to smooth relations between the youth group and the school, but this could not alter the basic fact that the GIL encroached on the time and prerogatives of the school to such a degree that the old conflict between party and state, instead of being put to rest, was exacerbated.[93]

Like the ONB, but on an even more ambitious scale, the GIL "complemented" the work of the school by planning innumerable excursions and lectures during school hours and by requiring attendance at propaganda films, parades, and PNF celebrations. Even the hours spent in the classroom were not entirely free from interference, because GIL political broadcasts were transmitted in the schools and youth group magazines were sold in the classrooms. Some PNF camps were scheduled during the school year, every Saturday afternoon was set aside for compulsory GIL meetings, and most Sundays (allowing time for church attendance) were dedicated to athletic competitions and military training. This invasion of school time did not go unremarked by parents, teachers, and school authorities. One typical police report from 1939 noted that parents were furious about continual changes in uniforms and convinced that "children should go to school to learn something useful and not to participate in the continual parades ordered by the groups."[94]

GIL activities also drew on the time and energy of the classroom teachers. By the mid-1930s membership in the PNF and AFS was virtually obligatory, and after the founding of the GIL teachers were also required to enroll in provincial and local courses in Fascist theory and physical education under its aegis. Beginning in the summer of 1938 national training courses were also held in centers all over Italy. Attendance was not strictly required, but promotions were contingent upon successful completion of these courses.

After the enactment of the School Charter, relations between the school and the GIL became the number-one item on the educational agenda. Meetings between party and ministry officials produced a document defining the "political function of the school at the service of the Revolution" that was distributed to all GIL and school authorities in July 1940. Entitled "Rapporti Scuola-GIL," the report was the most wideranging plan yet formulated for collaboration between the school and the PNF youth organizations. It worked, much to the dismay of the educational establishment, almost universally to the benefit of the latter.[95]

The plan stipulated that representatives from the GIL were to attend all ministerial meetings and planning sessions. In addition, the circular (with Bottai's begrudging approval) urged the adoption wherever possible of the single timetable, the *orario unico*, which meant that children would attend school only in the morning in order to leave the afternoon hours free for GIL activities. Winter vacations were to be dedicated totally to GIL events, and teachers were forbidden to give students any school projects during such vacation periods. The burden placed on teachers was even more weighty because they were required to join the GIL as officers and instructors and to participate in all GIL activities, though they never enjoyed the same status as career GIL instructors. In the words of one party circular: "The day of the technical teacher has passed. Today he teaches life in its Fascist fullness."[96]

This 1940 report came too late to be fully implemented in the schools, but its tone is indicative of the direction things would have taken if external events had not intervened. Although it never succeeded in completely stifling the life and vitality of the professional educational community, by the late 1930s the regime had become a ubiquitous and virtually unavoidable influence on the lives of Italian young people both inside and outside the classroom.

Statistical Data on the ONB and GIL

An analysis of statistical data supplied in party and ministry records and census figures permits some general observations on the PNF youth groups. Enrollment in the ONB and the GIL was influenced by factors of region, class, age, and gender.

In Fascist Italy the urban community was more adaptable to mass party techniques than was the agrarian sector. The strongholds of the PNF youth groups were in northwestern and central Italy; these groups were least successful in the primarily rural and underdeveloped south, where a much lower percentage of children went beyond the first few grades. In addition to the traditional suspicion of political organization in these areas, the regime's penetration was made more difficult by the fact that children in rural communities were needed on holidays and on weekends for work in the fields.

Whereas ONB and GIL enrollment, at least according to PNF statistics, approached 100 percent in the schools, the national average for all young people in the appropriate age brackets was consistently lower. A high percentage of those not enrolled in the schools were also not enrolled in the ONB and the GIL, even though membership was obligatory after the passage of the Carta della Scuola in 1939. A greater percentage of young people joined and remained in the PNF youth groups from the middle and upper middle classes than from the working class and rural youth; one reason was most certainly that more of these middle- and upper-middle-class youths stayed in school, where pressure to join and career incentives were the strongest.

All the available data also point to age and gender as factors in youth group membership. Enrollment in both the ONB and the GIL decreased in the groups for older males and females. School attendance was again the most important factor, because so many students left school between the ages of eleven and fourteen. This change was most striking among the females. Enrollment among females at all levels of the PNF youth

Table 6-4
Enrollment in the ONB, 1926–1936

Date	Balilla	Avanguardisti	Piccole Italiane	Giovani Italiane	Total
15 Oct. 1926	269,166[a]	211,189			480,355
25 Oct. 1928	780,937	325,127	365,781	66,253	1,538,098
31 Dec. 1929	856,814	344,844	418,691	60,605	1,680,954
28 Oct. 1930	981,947	371,529	670,183	98,002	2,121,661
28 Oct. 1932	1,427,318	410,239	1,184,424	119,344	3,141,325
28 Oct. 1933	1,559,106	442,223	1,319,753	125,067	3,446,149
28 Oct. 1934[b]	1,952,597	535,974	1,637,689	200,971	4,327,231
28 Oct. 1935[b]	2,121,003	677,970	1,802,549	298,836	4,900,358
28 Oct. 1936	2,326,951	787,256	2,003,775	381,285	5,499,267

Sources: Istituto Centrale di Statistica, *Annuario statistico italiano*, 1930–36, and *Compendio statistico*, 1930–32; PNF, *Bollettino dell'Opera Balilla*, 1934–35, and *Foglio d'ordini*, no. 11, 15 October 1926, no. 51, 28 October 1928.
Note: Until November 1929 the youth groups for girls were part of the Fasci Femminili (PNF) and not, legally speaking, part of the ONB, though they have been included here for the sake of convenience.
[a]PNF figures included Piccole Italiane in with Balilla for 1926.
[b]Totals for these years include figures for the colonies.

groups was consistently lower than among the males, though it dropped off most dramatically among the older females. Much of the decrease can be related to school attendance, because relatively fewer girls than boys went on to school past the age of fourteen, but there were social and regional factors as well. Female participation in politics and group activities was not encouraged in most regions of Italy and was positively discouraged in some regions, especially in the south, where early marriage and social pressure (no self-respecting young woman marched around in a uniform making a public spectacle of herself) combined to produce drastically falling enrollment statistics.

Statistical tables will illustrate some of these general observations. Tables 6-4 through 6-6 show the general evolution of the PNF youth groups throughout the Fascist period, from the early ONB groups through the Fasci Giovanili and up to the establishment of the GIL. In this period the groups developed from a relatively small organization enrolling about half a million young Italians into a mastodonic operation attempting to provide physical, military, and political education for some nine million young people.[97]

The statistics shown in Table 6-7 indicate impressive membership in the PNF youth organizations among secondary school students, ranging from a not-so-low low of 85.6 percent in 1930–31 to a total of 99.9

Table 6-5

Enrollment in the Fasci Giovanili di Combattimento
and the Gruppi Giovani Fasciste, 1931–1937

Year	Giovani Fascisti	Giovani Fasciste	Total
1931	480,845	30,986	511,831
1932	402,962	39,291	442,253
1933	456,472	57,125	513,597
1934	657,613	83,053	740,666
1935	740,099	128,191	868,290
1936	684,848	189,242	874,090
1937	1,163,363	256,085	1,419,448

Sources: PNF, *Foglio d'ordini*, 7 December 1931, 29 October 1936, 28 October 1937, and *Atti del PNF* 3 (1933–34): 31; Istituto Centrale di Statistica, *Compendio statistico*, 1935, p. 6.

percent in 1941–42. Such statistics are suspect, and almost certainly they were fudged a bit, at least in the earlier years. But the PNF did succeed in enrolling the vast majority of school students in its youth organizations, often simply by arbitrarily listing them as members. Membership statistics were reported by school authorities whose *libretti personali* recorded their success or failure and whose careers, therefore, depended to some extent on these numbers. After 1939 the statistics more closely mirrored reality, because GIL membership was obligatory as "scholastic service" for all Italian students.[98] All available evidence indicates, however, that the number of students who actively participated in the doings of the youth groups was far below the number enrolled on paper.

Tables 6-8 through 6-11 illustrate the influence of factors of region, age, and gender on youth group membership. From Table 6-8 it is evident that the enrollment among females in the various PNF youth groups ranged from only 6 percent in the Fasci Giovanili in 1931 to a high of 43.4 percent in the ONB in 1936. In Table 6-9 the age and gender factors are reemphasized: in a comparison between the 1936 census figures and the PNF youth group enrollment statistics, it becomes clear that enrollment among males was significantly higher at all age levels (though declining for both sexes in the older brackets) and that enrollments among older females declined most sharply of all. For ages eight to fourteen years, for example, 74.6 percent of the males but only 66 percent of the females were enrolled.

In Table 6-10 regional considerations also come into play. Enrollment

Table 6-6
Enrollment in the GIL, 1937–1942

Year[a]	Figli della Lupa	Balilla	Piccole Italiane	Avanguardisti	Giovani Italiane	Giovani Fascisti	Giovani Fasciste	Total for All Groups
1937		4,679,272		960,118	483,145	1,163,363	256,085	7,541,983
1938	1,387,386	1,728,263	1,669,045	876,550	386,867	1,168,693	360,577	7,577,381
1939	1,546,389	1,746,560	1,622,766	906,785	441,254	1,176,798	450,995	7,891,547
1940	1,764,380	1,862,406	1,567,524	664,015	452,972	1,028,179	529,829	7,869,305[b]
1941	1,969,637	1,926,491	1,623,035	872,447	603,199	793,532	398,471	8,186,812
1942	2,366,057	1,922,880	1,638,923	968,071	639,576	875,496	419,583	8,830,586

Sources: Istituto Centrale di Statistica, *Compendio statistico*, 1937–41, and *Annuario statistico italiano*, 1937–43; PNF, *Foglio d'ordini*, 28 October 1938–41, and *Bollettino del Comando Generale della G.I.L.*, 28 October 1938, 1 November 1939.

[a]Statistics are based on a year beginning 28 October.

[b]This figure was originally given as 8,495,929 but was corrected in the 1942 volume of Istituto Centrale di Statistica, *Annuario statistico italiano*, without explanation.

Table 6-7

Enrollment of State Secondary School Students in PNF Youth Groups, 1930–1942

	Total Students	No. Enrolled in PNF	% Enrollment
1930–31			
Male	94,650	81,046	85.6
Female	43,224	36,883	85.3
Total	137,874	117,929	85.5
1931–32			
Male	104,943	96,571	92.0
Female	48,991	46,531	94.9
Total	153,934	143,102	92.9
1932–33			
Male	147,658	137,737	93.2
Female	73,387	69,926	95.2
Total	221,045	207,663	93.5
1933–34			
Male	119,593	114,057	95.4
Female	78,695	76,377	97.1
Total	198,288	190,434	96.0
1934–35			
Male	134,941	132,468	98.2
Female	93,415	91,530	97.9
Total	228,356	223,998	98.1
1935–36			
Male	155,395	151,191	97.2
Female	114,305	111,938	97.9
Total	269,700	263,129	97.6

Sources: Istituto Centrale di Statistica, *Annuario statistico italiano* and *Compendio statistico*, 1932–43.

Note: Figures for 1931–32 through 1935–36 include state schools of all types. Data for other years include only *scuole governativi* (state schools rigidly defined in terms of administration and financing).

	Total Students	No. Enrolled in PNF	% Enrollment
1936–37			
Male	141,788	136,994	96.6
Female	106,159	102,551	96.6
Total	247,947	239,545	96.6
1937–38			
Male	150,316	149,211	99.3
Female	116,978	115,961	99.1
Total	267,294	265,172	99.2
1938–39			
Male	153,186	151,392	98.8
Female	124,470	123,189	98.9
Total	277,656	274,581	98.8
1939–40			
Male	155,075	153,961	99.2
Female	128,563	126,659	98.5
Total	283,638	280,620	98.9
1940–41			
Male	88,660	88,599	99.9
Female	70,789	70,679	99.8
Total	159,449	159,278	99.8
1941–42			
Male	88,429	88,385	99.9
Female	73,527	73,431	99.8
Total	161,956	161,816	99.9

Table 6-8

Females in Fascist Youth Groups as a Percentage of All Italian Females, 1928–1942

Youth Group	Year	%
	1928	28.1
	1929	28.5
	1930	36.2
Opera Nazionale Balilla	1932	41.5
	1933	41.9
	1934	42.5
	1935	42.8
	1936	43.4
	1931	6.0
	1932	7.6
	1933	11.1
Fasci Giovanili di Combattimento	1934	11.2
	1935	14.7
	1936	21.6
	1937	18.0
	1938	31.8
	1939	31.8
Gioventù Italiana del Littorio[a]	1940	32.4
	1941	32.1
	1942	30.5

Sources: Istituto Centrale di Statistica, *Compendio statistico* and *Annuario statistico italiano*, 1928–42.

[a]Figures for Figlie della Lupa are not averaged for the GIL because data are not available.

dropped off sharply not only among the older females when compared to the older males but also in the southern regions when compared to the central and northern regions. Reports from local PNF authorities also illustrated this regional variation. Statistics sent to Rome indicated, for example, that of the total membership in the GIL in 1940, older females accounted for 22.3 percent in Savona, 23 percent in Pisa, 17.3 percent in Milan, 16.3 percent in Turin, and 17.7 percent in Piacenza, but for only 8.4 percent in Matera, 7.7 percent in Palermo, 6.2 percent in Reggio Calabria, and 8.3 percent in Naples. There were some exceptions to this rule in some locales, but the overall generalization is sound.[99]

Table 6-11 reinforces this regional observation by comparing enroll-

Table 6-9
Proportion of Youth Group Members to Total Population in Certain Age
Groups, 1936

Youth Group	Total in Population	Enrolled in Group	%
	MALES		
Balilla (ages 8–14)	3,115,223	2,326,951	74.6
Avanguardisti (ages 15–17)	1,044,293	787,256	75.4
Giovani Fascisti (ages 18–21)	888,632	684,848	53.1
	FEMALES		
Piccole Italiane (ages 8–14)	3,038,473	2,003,775	66.0
Giovani Italiane (ages 15–17)	1,039,842	381,285	36.6
Giovani Fasciste (ages 18–21)	874,619	189,242	14.8

Source: Istituto Centrale di Statistica, *VIII Censimento Generale*, 3:114. Population figures are as of 21 April 1936; figures for PNF youth group membership are as of 28 October 1936. See Istituto Centrale di Statistica, *Annuario statistico italiano*, 1936.

ment in the ONB to total population statistics in all Italian regions.
Especially noteworthy here is the glaring gap in enrollment among the
Giovani Italiane in the southern regions of Campania, Basilicata, and
Calabria in the early years. In 1929, for example, the average enrollment
among young men in the Avanguardisti in those three areas was 586 per
100,000 inhabitants, whereas the average for young women in the Giovani Italiane was only 42 per 100,000.

Perhaps the most interesting statistical data are those published by the
PNF ranking the ninety-four provinces of Italy in descending order
based upon GIL enrollment as of 31 May 1939.[100] The figures, which
were originally divided into nine categories, bear out the regional infer-
ences based on the tables. Group 1 (from 71 percent down to 64 percent enrollment) included middle-sized industrial areas in Piedmont and
Lombardy (such as Bergamo, Cremona, and Novara) where fascism had
first enjoyed success. In groups 2 and 3 (ranging from 64 percent to 51
percent) were represented the large- and medium-sized cities of the
urban north and the central regions of Tuscany and the Romagna such as
Milan, Genoa, Bologna, and Brescia. The fourth group, which ranged
from 51 percent to 46 percent enrollment, contained almost all cities in

Table 6-10

Percentage of Total Enrollment in PNF Youth Groups Concentrated in the Older Age Brackets, 1933–1942

| | Opera Nazionale Balilla[a] | | | |
| | Avanguardisti | | Giovani Italiane | |
Region	1933	1935	1933	1935
Piedmont	23.7	27.7	9.7	16.8
Liguria	30.2	24.4	11.2	16.9
Lombardy	22.2	26.3	8.5	16.3
Trentino	15.8	22.7	11.4	18.0
Veneto	19.6	25.4	10.7	15.0
Venezia-Giulia	16.7	26.0	10.5	17.4
Emilia	17.8	21.8	6.8	16.6
Tuscany	19.6	25.8	8.3	14.7
Marches	16.2	17.1	7.8	10.2
Umbria	15.7	20.6	7.2	10.7
Latium	24.1	21.5	9.1	13.2
Abruzzi/Molise	27.3	20.4	7.1	8.1
Campania	21.6	21.6	8.3	13.0
Puglie	18.8	17.3	6.5	9.4
Lucania[c]	20.7	24.5	10.8	9.2
Calabria	37.4	23.6	7.9	6.9
Sicily	24.0	27.2	5.8	9.8
Sardinia	24.1	21.0	13.8	11.7
Kingdom	21.9	23.1	8.9	12.9

Source: Figures computed from relevant years of Istituto Centrale di Statistica, *Annuario statistico italiano*.

[a]Ages 15–17.
[b]Ages 18–21.
[c]Basilicata.

Gioventù Italiana del Littorio[b]			
Giovani Fascisti		Giovani Fasciste	
1939	1942	1939	1942
31.6	23.5	22.8	18.2
33.9	23.7	22.2	17.5
28.6	25.7	20.9	18.7
25.2	19.8	12.6	15.6
29.5	23.2	19.9	17.2
35.4	20.1	20.2	15.3
34.0	26.8	19.9	18.5
32.3	23.2	19.9	16.7
34.7	25.5	17.3	16.4
34.3	25.8	19.6	16.9
28.6	25.7	17.7	12.8
32.5	15.4	12.6	14.2
28.2	19.8	13.6	11.9
29.5	23.7	14.9	13.5
34.5	22.4	8.6	11.4
29.1	26.6	9.2	6.4
31.6	21.3	12.6	9.5
30.8	23.8	16.6	13.4
31.4	23.1	16.7	14.7

Table 6-11

Enrollment in the ONB per 100,000 Inhabitants, 1929–1932

Region	Balilla			Avanguardisti		
	1929	1930	1932	1929	1930	1932
Piedmont	2,590	2,527	3,967	786	852	1,076
Liguria	2,543	5,998	4,337	883	1,071	1,119
Lombardy	2,140	2,265	3,641	738	936	913
Trentino[a]	1,393	2,154	2,332	399	688	636
Veneto	2,004	1,895	2,671	776	886	779
Venezia-Giulia[b]	2,760	3,133	6,223	867	1,021	1,749
Emilia	1,619	1,902	3,676	748	880	880
Tuscany	2,263	2,661	3,791	1,403	852	1,123
Marches	2,711	2,936	4,423	890	1,154	1,025
Umbria	3,297	3,559	3,543	1,355	1,396	1,085
Latium	1,638	1,735	3,340	691	760	846
Abruzzi/Molise	3,167	4,030	3,508	1,147	1,027	881
Campania	1,120	1,480	3,049	619	732	958
Puglie	2,291	2,170	3,148	965	1,004	1,172
Basilicata[c]	1,767	2,028	3,219	596	687	896
Calabria	1,273	1,740	2,969	544	641	1,228
Sicily	1,796	1,939	3,160	706	814	1,112
Sardinia	2,506	2,468	2,612	1,273	1,162	750
Kingdom	2,049	2,345	3,466	825	887	996

Source: Istituto Centrale di Statistica, *Annuario statistico italiano*, 1930–32.
Note: Dates are as of 31 December 1929, 31 December 1930, and 28 October 1932.
 [a]Bolzano and Trent.
 [b]Fiume, Pola, Trieste, Zara, and Gorizia.
 [c]In 1932 Basilicata was called Lucania.

that central belt as well as the capital of Rome (ranked at number 39). The remaining provinces with lower enrollment (groups 5 through 9) contained an overwhelming proportion of southern provinces.

In the top half of all Italian provinces only two (Bari at number 45 and Salerno at number 46) were in the south. In fact, only two of the top thirty-nine provinces were south of Florence (Grosseto and Rome). In the bottom half of the list only a handful were from the north, and six of these were in the border areas of the Veneto, Venezia-Giulia, and the Trentino (Rovigo, Venice, Udine, Pola, Gorizia, and Bolzano), where fascism was traditionally weak and Catholic Action traditionally strong.

Piccole Italiane			Giovani Italiane		
1929	1930	1932	1929	1930	1932
1,937	2,448	3,652	253	332	443
1,421	2,114	3,763	255	380	495
1,198	1,707	3,240	143	237	256
601	1,403	1,980	120	248	197
429	1,031	2,001	71	178	240
1,499	2,500	5,673	252	510	637
785	1,394	3,023	132	215	270
1,001	1,435	2,971	244	373	325
2,144	2,242	3,703	259	362	185
2,758	1,766	2,722	290	436	263
750	1,232	2,842	118	248	321
720	1,675	2,812	75	160	290
331	1,801	2,291	48	125	295
1,293	1,596	2,497	176	171	262
503	1,293	2,688	44	116	148
260	1,239	2,391	33	126	270
1,006	1,236	2,497	124	143	165
450	1,550	2,232	126	291	247
1,001	1,601	2,876	145	234	290

Turin, though it consistently had a rather low percentage of party members, was near the top of the GIL list, at number 10, as were two other heavily industrial areas, Genoa at number 11 and Milan at number 14. The GIL clearly had greatest influence in the provinces with high per capita incomes and high school attendance.

CHAPTER SEVEN

Formation of the Fascist Ruling Class

The Fascist university groups—the Gruppi Universitari Fascisti—developed quite separately from the other PNF youth groups. The GUF, and the students who were members, enjoyed a special status during the Fascist period. In the long run, the efforts of the PNF to bring the university youth to its side were not successful. If, as one historian of the period remarked, the GUF members were for a time "among the most enthusiastic supporters of Mussolini's regime," it is also true that many of them ended up in the ranks of the active resistance.[1] Very few of the young men upon whom the regime had staked its future raised their voices or took up arms to protest the events of 25 July 1943.

Early History of the GUF

On 13 December 1923 Mussolini met at the Palazzo Chigi with representatives of the Fascist university groups. "The Fascist government," he said, "needs a ruling class. . . . I cannot suddenly produce all the officials needed in the state administration. They must come little by little from the universities."[2] The primary function of the GUF was political: the formation of a "natural ruling class" capable of articulating and disseminating a national Fascist culture.[3]

In 1919 and 1920 the GUF were little more than action squads allied with the local *fasci* or the Avanguardie Studentesche. In some locales where enthusiasm for the new movement ran high among the students, these university groups were established even before the *fasci*; in other places the *fasci* were set up on the initiative of the local students.[4] In May 1920 representatives from these scattered university groups attended the Fascist party congress, and the amorphous movement began to take on a definable shape as university students moved away from the Avanguardie—whose members were largely students from the secondary schools—and into their own organizations. The movement spread rapidly; by early 1921 GUF chapters were formally constituted in many of the large university towns.

The university squads waged a "patriotic crusade" that kept the universities in a constant state of agitation and violent confrontation in the early 1920s. Their main targets were Catholic and Socialist groups, though they battled any organizations that did not accept their general line: superheated patriotism and irredentism, antibolshevism, and support for the rights of ex-combatants. Often they turned to violence to publicize their causes and to punish the sins of their "antinational" opponents.

There was no dearth of opponents in these early days, for the GUF were only some of the many groups vying for the attention of the students in the frantic postwar period. In addition to such traditional goliardic groups as the Corda Fratres and the Catholic FUCI, others with well-defined political goals challenged the GUF for student leadership. In the early 1920s, for example, university Socialist groups were established in Genoa, Rome, and Naples; a republican association opposed the Fascist students in Milan; and the Ordine Nuovo group in Turin was actively disseminating Communist propaganda.[5]

Much of the early postwar unrest at the universities was the result of demands for special privileges for ex-combatants. In the fall of 1919 the University of Turin was in turmoil because of suspension of accelerated courses for those who had left their studies to serve in the armed forces. In November 1921 students went on strike and occupied the Turin Politecnico over the question of special examination sessions for veterans and student participation on academic and administrative councils at the university. Similar issues disrupted the academic peace in Bologna, Palermo, and Naples in the same period. In addition to the much-publicized assault on the editorial offices of *Avanti!* by students of the Milan Politecnico in April 1919, the GUF mounted widespread protests during the opening of the academic year 1919–20 against the new Chamber of Deputies and the *rinunciatari* of the Nitti government. Pitched battles between patriotic and left-wing groups were a familiar part of university life, especially during the 1920 celebration commemorating the intervention campaign of the "radiant days of May" and Italy's entry into the war.

In February 1922 representatives from university Fascist groups all over Italy met in Bologna with delegates from the PNF to map out a strategy and write a statute for the new organization, the Federazione Nazionale Universitaria Fascista, or FNUF.[6]

Most Fascist hierarchs looked with favor on the students' patriotic struggle at the universities, but many also feared that, left to their own devices, the GUF would become too autonomous and too revisionist. Future ruling class or no, the GUF leaders were clearly not supposed to make policy but to ensure PNF control of this important sector of Italian society. Having participated in the early armed struggle to install the new regime, many of the more outspoken leaders of the university groups clung tenaciously to their autonomy and pushed for a greater say in the decision-making process at the national level.[7]

Massimo Rocca and Dino Grandi attended the first meeting of the FNUF as delegates from the PNF. The founding statute of the new association aimed at establishing direct party control over the student groups. According to the FNUF constitution, all GUF chapters were to belong to the new national organization and all GUF members had to be members of the PNF. Defined as the fighting arm of the PNF in the universities, FNUF members were charged with the task of propagandizing *Italianità* and developing a "healthy national conscience" in the university students—and with muzzling antinational professors and students. The secretary of each local GUF was given an honorary position on the local *fascio*, but he had only a consultative vote. The secretary-general of the central committee of the FNUF, Ivo Levi, then political secretary of the Milanese GUF, was also allowed to sit on the national directorate of the PNF, but he had no real power to participate in decision making. The FNUF statute—which was rumored among the students to have been written by Mussolini himself—was approved at the first national congress of the new organization in Milan in June 1922, though not without some behind-the-scenes grumbling.

The essential powerlessness of the GUF was demonstrated in December 1922 when the universities exploded over Gentile's decision to suspend the extraordinary examination sessions for veterans scheduled for the next March. Many of the local GUF staged protests against the decision, but Mussolini sent Levi personal orders to desist. Despite an exchange of letters with the officers of several GUF chapters, however, Levi was not able to convince all of the Gufini to toe the party line.[8] The recalcitrant student leaders were eventually brought to heel, but not without some defections from the ranks. This was one of the first demonstrations of the division that was always to plague the Fascist youth movement: the clash between those who were content to serve as faithful executors of an "Idea and the Will of a Man" and those who desired some real autonomy and power for the university students in the direction of the movement.

After the March on Rome and the establishment of the Fascist militia, the GUF no longer served a combat function, and the PNF leadership set about taming the activism of the early recruits. But the passage from *squadrismo* to political action in the universities was not an easy or smooth one. Many of the GUF members were reluctant to lay down their weapons, undoubtedly realizing that their armed force provided them with a degree of independence and influence, if only potentially. After the "heroism" of the seizure of power—and apart from the unsubtle argument of the *santo manganello*—the groups seemed to have no clear-cut cultural or political program to inspire their activities.

Political lines were drawn on the issue of the Gentile reform, which was supported by the GUF and opposed by many non-Fascist students, who perceived it as an attack against academic freedom and a tool of political propaganda. Police quashed demonstrations at universities all over Italy, and a flood of open letters to Mussolini from anti-Gentilian students produced only an official statement that the regime would not tolerate "troublemakers."[9]

Political tensions at the universities continued after the opening of the academic year 1924–25. Some of the non-Fascist groups were essentially apolitical, but others were of a decidedly anti-Fascist cast. In 1924 Roman students set up the Unione Goliardica Italiana per la Libertà, and in Milan Socialist students gathered around Lelio Basso and the Associazione Milanese Universitaria.[10] In Florence many students gravitated to Gaetano Salvemini and Piero Calamandrei. The Tuscan universities at Florence and Pisa were generally thought to be hotbeds of anti-Fascist sentiment. The Neapolitan university journal *Il Gazzettino universitario* provided an independent voice until it was silenced in 1926.

Although the Gufini managed to infiltrate and capture some nonpolitical groups, they adopted less pacific methods with the outspokenly anti-Fascist students. The movement to purify the universities of this antinational rabble was supported by vitriolic editorials in some of the intransigent GUF papers—most especially in the pages of the Roman *La Rivolta ideale*, which called for pitiless strikes against these subversive parasites. One especially poisonous campaign was unleashed in this paper in 1925 against Francesco Severi, the rector of the university and a signer of the Croce manifesto. Severi's position was finally rendered untenable. He resigned in November 1925, to be replaced by Giorgio Del Vecchio, a Fascist of the first hour, who remained in the job until 1938; then, ironically, he was removed from office as a result of the regime's anti-Semitic legislation.[11] Severi was not the only target, however. During 1925 *La Rivolta ideale* had a regular third-page feature containing profiles of antinational professors. It also fought a no-holds-barred battle during the Matteotti crisis to purge the Italian schools of *Aventinismo universitario*.

As the political consolidation of the regime proceeded, so, too, did the consolidation of the power of the GUF, which sooner or later managed to silence or dissolve the other student groups or totally depoliticize their activities. The battle with the FUCI was the longest running and the most bitter.[12] But by the mid-twenties the early violence of the squadrist period began to die down and members turned to their main task: the creation of a national culture to replace the antinational culture of the liberal period. This goal they attempted to achieve in the array of newspapers published by the various GUF chapters and in the countless lectures, speeches, and demonstrations the group organized. "The violence of the billy club," said one historian, "became the violence of the word."[13] Despite the aggressive boasts that the universities had been "reclaimed," however, many realized even at this early stage that the battle for a cultural and political monopoly at the Italian universities would be an uphill struggle. An editorial in the Bolognese journal *Vita nova* in 1927 lamented: "Not only are the majority of the students not enrolled in their respective university groups, but they are more or less hostile to fascism. Who can wonder, then, that in our universities—which are supposed to be Fascist—the future opponents of fascism are being prepared."[14]

Organization and Activities of the GUF

Though the goal of the GUF was the political formation of the entire student body, membership was voluntary until the passage of the School Charter in 1939. Students in the special higher institutes and university students from twenty-one to twenty-eight years of age were eligible to belong, and former students were allowed to retain their GUF cards until they reached the age of twenty-eight.

Organizational ties to the PNF were very close. The party secretary, for example, served as national secretary of the GUF. GUF chapters were set up at all the universities and higher institutes and in the provincial capitals. Provincial PNF secretaries appointed the six-member provincial directorates of the GUF, and the local GUF secretaries also served on the party *federazioni*. Political reliability was the first requirement for GUF service. A survey of the leadership in 1934 showed that 56 percent of all provincial GUF officials had enrolled in the PNF before 1923. Of those remaining, 14 percent enrolled between 1923 and 1924, and 30 percent joined between 1925 and 1930.[15]

Smaller sections of the GUF—called Nuclei Universitari Fascisti, or NUF—could be set up in any town where at least twenty-five persons requested membership. By 1936 there were ninety-eight GUF chapters: twenty-six at the universities and higher institutes, seventy in provincial capitals, and two in the colonies. In addition, there were some four hundred NUF groups scattered all over the peninsula.[16]

The principle of "separate and not equal" that characterized the role of females in all other PNF youth groups and in the educational system as a whole also described the position of young women in the GUF. Relegated to a subordinate status by biological design (according to Fascist theory), women in the GUF were nevertheless a bit more difficult to

dismiss than their less articulate nonstudent sisters. The GUF leaders
recognized the professional and political role of the university women as
long as they participated in the movement in "sectors that do not coincide with the natural activity of the males."[17] Female GUF members
took courses in child care and hygiene; served as assistants in local
nursery schools, orphanages, and children's hospitals; and visited the
homes of needy families.

The fears about the moral repercussions of propinquity that produced
a reaction against coeducation in the schools and in the groups for
younger children carried over into the universities, and males and females in the GUF rarely participated in joint activities. GUF literature
frequently lauded the moral uprightness of members and the decadence
of foreign education. A medical student writing his thesis for the *laurea*
was dismissed by an irate Starace in 1934 for having sent out question-
naires to GUF members asking for information on the "medical and
social problems in the sex life of the young."[18]

The GUF were responsible for a wide range of activities at the universities, including sports, assistance programs, and political and cultural
affairs. In contrast to the ONB and the GIL, in the GUF military
activities were not much in evidence until the outbreak of world war,
though the MVSN included some special battalions of students known as
the Milizia Universitaria. University students were exempt from military
service until the age of twenty-six.[19]

Aside from some of the required political events, university students
were not really compelled to take part in the group's activities, though
GUF leaders emphasized the young Fascist's moral duty to support the
organization. In reality the GUF enjoyed a virtual monopoly over all
nonacademic aspects of university life, and students who wanted to
engage in sports or get involved in social, political, or cultural activities
during their years at the university had to have GUF membership cards.
Table 7-1 indicates the impressive growth of the organization.

The most popular events sponsored by the various groups were the
sports activities, which became much more a part of university life than
ever before. The main sports events of each year were the regional and
national competitions, the Littoriali dello sport. Anyone interested in
athletics, whether dilettante or serious, had to join the GUF, because
membership was a prerequisite for competition in national, international, and Olympic events.

In theory the aim of the assistance offices of the GUF was to help
students in need of financial aid or scholastic assistance. In practice,
however, the GUF did not provide day-to-day aid but concentrated
instead on grandiose projects that had very little impact—apart from
propaganda value—even when they materialized. Some of the GUF
provided low-cost cafeterias, periodic medical check-ups, and some

Table 7-1

Enrollment in the GUF, 1927–1943

Date	No. of Members
6 September 1927	8,854
25 October 1928	16,965
7 December 1931	55,303
28 October 1932	57,553
28 October 1933	57,509
28 October 1934	66,934
28 October 1935	70,325
28 October 1936	75,436
28 October 1937	82,004
28 October 1938	93,175
28 October 1939	105,883
28 October 1940	119,713
28 October 1941	137,148
28 October 1942	159,297
25 June 1943	164,667

Sources: Figures for 1927–31 are from PNF, *Foglio d'ordini*, 6 September 1927, 28 October 1928, 7 December 1931. Figures for other years are from annual issues of Istituto Centrale di Statistica, *Compendio statistico*; and the 28 October issue of the *Foglio d'ordini*.

scholarships and financial subsidies. These programs were administered by the university welfare and assistance agency known as the Opera Universitaria, originally established by the Gentile reform.[20] Dues from all student members of the GUF and contributions from the PNF were supposed to finance the assistance program, but judging from the frequency of complaints from the local GUF about lack of resources, the subsidies never satisfied the requests for aid. The most publicized assistance project of the GUF was the construction at each university of a student house, the Casa dello studente, which was supposed to provide living quarters, lounges, student halls, recreation rooms, and playing fields for deserving Gufini. In practice only a few rooms were ever available, and these were generally reserved for students judged politically meritorious by the local GUF authorities.[21]

Contacts with student organizations abroad were especially cultivated. GUF delegates attended international student meetings for many years, but in the thirties contacts with student groups abroad multiplied and foreign students from friendly or aligned nations received special

attention at Italian universities. GUF sections for foreign students were
set up at many universities, and members were often provided with
financial subsidies that included partial scholarships and travel discounts Formation
underwritten by government ministries. Particularly close relations were of the
established between the GUF and the Reichstudentenführung; in October Fascist
1940 *Die Bewegung*, the official organ of the German groups, devoted Ruling
an entire issue to the GUF.[22] Class

Starace was especially interested in expanding the range of GUF activities and in binding the university youth closer to the regime. During the 1930s there was great activity in the youth-oriented PNF initiatives: the establishment of political preparation courses and leadership schools; the encouragement of the university press; the creation of experimental theater, cinema, and radio sections in the GUF; the Littoriali of culture and art; and the propaganda activities of the Scuola di Mistica Fascista.

For students interested in drama, the GUF set up the Teatro sperimentale in Florence in 1934; it included an acting school and provided practical theater experience. The company, which became the Teatro nazionale dei GUF in 1941, eventually had branches all over Italy and sent touring companies out into the provinces.[23] Here, too, art was to be the handmaiden of politics, and many of the GUF productions were blatant glorifications of the party and the regime. Applications for positions with the GUF theater groups requested detailed information on the political background of the applicant; the group's leader, director Giorgio Venturini, had joined the PNF in 1923.

In addition to the radio sections discussed previously, the GUF also provided technical training for students interested in cinema. GUF cinema sections, called Cineguf, were set up in the major university towns in 1933, and by 1934 all university centers had film programs. Both Galeazzo Ciano and Vittorio Mussolini took a personal interest in the Cineguf, which were designed as schools in film technique but which also served as local censorship boards to guarantee that the films produced would correspond to the regime's political line. The groups did spread an interest in film. If the content of many of the films produced in the GUF sections was patently political, the groups were nonetheless the training ground—"nurseries for the Italian cinema of the future"—for many of the important filmmakers of the postwar period.[24]

It was not always easy to corral the creative energies of the film students in the Cineguf, and sometimes their impatience with overt political and artistic controls spilled over into opposition. Alberto Lattuada, then director of the Milan review *Corrente*, organized a film festival in May 1940, shortly before the Italian declaration of war. In spite of official prohibitions, the group showed Jean Renoir's *La Grande Illusion*. The audience applauded and sang during the "Marseillaise," a disturbance that prompted police intervention. The authorities ordered an inquiry, but because the performance had been sponsored by the GUF the investigation was finally hushed up.[25]

The cultural and political sections of the GUF were also charged with the task of producing colonial and racial propaganda. By the mid-1930s the colonial offices of the group were working closely with the Istituto Coloniale Fascista (ICF) to disseminate information on the colonies and to organize lectures and competitions on imperial and colonial themes. In May 1931 the ICF dissolved its provincial offices, and the task of colonial propaganda was turned over to the GUF. The GUF also sent out books and other "efficacious instruments of cultural propaganda" to *fasci* abroad in an effort to preserve the *Italianità* of areas such as Dalmatia and Malta.[26] After the passage of the racial laws in 1938, the GUF offices of demography and race took over primary responsibility for PNF racial propaganda.

Party Leadership Schools

Besides training and organizing the mass of young people, the regime also aimed at selecting the most promising of the younger generation for especially intense indoctrination as the future ruling elite. This initiative was slow in coming and, despite official ballyhoo, had a limited impact. The GUF had a key role in organizing the training, and the majority of the young men (women were not admitted to these rarefied circles) were GUF members. Starace announced the establishment of the new Corsi di Preparazione Politica per i Giovani in February 1935; the courses were inaugurated on 23 March 1935, the sixteenth anniversary of the founding of the Fascist movement.[27]

Young men from twenty-three to twenty-eight years of age who possessed the requisites of "intelligence, will, and character" were chosen from the party organizations to attend these provincial courses. The training lasted two years, combining theoretical studies on fascism with administrative experience in some PNF agency. Party leaders were sensitive to charges that the courses were a training ground for a future Fascist aristocracy, and emphasized that merit and service, not social class, were the main criteria for admission into the program. But it was difficult for those without substantial education to pass the required written and oral examinations. In essence, the courses were designed for those students whose social position and education had already marked them as future members of the party apparat and set them apart from the masses to be governed.[28]

Without a cadre of trained instructors the program could hardly be successful, and in 1939 the regime established a national training

school, the Centro di Preparazione Politica per i Giovani, at the Foro
Mussolini. Finally, almost seventeen years after the March on Rome, the
PNF had its leadership school, not a "school for hierarchs" but a school Formation
of "faith and experience." Though preference was given to veterans, any of the
male member of the party or the GUF from the appropriate age bracket Fascist
could take the entrance examination, provided that he could fulfill at Ruling
least one of the following requirements: successful completion of the Class
provincial training courses, a prize in the Littoriali, service in the PNF
organizations, or a diploma from one of the GIL academies or colleges.
Each candidate also had to undergo a test of "military character" and an
athletic competition in a combat sport such as boxing, wrestling, or
fencing.

Mussolini inaugurated the center on 3 January 1940—another historic
Fascist date, the fifteenth anniversary of the "clarification" speech. The
course of study lasted two years, including summers, which were devoted to travel and political experience in the provincial party administration. All students were required to live at the school and concentrate
on a wide-ranging curriculum that included, besides the usual Fascist
studies, foreign languages, colonial history, international relations, and
techniques of journalism and propaganda.[29]

The Center for Political Preparation never really succeeded in producing accomplished new ruling cadres. It was established very late, and its
inauguration coincided with Italy's entry into the war, which drew away
many of its best candidates. But beyond the purely logistical difficulties,
the center suffered from the basic problem that affected the regime at all
levels of its administration. Creative leadership required resourceful and
independent young men full of new ideas and fresh outlooks. The center
put a premium on very different qualities—obedience, blind loyalty, and
"faith"—and turned out yes-men who avoided rocking the boat at all
costs.[30]

The Scuola di Mistica Fascista—the School of Fascist Mysticism—
was another elite institution, though of a very different type. The school,
founded in 1931 and active until the fall of the regime, was named after
Arnaldo's son, Sandro Italico Mussolini, who had died of leukemia in
1930 at the age of twenty. Emphasis was on political commitment and
youth. Vito Mussolini (born in 1912), son of Arnaldo and nephew of the
Duce, served as the first president. Nicolò Giani, then a twenty-one-
year-old law student, acted as director, and Fernando Mezzasoma (born
in 1907) as vice-president. Guido Pallotta, secretary of the Turin GUF
and founder of its journal, *Vent'anni*, was also active on the administrative board of the school.

Arnaldo Mussolini played a crucial role. Stricken by the death of his
beloved son, he gave the school its characteristic religious and spiritual
tone. His speech "Coscienza e dovere," delivered at the school on 29

November 1931, was its ethical and political manifesto. The speech was a call to discipline, to personal honesty, to heroism—and above all to faith, to a religious conception of life and duty for the "new Italian."[31]

Originally founded as a section of the Milanese GUF, the school later became an agency of the PNF dedicated to the exegesis of Fascist doctrine and maintenance of the intransigent spirit of the movement's origins. Its task was to provide fascism with its apostles and missionaries. The *mistici* railed against careerism and the bureaucratization of the revolution; they called for a new aristocracy of true believers ready to fight to the death. "Believe, Obey, Fight" was not a convenient motto but a lifelong duty.

Here political activity was to become religious commitment. The *mistici* were celebrants in the cult of the Duce. The group, said Mussolini, is more "than a party, it is a religious order."[32] Like any religious cult, the school had its own sacred shrine and reliquary. In October 1939 the *mistici* took over the care and tending of the *covo*, Mussolini's first office at the *Popolo d'Italia* in Milan. In March 1940 they began to display their own relic: the revolver carried by the Duce before the March on Rome.[33]

The language of the *mistici* was based not on reason but on quasi-magical schema that would "give wings to the soul." "We return to the past," explained one initiate, "of Myth, of Dogma, of Faith . . . happy to abdicate reason to believe in Him who leads, in the Nation, in the hierarchy of the State." "We are mystics," said Giani, "because we are mad . . . and even absurd. . . . History has always been and always will be an absurdity . . . the spirit and will that bends and conquers the merely material."[34]

The activities of the school were varied, including public lectures, annual courses for teachers and students, and dissemination of Fascist doctrine through its journal, *Dottrina fascista*. The first series of courses for elementary school teachers, held in 1938–39, opened with Giani's speech "Why We Are Anti-Semites" and included such other offerings as "Mussolini, Creator and Duce of the Revolution," "The Party as Motor of the Revolution," and "Education of Intellect, Sentiment, and Will in the Preparation of the Citizen-Soldier."[35]

Also in 1938–39 the school offered a two-year lecture series for middle school students. These lectures usually enrolled between three hundred and five hundred students; because successful participants received a diploma that gave them precedence at the universities and vague promises of eventual positions in the PNF or GUF administration, many career-oriented young people may have seen the lectures as insurance for the future. Some prominent personalities were involved in the courses; in 1939, for example, Marinetti gave an address entitled "The Revolutionary Function of Art." Other lectures included "Racial Prob-

lems of the Empire," "The Eternal Characteristics of Fascist Poetry,"
"The Bourgeois Mentality and the Fascist Spirit," and "The Mission of
Women in the Fascist State."

Students presented public lectures at the school several times each
month, and the more inspiring talks were published in the school's
Quaderni. The school also sponsored annual contests for the best mono-
graphs on assigned themes. The topic for 1940 was "The *mistica* of
Fascist racism," a theme that won sixth-place honors for Giorgio Almi-
rante, who was to head the Movimento Sociale Italiano (MSI) in the
post–World War II era. Important public figures presented the keynote
speeches each year. Oswald Mosley, head of the British Union of Fascists, spoke in 1935. In February 1937 Ildefonso Cardinal Schuster of
Milan addressed the group, comparing the achievements of Mussolini to
those of Augustus and Constantine. In 1940 the school opened a series
of lectures by university professors called the *Lecturae ducis* (modeled
on the famous series of Dante lectures), illustrating the most apodictic
statements of the Duce.[36]

The school's first annual national conference took place in 1940 and
drew about five hundred participants, many of them clearly non-Fascist
or even anti-Fascist in outlook. A report written by Gastone Silvano
Spinetti to Mussolini after this meeting is enlightening. Spinetti, then an
employee of the Ministry of Popular Culture, divided the audience into
three groups: *squadristi* and World War I veterans; university professors
and other older men; and the young, many veterans of the Ethiopian war
and the Spanish civil war. These groups, he claimed, did not share the
same views on the role of youth in the regime. The *squadristi* called for
firm discipline and blind obedience to the will of the leader. The second
group seemed skeptical and without true faith. The young, Spinetti said,
were firmly convinced both that only discussion and questioning would
produce a firm basis for the future development of the regime and that
they were the ones best equipped to guide that evolution. Echoing
familiar themes that Bottai had been voicing for years, Spinetti called
for toleration of the activism and energies of youth, who should, he
claimed, be encouraged to build and not only to obey passively.[37]

Zangrandi has compared these national meetings of the Scuola di
Mistica Fascista to the Littoriali, for despite the propagandistic intentions of the regime, the meetings did draw many non-Fascists, who
attempted to make them open forums on fascism.[38] On the whole,
however, the school had very little effect on the policies of the regime or
on Italian cultural life in general. Financial subsidies mounted steadily
during the last half of the 1930s, but by then even some of the school's
founders could no longer hope for a new beginning, and the retreat into
irrationalism in politics was something of a last resort. The school
officially supported intervention in 1939, and when war was declared

169 of its members volunteered for service, including the school's director, vice-director, and president. By the spring of 1943, 15 had died at the front, among them Giani, Pallotta, and Berto Ricci.[39]

Largo ai giovani

The Fascist regime failed in its attempt to create a new Fascist ruling class among the university youth—a failure attested to not only by the young people involved but by party leaders as well. For most of the Fascist period the majority of university students were not openly disloyal, though much of the autobiographical testimony from the period would tend to paint that picture. Such accounts, however, were written by the highly politicized, often those who worked in clandestine organizations and took up arms. But even the less-politicized university students did not all respond with the enthusiasm the regime had hoped to elicit. Even among many of the students who still called themselves Fascists in the thirties, there was a marked resistance to the regime's indoctrination program, a growing disillusionment with the clash between rhetoric and reality.

Articles in the Fascist press frequently pointed to the lack of political faith among the young and the diffuse political opportunism or *qualunquismo* that seemed to characterize many of these young men upon whom the regime had staked its future. In 1937 Camillo Pellizzi wrote in *Critica fascista* that the GUF had become "what no one ever wanted it to be: a career springboard."[40] A police report on the situation of the GUF in Turin in 1931 also expressed typical concern about the morale and reliability of the Gufini. Enrollment, the agent reported, "is seen as a necessary and indispensable condition in order to be able to continue studies with a greater chance of success and to avoid problems, so all belong. But few are enthusiastic."[41] In July 1931 Carlo Scorza reported to Mussolini that after nearly a decade of Fascist rule, "The masses in the university are still not what the Duce wants. . . . I have found among the university students a lively sense of autonomy in their relations with the party, and a spirited disregard of disciplinary and hierarchical ties." Scorza blamed part of the party's failure on anti-Fascist university professors, who exerted a "special fascination" over the students. As evidence for his claims, he pointed to the high incidence of antifascism among university teaching assistants.[42]

Scorza had put his finger on a very crucial issue, what was in the 1930s referred to in the party press as the *problema dei giovani*. As we will see below, during the 1930s there was a great deal of ferment among Fascist university students aimed at a "refounding" of fascism that would allow the masses, and especially the youth, greater initiative and creativity and a more conscious participation in the life of the nation. Critical of much in the past but still hopeful for the future, these young people took the revolutionary rhetoric of the party more seriously than the PNF leaders did. An ever more widely diffused feeling of dissatisfaction with the regime's failure to live up to its original revolutionary promises and an impatience with its lack of vitality and dynamism were clearly evident by the mid-thirties—as well as a growing belief that if reform were to come it would not begin inside the party.

Toward these restless students the regime adopted the slogan *largo ai giovani*, a policy of concessions to the idealistic fervor of the young. The regime presented fascism to the youth as a continuing revolution that would soon produce well-being and social justice for all. It could not, at the same time, show its authoritarian and repressive face if these young students were really to feel they had a role to play in the future. And so the regime's leaders tried to find a middle way, downplaying force and coercion and emphasizing spontaneity and creative initiative. The regime walked a kind of political tightrope with these young people: attempting to balance force and consent, to harmonize totalitarian political and social control with the active participation of the young. Fascist leaders attempted to exercise a kind of "repressive tolerance" of youthful activism by providing institutional mechanisms—such as the Littoriali and the GUF press—that would allow the young to let off steam without challenging the stability of the system. For a time this squaring of the circle had some success. Zangrandi recalled that in some ways the years of Fascist control were not difficult enough for his generation, especially for the students, intellectuals, and professionals whom the regime wanted to co-opt: "This deceptive 'freedom' . . . left us inside a wall, not of Fascist orthodoxy but of the most general obscurantism . . . that contributed not a little to making us lose time, to preventing us from understanding earlier the true nature of fascism. This made the road toward the full acquisition of conscience not only laborious, tortuous, uncertain, full of perplexities and of 'relapses' and temptations but also—for these very reasons—very long."[43]

Inherent in this policy of *largo ai giovani* was a kind of political double standard: one to judge irreconcilable anti-Fascists of the older generations and one for the privileged younger rebels. Youthful intemperance was indulged and sometimes subsidized; lessons from the *santo manganello* or exile were usually thought to be more fitting punishments for the stubborn heretics among the older Italians. University students rarely saw the open face of the police state in quite the same way as their elders, though the threat was always present. They were allowed "open discussion" and "constructive criticism"; the slogan of the day was *discutere con fede*, "discuss with faith." In place of a policy of open repression that would have been counterproductive, the regime adopted a policy of vigilant paternalism. Giuseppe Bottai was especially eager to encourage a creative ferment among the young: "The young must speak . . . tell us their ideas. . . . The Fascist Revolution is a revolution of the young and it is to the young that its continuity is entrusted."[44] Bottai was probably quite sincere, but for most in the hierarchy—and certainly for Mussolini himself—the policy of *largo ai giovani* was not an encouragement of creativity but a smokescreen covering up the regime's fundamental desire to repress dissent.

This policy of *largo ai giovani* helps to explain the complex evolution of movements of dissent within fascism during the 1930s. The regime's apparent toleration of criticism convinced many young people who might otherwise have turned to anti-Fascist activities that there was a way to work within the system to realize the revolutionary promises of fascism. In this sense, *largo ai giovani* paid dividends. But the young people who formed this loyal opposition were opposed by others who could not be deluded by a policy of official toleration within limits into believing that any change within the Fascist framework could bring true social reform. Convinced of the repressive nature of the regime, these young people fought not to "renew" fascism but to destroy it. Somewhere between these two positions were the young people who began as convinced Fascists working for the revitalization of the movement and ended by accepting the futility of their hopes for a new beginning—the young people who, in Zangrandi's well-known phrase, made "the long voyage through fascism."

Gastone Silvano Spinetti was one of the spokesmen of the leftist Fascists calling for internal renewal. He was much influenced by the moral and spiritual outlook of Arnaldo Mussolini, and one of his first professional tasks was to edit Arnaldo's speeches and writings. Spinetti called his movement *universalfascismo*, and in the pages of *La Sapienza*—a journal he began in early 1933 with Giorgio Prosperi—he urged a retreat from Gentilian idealism and a return to the principles of 1919. Contributors to the journal frequently criticized the centralizing and statist tendencies of the regime. The crisis facing the modern world, they argued, demanded not merely an institutional resolution but a moral transformation. The logical leaders of this moral reformation were the youth. Echoing Mussolini's 1930 claim about the universality of the Fascist spirit, the proponents of *universalfascismo* saw in their own freedom to criticize an openness that assured them that the youth would soon be able to assume the guidance of the revolution and realize the spiritual renewal of Italy and its preeminent role in resolving the crises of modern civilization.[45]

Many of these themes of independence and renovation were emphasized in Berto Ricci's Florentine journal, *L'Universale*, and in the Roman review *Il Saggiatore*, directed by Domenico Carella and Giorgio

Granata.[46] Like *La Sapienza*, these two journals harked back to Mussolini's early theme of the "new Fascist man." Deeply convinced of the
decadence and degeneration of Western civilization, these young men
believed that the crisis demanded new men and not merely institutional
tinkering. Calling for transcendence of both nationalism and Christianity, for example, Ricci dreamed of a new empire based on Italy's
universal mission and creative genius—a new civilization of the spirit,
not of armies and industrial production. *L'Universale* ceased publication
in 1935 when Ricci left for the African campaign. Just after Italy's entry
into the war in 1940 Ricci, still hoping for the promised internal revolution, wrote in *Rivoluzione*, the GUF paper in Florence, that the conflict
would sweep aside the "old world of the rich and poor, of landowners
and landless, of employers and employees."[47]

Zangrandi's reminiscences of Berto Ricci painted a fascinating picture
of the inner turmoil of a young leftist Fascist attempting to reconcile his
desire for social and political renovation and his insistence on fidelity to
fascism. Zangrandi visited with Ricci often during the 1930s, when the
young Florentine was a poor schoolteacher. Solitary and isolated, Ricci
was "walking on the razor's edge," closely watched by the authorities
despite the almost reverential air of the Fascists who claimed him as their
own. The two men met clandestinely for years, and Zangrandi claimed
that after 1940 Ricci's position was "decisively outside fascism" but that
his emotional ties to old hopes and dreams prevented him from making
the open break others had accepted. Inspired by his "presumed coher-
ence, romanticism, and desperation," Ricci volunteered for the front in
1940. He died in Libya in 1941 at the age of thirty-six. Zangrandi called
his death a suicide.[48]

The group that formed around Ruggero Zangrandi was typical of
many other groups that began as leftist movements inside the PNF and
then moved outside and against the regime. The "Zangrandi group" is
the most famous because it was the subject of the controversial book *Il
lungo viaggio attraverso il fascismo*, in which Zangrandi chronicled the
vicissitudes of a broad stratum of Italian youth born in the Fascist
period.[49]

Zangrandi was for years a close friend of Vittorio Mussolini, the
Duce's eldest son, with whom he attended the Liceo Tasso in Rome. The
two met in 1929, their common Milanese backgrounds an initial bond.
They soon began collaboration on a school newspaper, *La Penna dei
ragazzi*, the first issue of which appeared in January 1930. The undertaking was at first of very modest proportions—they printed only fifty
copies of the first four-page issue—but by 1933 some twenty-five hundred copies of a twenty-page version were being printed. The tone of the
paper could hardly be called anti-Fascist, but the youthful enthusiasm of
the editors sometimes got them into hot water with the authorities—in

this case, Mussolini himself. In October 1932 Zangrandi published an article extolling the virtues of pagan Rome, an unwelcome effusion given the recently quieted conflict between church and state. The Duce personally called Zangrandi to his office and gave him a copy of the article annotated by Pius XI. The point was made, and for a short time at least Zangrandi toed the official line.[50]

In 1934–35 the two continued their collaboration and published *Anno XII* and *Anno XIII*, a name suggested by the Duce himself. The editorial and circulation offices of the new review were located in the official residence at Villa Torlonia, and Vittorio Mussolini was listed on the masthead as "founder and director." Nonetheless, or perhaps precisely because of the tacit protection that relationship implied, the papers were characterized by an outspoken and nonconformist tone. Such future anti-Fascist activists as Paolo Alatri and Bruno Zevi appeared frequently as contributors, a fact that has led to speculation that official tolerance of the papers was a ruse to flush out potential dissenters.[51]

Zangrandi's friendship with Vittorio provided him with some professional perquisites and a rare opportunity to observe the Fascist holy family in private moments—not always an edifying experience. He began writing short articles for the *Popolo d'Italia* in the fall of 1933, at the age of eighteen, and over the next few months had over twenty published on the paper's semiofficial editorial page. But Zangrandi's meetings with the Duce were a source of deep disillusionment. Mussolini's informal visits with the young men working at the Villa Torlonia soon convinced Zangrandi that the Duce "was not normal." He spoke to the few young men present, remembered Zangrandi, as if he were a Shakespearean actor addressing an audience. He always wanted to win at games, though he was a bad player. He was cynical and totally lacking in humor. And everyone, his children included, addressed him at home as "president." One day, walking in the Villa Borghese gardens, Vittorio told Zangrandi: "It's useless. Fascism is all a bluff. Papa has not been able to do any of the things he wanted; the Italians are Fascists out of cowardice and they don't give a damn about the revolution."[52] For Zangrandi, however, the suspicion was maturing that it was Mussolini himself who didn't "give a damn about the revolution."

In March 1933 Vittorio and Zangrandi organized what they called the Movimento Novista Italiano. The Novist manifesto appeared in May 1933. The real doctrinal bent of the movement, if any, was never very clear. Zangrandi claimed later that it was a vehicle for activist youth to give vent to their "anxiety for renewal . . . their need to discuss . . . their desire for action." Novism, claimed the manifesto, "rejects dogmas, schemes, prejudices of any sort . . . it puts man before the citizen, humanity before Italy. . . . Novism fights for moral and intel-

lectual freedom for all, against revealed religions . . . injustices, hy-
pocrisies."[53]

201

Formation
of the
Fascist
Ruling
Class

Novism was not a conscious movement of opposition but rather a
spontaneous impulse toward independence and nonconformity. The
Novists criticized the sterility of official culture and the cancers of
careerism, servility, opportunism, and profiteering that they claimed
were sapping the vitality of the revolution. The movement soon gained
adherents and spread to other cities, assuming clandestine airs that
brought it to the attention of the police. Evaluations of the Novists by the
eyes and ears of the regime varied. One concerned agent reported in June
1933 that they "pass themselves off as Fascists, but they are not." A
report filed in October 1933 dismissed the Novist leaders as "young men
of Fascist sentiments but of a restless temperament who want to do
something new." Whatever the judgment, it is clear that the activities of
this group—and of others at the Liceo Tasso, which was thought to be a
hotbed of youthful activism—were closely watched by the police.[54]

The regime was willing to tolerate a certain degree of youthful exuber-
ance, but it was also ready to nip such activism in the bud if it threatened
to get out of hand. In October 1933 Zangrandi was called to order by
Arturo Marpicati, then vice-secretary of the PNF and one of the targets
of the Novists. Marpicati was especially interested in ascertaining if the
movement was being encouraged by any members of the Fascist hierarchy (his main suspect was probably Bottai), or if the Novisti had read
any Russian books! During Marpicati's questioning, Zangrandi remembered, he had to ask himself for the first time the fundamental question:
What is my relationship to fascism?[55] In December 1933 the Novist
movement was dissolved, but the basic question—"to be or not to be
Fascists," as Zangrandi expressed it—remained unanswered. The long
voyage through fascism began for many with the attempt to find an
acceptable response.

The shared Novist experience had woven a network of like-minded
young men, and this nucleus formed the shifting and ever-changing
group of activists that came to be known as the Gruppo Zangrandi. By
1935 the group had adopted the tactic of the *doppio binario*, the "double
track." Zangrandi described this as the trick of the Trojan horse: to work
within the Fascist groups and at the same time to engage in clandestine
activities against the regime. It was, he later admitted, an ambiguous
position and one that lost his group many of its best supporters in the late
thirties. But the Zangrandi group, by then spread all over Italy and
equipped with a press office and a fairly sophisticated underground
network, persisted on this double track until the repressive face of the
dictatorship could no longer be ignored. In March 1939 the group was
dissolved, to be replaced in December 1939 with the clearly anti-

Fascist Socialist Revolutionary party, the Partito Socialista Rivoluzionario (PSR). By 1942 the new party had forty cells in Italy, most of them under constant police surveillance. The PSR leaders, Zangrandi included, were arrested beginning in June 1942. In October 1943 Zangrandi was deported to a Berlin prison, where he remained until the end of the war.[56] His reminiscences must of course be read with the same caution as is required by any other personal testimony from the period. But it does seem clear that many of the active members of the youth resistance, including many who eventually participated in the clandestine activities of the Partito Comunista Italiano (PCI), were influenced by the Zangrandi group—sometimes as a reaction to what they considered the group's dangerous *doppio binario* tactic.

The Littoriali

The most controversial activity organized by the GUF was the annual competitions known as the Littoriali. The GUF sponsored three types of events: in sports, in culture and art, and in professional and technical fields for nonstudents. The Littoriali were intended both as a means of selecting future leaders for the regime—in the case of the art and culture competitions—and as a showcase for the accomplishments of youth under fascism.

The first organized competitions for university students, the Littoriali dello sport, were held in Bologna in 1932. In annual meetings thereafter the number of participants grew regularly. Successful competitors were heavily subsidized by the state to attend later meets and international university competitions, and there were frequent rumors that the academic credentials of some were falsified to allow them to compete.[57]

Although the Littoriali dello sport were usually free from the sort of unorthodox behavior that often characterized the cultural and artistic events, there were occasional outbursts against some of the less popular PNF leaders. During the 1934 meeting, for example, the assembled contestants sang disrespectful ditties at the expense of Starace, who was seated in the reviewing stand. As a result of this indiscretion, five Gufini were suspended and the party secretary—always the favorite target of university high jinks—stormed out of the ceremonies.[58]

The Littoriali del lavoro were first held in 1936. Male and female contestants competed in four areas: agriculture, commerce, industry, and artisanry. In addition to these technical fields, all competitors also had to prepare a written theme on fascism, a task for which they had been prepared during the year by GUF members who taught provincial courses on Fascist doctrine. In theory these meets were supposed to bring the classes closer together, but in practice social lines were still drawn; as nonstudents these young men and women were not allowed to take part in the Littoriali of culture and art, for example. Young men competed in a variety of fields, but the great majority of the sessions for young women were designed to demonstrate *lavori femminili*: they competed in darning, spot removal, ironing, preparation of an autarkic dinner, and embroidery, among other fields.[59]

203

Formation
of the
Fascist
Ruling
Class

The most prestigious of these annual competitions were the Littoriali della cultura e dell'arte, involving written themes, artistic presentations, and oral debates in a wide variety of fields. Suggested originally by Bottai or by Alessandro Pavolini (depending on the source), these meetings were held every spring from 1934 until 1940. Females participated only after 1939, but their competitions continued even during the war, when the government suspended those for males.[60]

Two elimination rounds preceded the national meets each year: the *agonali*, held in nonuniversity cities, and the pre-Littoriali, held in the university GUF chapters. Two winners in all fields from the pre-Littoriali were then allowed to compete at the national level. Themes for discussion were published months in advance to give the contestants sufficient time to prepare their entries, though school authorities often complained that such preparation cut into study time. The first-place winner in each field won the title of *littore*.[61]

Students competed in only six fields at the Florence Littoriali of 1934, but by 1940 there were over twenty events, ranging from literary and art criticism, theater, film, and journalism to foreign policy, Fascist doctrine, racism, and scientific and technical panels. The selection of judges in the early years gave the meetings an air of intellectual legitimacy; in 1934, for example, the panels included Enrico Fermi, Edmondo Rossoni, Ugo Spirito, Giuseppe Ungaretti, F. T. Marinetti, and Luigi Volpicelli. As time went on, however, the judges were chosen more for political merits than for any professional expertise.

No minutes or detailed records of the written or oral presentations exist, but the subjects proposed for the various competitions illustrate the general tone the authorities wanted to encourage. For the oral debates held in Venice in 1936 students wrote themes on topics such as "The importance of the Mediterranean in the life of Europe and Italian politics," "The function of the theater in Fascist propaganda," and "The party as military force." In 1940 oral presentations from fifteen fields included "Race in the formation of Fascist conscience," "Film and propaganda," "The last two centuries in the light of fascism," and "Roman and Fascist colonization."[62]

The Littoriali were the working out of the regime's policy of *largo ai giovani*, with consequences that are still debated. There is abundant testimony to indicate that many of the participants saw them as a breeding ground of antifascism. One participant termed them a kind of "moral suicide" for the regime, an opportunity for many young people to form political and social ties that would bring them ultimately to armed resistance.[63] Antonello Trombadori—postwar art critic and senator, member of the PCI after 1941, activist in the GAP (Gruppi d'Azione Popolare)—was a prizewinner at the Littoriali who defended participation by anti-Fascists. "All the most active anti-Fascist militants working then among the student youth," he said, "had something to do with [the Littoriali] . . . where a feverish and organized anti-Fascist activity was being carried out."[64] Pietro Ingrao, a prizewinner in the poetry competition in 1934 and a postwar president of the Chamber of Deputies from the PCI, argued that despite the regime's attempt to use them for propaganda purposes, the Littoriali served to establish an important network among anti-Fascist youth and to nourish ongoing debates outside the conference halls that "took off from corporativism and literary questions to arrive at De Sanctis, Croce, and Marx."[65] Palmiro Togliatti recognized the possibilities for infiltration the Littoriali presented; in his view, they allowed the students to go beyond the limits allowed by the regime "to a corrosive criticism of the ideological edifice of fascism." In his history of antifascism, Paolo Alatri claimed that the Littoriali constituted a "singular chapter in the history of antifascism." Edward Tannenbaum maintained that the oral debates at the Littoriali were the "freest forum in Fascist Italy" and that the experience "stimulated among some students a degree of non-conformity bordering on anti-Fascism."[66]

If all these claims are justified, then why did the regime allow and even encourage the Littoriali? The meetings were a kind of two-edged sword: to allow the students a forum for their dissent within the Fascist framework, the regime had to accept the risk of criticism, occasional heterodoxy, and even the possibility of open rebellion. For these young people at a traditionally questioning age, the regime adopted a safety valve, an organized and controlled arena for letting off steam that could create the illusion of real participation and prevent youthful dissent from developing into open political struggle and defection. Ugoberto Alfassio Grimaldi, a participant at the Littoriali and later Partito Socialista Italiano (PSI) leader, referred to the meetings as "antifascism in black shirt." "The Littoriali," he said, "were the occasion for the first spontaneous formation of a critical conscience and of opposition. Ingenuous, to be sure, . . . but not useless: fascism, in the crucial moment of its existence, had with it very few of those *littori* whom it had coddled."[67]

It is difficult in the absence of detailed records to make any definite statements about the degree of antifascism present in the debates or to estimate the exact proportion of young people whom the yearly contests mobilized solidly behind or against the regime. It is clear that the meetings drew students with widely varying political views and that the incidence of anti-Fascist activity increased sharply in the later years, peaking with the meetings of 1937 and 1938 in Naples and Palermo. After these experiences the authorities exercised a tighter control over the contests, and many of the more militant elements dropped out and turned to clandestine activities.

For at least the first two years, at the meetings in Florence in 1934 and in Rome in 1935, the discussions at the Littoriali did not stray far from the orthodox line. Several young men later active in the anti-Fascist movement did compete in these meetings, however. In the Florentine contests Aldo Moro won prizes in both written and oral debates, and Pietro Ingrao won second place in the poetry competition. Intolerance of the regime's more unsubtle propaganda efforts did occasionally, however, spill over into open derision. A sentimental film directed by Alessandro Blasetti and written by Pavolini, entitled *18BL*—the stirring story of a truck that saw action on the Piave, during the March on Rome, and in the Pontine marches—was whistled down by assembled students in Florence.[68]

With the meetings in Venice in 1936 the tone began to change, at least in part because of the students' increasing disgust with the pettifogging pomposity of Starace, who had always been the butt of their jokes. (The party secretary, according to a story then current in student circles, went to bed with his medals pinned to his pajamas.) Both Starace and Minister of National Education De Vecchi, also thought to be a man of incurable ignorance by many of the university students, were roundly booed by the assembled throng on the opening day of the meetings. The PNF secretary was even treated to a bit of roughhousing (the students pretended to be carrying him on their shoulders in triumph) that wounded his pride and wrinkled his starched uniform.[69]

What Zangrandi referred to as the "critical biennium" began with the meetings in Naples in 1937. At these meetings, and at those held in Palermo the following year, the tone was no longer one of cautious revisionism but often one of open criticism. All shades of opinion were still represented, but an increasing number of students had come to use the Littoriali as a forum for anti-Fascist propaganda and proselytizing. The Communists were especially active because the leadership in exile had by then sanctioned participation in the Fascist mass organizations.[70]

The Zangrandi group was represented en masse at the Naples contests, but the real conspiratorial work was done by future Communists such as Mario Alicata and Bruno Zevi. At the Naples and Palermo meetings they began to make broad contacts with other anti-Fascists, especially with such young Communists as Antonio Amendola, *littore* of literary criticism in 1935. During this same time Alicata and Zevi, like many others, began to turn away from the tactics of the Zangrandi group and toward more active opposition.[71]

The most interesting meetings were those held in Palermo in 1938, which threatened on more than one occasion to degenerate into active rebellion. Troubles had been brewing even before the national contests. During the pre-Littoriali in Rome, debates on foreign policy had become a platform for anti-Nazi statements, and when Virginio Gayda—then director of the *Giornale d'Italia*—came to speak on the *Anschluss*, he was loudly whistled down.[72] The national meetings, to which the Hitler Youth had sent official delegates, were characterized, remembered one participant, by an "anti-German, antiracist, and generally anticonformist ferment."[73]

One of the most turbulent sessions was the panel on art, where the polemics became so heated that the judges intervened at one point threatening the participants and accusing the most outspoken of antifascism. The meeting, which Zevi called a "real revolt," was brought to order by GUF Secretary Fernando Mezzasoma, who attempted to pour oil on troubled waters by asking a rhetorical question: "The premise that we must accept is that we are all Fascists here, is that not true?" At that point, one-third of the contestants silently left the meeting hall.[74]

Other sessions at Palermo also worried the authorities. The radio competition evolved into an antiracist demonstration that once again brought Mezzasoma to the rostrum. One young contestant read a long quotation from Joseph Stalin, though he attributed the piece to Mussolini. A competitor from Ferrara, who called during his oral presentation for the boycott of all Jewish authors, was shouted down and prevented from finishing his speech.[75] Eugenio Curiel, then working clandestinely for the PCI, reported that during the foreign policy panel the participants overwhelmingly favored the development of the Four Power Pact, the principle of friendship and cooperation among all Latin peoples, and pacifism—surely not popular themes among many in the PNF leadership in the spring of 1938.[76]

The contests held in Trieste in 1939 and Bologna in 1940 were generally quieter than earlier meetings. The change was due largely to the intervention of Starace, who, less indulgent toward youthful displays of "spirit" than many other party hierarchs and probably eager to salvage his own dignity, ordered local PNF authorities to control the selections made during the pre-Littoriali to ensure that only elements of secure political faith were sent on to the national competitions. There were some isolated examples of opposition—the contestants arguing for cultural autarky during the Trieste meetings were booed out of the hall, and Giaime Pintor refused publicly to discuss the theme chosen by Marinetti, "The figure of Mussolini as object of poetry"—but the general tone was reasonably well in line with the regime's desire to make the meetings a propaganda showcase.[77]

An appraisal of the importance of the Littoriali is difficult because most of the testimony on the subject comes from leftists who used the meetings for their own ends. Young loyalists were present at these contests, but they have not often been forthcoming with personal testimony. One who did write on the experience was Nino Tripodi, who competed at the Littoriali and was elected as a deputy of the neo-Fascist MSI in the postwar period. Tripodi denied that the Littoriali were a kind of "anti-Fascist congress," as *L'Unità* expressed it.[78] Obviously, not all of the nonconformity and rowdiness of the meetings can be attributed to conscious antifascism; some of the disruptions may have had more to do with normal generational conflict, with youthful opposition to the world view of their fathers, than with strict ideological divergence. Some anti-Fascists refused to attend the meetings at all. The *liberalsocialista* Aldo Capitini, for example, would not take part in the debates for fear that his participation would "generate in the very young . . . the illusion that freedom of speech existed in Fascist Italy."[79] Certainly Mussolini himself was not pleased with some of the developments at these meetings. In an interview with Bottai after one especially disturbing session, he expressed his anger and vowed to punish those "who stand with one foot in the party and the other out." "No, Duce," Bottai is said to have responded, "they want to stand in the party with both feet, but also with their heads."[80]

The fact remains that many of the young men later active in the resistance made their early political contacts at the Littoriali. These activists were in the minority, but for many others participation provided a network of contacts and planted the seeds of doubt that matured later. Giuseppe Melis Bassu, who competed at the 1940 meetings, remembered that, coming as he did from the provincial town of Sassari, the "contacts that I made in those days . . . opened my eyes to many things." The Littoriali were important in the story of the "generation of the lictor" because they represented for many the first step "toward open criticism of the regime."[81] They were, as another remembered, "centers of connection and gathering." From 1935 on "fascism was losing its influence on the young. For them, 1935–37 were years of clarification. Many had already begun to use the facade to hide their clandestine activity."[82]

The GUF Press

Together with the Littoriali, the GUF newspapers were the most evident indicator of the special status of the university students under fascism. The motto *largo ai giovani* carried over in the regime's dealings with the young journalists writing for these papers; they enjoyed a kind of conditional toleration that assumed their good faith until clear evidence of heterodoxy surfaced. Virtually any topic could be discussed if the author used certain obligatory formulas. Debates about Italian society were

207

Formation
of the
Fascist
Ruling
Class

permissible, for example, as long as they had as their goal the fulfillment of the "revolutionary" promises of the movement. Overt criticism of the Duce was outside the acceptable bounds, but the actions of the government could be criticized by saying that the will of the leader had been misinterpreted by corrupt or incompetent underlings—a formula that Mussolini seems to have accepted, perhaps because he hoped that it would keep the more ambitious hierarchs on their toes.

Harsh measures were taken, however, against repeated offenders and against those whose diatribes were blatantly heterodox. Punishments ranged from oral reprimands and suspension to expulsion from the party organizations and (in wartime) to orders to the front lines. The authorities did keep a close watch on the activities of the Gufini. Two copies of all GUF papers had to be sent to the Press Office of the national organization, and copies of all articles written by GUF members had to be forwarded to the PNF national headquarters.[83] Many party leaders recognized that the contributors to these papers sometimes stepped out of bounds, but only a few were willing to admit the causes of this youthful unrest. In June 1941 Ciano admitted that the "regime has also made a mistake; for twenty years it has neglected these young men, and has had them in mind only to deck them out in uniforms, hats, and capes, and herd them against their will into the squares to make a lot of noise."[84]

Only the GUF university chapters published their own papers, but the provincial groups were usually allowed a weekly or biweekly page in local papers. These were predictably conformist in tone: accounts of the activities and ceremonies of the local groups and celebrations of the mythology and martyrology of the regime.[85] The tenor and quality of these party-subsidized pages varied greatly, depending not only on the political proclivities of the editorial staff but also on the intelligence and disposition of the local PNF leaders and on the character of the reigning PNF secretary.

The GUF papers dealt with a wide range of topics, but certain themes recurred frequently. The first was a moral one: the desire to carry through the spiritual renewal of the nation. The pages of many of these GUF papers were filled with forthright denunciations of the corruption and the *dolce vita* of some of the luxury-loving hierarchs. There were repeated criticisms of the sterility of party rhetoric, diatribes against the *arrivisti*, against the loss of revolutionary purity and the aridity of official culture. In the beginning, even World War II was portrayed by some as an opportunity to return to the pure origins of the movement through a cleansing blood purge, a trial by fire that would sweep away the old bourgeois society protected even under the Fascist regime.[86]

A second theme was preoccupation with the failure of Fascist corporativism to produce social justice. Evident in the most outspoken of these

GUF papers was a social conscience, an awareness, however embryonic, of the human reality of the economic system and the situation of the Italian working classes. In *Lo Stato operaio* in 1936 Celeste Negarville wrote, "These are students who are shouting their enthusiasm for the demagogic 'go to the people' which for them . . . is not demagoguery."[87]

What began in many as a general sense of dissatisfaction resulted in overall condemnation of the system by some. The nonconformist, and eventually anti-Fascist, young men who wrote for these papers represented various shades of political opinion; many who would later be active in liberal socialist groups and in the Communist underground movement got their first journalistic and political experience while working on the GUF papers.

In general, the papers were characterized by a kind of journalistic split personality. The political front pages were usually distinguished by the numbing conformity that afflicted other Fascist newspapers, but the cultural and artistic criticism showed a vivacity and curiosity lacking in most other publications. The regime's censors closely monitored the political articles and, having spied the ritual obeisances to the Duce and his regime, very often did not delve deeply into the material on the back pages. Often the most nonconformist of the GUF papers contained on their front pages the same prolix tirades and the same granite-jawed Duce as all the other newspapers. A closer look at some of the articles inside, however, sometimes reveals a very different outlook.

The earliest GUF papers were propagandistic and controlled by extremist elements who used them as weapons against the regime's enemies. *La Rivolta ideale* began publication in early 1925. Designed to serve as the tool of the *squadristi* at the University of Rome, the paper was distinguished more by its violent and vulgar language than by its high journalistic quality. Close behind in political orientation were *Libro e moschetto* and *Roma fascista*. *Libro e moschetto* began in 1927 as the paper of the Milanese GUF, but in 1937 it became the official journal of the PNF youth organizations and Starace took over as director.[88] The paper continued to be among the purest of the pure even after Starace's departure and was in the forefront of the campaign for intervention. After the declaration of war, thousands of copies of *Libro e moschetto* were regularly sent to the frontline troops. In June 1940 the word *libro* was ceremoniously canceled from its title and it became the *foglio di trincea*—the "paper of the GUF in arms." *Roma fascista* was one of the most hard-line of all the youth papers. First published in July 1924, during the Matteotti crisis, the paper never quite outgrew its squadrist origins. One contemporary critic referred to it as "the most orthodox and the most idiotic" of all the GUF papers.[89]

Among the most original of the GUF papers was *Vent'anni*, founded by Guido Pallotta in Turin in 1932. Pallotta had taken part in the Fiume expedition and had then served as secretary of the Turin GUF and vice-secretary of the national organization. An articulate spokesman for the *mistici*, he claimed that for the young fascism should be "disdain of every material good: idealism . . . an idea for which every university Fascist would give his life, just as one throws flowers at the feet of a beloved."[90] Pallotta became something of a hero to many other young journalists, and his articles were frequently carried in other GUF papers. His death at Sidi-el-Barrani in December 1941 gained him a place in the Fascist pantheon, but the paper that he had left behind in June 1940 became steadily more official after his departure. Pallotta was an outspoken critic of profiteering and careerism among the PNF leaders, vices he satirized in broad terms. Despite a return to strict orthodoxy on most issues, *Vent' anni* continued this tradition after Pallotta left for the war. An article published in February 1941, for example, defined the "gentleman dressed up as a Fascist" as the man "who thinks that the heroic climate is the after lunch nap . . . who feels proud of being born in this epoch (but with the advantage that he is too old for service) . . . who thinks that the Via dell'Impero was built to allow him to pass the evenings in his car with his secretary."[91]

Racist and anti-English propaganda became a staple of *Vent' anni* during the war. Cartoons showed France being caressed by leering black soldiers; other articles repeated the accusations of a Judaic-masonic front running the Allied governments. The British monarch was referred to as "King Isaac George," and Roosevelt as "Shylock Delano." Two headlines from 1940–41 were typical of the paper's anti-English tone: "The English Are the Refuse of All Races" and "Prostitution and Lying: The Fundamental Virtues of the English Race."[92]

Il Campano, the paper of the Pisan GUF, echoed many of the themes found in *Vent' anni*. Founded in 1926, *Il Campano* was the frequent target of attacks from the harder-line papers, such as *Battaglie fasciste* of Perugia. Denunciations of party leaders often appeared in the pages of *Il Campano*: condemnations of the mania for bureaucratic paper shuffling, the use of titles and phony honors, the exaggerated affection for medals, and the love of high-flown rhetoric that "is the enemy of greatness and sincerity."[93]

Il Barco, the monthly paper of the Genoa GUF, began publication in September 1941. Despite its late date, however, the paper managed to avoid being swallowed up by the war hysteria and the rush to conformity that characterized some of the other papers. *Il Barco* never used the quasi-obligatory Roman numerals in its dates, for example, and unlike many other papers it included more purely cultural articles as the war dragged on. Entire issues were devoted during 1941–42 to dance and theater.[94] The myth of the great revolutionary war was much in evidence. The war would be the means to purge the regime, and after it the young "will begin another war, the second Revolution against the enemies of fascism, against the centralizers, the plurality of offices, against the capitalists." Only the young could accomplish such a moral regeneration: "We need new men and we need them fast. We need a moral reclamation. The generation that now commands is in decline."[95]

211

———

Formation
of the
Fascist
Ruling
Class

L'Intervento, the GUF paper in Sassari, presents an interesting case study of local and provincial developments. The paper was first published in August 1940, though the "Pagina del GUF" of the newspaper *L'Isola* had been in existence since early 1939. After the summer of 1941, the editorial staff included Giuseppe Melis Bassu and Antonio Pigliaru, whose conflicts with local and national party authorities often got them into hot water and eventually led to their removal. In the fall of 1942 they were called to arms, and the paper returned to a "rigidly conformist track." Melis Bassu recalled thirty years after the events that censorship came by way of a "pencil that drew a cross through what was not pleasing to the local hierarchs." But he also maintained that while the political articles were "severely controlled," because of the "crass ignorance of our superiors and controllers, the cultural pages had a much greater liberty."[96]

The best representatives of the GUF *giornali di fronda* are *Architrave*, published by the Bologna group, and *Il Bò*, the organ of the Padua GUF.

The same fertile region of Emilia that produced the colorful dissident *ras* Leandro Arpinati also produced a unique GUF paper, *Architrave*, first published on 1 December 1940. The history of *Architrave* is a rather convoluted one, because the paper went through several changes of the guard as a result of official displeasure at its increasingly heterodox tone. First published as Italian troops were bogged down in Albania during their attack on Greece, the paper had war as one of its major themes. But in its pages there was little of the overblown heroism of the harder-line papers and much that reflected the clash of generations.[97] The contributors to *Architrave* saw war as something of a rite of passage for the younger generation, which, in their view, had always been shunted aside by the older leaders in power. War was, in a sense, their opportunity to win their spurs. Renzo Renzi, cinema critic for the paper and later activist in the rank of the *liberalsocialisti*, put it this way: "It seemed to me . . . that decorations brought with them a greater freedom. . . . Who, in a militarist regime, touches the man who has participated in many battles?"[98]

The Gufini at *Architrave* were eager to proclaim their right to take the place of the older generation, to begin a Fascist reformation. Their goal, said one editorial, was "to bring the revolution into the moral arena, to create the conditions under which man can keep himself whole. . . . We must above all fight the man who is out only for his own interests, the old man lying down in the shadow of an immoral system."[99]

The editors at *Architrave* frequently made use of Marxist terminology forbidden for years. Roberto Mazzetti, a teacher known for his views on leftist corporativism who directed the paper for the first six months, was familiar with the Marxist writers and set the tone for his younger charges. Agostino Bignardi, at the time *Architrave*'s chief editor and later national secretary of the Italian Liberal party, called for the creation of a new society based on work "by suffocating every form of pseudo-corporative super-capitalism and bringing a full valuation of the purity of collective life."[100] Gianni Guizzardi, then a director of the Scuola di Mistica Fascista, echoed the same theme: "Justice among men and among peoples is what the mass demands and what we young men demand. . . . Those who survive, those whose bones will be brought home from Libya, from Albania or elsewhere, will . . . not want to have spilled their blood in vain."[101]

The most unusual sections of *Architrave* were those devoted to literary, cinema, and art criticism. The literary columns often contained articles from young authors of such dubious political pedigree as Alfonso Gatto and Pier Paolo Pasolini. As cinema critic, Renzi most often limited his comments to films that were anything but orthodox, sometimes for general contrariness: "Generally I spoke badly of Italian films, sometimes because they had ordered us to speak of them in glowing terms . . . in part so as to balance the exaggerations of the official rhetoric."[102]

The real trouble for the young editors of *Architrave* came with the sixth issue, dated April 1941. The journalistic straw that broke the camel's back was an attack on corruption in the party by Eugenio Facchini. Summoned to Rome by Mezzasoma and unable to produce any concrete evidence of that corruption, Facchini was ordered to the Russian front.[103]

The interim editorial staff followed a fairly hard party line, but in the spring of 1942 the group was reconstituted. The new editorial board, headed by Pio Marsilli and Vittorio Chesi, was quite openly anti-Fascist. They published only four issues, three of which were sequestered by the authorities. Chesi rejected the possibility of a reform from within and gathered around him "elements decisively hostile to fascism." New editorial policy forbade the use of Mussolini's picture on the front page of the paper, and the staff refused to use any of the party's familiar catchwords.

If the paper was by this time causing consternation among the local PNF leaders, it had become very popular among the youth in Bologna. Early circulation was about two thousand copies, but by June 1942 twelve thousand were being distributed. The issue for July 1942 was sequestered, but only after seventeen thousand copies had been sold. The issue of September 1942 was also taken off the stand by the authorities, and this time the GUF officials replaced the entire editorial staff.[104]

Marsilli and Chesi were taken to Rome after refusing to give any assurances of a new editorial posture, and there they were interrogated by Mezzasoma and Carlo Ravasio from the PNF press office. During this interrogation Chesi realized that the orders for action against *Architrave* had come from the Duce himself: scrawled across the front page of the September 1942 issue, in Mussolini's unmistakable hand, was the query: "Who is this imbecile?" The two were bound over for trial and condemned to three years of *confino*. By this late date, however, the regime's leaders could not help but realize the depth of feeling among the young: to avoid outbursts of violence among the students in Bologna, the sentence was never carried out.[105]

The tone of the last issues of *Architrave* was resigned and bitter. Massimo Rendina, one of the new editors, wrote in the issue for January 1943: "Already the rhetorical illusion of an easy victory and of a lightning war has sunk into the abyss of the past."[106]

The young contributors to *Architrave* took different roads after the fall of the regime. Its founder, Umberto Righi, died in a Nazi concentration camp. Several regular collaborators were shot by the Fascists, and many of the editorial staff—among them Chesi, Rendina, Marsilli, and the future PCI senator Paolo Fortunati—fought in the Resistance. Renzo Renzi and Nino Gardini, one of the editors in the later period, ended the war in a concentration camp. A few went over to the other side and collaborated in Mussolini's Italian Social Republic at Salò. Perhaps the most surprising case was that of Eugenio Facchini, whose constant antiregime diatribes had put him in the front lines in Russia. Facchini became the Fascist provincial secretary of Bologna, where he was later assassinated by partisans.[107]

The most interesting of all the university Fascist newspapers was Padua's *Il Bò*. Members of the Zangrandi group, the *liberalsocialisti*, and the Communists all controlled this paper at some time, and it produced in Eugenio Curiel one of the most fascinating young men of the Fascist period.

Il Bò was first published on 8 February 1935, and it continued to appear biweekly until 1940. Its first editor was the *federale* of Padua, Agostino Podesta, but in 1936 Esule Sella came to the editorial offices. Sella, who had collaborated with Zangrandi on the two youth journals *Anno XII* and *Anno XIII*, had a well-developed underground organization and managed to make use of his contacts to fill the paper with a stream of nonconformist articles from all over Italy. By 1936 *Il Bò* had a wider national echo than any other GUF paper.[108]

The real problems began with the publication of an article by Sella in the issue dated 1 October 1937. The article, dealing with the juridical position and powers of the PNF secretary, was received with something less than equanimity by Starace, who angrily telephoned Mezzasoma demanding Sella's ouster.[109] The next issue of the paper commemorated Sella's passing with a black mourning band around the editorial box. Zangrandi's group continued to contribute articles for some time, but gradually the leading roles were taken by Eugenio Curiel and Ettore Luccini, both of them working for the PCI.

Curiel represented many of his generation who, in the words of his biographer, took "the long voyage from fascism to opposition and struggle."[110] Born in Trieste in 1912, Curiel took his degree in mathematics and physics at Padua with high honors and began teaching there in 1933. The Ethiopian war convinced him of the need to take action against the regime, and his leanings toward Marxism were encouraged by his roommate, Atto Braun, with whom he established a Communist cell in Padua. They made contact with the PCI in Paris through a friend of Curiel's studying at the Sorbonne, and Curiel personally visited party leaders in the French capital in April 1937. He returned to Padua—rebaptized with the *nom de guerre* Giorgio Intelvi—with instructions to begin "legal activity" within the Fascist mass organizations. Curiel and his comrades in the Padua cell—Renato Mieli, Guido Goldschmied, Braun, and later Ettore Luccini—soon became active in the editorial offices at *Il Bò*. Their activities also included some patently illegal endeavors: collection of funds for republican Spain; diffusion of propaganda tracts, copies of *L'Unità*, and Marxist texts; and contacts with Catholics and other anti-Fascists designed to establish a united front against the regime.[111]

Given the lack of literature at his disposal, Curiel did not know many of the writings of Marx and Engels or Gramsci. But he did clearly identify with the working class in Italy, and he was convinced that Marxism should be a "critique of reality": a combination of theoretical research and practical political activity that together would realize the ideal. He was familiar with the best thinkers of the European tradition and was eager to apply Italian Marxism in a wider Italian and European cultural perspective. For Curiel the Resistance would be the fulfillment of the promise of the Risorgimento. Between the two there existed a continuity of ideas and ideals: both stressed freedom, independence, and unity. But the Resistance, unlike the Risorgimento, would be a truly national and mass movement, tied inextricably to the life of the Italian people.[112]

Curiel began to contribute articles to *Il Bò* on 1 August 1937 and soon took over management of the important corporative/syndical page. The last of his fifty-four articles appeared on 20 August 1938, when the anti-

Semitic legislation cut short his university career.[113] Curiel wrote on a
wide variety of subjects, including discussions of foreign policy and of
labor and economic topics that, as Paolo Spriano remarked, were "trans-
parently polemical." One of his articles, "Cina e Giappone," published
in August 1937, elicited an official protest from the Japanese embassy in
Rome—and a thank-you note from the Chinese ambassador.[114]
The bulk of his articles dealt with the problems and future of the
syndical movement in Italy. For Curiel the workers were the base of the
corporate state, and the syndicates the fundamental instruments of true
social reform in Italy. His articles aimed at politicizing the activities of
the working class and at establishing worker control of the factories.
Curiel called for salary increases, denounced inferior working conditions, and encouraged political struggle to better those conditions. He
hoped to diffuse a new understanding of the problems of the working
class in the university students and succeeded in organizing committees
of students who volunteered to go into the factories and meet with the
workers. Curiel's plan was to use Fascist organizations themselves for
the political education of the workers, but the meetings were not very
productive because the workers were suspicious of the young students,
whom they saw as agents of the owners—a suspicion not allayed by the
fact that the Gufini had to come into the factories wearing their PNF
uniforms.[115]
Curiel participated in this *lavoro legale* until the racial laws forced
him to leave the university. Afterward he lived in Milan and continued to
make contacts with various non-Communist, anti-Fascist groups. He
was arrested in June 1939 and sentenced in January 1940 to five years'
confino on the island of Ventotene. There he spent three years and eight
months, dedicating his time to reflection, study, and conversation with
the other political internees. After the fall of the regime, the Badoglio
government liberated those confined, and Curiel left the island in August 1943. The rest of his short life was taken up with feverish political
activity. He served during this period as one of the editors of the party's
clandestine papers, *L'Unità* and *La nostra lotta*. In November 1943 he
founded the Fronte della Gioventù, which he envisioned as a unitary
anti-Fascist group that would transcend purely party interests and be a
genuinely democratic and national movement of youth against fascism.
The first directing committee of the Fronte was indeed composed of
representatives of various non-Communist parties, though many never
lost their suspicion that the group was intended to further the political
interests of the PCI, which sent a large group of delegates.[116]
On 24 February 1945, as he was walking to an appointment with some
of his colleagues in Milan, Curiel was murdered by Fascist gunmen. He
was awarded the medal of valor posthumously in 1946.[117]
Curiel was a symbol, then, of the process of awakening among the

young born to fascism—a process evoked in striking terms by Giuseppe Melis Bassu: "At a given moment it is inevitable that in every man there awakens . . . autonomy of judgment, the right to doubt, skepticism about revealed and pre-fabricated truths, intolerance of everything that smells like rhetoric. . . . The official fascism of the time never came to understand just what vipers it was nursing in its bosom."[118]

CHAPTER EIGHT

"The Long Voyage"

The deepest, the only theme of human history, compared to which all others are of subordinate importance, is the conflict of skepticism with faith.

—Goethe

Much of the discussion about the success or failure of Fascist socialization and indoctrination revolves around the questions of consensus and dissent. Neither term is easily defined. "Consent" can mean very different things, depending on the personality traits and on the social and cultural circumstances of the individuals involved. Given the monopoly of the instruments of social control and coercion in the hands of the Fascist state, the silence of many cannot always be taken as consent. The absence of vehicles to make opposition known, the distrust among many Italians of any kind of political involvement, and the repression of dissent by the regime must be taken into account when analyzing apparent conformity. In Italy the squadrist violence of the early days was soon replaced by what Giorgio Amendola called a "rational form of repression."[1] The threat of trial by the Special Tribunal was always present, but for most Italians the ultimate sanction was not fear of death but loss of income. This concern about the future reinforced the general tendency toward at least outward conformity and passive acceptance. "Dissent," too, is a slippery term, applicable to a whole complex of reactions ranging from active clandestine opposition to a silent determination to preserve one's conscience from infection by Fascist ideas. Dissent often arose first as a moral or cultural reaction, only later developing into full-fledged political resistance. It could also mean skepticism: not "believing in the parades, seeking to get out of them," as Amendola said, "but not yet maturation of an anti-Fascist position."[2] The young were often accused of just such skepticism.

By the 1930s the *problema dei giovani* had become an issue in the press. In the pages of *Critica fascista* and other journals, commentators noted a kind of cosmic *me ne freghismo* among many of the young, whose participation in the regime's youth groups and other activities they described as superficial and opportunistic. Perhaps these observers took the regime's rhetoric about "going to the people" too seriously. The passive conformity of the many did not threaten the continuance of a regime based fundamentally on depoliticization of the masses. The silence of the majority was a kind of passive consensus for the regime, so long as the people did not translate their doubts into opposition.

But many young people began to do just that. Increasingly during the 1930s disillusionment developed into criticism, agitation, and eventually genuine antifascism. Many young people decried the closed nature of the regime, its repression of real debate, and its failure to undertake a true revolution. As they realized that the situation could not be changed from within, many of them began to search for a political alternative.

Open opposition did not really develop into a widespread phenomenon until the late 1930s and the war years. But the events of 1937–39 detached an ever-growing number from the regime. Indoctrinated for years to identify fascism and fatherland, some could not distinguish between country and government until after 1940. Those who clung to the hope that a new fascism could emerge from the supreme test were finally swamped by the delusions and defeats of war.

Documentation of this evolution for the Italian youth as a whole is sketchy and impressionistic. Police records on investigations of suspected subversives were not divided according to age, and as a consequence the young do not usually appear as a separate category in official files. But there is abundant evidence to trace the evolution of dissent among the educated youth: special police investigators infiltrated the GUF, the universities, and the *licei*. The information in such official sources can be augmented and complemented with a wealth of autobiographical literature published after the war. Such sources have a built-in class bias; they do not tell us a great deal about the state of mind of the Italian youth in general. But the regime expended a great deal of attention and energy on precisely this sector, the educated youth. In this sense, the testimony of growing disillusionment among these young people is, though perhaps not typical of the entire youth population, certainly a telling comment on the regime's failure among those members of the younger generation it sought most assiduously to win over.

The problema dei giovani

The role of the young in Fascist society—the *problema dei giovani*, as it was usually called—was one of the most frequently debated issues in the Fascist press. As seen by the Fascists, the *problema dei giovani* was the historical problem of the continuity of the regime in a new ruling class formed under fascism. It involved questions about the formation of the new generations: how to make them feel their solidarity with the older generations, how to find a place for them in the new national picture.

The Fascist regime never found the correct formulas. The *problema dei*
giovani became an issue soon after the consolidation of the regime, and
it persisted until the regime fell. It arose out of the contradictions within
the regime itself. How could the leaders of the Fascist system harmonize
their need for rigid mechanisms of social control with their need to
mobilize and prepare a new elite? How could they resolve the conflict
between freedom and discipline, between the participation and involvement demanded from the young elite and the internal controls exerted
over them?

One aspect of the *problema dei giovani* was generational. If promises
of a creative role for the young in the future served as a magnet attracting
some to fascism, such promises were sometimes a source of concern for
the old guard, who feared that *largo ai giovani* might well mean "out
with the old." In a less self-interested vein, many feared that the excessive emphasis on youth could well push fascism beyond the plotted
course and toward some dangerous social and political adventures.

Fascist rhetoric continually hammered on the mystique of youth, but
reality often told a different story. The young saw an abyss between those
who had carried out the March on Rome and those who, because of their
age, had to accept a ready-made "revolution" and a fascism received as
holy writ. After the purges of 1922-25, the key posts were occupied by
the young of the twenties, and there seemed little hope of changing the
guard very soon. The Fascist inner circle was almost always composed
of veteran black shirts—the men of the first hour whose party cards
carried the precious stamps *Marcia su Roma* or *squadrista*. Provincial
ras whose positions had allowed them to carve out virtual fiefdoms—
men like Farinacci, Ricci, Turati, or Starace—were hardly attractive
models for the new generations, especially for the student youth.[3] Before World War II few important positions were given to the young
hopefuls the party touted so enthusiastically. But the young men passed
over for positions of responsibility in favor of the older "men of action"
were the young men who were sent to the front lines when the wars
came.

The general economic scene also served to discourage and alienate
many of the young *laureati* struck by the disparity between the aspirations encouraged by the regime and the real possibilities for employment. This was not a problem unique to Fascist Italy, but it was exacerbated there by the exaltation of youth in the press. Bottai was especially
sensitive to the connection between youthful discontent and unemployment or underemployment among the students, a problem he hoped to
solve by the introduction of a *numerus clausus* at the universities. The
quotas were set in place only in January 1943, however, and certainly
did nothing to placate the many young people who, seeing the doors
closed in their faces, sometimes opened other doors to opposition.[4]

Alarm about the progressive alienation of the young was manifested early in the history of the regime, particularly in the pages of *Critica fascista*. The opening salvo in the debate came in an article entitled "Un regime dei giovani," published in this journal in June 1928. Here Bottai deplored the growing chasm between those who had made the revolution and those who found fascism-as-regime increasingly extraneous and suffocating. Pushing actively for the inclusion of more young people in the PNF and state administration, Bottai argued that instead of multiplying the number of parades and rallies, the regime should give the young some real duties to perform. He called also for party assemblies so that the younger rank-and-file members could make their ideas known to the older PNF stalwarts.[5]

In another editorial published in August 1928, entitled "Il regno della noia," Bottai pressed this point in even stronger terms: the "old-timers," he declared, saw the party as sort of a steamroller compressing ideas, feelings, and ways of thinking and acting into a dreary sameness, a "Bourbonism of the zealots . . . who are working to make Italy a huge Prussian barracks." The same issue contained an article advancing the notion of yearly elections to renew party leadership, an idea greeted with less than universal enthusiasm by the PNF hierarchs.[6]

Much of the debate among these revisionists centered around the vacuousness and hyperbole of the official press. Calling for a new journalism that would stimulate debate and a true circulation of ideas, Berto Ricci deplored the superficiality and the exultant propagandistic tone of the nation's papers: "An assembly is not Austerlitz, a holiday train is not the March on Rome. We ask from the press good sense and moderation."[7] A commentator in *Critica fascista* dismissed the style of much of the press as "banal pindarism" and lamented that journalism seemed often to be nothing more than "trombone blasts."[8]

By 1930 articles in *Critica fascista* openly referred to the growing apathy and skepticism of the young. Romano Bilenchi accused his own generation of melancholy, careerism, social climbing, and chronic bourgeois sympathies. The stirring old squadrist motto *me ne frego* was ironically applicable to the young, he said, whose involvement in fascism was reduced to a shrug of indifference. The party, he maintained, was not much more than an employment agency for many. Agostino Nasti criticized the lack of true cultural preparation among many young people. Familiar only with textbook answers and political tracts, they had become "repeaters of rhetorical formulas" and insincere readers of "superficial and bombastic speeches." "The problem of the young," said Bottai in 1933, "is the central problem of fascism."[9] "Although a minority have a truly Fascist style of life," claimed another article in *Critica fascista*, "the great majority are apathetic . . . about all the problems of national importance. But this apathy is made more profound by the fact that it is . . . disguised as pure faith, discipline, and perfect political orthodoxy."[10]

Police reports during the early 1930s frequently assessed the state of mind among university students. Speaking of high enrollments in the GUF, an agent in Turin in 1931 wrote: "Everyone belongs, few, however, are really enthusiastic." "Enthusiasm is scarce and observed with irony," commented another report. An agent in Naples reported that the student mass "views the GUF with apathy and indifference," convinced that the regime's organizations aimed only at creating a "standardized student lacking in thought and initiative." The regime, continued the same report, claimed that it wanted to increase the role played by the students, but in the view of many of them it "ends up by clipping their wings and protecting the rubbish."[11] The agent in Milan reported widespread rumors of misdeeds and corruption among party leaders and a belief among the students that these leaders were "ignorant and incompetent and in reality much below the level of any educated and honest high school student." Letters from Ancona and Milan in 1934 commented that the students were tired of reading the same "swollen words" and "bombastic praises" in the press, and that they were especially sensitive to the fact that there would be no jobs for them when they finished their studies. A long report from Rome warned of an intellectual reawakening among the students, who were not content to become sheep or, as they put it, "wild beasts in the circus."[12]

A series of articles by Camillo Pellizzi in the form of letters exchanged in late 1931 and 1932 with Mino Maccari, the director of *Selvaggio*, provided a lucid analysis of the political evolution and moral situation of the youth. The young, Pellizzi argued, saw a Fascist elite still holding onto the mentality of the past, a mentality that, although necessary in the circumstances of struggle, had become deleterious and negative. They were taught that all pressing social and political problems had already been resolved, but they felt that those same problems were still very much open issues. Told that they were to play a real role in Fascist society, they were at the same time discouraged from taking part in decision making and reduced to the role of executors of policy made on high. Given the methods adopted by the regime, claimed Pellizzi, it was an illusion to speak of the formation of a real ruling class; for the young, he said, the regime could be summarized in three words: "Mussolini, *squadrismo*, and bureaucracy." If the regime did not realize a true revolution, Pellizzi predicted in his second letter, the young would begin to turn to solutions antithetical to fascism: "Do you know, Maccari, what are the secret sympathies of the more intelligent and lively among the younger generations? . . . they are for communism. . . . They can't read a paper or a journal that doesn't repeat every day the same things; no hierarch opens his mouth without repeating the same refrains; no

Fascist book is published that doesn't re-fry another time the same food. Nothing has contributed to developing in these young people the feeling of spiritual autonomy, of freedom."[13]

Aware of the insistent discussions of the *problema dei giovani* in revisionist circles, Mussolini himself contributed to the debate in early 1930.[14] "The Regime is, and intends to remain, a Regime of the young," he began. While paying lip service to many of the issues raised, Mussolini also tacitly underlined his fundamental differences with the revisionists. Emphasizing the absolutely essential role of the single party in national life, he went on to vindicate the regime's approach to the young: what was needed, he claimed, was dedication to the principle of the totalitarian spiritual and political preparation of the new generations.

This was a revealing article, one that set the tone for the regime's approach to the youth for the remainder of its history. In the second lustrum of the 1930s, the Duce would seek to infuse the regime with new popularity and direction through a policy of military prestige and expansion. For the first half of the 1930s Mussolini, always suspicious of the older generations still too tied to the pre-Fascist climate, counted on being able to reinvigorate the younger generations and build his consensus around them. The debates on the *problema dei giovani* convinced him of the need to make new overtures, but the content of those debates did not really affect the regime's policies. Mussolini's words seemed to indicate an understanding of and support for the needs of the young, just as his subsidies to the young journalists of the GUF seemed to indicate his willingness to hear and respond to their ideas. But he was deaf to the insistent demands of the revisionists for real liberalization. The consensus he envisioned was not a rational consensus, based on real participation and understanding, but rather an irrational consensus based on quasi-religious ecstasy and faith. The real repository of Fascist faith was the generation of the March on Rome; the youth had only to learn the "word according to fascism" and to offer "the obedience of the enthusiastic, the ardor of volunteers, and an unconditional and absolute devotion."[15]

The real focus of interest could never be the realization of individual potential; rather, it would be the stability of the collective life as defined by the leader. In the conflict between individual initiative and social control, Mussolini opted for the latter, calling for the active consent of the few and the passive acceptance of the many. Revisionist calls for a real *largo ai giovani* would have meant a radical transformation that was never on the Duce's agenda. The regime eventually ended up in a blind alley: without liberalization it risked the defection of the future ruling class; with such liberalization it ran the risk of encouraging the deviations of a new ruling class whose "fascism" would have had little in common with the Mussolinian version. In either case, the regime as constructed by the old guard would not have survived. With the advent of the most exaggerated aspects of the *stile* Starace in the mid-thirties, the revisionist dream of a ruling class of thinkers and doers, though still much bruited about in the press, was clearly an illusion.

Antifascism and the Young

Although the topic of antifascism is really a separate study, some general comments on the evolution of youthful participation in such activities will indicate the range of political alternatives available to Italian youth. Though conscious political opposition did not really occur among many Italians until the war years, there were clearly discernible movements of dissent among the young before the war. Sometimes the young became involved with groups tied to pre-Fascist parties, and sometimes groups arose on the initiative of the young themselves—what Zangrandi referred to as "spontaneous generation"—who only later made contact with adults in anti-Fascist organizations. A distinction needs to be made between political antifascism in exile and anti-Fascist activists working inside Italy. With the former the young could have few contacts; only when a growing number of anti-Fascists began to see the need to bring the struggle home into the mass organizations of the regime did many young people begin to see a real possibility of embarking on the "long voyage."

The Anti-Fascist Concentration, founded in Paris in 1927, was in some ways a continuation of the policies of the Aventine and was closely tied to the entire pre-Fascist political scene; it was therefore outside the experience of many young Italians by the 1930s. In general these groups exerted a minor influence over the youth in Italy. The exiles, as Giorgio Amendola maintained, tended to become "detached from their bases, incapable of understanding the course of events in Italy, they became truly *fuorusciti*, outside the living Italian reality."[16] Others, with a variety of political views, felt that they had to undertake concerted action to bring fascism down, and that such activity had to occur inside Italy. These groups began to attract increasing numbers of Italian young people in the 1930s.

Giustizia e Libertà became the point of contact and organization for many non-Communist anti-Fascists who wanted to engage in active work to overthrow the regime in Italy. Organized formally during the autumn of 1929 by, among others, Emilio Lussu, Carlo Rosselli, and Alberto Tarchiani, Giustizia e Libertà served to pull together members from groups scattered all over Italy: the Non Mollare group in Florence, the Milanese group around Ferruccio Parri and Riccardo Bauer, the Rivoluzione Liberale group formed by Piero Gobetti. Tied together by a common moral, political, and social revolt against fascism, the Giellisti often differed on precise ideological issues because the group included Socialists of various stripes. Very soon Giustizia e Libertà came into conflict with the Anti-Fascist Concentration: the Aventine parties had been legalitarian, said Lussu, whereas Giustizia e Libertà would be activist in method, republican in principle, and revolutionary in aim.[17] Despite some early cooperation—the Giellisti were given the go-ahead by the Concentration in 1931 for activity in Italy—the differences in tactics eventually led to a break between the two and contributed to the dissolution of the Concentration in 1934.

Rosselli was not really a profound theorist, but his energy, optimism, and broad humanistic education helped him to inspire and galvanize others. He also spent much of his personal fortune financing the activities of the group.[18] Rosselli had been sentenced to five years' imprisonment for his involvement in Filippo Turati's escape from Italy in 1926. Together with Lussu and Fausto Nitti (a relative of the former prime minister), and with the outside help of Tarchiani—a former editor of *Corriere della sera*—Rosselli escaped from Lipari and returned to Paris. There he published *Socialismo liberale*, an elaboration of his *tesi di laurea* written under the direction of Gaetano Salvemini. Drawing on a wide range of philosophical and political influences—Croce, Gobetti, Turati, and Salvemini in particular—Rosselli sought to reconcile the liberal tradition of the Risorgimento with the desire for social justice embodied in Socialist thought and Christian teachings. By downplaying Marxian economic determinism and portraying socialism first of all as moral revolution, Rosselli hoped to provide an alternative between laissez faire capitalism and Russian-style socialism: a new socialism that would aim above all at the elevation of man and human freedom.

The tactics adopted by the Giellisti included both cultural and literary antifascism and violent strikes against the institutions of government in Italy. Members of the group, such as Carlo Levi, Cesare Pavese, Franco Antonicelli, Vittorio Foa, and Massimo Mila, were involved in the publication of *La Cultura* and *Quaderni di Giustizia e Libertà* in Turin. Other activities were much less cerebral, including bomb explosions and attempted assassinations. Fernando De Rosa, for example, shot at Prince Umberto in Brussels in 1929. These early activities produced little national resonance or effective penetration of the masses, but they did provoke a massive counterattack by the police and opposition from the Anti-Fascist Concentration. The Giellisti defended their adoption of violent tactics by pointing out that there were no legal means of defense against a tyranny that controlled the media and the tools of physical coercion. Accused often of antipatriotic strikes, they maintained that they were working against the state but in the interests of the nation.[19] Giustizia e Libertà paid a high price in arrests, and during the 1930s

many of the leading Giellisti were put out of commission, temporarily or   225
permanently. Many members of the group, however, served in partisan   _____
bands, and many Giellisti were active in the founding of the Action party   "The
in 1942 and the staffing of its paper, *L'Italia libera*, beginning in 1943.   Long
Voyage"

One of the most dramatic gestures organized by Giustizia e Libertà
was the flight of Giovanni Bassanesi over Milan in July 1930. The
masterminds of this operation, Tarchiani and Rosselli, hoped to bring the
message of the Giellisti to as many Italians as possible without risking
the cadres needed to bring the leaflets in personally, a tactic they admitted had produced scarce results. Bassanesi, a young liberal Catholic
from Aosta, was tutored in the rudiments of aeronautics, and during
the afternoon of 11 July 1930 he flew low over Milan and dropped
some hundred thousand leaflets urging resistance against the regime. He
crashed on his return flight and was arrested, along with Tarchiani and
Rosselli, for violation of Swiss territorial sovereignty. Their trial in
Lugano became something of an international forum for antifascism,
and the defense speeches by Turati and Sforza received great media
attention. The accused were eventually given suspended sentences.[20]

The influence of Giustizia e Libertà on Italian youth came through a
movement known as *liberalsocialismo*, associated with Guido Calogero
and Aldo Capitini. The movement had as its focal point the Scuola
Normale Superiore in Pisa, a prestigious institution founded by Napoleon in 1810 and imbued with strong traditions of academic freedom and
intellectual nonconformity.

One contemporary referred to the Scuola Normale as an "oasis," and
another, who studied there in the 1930s, recalled the profound influence
of professors such as Calogero, Delio Cantimori, Cesare Luporini, and
Luigi Russo on the students. The atmosphere of the school, claimed
Mario Pomilio, encouraged the "desire to understand, the eagerness of
discovery," and eventually this encouragement of criticism became "an
open and free taste for discussion." "Freedom," said Pomilio, "began
just on the other side of the door, as if there one enjoyed a kind of
extraterritoriality and the suspicion and fear of the spies remained behind
us." Croce was the spiritual and intellectual guide for many of these
young students; the writings of Marx were unknown to most, and the
influence of Gentile problematical: "We accepted his theoretical prem-
ises," claimed Pomilio, "but not the political stances." Gentile served as
director of the Scuola Normale for a time in the 1930s and, despite these
political stances, was largely responsible for "the freedom we enjoyed":
he "protected as a philosopher . . . a freedom of criticism that, as a
politician, he should have denied us," remembered Pomilio.[21]

Aldo Capitini, a theistic but anti-Catholic proponent of Gandhian
nonviolence, studied at the Scuola Normale from 1924 to 1928 and came
to antifascism after the 1929 Concordat. He held teaching and adminis-

trative posts at the school from 1930 until 1933, when he was fired by Gentile for refusing to apply for the required PNF membership card and—according to Capitini himself—because Gentile objected to his vegetarianism.[22] Even at the Scuola Normale, it appears, there were limits.

The movement spread out from Pisa in the late thirties, and by 1939 there were nuclei of *liberalsocialisti* all over the peninsula; the movement's strength, however, remained in central Italy between Florence and Pisa. The groups resembled Socratic schools; each was headed by a professor or teacher who set the tone for that particular nucleus. The Pisan group, for example, formed around Calogero, those in Umbria around Capitini. Carlo Ragghianti worked with the Emilian groups and Mario Delle Piane with the Siena nucleus; in Florence the leaders were Piero Calamandrei and Enzo Enriques-Agnoletti. Guido De Ruggiero worked with the *liberalsocialisti* in Naples, and in Bari Tommaso Fiore headed the group that met at the Laterza publishing house. Here the influence of Croce was especially deep, though he himself did not participate. Some *liberalsocialisti* also worked within the regime's youth organizations; Guido Aristarco and Renzo Renzi were on the staff of the Bolognese GUF paper, *Architrave*.

The movement as a whole is difficult to categorize, but the various groups became the natural meeting places and passage points for many young people who began to move around the unfamiliar terrain of antifascism. The *liberalsocialista* movement never became a party per se, but except for the groups with ties to pre-Fascist political parties, these nuclei were among the few in Italy that began to weave a network of support among the young. Many of the *liberalsocialisti* eventually joined the Action party during the war. Carlo Ragghianti became president of the Florentine Committee of National Liberation in 1943; Calamandrei, Enriques-Agnoletti, Delle Piane, and Calogero all served with distinction in Action party units. Capitini, whose pacifism prevented him from participating in the fighting, continued his writing and anti-Fascist activities with the Action party after his release from prison in 1943.[23]

Much less influential was a group called Giovane Italia. Republican in orientation and, according to police reports, responsible for several well-publicized terrorist attacks, Giovane Italia never succeeded in drawing many followers in Italy, but it did draw headlines. One of the group's most famous attempts was the *caso Bovone*. Domenico Bovone, a young Genoese, was apparently in the process of constructing a powerful bomb in his apartment when it exploded in September 1931, wounding him and killing his mother. Later investigations and testimony led police to conclude that Bovone had been preparing an assassination plot against Mussolini. He was tried by the Special Tribunal and executed.[24] Many of the group's members were arrested in 1931–32, but their activities dramatized the regime's contention that antifascism was but another name for terrorism.

Not all of the anti-Fascist activity among the young occurred on the left. The Alleanza Nazionale per la Libertà had a short but colorful history. The group began its activities in June 1930 under the leadership of Mario Vinciguerra, with the assistance of Lauro De Bosis and Renzo Rendi (who is to be distinguished from the *liberalsocialista* Renzo Renzi) and with the encouragement of, among others, Croce and Father Enrico Rosa of *Civilità cattolica*, who secretly distributed the Alleanza pamphlets at Catholic Action meetings.[25]

Mario Vinciguerra was a representative of the older liberal tradition. Born in Naples in 1887, he was a scholar and journalist who had served for a short time as the secretary of the Liberal party. During the 1920s he had worked on the editorial staff of *Il Resto del Carlino* and *Il Mondo* with Giovanni Amendola.

Lauro De Bosis—a young poet, dramatist, and translator of Greek tragedies—had been influenced, like so many other Italian young people, by the Fascist myths of rejuvenation and rebirth. He had seen fascism as a "generous attempt to renew decadent bourgeois society."[26] De Bosis's respect for the historical contribution to unity and national sentiment made by the Savoyard dynasty convinced him that the crown would prevent fascism from degenerating into excess. He later recanted: "One cannot both admire fascism and deplore its excesses," he said. "It can only exist because of its excesses. Its excesses are its logic."[27]

De Bosis's father, Adolfo, was a well-known poet; his mother was an American from New England, and between 1924 and 1930 he lived in the United States. He served as secretary of the Italy-America Society, a Fascist propaganda agency, from 1924 to 1926 and also taught at Harvard, where he met Salvemini and Sturzo. In 1927 his prophetically titled lyrical drama *Icarus* won the Olympic Prize at Amsterdam. By 1930, on his return to Italy, he fully realized the repressive nature of the regime and vowed to enter the arena of battle. De Bosis was especially concerned about the youth and the indoctrination they received in the ONB, which was, he said, "imposing on them the uniform of executioners and giving them a barbarous and warlike education." "For several years," he added, "Italy has been turned into a great prison where children are taught to adore their chains."[28]

The platform of the Alleanza Nazionale was hardly radical. Its authors sought to take some of the wind out of the sails of the Left by convincing the public that antifascism should not be equated with Marxism. As liberal "men of order" they aimed at reconstruction of a moderate movement, inspired by monarchist and Catholic sentiments. The traditional forces of state, church, monarchy, and army should not, they felt, be driven away from the struggle against the regime, but should be brought into the forefront of that struggle.

Beginning on 1 July 1930 the group sent out nine leaflets, one every fifteen days. They were distributed in batches of six hundred copies, with instructions asking the recipient to pass copies on to six others.[29] De Bosis left Italy late that year for the United States, where he hoped to publicize the cause and find some financial support. The remaining members of the group were all arrested in December 1930. De Bosis's mother was convinced by the authorities while incarcerated to make a public appeal for clemency, a fact much played up in the press. Vinciguerra and Rendi made no such appeals and were speedily sentenced by the Special Tribunal to fifteen years, with two and a half years to be served in solitary confinement. Horror stories soon began to circulate about the brutal treatment meted out to them during their interrogations. Their case aroused a good deal of publicity abroad; an international call for their liberation was organized in December 1933 and signed by, among others, Paul Valéry and Aldous Huxley. They were both given amnesty in December 1936.[30]

The arrest of his family and friends convinced De Bosis to undertake a mission of solidarity with them. Perhaps inspired by the flight of Bassanesi—the Alleanza Nazionale did have many contacts with the Giustizia e Libertà activists—De Bosis decided to "bear a message of liberty across the sea to a people in chains" in a plane named *Pegasus*. After working for several months to raise the money for the small craft and taking several flying lessons, De Bosis took off from an airfield in Marseilles on 3 October 1931. He reached Rome at about eight o'clock in the evening and flew low over the city, dropping some four hundred thousand propaganda leaflets exhorting the people to make common cause with the monarchy against fascism in the interests of the ideals of the Risorgimento. "If my friend Balbo has done his duty," wrote De Bosis before his flight, "they are waiting for me. So much the better; I shall be worth more dead than alive."[31] Balbo's planes did take off in pursuit. It is unclear whether he was shot down or ran out of fuel, but thirty-year-old Lauro De Bosis was never heard from again.

The gesture served to infuse a certain amount of hope into anti-Fascist groups then working in Italy. In the words of Max Salvadori, then involved with Giustizia e Libertà: "The trip filled us with joy, it gave us courage, it lighted the way that for some time had become dark, ever darker."[32] "It is necessary to die," wrote De Bosis in his prose epitaph, *The Story of My Death*. "I hope that many others will follow me and will at last succeed in rousing public opinion."[33]

The Movimento di Unità Proletaria (MUP) was one of the few anti-Fascist movements arising spontaneously among the youth inside Italy to succeed in affecting the development of one of the pre-Fascist parties, in this case the Socialist. The MUP was founded in 1939 by anti-Fascist youths in Rome and Milan who made contacts with members of the PSI in exile and sought to persuade them to go beyond the old divisions to carry out some effective work among the proletariat inside Italy. Ideologically midway between the young Communists and the *liberalsocialisti*, the MUP in 1943 played an important role in the fusion of the old maximalist-minimalist currents and the establishment of the new unitary socialist party, the Partito Socialista Italiano di Unità Proletaria (PSIUP). Under the auspices of the MUP, a group called the Associazione Rivoluzionaria Studenti Italiani (ARSI) was founded at the University of Rome. Just after the liberation of Rome the ARSI began to publish a journal, *La nostra lotta*, that later became the official organ of the Fronte della Gioventù under Eugenio Curiel.[34]

The increasingly active role played by the Italian Communist party in the 1930s also added to the anti-Fascist ferment among the Italian youth. In 1926 Antonio Gramsci had predicted the course events would take in Italy: "It will be within the breast of fascism itself that the conflicts will tend to arise, since they cannot appear in any other way."[35]

Since 1931 the PCI had adopted this strategy of struggle within the Fascist organizations as party policy. This line was frequently stressed in the pages of the theoretical organ *Lo Stato operaio*, printed in Paris and distributed clandestinely in Italy after 1927. But, as Giorgio Amendola later admitted, the new party line was rarely applied in the first few years because of a "sectarian resistance among the militant Communists who would have nothing to do with fascism, even to make use of the Fascist organizations to fight against the regime." These militants, animated by an adamant refusal to cooperate with bourgeois forces, insisted on the autonomy of Communist groups and their absolute antagonism to the mass organizations of the regime.[36]

In the view of many this was a policy guaranteed to spread the anti-Fascist gospel only among the already converted and to keep the message from the masses, and especially from the youth. "There is no doubt," said Palmiro Togliatti in a 1934 editorial, "that the major part of these young people are today malcontent and ready to rebel. But . . . how will this instinct to rebellion be expressed if we . . . reject these young people, if we brand them all in a block as traitors, if we do not undertake an organized effort (*organized where they are*) to conquer them?"[37]

By 1934–35 the situation began to change. The French Communist party began its involvement in the Popular Front, and the PCI signed a Unity of Action Pact with the Socialists in Paris. In July 1935 the decisions taken at the Seventh Congress of the Comintern also helped to push the PCI in the direction of work inside fascism. Using the analogy of the Trojan horse, Georgy Dimitrov delivered a speech at the Moscow meeting condemning sectarianism and calling for the "exploitation of the legal possibilities" for the overthrow of fascism. Communists, Dimitrov continued, "must work in these Fascist organizations . . . and must rid themselves once and for all of the prejudice that such activity is unseemly and unworthy of revolutionary activists."[38] Giorgio Amendola remembered being convinced by his younger brother Antonio, who came to visit him in exile on Ponza. Berating Giorgio for his anachronistic ideas on the political struggle, Antonio explained that "there are young people in those Fascist groups . . . who think they are Fascists but are not Fascists. . . . When [they] realize that fascism is not Socialist corporativism but the domination of the ruling classes . . . that fascism is not patriotism but the negation of the fatherland, then from these young people the revolt will come, it will come!"[39]

Giancarlo Pajetta referred to the party's decision to adopt the tactics of *lavoro legale* as the PCI's "secret weapon." "We believed in the young," he said, "because we understood that their desire to understand would soon become conscience, and that it would bring them to know us and to work with us."[40] In a report to the PCI headquarters in exile, Curiel attempted to assess the tendencies he saw among the young intellectuals. "They are tired," he wrote, "of singing again the same Mussolinian song. . . . These young people are not yet many and they are isolated, their ideas are imprecise and confused. . . . But they are sincere, they want . . . to fight for liberty. . . . They want Italy to be free and happy."[41]

Organization of the youth proceeded slowly during the second half of the 1930s. But by the mid-thirties small groups of Communist students had begun to form on the initiative of the young, who gradually began to make contacts with the PCI in exile. Much of this early organization centered around the group of Roman Communists, students from all over Italy who attended schools in Rome. Many of these young intellectuals came to Marxism through literary and historical studies; some got their earliest introduction at the *liceo*, influenced by such anti-Fascist professors as Pilo Albertelli and Gioacchino Gesmundo, both later to become victims of the German reprisal at the Fosse Ardeatine in March 1944.

Some of these young people met at the Amendola house, where younger sons Antonio and Pietro organized group discussions; others— including Aldo Natoli, Paolo Bufalini, and Paolo Alatri—gravitated to activities at the home of Giuseppe Lombardo-Radice, organized by his son Lucio and his daughters Giuseppina and Laura. Members of this Roman group took part in the 1934–35 Littoriali, but most of the concerted anti-Fascist activity got under way as a result of their opposition to the African war and increased in intensity with the Spanish civil war and the Nazi alliance. Mario Alicata, a student in a Roman *liceo* in 1935, began to make contacts with Zangrandi, Bruno Zevi, and others in that year. He remembered the period 1936–37 as a crucial time when the Zangrandi group began their infiltration at the Littoriali and Curiel made his first contacts with the PCI abroad and started his work at *Il Bò*. Bruno Sanguineti, a member of the Lombardo-Radice group in Rome, was by 1936 also in touch with the PCI in France. When Giorgio Amendola returned from prison in 1937 he, his brothers, and Bufalini organized a drive to collect funds for republican Spain.[42]

These and other activities brought the groups to the attention of the authorities and led to a series of arrests. In 1940 Pietro Amendola, Natoli, and Lucio Lombardo-Radice were sentenced to prison terms by the Special Tribunal. In their absence the work went on under the guidance of Bufalini, Pietro Ingrao, Alicata, Antonello Trombadori, and Antonio Giolitti. In 1941 both Bufalini and Trombadori were also arrested. By this time organized activity was being guided by PCI contacts sent from Paris; Celeste Negarville worked with the student group in Milan, for example.

The Roman group was not an isolated example; during the second half of the thirties others sprang up in several large cities, usually first on the initiative of the students and later under the coordination of party delegates. Many of the Communist sympathizers working on the review *Corrente di vita giovanile* in Milan were arrested in early 1943. In Naples, under the leadership of the young Giorgio Napolitano, the Communist group worked within the GUF. In 1940–41 it took over much of the editorial responsibility for the GUF journal, *9 Maggio*, often publishing articles from Marx under their own names. A group of Catholic Communists began to form after 1939 in the larger Italian universities in Milan, Turin, Rome. The most active of these was the Roman group, led by Franco Rodano and Laura Lombardo-Radice. The group took the name Sinistra Cristiana in 1945, and some of its members entered the PCI shortly thereafter.[43]

Conformity versus Active Participation

An individual's response to Fascist socialization was a function of two variables: the individual's propensity for political participation and involvement and the degree to which he or she accepted the Fascist political system. Responses to Fascist indoctrination varied from active support to open opposition (with many intermediary points along the way) on the basis of these two personal (internal) factors. But the individual's degree of acceptance also depended on external influences, and thus the youthful response to Fascist socialization over time came to resemble a parabola, with the ascending curve representing growing consensus or acceptance and the descending curve representing growing dissent or alienation. The culmination of the descending curve of the parabola was rejection of and opposition to the system among the minority of the youth with a high propensity for political activity. There is a rich autobiographical literature discussing precisely why the young accepted the regime and why, at varying points, many of them joined the opposition.

Passive acceptance of the regime and conformity to its regulations resulted from many causes, not the least of which was fear. But other factors were also important. One of the common threads running through many of the autobiographical accounts is that of fascism-as-normality: the regime was accepted because it was fact. Only a slow process of maturation brought many young people to the realization that there were alternatives. This is the burden of Zangrandi's *Il lungo viaggio attraverso il fascismo* and much of the other testimony from the period.[44] The young born into fascism, in the words of Zangrandi, "found themselves growing up in an ocean of silence in which only the Fascist sirens sang their songs."[45] An informational gap separated these young people from the worlds outside the PNF youth groups and the schools. The testimony of one born and raised under fascism emphasized this lack of contrast: "Until my last year in high school . . . I cannot say that fascism was for me much more than a word. I lacked any sense of its opposite, the experience of a different reality."[46]

The general silence of the old ruling class and the intellectuals has been condemned in much of the postwar testimony from the young; that charge forms the burden of Zangrandi's *Il lungo viaggio*. The young saw that king and church supported the regime; they knew that illustrious members of the pre-Fascist political parties had voted with the PNF and that only a handful of professors had refused to sign the party's loyalty oath.[47] Those who had fought fascism were in exile, imprisoned, or dead. "And around their struggles, around their sacrifice . . . a void was constructed." It seemed to the young that there was for a long time "no trace of opposition either in Italy or outside."[48] For years, said Ugoberto Alfassio Grimaldi, "the reality was fascism; antifascism was archaeology and whining . . . the very rare leaflet . . . sounded out of place and said strange things."[49] Davide Lajolo wrote: "I never had the good fortune to meet an anti-Fascist who said one word to make me understand that fascism was just the opposite of the enthusiasm and anxiety that burned in me."[50]

The technique of divide and rule, enhanced by the use of police-state tactics and fear, aimed at keeping individuals or small groups isolated as "islands of separateness" to confront the totalitarian state alone. A member of the Zangrandi group said of his early anti-Fascist activities: "I doubted that we could succeed. We were so few and the tyranny so strong and deeply rooted. . . . I did not know that there were many others . . . who were struggling for the same idea."[51]

All of these negative factors were important in producing conformity and passive acceptance, but from some of the young the regime attempted to elicit more active participation. Here the regime's myths and slogans were most important, especially the myth of fascism as continuing revolution. For some time these myths made a strong appeal to the idealism and the reformist zeal of many of the young intellectuals. For these young people the early Fascist excesses were not reality. They saw instead the frenzy of reconstruction, the reclamation and public works programs, the modernization of industry—all of these things intimately linked with Mussolini, who seemed determined to see that Italy looked forward and not backward. For these young people fascism was not billy clubs and castor oil; it was, rather, enthusiasm, building, cooperation in the grand plan for the future. It opened to them a world of welcome struggles, passions, and idealism that exerted a powerful pull. Lajolo expressed this youthful response to the revolutionary rhetoric of fascism: "We had to make Italy a great country. Get rid of the rich, do away . . . with the cowards . . . go to the people. . . . What youth with blood in his veins does not love to see justice where there is injustice, who does not feel love for his country, who does not feel himself shiver with pride if he is called to make history? These great, immense words: history, fatherland, justice—they filled us with enthusiasm."[52]

Costanzo Casucci, historian and until recently director of the Archivio Centrale dello Stato in Rome, argued that many in his generation became anti-Fascists in the 1940s precisely because they had taken fascism's revolutionary rhetoric and promises so seriously until then.[53] Youthful opposition was, according to Giuseppe Melis Bassu, a "pre-political stance, a prevalently moral one." The young called for purity and disinterest and "dedication to the idea as the antithesis to the ever more evident corruption of the apparatus, both of the party and the state."[54]

When the young learned that their hopes would not be realized, the long voyage began. The disillusionment meant only passive resistance for some; it led others into open opposition outside and against the regime. But that youthful revolt would not have been possible without a long period of brewing discontent and alienation under fascism. The disillusionment of many was further compounded by the pressures of external events. Internal processes and external events worked on one another: the internal evolution led to the acquisition of a certain maturity and political conscience that allowed many of the youth educated and indoctrinated under fascism to respond to external stimuli by pulling away from the regime. These events could be plotted as points on the downward curve of fascism's relationship to the Italian youth.

Believe,
Obey,
Fight

From the late twenties until the African war the socialization process was still on the upward swing. If the great majority of Italy's young were depoliticized and only passively attached to the regime, there was still a vocal minority who were highly politicized in the Fascist sense. At this stage the majority of the young showed little interest in alternative political solutions. During this period it is not really possible to speak of a resistance movement among the young, though youthful opposition based on the unique experiences of those raised in the Fascist climate was beginning to grow.

In 1932 the regime celebrated its tenth anniversary amid great panoply. There were few threatening clouds on the horizon. Few people knew anything about the *fuorusciti*, memories of early Fascist violence had blurred, and most of the early anti-Fascists had been silenced. At home the regime seemed active and vital: the "battle of grain" was under full swing, marshes were being reclaimed, building was changing the face of towns all over Italy. In foreign affairs fascism seemed oriented toward prestige, but also toward peace and European equilibrium. The regime still indulged in polemics against Germany and the Nazis, and in July 1933 the signing of the Four Power Pact gave Mussolini the international stature he felt he deserved. His decisive reaction to the July 1934 murder of Austrian Chancellor Dollfuss gave many Italians pride in their country and convinced them of the profound contrast between the two dictators. The Stresa accords signed in April 1935 tied Fascist Italy closer to the two great democracies. It was, in the words of Zangrandi, the epoch of "*il bel fascismo.*"[55]

Evidence from police agents and informers for this period indicated that the regime expended a great deal of time and attention infiltrating student groups and the university communities. Scattered reports in the late 1920s and early 1930s tied the activities of some student groups to Giovane Italia and Giustizia e Libertà. Agents also noted the appearance of anti-Fascist graffiti and leaflets at some universities during this period. An agent in Milan in 1931 reported, for example, that a small number of students were "microbes of infection" disseminating subversive propaganda tracts.[56] Police commented on antiregime activities during this period among the students in Rome, Turin, and Milan and reported on contacts made by some students with anti-Fascist groups in France and Switzerland.[57] But these reports were occasional and scattered. The frequency and intensity of these investigations and reports increased with the Spanish civil war in 1936 and especially with the Nazi alliance and the developments of 1938–39.

Most observers agree that the Ethiopian war marked the apogee of
Mussolini's prestige and popularity in Italy.[58] The propaganda campaign
waged by the regime in support of the aggression in Ethiopia struck
some responsive chords among the young. The war was billed as the
supreme moment in Italian history: Italy, an overpopulated proletarian
nation, was challenging the plutocracies for its legitimate place in the
sun. Victory would vindicate Italy's claim to great-power status and
would bring freedom and civilization to the victims of a feudal caste
system in Ethiopia. The imposition of sanctions by the "fifty-two traitor
nations" produced an austerity campaign and a reign of xenophobia in
Italy. This clash was painted as a clear-cut case of the good guys against
the bad guys: the decadent and spineless "perfidious ex-allies" against
the idealistic and heroic Italians fighting for survival. Posters branded as
traitors all those "nostalgic for roast beef" (wishing them a "fitting
arteriosclerotic punishment") and urged the consumption of meatless
"sanction soup" each Friday. The game of bridge became *ponte*, and the
luxurious Hotel Eden in Rome got a new name. Children heard tales of
Italian heroism and sang "Faccetta nera" in school. In that moment of
triumph when the Piazza Venezia and all the squares in Italy were
crowded with citizens hailing the reappearance of the empire "after
fifteen centuries . . . on the fateful hills of Rome," Mussolini seemed to
have succeeded in making many people believe that Italy had finally
become a great military power—the Italy of *otto milioni di baionette*.[59]

The spectacle of the great joining ranks behind Mussolini must have
been impressive to the young. The so-called *giornata della fede* on 18
December 1935, when the women of Italy gave their gold wedding rings
to the Fascist cause, was a true propaganda triumph for the regime.
Luminaries such as Marinetti, Gentile, and D'Annunzio sang the praises
of the new empire. The king sent a message to Mussolini: "In the present
moment every Italian must be present to serve." What better testimony
to the unity of regime and fatherland? Luigi Pirandello sent his Nobel
Prize medal to the cause; Luigi Albertini and Benedetto Croce sent their
gold senator's medals: "Croce offering his little medal—a gesture that
destroyed a whole library of his writings."[60] Both Bruno and Vittorio
Mussolini served, and Vittorio contributed to the literature on the glories
of war in 1937 with the publication of his book *Voli sulle Ambe*, exalting
the sporting and aesthetic aspects of combat.[61] Italian prelates were
photographed blessing troops as they left for the holy war; on 8 December 1935 the bishop of Civita Castellana sent Mussolini his gold pastoral
cross, saying: "I thank Almighty God for permitting me to see these days
of epic grandeur."[62]

Even many anti-Fascists had to concede the influence of nationalist slogans during the African war, especially among the youth. The "myths of the proletarian war . . . of the war for 'social justice among the nations,'" admitted a contributor to *Lo Stato operaio*, "mask the real cause of the misery of the Italian people and the real cause of the war, [but] find a certain echo among the masses who live in misery and without a tomorrow, in particular among the youth."[63] The anti-Fascist groups stepped up their propaganda against the war of aggression, but their leaders admitted that the popularity of the regime during this time made real penetration into Italian society quite difficult.

If the short-term reaction to the war was largely favorable, the long-term effects—the seeds of discontent and mistrust that the policy of aggression sowed—were not. Even in victory the basic weaknesses of the regime became evident. With "the euphoria of empire," wrote Enzo Santarelli, "went the disease of the regime."[64]

The direct repercussions of the Ethiopian war have often been discussed. Though Italy's losses in human terms were relatively light, the war cost the equivalent of almost a year's national revenue. The loss of war matériel severely strained the Italian budget, as did the possession of the new colony, which demanded defense of supply routes to the Red Sea. Mussolini's actions also narrowed Italy's range of options in foreign affairs, a move that brought his country ever closer to alliance with Nazi Germany.

More subtly, however, the victory served to institutionalize what Denis Mack Smith called the "religion of *ducismo*." The proclamation of empire increased the distance between the regime and the masses and even between the leader and his closest collaborators. "Peasants knelt to him in the fields, women held up their children for him to bless, and cabinet ministers were expected to stand in his presence for hours at a time."[65] Mussolini's conviction of his own historic and charismatic function became crystallized as regime and party policy: the myth of the "founder of empire" was intimately tied to the myth of Rome and the Fascist new civilization. Under the indefatigable Starace, every aspect of cultural life was deformed to these ends. An enormous and ever-growing propaganda machine constructed the dreams of universal empire bit by bit out of words and illusions and put the finishing touches on the quasi-divine image of Mussolini. Fascism, said one of the faithful, "was by then not much more than Mussolinianism."[66]

Members of the cabinet and other hierarchs noted the changes. Emilio De Bono wrote in his diary: "The Leader? And who understands anything about him anymore!" In a harsher vein, he exclaimed: "Now he limits himself to playing a walk-on role in all the buffooneries that Starace thinks up."[67] Having waged a war based on his intuitive feeling that England would not fight, Mussolini emerged from the conflict with a rooted belief in the infallibility of his political *fiuto*. In this atmosphere policy making became fiat. Mussolini was hypersensitive to criticism and was impressed only by the most inflated praise. When he spoke to his cabinet members he seemed to be addressing the throng; every pronouncement, said Bottai, was ex cathedra.[68] Cutting himself off from all around him, he lived in a self-imposed solitude save for his increasing involvement with Clara Petacci.

After 1935 it became almost impossible to escape the mass organizations of the regime, where political participation was ever more reduced to "Believe, Obey, Fight." "Fascism, made more and more presumptuous and overbearing by its successes . . . persecuted the citizen in an ever more inescapable manner, it oppressed his present and his future, it did not allow him peace or truce."[69] If for some time many of the young were seduced by the mirage of glory and grandeur offered by the Fascist regime, many others began at this time to have their first doubts about the nature of that glory and grandeur. In the most direct sense, the war brought the young closer and closer to the regime: the activities of the ONB were stepped up, the tenor of the propaganda in the groups, on the radio, and in the textbooks became increasingly grandiloquent. The African war was thus a two-edged sword. It was a time of triumph and euphoria, but it was also the beginning of the end of fascism in the minds and hearts of some of its best young people. One young man's illusions were dispelled by the war and replaced by a "kind of ironic skepticism, under the mask of external conformity and with a kind of secret shame for feeling myself a participant, even as an extra in the last row, in the gigantic farce I laughed at deep inside myself." Zangrandi wrote of the reaction of his group of friends as they walked away from the mob scene in Piazza Venezia on the day the empire was proclaimed: "We came away anxious and worried . . . because we sensed that the road down which we had begun to walk was a dangerous road for the country."[70]

The Spanish Civil War

Italian involvement in the Spanish civil war polarized the international community and public opinion inside Italy. The Italian populace was increasingly affected by the poor economic showing of the regime. The Ethiopian war had severely strained the economy; the state budget deficit rose alarmingly between 1934 and 1936. As the economy was geared increasingly toward war, private monopolies flourished, convincing many Italians that corporativism worked only to the advantage of industrialists and an ever-burgeoning government bureaucracy. Real wages for both agricultural and industrial workers fell slowly but continuously.[71] Jobs provided by the war helped put some back to work, but in 1936 unemployment hovered at around one million. The diet of Italians was also affected: they consumed less protein, milk, and sugar and fewer calories than they had ten years before. The volume of foreign trade declined. Italy's total imports in 1936 were less than one-third of the 1929 level. Total exports in the same year amounted to only about 38 percent of the 1929 total. The decline in trade with Britain and France led to an increase in trade with Germany. In 1929 Germany accounted for 20.3 percent of Italy's exports; by 1936 Germany received 41.4 percent. Imports from Germany accounted for 23.7 percent of the total in 1929; by 1936 they had reached 43.6 percent of the total. Autarky was not yet fully effective in 1936, but it produced distortions in the Italian economy as production in some areas was speeded up without regard to costs. Coal was three times as expensive in Italy as in England; steel costs were double those in Britain.[72]

Already exasperated by the evident contrast between the economic promises of the regime and its real achievements, many Italians were less and less willing to take to their hearts the cause of Western civilization against the Bolshevik hordes. Most important, the Spanish civil war "unveiled new ties with Germany—ties that stirred up many worries, reawakened old anti-Teutonic feelings, foreshadowed racism. The descending parabola began then."[73] The war produced in Italian public opinion, said Zangrandi, a "laceration that, shortly thereafter, the ever closer alliance with Germany and racism made even deeper."[74]

For many young people the long voyage reached its terminus in the Spanish civil war. Over three thousand Italians fought on the Loyalist side. It was, therefore, in the political and military sense a valuable training ground for future Resistance fighters. But it was more than that: it was an opening to a new world of international antifascism, a conflict that forged a new unity among anti-Fascist activists inside and outside Italy. In groups gathered around radio sets, thousands of Italians heard new voices in their homes, voices that told a very different story from the one they had heard for years on the Italian radio. Regular broadcasts from abroad, either directly from Spain or through BBC or Russian sources, allowed Italians to follow events in Barcelona or Madrid.[75] On 13 November 1936 they heard Carlo Rosselli promise: "Today in Spain, tomorrow in Italy." In June 1937 they also heard that Carlo and his brother Nello Rosselli had been murdered, and clandestine broadcasts covered the march of over two hundred thousand mourners following the two caskets through the streets of Paris to their final resting place in Père Lachaise. Buoyed by the testimony of international opposition and confronted with such evidence of the reactionary nature of fascism, many saw the future stretching out as a series of international crises, struggles, and wars.[76]

There is ample evidence, from inside the regime and outside, to support the conclusion that disaffection increased during the Spanish civil war, even among those formerly loyal. Reports from prefects and agents of the OVRA, the secret police, while trying to put the best possible face on things, clearly indicated growing discontent, especially among the working class disaffected by the economic situation and energized by the exploits of the reds in Spain.[77]

Officials were especially disappointed in the number of volunteers who signed up to serve in Spain. Very soon the ranks of the CTV, the Corpo Truppe Volontarie, were swelled by "volunteers" enlisted by the government authorities. Information available for the period of spontaneous enlistment (July 1936 to January 1937) indicates that the total number of volunteers was 3,364—less than 5 percent of the 78,846 who eventually served. Detailed data is available on 2,423 of these early enlistees. About half of them were over the age of thirty. That is, only about 1,200 Italian men under thirty enrolled voluntarily in the early stages of the conflict; of these about 4 percent were students.[78]

Beginning with the Spanish civil war, and especially in 1937–38, there developed in Italy what Lucio Lombardo-Radice referred to as "the new antifascism" among the young.[79] Many young people from the ONB and the GUF began spontaneously to print and distribute leaflets, to organize demonstrations, and to form study groups, very often of a Marxist orientation. Increasingly disillusioned with a war that the regime defined as a clash between Rome and Moscow, many began to see the conflict from the other side. Few young people in Italy as yet had close ties with the official PCI organizations inside or outside Italy, but the Communists were still the only active anti-Fascist group with a real national network.

Guido Leto, head of the OVRA, claimed that the work of the Special Tribunal, which had been "languishing" before the Spanish civil war, took on a new intensity. Most of the victims, he claimed, were Communists, because "all other parties and groupings were almost nonexistent" at this stage.[80] The number of Italians sentenced by the Special Tribunal and the police increased in the period 1938–39, an increase that is directly related to opposition to the Spanish civil war, as most of those sentenced in this period had been arrested earlier. The Special Tribunal sentenced 310 people in 1938 and 365 in 1939, higher totals than for the preceding six years.[81] Many of those sentenced were young. Records for January 1939 to July 1943, for example, indicate that the Special Tribunal tried 1,590 offenders. Of these 752 (about 47 percent) were under the age of thirty, 328 (almost 21 percent) were under twenty-five, and 119 were under twenty. Of the total number, 99 were students.[82]

Sometimes the opposition of the young intellectuals came initially over seemingly nonpolitical issues. Leonardo Sciascia recalled that he and his friends were influenced by artistic movements in Europe and America during the Spanish civil war. "The first revelation," he said, "came to us when [we heard] that Garcia Lorca had been shot by Franco's forces, that Dos Passos, Hemingway, and Chaplin were fighting on the side of the republic."[83] For many of these young students, the struggle against fascism was part and parcel of the struggle to deprovincialize Italian culture, to bring a new cultural spirit to an Italy that seemed barricaded inside its sterile and arid rhetoric.

Police agents and informers reported for 1937 "intense anti-Fascist propaganda" in Milanese and Turinese student circles and dissemination of Giustizia e Libertà pamphlets in Milan and Genoa.[84] The chief of police noted that anonymous letters sent from Turin signed by "one hundred university students and professors" protested the German and Italian intervention in Spain and referred to the "threats and aggressions of international fascism." Another file reported the arrest of over sixty students at the Milan Politecnico for "Communist activity." An agent in Switzerland warned about the infiltration of the GUF by Giellisti, who, he said, were especially active in Florence, where anti-Fascist works were in widespread circulation.[85] An official observer in Milan described the atmosphere in the student community as one of "fatigue and coldness"; another agent warned about a "noticeable relaxation in Fascist faith."[86] A letter from Pavia commented that there was a "very widespread feeling of discontent against the party" and especially against Starace, who, the writer added with some understatement, "does not enjoy the sympathy of the students."[87]

The German Alliance

In the first half of 1938 two events further pointed up the changed Italian relationship to Hitler's Germany: the *Anschluss* in March and the Fuehrer's visit to Rome in May. Mussolini's inability to take action against Hitler's move into Austria conjured up an image of an increasingly impotent Italian government and gave the lie to his oft-repeated promises to defend Austrian sovereignty. The regime's immobility elicited much unfavorable comment in student circles all over Italy. There was a "growing antipathy," one typical police report said, "to the entire Axis policy of the Mussolini-Ciano family." Milanese and Roman investigators commented on a "marked anti-Hitler note" among the university students there.[88]

Hitler's visit to Rome, covered with the familiar rodomontade in the Fascist press, was greeted unenthusiastically by many Italians. The frantic preparations—including the construction of Italian-style Potemkin facades and military equipment along the parade route—were commented on widely and produced a much-quoted poem by the famous Roman dialect poet Trilussa:

Roma de travertino	Rome of travertine
refatta de cartone	remade of cardboard
saluta l'imbianchino	hails the house-painter
suo prossimo padrone[89]	her next master

The decision that aroused the greatest dismay, however, was the adoption of racial legislation in 1938, a decision that even a once-sympathetic judge termed "the gravest error and the one most pregnant with consequences for the regime." The passage of the anti-Semitic laws was received by the populace at large with dismay, disgust, or contempt; even among some members of the Duce's own family the reaction was negative.[90]

Fascism had appealed to many young people as an affirmation of Italian national uniqueness. The anti-Semitic campaign reeked of the most servile imitation; it was for the young, and for many Italians, a foreign tradition and an alien importation. If fascism had once meant national glory and national pride, after the passage of this legislation it seemed to many to mean subservience to the German overlord. Despite Farinacci's attempts to take the sting out of the pope's comments charging imitation of Nazi Germany, the opposition of the Vatican made a clear impression, as did Enrico Fermi's denunciation of the laws while in Stockholm to receive the Nobel Prize and his decision not to return to Italy.[91] Mussolini had taken an active role in the promulgation and defense of the laws; few could any longer say, "If the Duce only knew."

The negative reaction among the youth was not universal. Some attempted in the pages of the GUF papers to defend anti-Semitism as a spiritual manifestation that would draw the national community closer together. But for many others in the GUF, this was the last straw. Rosario Assunto remembered the reaction of many as one of "nausea and moral irritation."[92] Primo Levi was a nineteen-year-old student in chemistry at the University of Turin when the laws were passed. He remembered that many students, even loyal Fascists, were perplexed by the laws, which seemed a "stupid aping" of Nazi ideology. Levi enrolled during the war in partisan bands with Giustizia e Libertà, was captured by the Fascist militia in late 1943, and was transported to Auschwitz until liberated by the advancing Soviet armies.[93] Lucio Lombardo-Radice recalled in a conversation with Paolo Spriano in 1970 that many young people, among them Giaime Pintor, passed into the anti-Fascist movement at this time.[94] Criticism of the racial policy was at the heart of many of the debates at the Littoriali in Palermo in 1938. "At that point," said Zangrandi, "a choice and a decision became necessary: there was no longer any room for illusions, it was no longer reasonable to speak of 'errors' or 'delays' or to hope that the situation could be put back on the right track."[95]

Believe,
Obey,
Fight

The progressive deterioration in the quality of leadership in the PNF had become evident to many by the 1930s, though the process had been under way for years. Mussolini's decision to break the independence of party activists led to the effective depoliticization of the PNF. Party statutes provided for regular meetings of the *fasci*, for example, but they rarely took place, and the local groups had no real decision-making power in any case. After passage of the law requiring party membership for state employees, the ranks were swelled with a mass of bureaucrats and careerists who joined because for them the PNF card was, as Carmine Senise said, the *"tessera del pane."* By the late 1920s, said Adrian Lyttelton, "pure careerism of a pedestrian kind predominated over a more adventurous and aggressive spirit; Fascism developed middle-aged spread."[96] As the party was more and more cut off from real power and decision making, it busied itself with counting burgeoning enrollment figures and stage-managing the activities of the proliferating auxiliary organizations.

By the mid-1930s the reforming zeal of many of the best had degenerated into facile platitudes. Cracks showed in the monolithic facade of fascism as the revolutionary demagoguery of the movement was put to the test in a confrontation between its social pretensions and the demands of its imperialistic policies. The political process had resolved itself into a clash of factions swirling around the Duce, who was flattered grotesquely by a servile and fawning press. PNF secretaries followed one another in dreary succession after the dismissal of Starace. On 28 October 1942, the twentieth anniversary of the March on Rome, Galeazzo Ciano described the malaise of the PNF: "The inefficiency of the party is felt more strongly than ever, because the party is headed by incapable, discredited, and questionable men."[97]

Mussolini had never been much interested in the moral qualities of his appointees. Convinced of his own genius and equally convinced of the base nature of most men, he wanted to be surrounded by "sycophants, dissemblers, and place-hunters." Two required characteristics in the inner circle seemed to be a belief in his infallibility and a readiness to laugh at his jokes. "It appears," claimed Mack Smith, "that he sometimes selected ministers by simply running his eye down a list of deputies until he recalled a face or a name that sounded well—better still if they were less tall than himself."[98] Except when it served his purposes of the moment, he did not take action against the much-rumored corruption, even—as with the Petacci family—when it threatened to erupt into public scandal.[99] The party press cultivated an image of probity, but in the end, said Mussolini's own police chief, "public opinion came to equate the word *gerarca* with thief or worse."[100]

The Duce's methods of dealing with associates eroded morale among party and state officials. Mussolini was always suspicious of the popularity of his subordinates—especially of Bottai and Balbo—and in order to prevent any of them from building up an independent power base, he moved them around from post to post. One sure way to incur his wrath was to appear too often in the press—or to presume too familiar a relationship with the Olympian leader. Mussolini often seemed to take delight in sowing discord among his ministers; he encouraged them to tell tales on one another and then repeated the stories to the offended party. He did not usually have the courage to relieve people of command personally, so they often heard about his frequent "changings of the guard" on the radio or from the newspapers.[101]

The almost laughable excesses of the Starace era served further to discredit the Fascist ruling class. Guido Leto noted the general derision of the people treated to the spectacle of hierarchs jumping through hoops of fire. "All of this roused a sense of hilarity in the public that sometimes changed into a painful stupor when they thought about the fate of a country entrusted to people deemed suitable if they had muscles and wind."[102] A contemporary observer noted: "One usually associates a governing class with a class of intellectuals. But here physical fitness and a commanding presence are the first requisites."[103] Much of the student antipathy to these "men of action" was, as we have seen, directed at Starace. At the University of Padua in 1936 some enterprising young students organized a funeral for the still energetic party secretary, who, when the news reached him, reacted with predictable fury.[104]

The students' nemesis was finally removed in October 1939 and replaced by Ettore Muti. The new PNF secretary was a much-decorated war hero who was totally ignorant of politics and abhorred offices and telephones. Under both Muti and his less-than-memorable successor, Adelchi Serena, the PNF continued its downward spiral.

Things only worsened after Serena's "resignation" and departure for the front in late December 1941. News of the appointment of Aldo Vidussoni, a twenty-six-year-old law student from Trieste, stupefied party leaders and shocked even the appointee, who heard the news on the radio and assured his friends that a mistake had been made. He had nothing to recommend him except war wounds (he had lost an eye and a hand in Spain) and a gold medal for valor. He was abysmally ignorant but fanatically loyal. Even sympathetic commentators termed Vidussoni's appointment a "dangerous experiment" to bring the new generation to the forefront of the Fascist movement.[105] The less sympathetic snickered that the motto of the GUF should be changed from *Libro e moschetto* ("Book and Musket") to *Libro e maschietto* ("Book and Little Man"). Bottai publicly called Vidussoni a "nincompoop" but Ciano was willing to give the new secretary the benefit of the doubt for a time.

Admitting that Vidussoni was "enthusiastic and loyal but a novice," Ciano predicted that he would "sweat blood in that environment of old whores which is the Fascist Party." By early 1942 Ciano too had given up. He described Vidussoni as a "perfect specimen of Fascist youth: mutilated, depraved, ignorant, and moronic," and a "perfect imbecile."[106]

Vidussoni's appointment—made because he had been the lover of one of Mussolini's former mistresses or because he was an intimate of the Petaccis, depending on which contemporary story one chooses to believe—clearly indicated the bankruptcy of the PNF. Mussolini stuck by Vidussoni longer than predicted because he found the secretary's slavish adulation increasingly necessary as he grew more insecure. In April 1943, however, the last PNF secretary was appointed. Carlo Scorza's reaction to his nomination indicated the desperation of the situation: "I feel," he said, "as if I've been called to the bedside of a dying man."[107]

Scorza, five times a war volunteer and eight times decorated, had served the party in various capacities during his long career, most notably as secretary of the GUF and the Fasci Giovanili. But opponents also remembered his service in suppressing dissent, especially his involvement in the fatal attack on Giovanni Amendola in 1926. Calling Scorza's appointment the "clearest, the most evident, the most clamorous declaration of the failure of the Fascist party and of Mussolini's regime," Togliatti broadcast a speech charging that in any other country the new secretary would be wearing a "shaved head and a prisoner's striped uniform."[108] Despite his immediate attempts to breathe new life into the moribund PNF, Scorza could do little. "But who," asked Leto, "could have resuscitated in the Italians and in the souls of many Fascists their political faith? Fascism was really dead long before 25 July 1943."[109]

In a perceptive twenty-one-page letter to the Duce dated 7 June 1943, Scorza analyzed the ills and failures of the party and assessed (in anything but rosy terms) the popular attitude toward the PNF. He blasted the bureaucrats, whom he described as "not honest and not Fascist," the unpreparedness and incompetence of the armed forces, and the chaos prevalent in the economic sector. He called repeatedly for a "moralization of the national life." In regard to the youth, Scorza maintained: "The youth have a somewhat limited belief in fascism for various reasons by now well-known. But the vast majority of the young can be recaptured as soon (only a few months more, Duce!) as we have changed the climate of the party."[110]

Scorza was correct about the disbelief among the youth, but he was less astute when he counted on the prestige of Mussolini to heal the breach. By the war years the character flaws and physical problems that had plagued Mussolini for years were all too obvious to those around him. Since the Ethiopian war the Fascist system of government had revolved around the Duce's personal whim and "mystical" style. Mussolini was a man tragically out of touch with reality. He had no tolerance for real administration but an inexhaustible capacity for trivial detail. He was supposed to be all-powerful, and yet he constantly changed his mind. He wanted no bad news, but because after a certain point the news was almost all bad, he heard little truth.[111]

Morale among the inner circle plummeted. By mid-1941 Bottai described Mussolini's attitude to his subordinates as "cold and almost hostile." Ciano added, with some understatement, "among our Fascists one can perceive a marked uneasiness."[112] Unable to trust any of his collaborators, Mussolini resorted to rule by fear. Ministers and party leaders were required to dance attendance on the *capo* daily, waiting long hours in the anterooms of the Palazzo Venezia. He often left the infamous "green cards"—the secret police reports—on various officials in plain view on his desk to intimidate them. Cabinet meetings were little more than monologues.[113] In October 1941 Bottai commented: "The Duce has decayed intellectually and physically. He doesn't attract me anymore. He is not a 'man of action'; he is presumptuous and ambitious and expects only to be admired, flattered, and betrayed."[114] Lamenting the situation one day to Balbo, Bottai remarked, "We have a Duce but not always a leader." "A leader, come on," Balbo replied. "He's a rag."[115]

Mussolini explained the failures by blaming others: the military leaders in particular and the Italians in general. He had set out to make a new race, but in his more lucid moments he recognized the folly of that hope. The Italians, he said, were not the proper material: they were too incurably bourgeois, trivial, cowardly, and pleasure-loving ever to be his new Fascist men.[116]

By 1942 there had been a clear decline in his intellectual and physical powers, what one biographer termed a "moral and physical collapse."[117] He was nearly sixty years old, though the papers were still forbidden to refer to his age or his health problems. His mood changes were more extreme, and he was often depressed. The intense pain of his stomach ailment (most of it probably psychosomatic) kept him bedridden for long periods and out of touch with developments.[118] Even when he was physically present, he seemed psychologically absent, uncertain, and unresponsive, "like a sleepwalker who no longer knew his own mind and did not understand the immense disaster he was bringing on the country."[119]

Without firm principles and without any real ideas and ideals, fascism had been the personal creation of a man. But hundreds of journalists pushing the same old myths could not, after a certain point, polish his fatally tarnished image. The success of the regime had depended on Mussolini's ability to convince himself and others that he was superhuman. But by the war years he was no longer above it all: "Hated and despised," said Bottai in May 1943, "he is the personification of defeat."[120] Murmurs blamed him for every injustice, every defeat, every sacrifice, and all hardships. "Mussolini," said an American correspondent covering Italy, "the man who could do no wrong, is the object of scorn, the butt of jokes, or at best (and he must hate this more than anything) a man whom some of his people pity rather than condemn."[121] Once the Mussolini myth died, the end of the regime was not far away. When it came it was an anticlimax: "His arrest brought down the imposing edifice of Fascism like a house of cards; even the elite troops of the militia did not lift a finger: the Party, so long isolated, disappeared from the life of the nation as if it had never been. No abyss opened up; life seemed to go on without interruption—and so, of course, by order of Badoglio, did the war."[122]

The Youth and World War II

The brewing discontent present among Italian youth boiled over during World War II. After twenty years of intense indoctrination there were still, to be sure, some believers, but for many the events of the war buried for good the regime's myths of war and Roman glory. Fascism failed to convince most of the young that they should champion war over peace. The regime could enroll millions of young men and women in youth groups, it could bombard them with propaganda, it could make them march and carry rifles, but it could not make most of them accept a war for which their nation was unprepared and an alliance they scorned. Fascism had failed to mass-produce the "new Fascist man"; it had failed to change the character of Italians, whom, even Mussolini admitted, "a tenacious therapy of twenty years has succeeded in modifying only superficially."[123]

There is ample evidence to indicate that the leaders of the PNF realized the total unpreparedness of the nation and the depth of the anti-German sentiment among the youth and the population at large. Both Ciano and Bottai frequently noted the pessimism among the military officers, the disastrous situation of Italian armaments, the inability of the nation to withstand a serious attack. Ciano called press releases about Italian invincibility a "tragic bluff" and wondered of the Duce: "Does he fear the truth so much that he is unwilling to listen?"[124] The chief of police, Carmine Senise, admitted that the populace had always been against the war: "Everyone was against it, even the majority of the Fascists . . . the only one favorable was Starace who uttered the historic phrase 'For me war is like eating a plate of macaroni.' "[125] Ciano wrote in his diary in September 1939: "The country is and remains fundamentally anti-German. Germanophiles can be counted on the fingers of one hand. They are objects of scorn."[126] Zangrandi remembered the reaction to Mussolini's declaration of war. "The majority of the young," he said, "remained inert, as if plunged into a condition of obsessive paralysis." An ever-deeper "chasm . . . divided the few and foolish fanatics from the mass of the population, now conscious and foreseeing."[127]

For the young men who were supposed to fight the war the dilemma was an especially cruel one. How could they make the distinction between their country and the individuals who governed it? How could they hope for defeat without admitting the huge costs? Only gradually, as failures and the evidence of criminal irresponsibility multiplied, could many accept defeat as "the obligatory road . . . towards liberation."[128]

The widening rejection of the war among the students became obvious as the number of volunteers from the universities slowed to a trickle. A foreign correspondent in Rome reported that in the winter of 1940–41 only eighty-seven students out of some seven thousand volunteered in Rome and that in Genoa, out of more than three thousand students, only about thirty enlisted. The story was much the same in Turin and Milan. General Mario Roatta recalled in his memoirs that in June 1943, when the army called for volunteers from the GIL, there was not one volunteer in sixteen provinces.[129] Some officials resorted to other tactics. Eager to impress the authorities in Rome, GUF secretaries routinely petitioned the government to call up their members en masse; these GUF draftees were formally listed as volunteers.[130]

Early in 1941 the government decided to lift deferments for university students, a decision that produced an uproar in formerly privileged student circles. Police agents from all over Italy reported demonstrations against the proposal, and against the war in general. A report from Milan, for example, quoted many students as feeling that the war was only to satisfy the "interests of Germany and the blind pride of those who control the fate of the two Axis powers."[131] One agent in Padua quoted the students as saying: "They order us to shout 'Long live the Duce and long live the war.' That's all right; we're ready to do that. But to order us to go get ourselves killed under the command of cretinous generals is another thing. We are quite capable of also shouting 'Down with the Duce and down with the war.' "[132] Party Secretary Serena was whistled down at the University of Rome in February 1941 by students shouting, "We'll go to the front when Serena puts on khaki."[133]

According to the new law, students were supposed to present themselves by June. In May the opposition in many university circles became particularly heated. The universities in Naples and Rome were closed for a time that month after signs appeared saying, "Down with the war and long live England."[134] Similar incidents occurred at other schools as well. The antiwar protest at the University of Rome degenerated at one point into a virtual riot; signs all over the campus said, "Down with Mussolini," "Down with Hitler," and "We don't want to be butcher's meat."[135] The Roman GUF was infiltrated by anti-Fascist students who, organizing what was supposed to be a patriotic demonstration in favor of the war, covered the school with streamers inscribed with antiregime slogans. Eventually about fifty students were arrested, and many of these were tried before the Special Tribunal.[136] The informer in Forlì reported students there singing, "Se non ci conoscete, guardateci l'elmetto. Noi siamo i volontari della cartolina precetto." In Parma a group of students on troop trains were quoted as saying that the lack of uniforms and arms proved that "we entered the war without preparation. . . . The Germans have good cause to disdain us and treat us as though they are our masters."[137]

Characteristically, Mussolini blamed everyone but himself. When he was not laying the responsibility for the mounting defeats at the feet of his own military leaders, he took refuge in the innate flaws in the Italian character. "Even Michelangelo had need of marble to make statues. If he had had only clay he would have been nothing more than a potter. A people who for sixteen centuries have been an anvil cannot become a hammer within a few years." Sometimes he was more realistic: "I must . . . recognize that the Italians of 1914 were better than these. It is not flattering for the regime, but that's the way it is." "This war is not for the Italian people," he said in 1942. "[They] do not have the maturity or consistency for a test so grave and decisive. This war is for the Germans and the Japanese, not for us."[138]

The war was a catharsis. It opened the eyes of many young people to the desperate situation of the armed forces and thus to the moral and political bankruptcy of the regime. Giuseppe Melis Bassu remembered that even as early as the Christmas of 1940 he received a postcard from an old friend who had once been secretary of the Sassari GUF. "Anyone who comes here," said the young man at the front, "changes opinions and feelings on many things . . . our imprepration is great, our delusion immense."[139]

Some young men remembered the barracks themselves as the forum for their first anti-Fascist indoctrination. The Palermitan student Marcello Cimino, called up in the division of "university volunteers" in 1941, recalled that his first contacts with Marxist literature came in study groups formed at his army post. Franco Fortini claimed that his real involvement with anti-Facist activities began during that same summer while he was serving his first few months in the military. Government authorities also reported widespread infiltration by Marxists into the young officer cadres during this period.[140] The PCI activist Emilio Sereni recalled that, in order to capitalize on the growing discontent among these soldiers, the anti-Fascist groups in the military began to change their appeal. Attempting to fuse the political antifascism of the parties with the opposition born at the front, they began to circulate among the troops papers such as *Parola del soldato*, portraying the anti-Fascist struggle as a national struggle, as the fight for national independence threatened by fascism and Nazism.[141] In April 1942 Bottai noted in his diary: "You can feel the uneasiness growing. . . . Young people are stopped . . . arrested, sent to *confino*. And these are 'our' young people, out of the Avanguardie, from the university groups, from the party's political preparation schools."[142]

For some the distinction between regime and country came more slowly. Davide Lajolo—sincere Fascist, volunteer in Spain—felt bound by a sense of duty until the Germans came as invaders. "Didn't I realize my errors, even after years of war?" he asked. "Sure, when in Greece battalions . . . were massacred and from Rome arrived only orders and cardboard shoes . . . and medals for those safely behind the front. Certainly I realized. But what of the companions who had died? What of the sincere oaths taken on crossed hands? Terrible torments of conscience." He finally joined the partisans, convinced of the need to settle two accounts: "with those who had deceived me and made me carry a rifle in the most crazy and unjust wars and with myself—to redeem at last my dignity, to learn to understand and truly love my country, the real country, the one made by us." In the resistance, through the "blood and suffering, I liberated myself finally from the sad burden." There are, he recalled Teresio Olivelli as saying, "no liberators, only men who liberate themselves."[143]

The story of Falco Marin did not end so happily. Marin, son of the author Biagio Marin, was a convinced Fascist who, during the war years, began to write letters home to family and friends confessing his doubts and delusions. Late in the spring of 1943 he joined an anti-Fascist group. His last letter to his family, dated 16 July 1943, concluded: "The tyrannical government that by now puts all its hopes in its . . . powerful ally, continues to sell humbug in its newspapers. . . . But still not all hope is lost. We might still be in time to save something, at least for tomorrow. . . . Under the tragic push of events, in the violent and cruel struggle, the people could find some new forms of organization upon which tomorrow to build a truly free country." Twenty-four-year-old Marin was killed on the morning of 25 July 1943, just hours before the news of the fall of the regime began to circulate in Italy.[144]

For many the long voyage was complete. The regime branded these young men traitors for refusing to accept Nazi domination and carnage. But, in the words of one contemporary: "Those young men betrayed nothing and no one. The truth is that, faced with naked reality, they realized that no voice inside spoke to them seriously. Those presumed ideals . . . by which they believed themselves dominated were not ideals clarified and meditated upon in the intimacy of their consciences . . . but rather words repeated because they had been heard so often, names without objects. For those they could not die."[145] In the conflict between skepticism and faith of which Goethe spoke, skepticism had won over much of the Italian youth.

*　　*　　*

After twenty years a new political elite trained under fascism to assume the responsibilities of command should have been stepping onto center stage. But that second generation never materialized. The Fascist regime failed to produce an army of young Italians loyal to, and prepared to fight for, the Duce and the party. The Fascist myths used for a time with such effect by the party's propaganda machine lost their appeal as the regime's internal failings and external defeats multiplied.

Mussolini had called Gentile's educational reforms the "most Fascist of all reforms," but education in Italy from 1922 to 1943 underwent no real revolution that completely destroyed the old system. The Italian school was decked out in Fascist garb for twenty years, but in its spirit and in its heart it remained more or less traditional. In education, as in many other aspects of the Fascist experience, the divergence between theory and practice was great.

That is not to say that fascism had no effect on the Italian educational system. Fascist reforms centralized the educational system and gave the ministers of education more power than ever before. The regime created some new schools and abolished others. During the Fascist period the number of both schools and students rose, and the educational system was adapted to the needs of a wider segment of the population by increases in the availability of technical and vocational training. The physical education of youth, too long neglected under liberal regimes, was emphasized as never before or since. The Catholic church enjoyed a new status in the Italian schools, where religious instruction was compulsory for elementary and secondary students. Many of these changes, however, were in line with ideas discussed by neo-idealist educators for years. Except for some of the ideas embodied in the 1939 Carta della Scuola (most of which were never implemented), the Fascist structural reforms were more in line with normal evolution than with total revolution.

Italian teachers were affected by the Fascist reforms. They were required to enroll in the PNF, wear the black shirt on special occasions, and join Fascist teachers' associations. By World War II the teachers had adapted themselves to the external demands of the regime, and their ranks had been swollen by some new recruits attracted to the profession by the lure of a political career in the ONB/GIL. But except for these politically ambitious careerists, most men and women who became teachers during the Fascist period seem to have done so for the traditional reasons. Most Italian teachers, especially those reared in another era, performed the ritual obeisances the party required in order to keep their positions but did not become stalwart supporters of the regime.

The political and social tenets of the new Fascist faith did permeate the teaching in the schools. After 1930 all children educated in Italy read the same state-approved textbooks. All of the young people enrolled in the regime's youth groups were required to study the same training manuals and handbooks; they were all exposed to the same lessons taught in the Fascist culture and military culture courses from the primary grades to the universities. Curriculum changes at all levels of the school system brought teaching more into line with the Fascist world view. The precise extent to which the lessons learned from these Fascist texts and lessons have affected the present generation of Italians is an open question. Surely, however, it is here—in the rote memorization of the party's history, in the repetition of its credo, in the inculcation of an authoritarian turn of mind—that the influence of fascism on the national psyche was most profound.

Mussolini's goal, he said, was to build a new civilization and a "new man," the Fascist citizen-soldier. To accomplish this goal he had to make Italian youth "Believe, Obey, Fight." If for some time the imaginations of many young people were captured by the myth of the leader and the seductive mirage of a new Roman Empire, the mammoth propaganda campaign could not obscure reality forever. The regime claimed to be a modernizing force that would bring Italy into the ranks of the industrial great powers. Party rhetoric promised to realize social justice in Fascist corporativism. Mussolini claimed that fascism had finally fulfilled the promise of the Risorgimento by truly bringing the masses into the life of the nation. He promised that the new spirit of national solidarity and purpose would increase national prestige and ensure a glorious future. Italian fascism fulfilled none of these promises.

The PNF failed to capitalize on the early enthusiasm among the young by channeling that enthusiasm and energy into productive directions. Fascism became an exterior cult of form—songs, uniforms, parades—without any serious moral imperative. Even Mussolini recognized this failure in 1945: "The hard times came when the enthusiasm was . . . squandered and we told ourselves that all had been accomplished. . . . [We] indulged in too much rhetoric, at the expense of an austere lifestyle. Too many high positions, too many baubles, too many songs, even for the youth who were supposed to be the bearers of a new way of life. I recognize that even I let myself be led astray by the triumphal march of enthusiasm."[146]

The internal inconsistencies of the regime, the contrast between what fascism promised to the young and what it offered to them, the reality of life under fascism—all this served to drive many young people into opposition. As they embarked on their "long voyage through fascism," many of the young born and raised in the "new Fascist climate" realized that the regime had given them nothing to believe in, no one to obey, and nothing for which to fight.

ABBREVIATIONS

ACS	Archivio Centrale dello Stato
DN	Direttorio Nazionale
EIAR	Ente Italiano Audizioni Radiofoniche
ERR	Ente Radio Rurale
GIL	Gioventù Italiana del Littorio
GUF	Gruppi Universitari Fascisti
ICS	Istituto Centrale di Statistica
INCF	Istituto Nazionale di Cultura Fascista
MCP	Ministero della Cultura Popolare
MEN	Ministero dell'Educazione Nazionale
MI	Ministero dell'Interno
MI, DGPS, DAGR	Ministero dell'Interno, Direzione Generale Pubblica Sicurezza, Divisione Affari Generali e Riservati
MI, DGPS, DPP	Ministero dell'Interno, Direzione Generale Pubblica Sicurezza, Divisione Polizia Politica
MPI	Ministero della Pubblica Istruzione
MRF	Mostra della Rivoluzione Fascista
ONB	Opera Nazionale Balilla
PCM	Presidenza del Consiglio dei Ministri
PNF	Partito Nazionale Fascista
PNF, SPEP	Partito Nazionale Fascista, Situazione Politica ed Economica delle Provincie
SPD, Ord.	Segretaria Particolare del Duce, Carteggio Ordinario
SPD, Ris.	Segretaria Particolare del Duce, Carteggio Riservato

![black rectangle]

Note: Unless otherwise indicated, all translations are my own.

Introduction

1. On political socialization of youth in Fascist systems see Germani, "Socializzazione politica dei giovani," pp. 11–58.

2. On the organization of consensus and propaganda see Guaitini and Seppilli, "Organizzazione del consenso," pp. 145–82; Cesari, *Censura nel periodo fascista*; Victoria de Grazia, *The Culture of Consent: Mass Organization of Leisure in Fascist Italy* (Cambridge: Cambridge University Press, 1981), pp. 1–23; Cannistraro, *Fabbrica del consenso*, and "Burocrazia e politica culturale," pp. 273–98; and Aquarone, *Organizzazione dello Stato totalitario*, pp. 270–71.

3. These varying responses are schematized in Germani, "Socializzazione politica dei giovani," pp. 56–58.

4. Addis Saba, *Gioventù italiana del littorio*, p. 52.

5. Zangrandi, *Lungo viaggio*.

Chapter One

1. The Futurist Manifesto is included in Joll, *Three Intellectuals*, pp. 179–84. The program of the Futurist party is reproduced in De Felice, *Mussolini il rivoluzionario*, pp. 475–76. On the influence of futurism on fascism see E. Gentile, *Origini dell'ideologia fascista*, pp. 109–29.

2. Venturi, "Regime fascista," pp. 186–87.

3. Renzo De Felice especially emphasizes the influence of Le Bon and Sorel: De Felice, *Mussolini il fascista*, 2:367.

4. B. Mussolini, *Opera omnia*, 22:156; B. Mussolini, *Autobiography*, p. 36.

5. Widener, *Gustave Le Bon*, p. 71.

6. Le Bon, *Crowd*, pp. 115–32. On the role of the leader see ibid., pp. 133–59.

7. Ludwig, *Colloqui con Mussolini*, p. 68.

8. On the influence of Sorel in Italy and on fascism see Roth, "Roots of Italian Fascism," pp. 30–45, and *Cult of Violence*.

9. H. S. Hughes, *Consciousness and Society*, pp. 90–96.

10. Sorel, *Reflections on Violence*, pp. 78, 140.

11. On the relationship between revolutionary syndicalism and fascism see Roberts, *Syndicalist Tradition*.

12. Pareto, *Rise and Fall*, pp. 37–38.

13. Rocco, "Political Doctrine," p. 405.

14. A. Gatti, "Abbozzo per un ritratto di B. Mussolini," *Popolo d'Italia*, 27 March 1938, quoted in Simonini, *Linguaggio di Mussolini*, p. 37 (n. 44).

15. Addis Saba, *Gioventù italiana del littorio*, pp. 155–56.

16. B. Mussolini, *Opera omnia*, 6:427.

17. B. Mussolini's speech in Naples, 24 October 1922, published in *Popolo d'Italia* for 25 October 1922 and *Opera omnia*, 18:453. See also Finer, *Mussolini's Italy*, p. 218.

18. On the role of myth in Fascist Italy see Isnenghi, *Educazione dell'Italiano*, pp. 7–22; and Guaitini and Seppilli, "Organizzazione del consenso," pp. 145–79.

19. Mack Smith, "Mussolini, Artist in Propaganda," p. 224.

20. B. Mussolini, *Opera omnia*, 20:207.

21. On these *veline* see Flora, *Stampa dell'era fascista*; Matteini, *Ordini alla stampa*; Cannistraro, *Fabbrica del consenso*, pp. 445–50; Simonini, *Linguaggio di Mussolini*, pp. 191–94, 215–20; and Foresti, "Proposte interpretative," pp. 136–37 (n. 22).

22. Quoted in Luigi Rosiello, introduction to Leso et al., *Lingua italiana*, pp. 8–9.

23. Trabalza and Allodoli, *Grammatica degli Italiani*.

24. For a study of propaganda and cartoons see Carabba, *Fascismo a fumetti*.

25. For a list of foreign words and expressions banned from the newspapers and comments on the Fascist view of dialect see Foresti, "Proposte interpretative," pp. 143 (n. 67), 144 (n. 69), 146–47 (n. 72); and Simonini, *Linguaggio di Mussolini*, pp. 208–11. Giovanni Gentile accepted the use of dialect by children in the elementary schools as the truest expression of the child's experience, but this attitude changed as his reform was "touched up" in the late 1920s and 1930s.

26. For some very graphic illustrations of this imagery see Vittori, *C'era una volta il duce*; Silva, *Ideologia e arte*; and Ciani, *Graffiti del ventennio*.

27. Quoted in Tamaro, *Venti anni*, 2:459. A particularly detailed and interesting examination of the Mussolini myth is Biondi, *Fabbrica del Duce*. See also Melograni, "Cult of the Duce," pp. 221–37; Mack Smith, *Mussolini*, pp. 102–3, 123–31, 163–69; and Cantalupo, "Classe dirigente," pp. 3–13.

28. Montgomery, "Mussolini," p. 742.

29. "Elogio di Lord Curzon a Mussolini ed alla sua politica," *Popolo d'Italia*, 2 March 1923, quoted in Melograni, "Cult of the Duce," p. 233.

30. De Felice, *Mussolini il fascista*, 2:370, 372.

31. Bottai, *Vent'anni e un giorno*, p. 118.

32. For the contents of this circular see Aquarone, *Organizzazione dello Stato totalitario*, pp. 485–88.

33. On Mussolini's view of the PNF see Nello, "Mussolini e Bottai," pp. 335–66.

34. Melograni, "Cult of the Duce," p. 223.

35. Testimony of Ugoberto Alfassio Grimaldi in *Autobiografie di giovani*, pp. 68–69.

36. B. Mussolini, *Autobiography*, p. 27.

37. Biondi, *Fabbrica del Duce*, p. 5; E. Panetta, *L'anello di Salomone* (Florence, 1939), quoted in De Felice, *Mussolini il duce*, 2:225.

38. B. Mussolini, *Autobiography*, p. 123.

39. Sarfatti, *Life of Benito Mussolini*, p. 230.

40. B. Mussolini, *Autobiography*, pp. 56–57.

41. For a psychoanalytic approach to Mussolini's superman myth see Berneri, *Mussolini*, pp. 69–78.

42. G. Ciano, *Diario, 1939–1943*, p. 416 (quoted from the translation, p. 360).

43. Diary of Giuseppe Bottai, quoted in De Felice, *Mussolini il duce*, 2:277.

44. Gravelli, *Uno e molti*, p. 28. See also Carlini, *Filosofia e religione*; Sulis, *Imitazione di Mussolini*; Orano, *Mussolini al fronte della storia, Mussolini da vicino*, and *Mussolini fondatore dell'impero*; P. Ardali, *San Francesco e Mussolini* (Mantua: Paladino, 1926); and A. R. Viggiano, *Il Duce* (Rome: Studio Editoriale Romano, 1926).

45. Quoted in Luigi M. Lombardi Satriani, "Il credo fascista," in Vittori, *C'era una volta il duce*, p. 11. On the Mussolini myth as presented to the young see A. Mussolini, *Ammonimenti ai giovani*; B. Mussolini, *Diuturna*; Marziali, *Giovani di Mussolini*; Perroni, *Duce ai Balilla*; Agnesi, *Tappe fasciste*; and Marchello, *Morale eroica*.

46. *Giornale d'Italia*, 12 September 1926.

47. See fig. 87 in Vittori, *C'era una volta il duce*.

48. Gambetti, *Anni che scottano*, p. 275.

49. Mack Smith, *Mussolini's Roman Empire*, p. vii. On Mussolini's posturing and exhibitionism see also Mack Smith, *Mussolini*, pp. 106–16, 131–37.

50. Quoted in Barzini, *Italians*, p. 146.

51. Bastianini, *Uomini, cose, fatti*, p. 51. For the reactions of other collaborators see Leto, *OVRA*, p. 145; and Senise, *Quando ero capo della polizia*, pp. 93–94. See also Aquarone, *Organizzazione dello Stato totalitario*, pp. 302–11.

52. Quoted in De Felice, *Mussolini il duce*, 2:272. On Arnaldo's influence on his brother see Mack Smith, *Mussolini*, pp. 109–10.

53. Roberto Cantalupo, *Fu la Spagna: Ambasciata presso Franco Febbraio–Aprile 1937* (Milan, 1948), p. 55, quoted in De Felice, *Mussolini il duce*, 2:273.

54. Pini, *Filo diretto*, pp. 18–20. For another view on Mussolini's appeal to youth see Bartoli, "A diciotto anni anch'io credevo in lui," p. 56.

55. B. Mussolini, *Opera omnia*, 2:278, 26:187.

56. B. Mussolini, *Autobiography*, p. 37.

57. On the appeal of the Roman myth to youth see Preti, *Miti dell'impero*, pp. 39–44.

58. B. Mussolini, *Opera omnia*, 27:269.

59. Cannistraro, "Mussolini's Cultural Revolution," p. 127.

60. MEN, *Annuario 1935*, p. 13.

61. PNF, GIL, *Capo centuria*, p. 245.

62. On Mussolini's use of military rhetoric as a Socialist see Cortelazzo, "Mussolini socialista," pp. 63–82.

63. B. Mussolini, "Political and Social Doctrine," pp. 6–7.

64. B. Mussolini, *Opera omnia*, 32:185-86.

65. A. Mussolini, *Ammonimenti ai giovani*, p. 40.

66. B. Mussolini, *Opera omnia*, 7:8, 24:235.

67. Ibid., 10:140-41.

68. MEN, *Annuario 1935*, pp. 295, 305, 61.

69. On the *arditi* see De Felice, *Mussolini il rivoluzionario*, pp. 475-81; Simonini, *Linguaggio di Mussolini*, pp. 131-35; E. Gentile, *Origini dell'ideologia fascista*, pp. 98-109; Mack Smith, *Mussolini*, pp. 30-34, 36-38, 46-47; Nozzoli, *Ras del regime*, p. 44; and Guerri, *Giuseppe Bottai*, pp. 24-30.

70. Quoted in Leeds, *Italy under Mussolini*, p. 10.

71. Vittorini, *Garofano rosso*, pp. 35-37, 49.

72. This aspect of Mussolini's appeal is discussed in detail in two biographies: Hibbert, *Benito Mussolini*; and Monelli, *Mussolini piccolo borghese*. On foreign reports of Mussolini's sexual adventures see De Felice, *Mussolini il duce*, 1:303, 2:275-77. Mussolini's daughter, Edda Ciano, discusses the relationship between her parents and her mother's "scenes of jealousy" in *Mia testimonianza*, pp. 36, 50. Mack Smith discusses Mussolini's "sadistic" relations with women in *Mussolini*, p. 115.

73. From "La donna e il voto," speech to the Chamber of Deputies on 15 May 1925, quoted in Tomasi, *Idealismo e fascismo*, pp. 134-35.

74. Ludwig, *Colloqui con Mussolini*, pp. 168-69.

75. For examples of promaternity articles see Pompei, "Educazione virile"; and Sammartano, *Funzione della scuola media*, p. 70.

76. For examples see Cesari, *Censura nel periodo fascista*, pp. 35-36; and Meldini, *Sposa e madre esemplare*.

77. Vahdah Jeanne Bordeaux, *Benito Mussolini the Man* (New York: Doran, 1927), p. 248, quoted in Gregor, *Italian Fascism*, p. 287.

78. Quoted in Meldini, *Sposa e madre esemplare*, p. 77. See also Macciocchi, *Donna "nera,"* especially pp. 59-62; Antonio Morreno, "The Position of Women in the Fascist State," in Keene, *Neither Liberty nor Bread*, pp. 154-59; Margherita Armani, "Il fascismo e la donna," in Pomba, *Civiltà fascista*, pp. 615-37; and De Grand, "Women under Italian Fascism," pp. 947-68.

79. Quoted in Gregor, *Italian Fascism*, pp. 288-89.

80. B. Mussolini, *Opera omnia*, 7:122, 51, 30, 341, 22:197.

81. Ludwig, *Colloqui con Mussolini*, pp. 121-23, 72.

82. Erik Erikson, *Young Man Luther* (New York: Norton, 1962), p. 186. See also Mosse, *Nationalization*.

83. On Fascist ceremonies see ACS, PNF, DN, busta 62. Dino Alfieri described the organizational details of another celebration in Mazzatosta, *Regime fascista*, p. 38.

84. Quoted in Delzell, *Mediterranean Fascism*, p. 45. On the influence of the myth of revolution on Fascist propaganda see E. Gentile, *Origini dell'ideologia fascista*, pp. 253-94.

85. Vittori, *C'era una volta il duce*, figs. 32-34.

86. B. Mussolini, *Autobiography*, pp. 280-81.

87. *Il Resto del Carlino*, 29 April 1924; Vittori, *C'era una volta il duce*, back cover.

88. Finer, *Mussolini's Italy*, pp. 396–99; Tannenbaum, *Fascist Experience*, p. 65.

89. ACS, PNF, DN, busta 259, "Mostra della Rivoluzione," minutes of a meeting of the PNF national directorate in July 1931.

90. Nicolò Giani, "Civiltà fascista, civiltà dello spirito," quoted in Guido Quazza et al., *Fascismo e società italiana* (Turin: Einaudi, 1973), pp. 235–36. On the School of Fascist Mysticism see also Marchesini, *Scuola dei gerarchi*, and "Episodio della politica culturale," pp. 90–122.

91. Bottai editorial in *Critica fascista*, 1 January 1929, quoted in Ledeen, *Universal Fascism*, p. 67. On Bottai and the youth see Guerri, *Giuseppe Bottai*, especially pp. 133–46.

92. Marpicati, "Azione educativa."

Chapter Two

1. B. Mussolini, "Discorso al Congresso della Corporazione della scuola, 5 dicembre 1925," in *Opera omnia*, 22:23.

2. The relationship between the Gentile reform and earlier developments in Italian education is discussed in Argento, "Continuity and Change," pp. 94–105.

3. Renzo De Felice, introduction to Mazzatosta, *Regime fascista*, p. x. Some other important recent studies on educational policy under fascism include Tomasi, *Idealismo e fascismo*; M. Bellucci and Ciliberto, *Scuola e la pedagogia*; Canestri and Ricuperati, *Scuola in Italia*; Gentili, *Giuseppe Bottai*; Isnenghi, *Educazione dell'Italiano*; Natale, Colucci, and Natoli, *Scuola in Italia*; Ostenc, "Tappa della fascistizzazione," pp. 481–505, and *Education en Italie*; Quazza, *Scuola e politica*; Ricuperati, *Scuola italiana*; Tomasi et al., *Istruzione di base*; and Amato et al., *Scuola nel regime fascista*.

4. Borghi, *Educazione e autorità*, p. 91. The text of the law is reproduced in Canestri and Ricuperati, *Scuola in Italia*, pp. 31–49.

5. Canestri and Ricuperati, *Scuola in Italia*, p. 21.

6. For a discussion of the details of the Casati law see Antonio Santoni Rugiu, "Scuola e politica ieri e oggi," in Quazza, *Scuola e politica*, pp. 9–29; Canestri and Ricuperati, *Scuola in Italia*, pp. 18–30; Minio-Paluello, *Education in Fascist Italy*, pp. 4–13; and Sotto-Commissione dell'Educazione della Commissione Alleata in Italia, *Politica e la legislazione scolastica*, pp. 17–33.

7. See Ricuperati, *Scuola italiana*, pp. 8–10; and Borghi, *Educazione e autorità*, p. 11.

8. Binchy, *Church and State*, pp. 440–41; Minio-Paluello, *Education in Fascist Italy*, pp. 48–49.

9. Tomasi et al., *Istruzione di base*, pp. 10–16; Canestri and Ricuperati, *Scuola in Italia*, pp. 22–25.

10. Tomasi et al., *Istruzione di base*, pp. 14–30. See also Schneider and Clough, *Making Fascists*, pp. 83–85; and Tannenbaum, "Education," pp. 235–36.

11. Figures from ICS, *Sommario di statistiche storiche italiane*, p. 48.

Slightly different figures are used in Tannenbaum, "Education," pp. 234–35; and Fornaca, "Scuola e politica," pp. 31–76.

12. Figures compiled from Sotto-Commissione dell'Educazione, *Politica e la legislazione scolastica*, pp. 428–29; and Minio-Paluello, *Education in Fascist Italy*, pp. 28–29.

13. Canestri and Ricuperati, *Scuola in Italia*, p. 24.

14. On these teachers' organizations see Borghi, *Educazione e autorità*, pp. 104–18, 136–56; Bertoni Jovine and Malatesta, *Breve storia*, pp. 127–38; and Tomasi et al., *Istruzione di base*, pp. 16–18.

15. The activities of these groups and their fate under fascism are discussed in Ulivieri, "Maestri," pp. 163–211.

16. Lyttelton, *Seizure of Power*, pp. 402–3.

17. Tannenbaum, "Education," p. 238.

18. The speech was published in *Rivista pedagogica* 12 (1919): 5–6 and is quoted in part by Borghi, *Educazione e autorità*, pp. 207–8. See also Harris, *Social Philosophy of Giovanni Gentile*, pp. 160–61.

19. Tomasi, *Idealismo e fascismo*, pp. 33–39, deals with the relationship between Croce and the neo-idealist educational reformers.

20. Bertoni Jovine and Malatesta, *Breve storia*, p. 123. The motivations for Mussolini's appointment of Gentile are discussed in Tomasi, *Idealismo e fascismo*, pp. 74–76, 181; and Ricuperati, *Scuola italiana*, pp. 7–8.

21. De Felice, introduction to Mazzatosta, *Regime fascista*, p. ix.

22. For a discussion of the early collaboration between Croce and Gentile see Jacobitti, "Hegemony before Gramsci," pp. 66–84.

23. Short biographical sketches of Gentile are included in Ferrarotto, *Accademia d'Italia*, pp. 119–20; and Tomasi, *Idealismo e fascismo*, pp. 14–15. On the Gentile manifesto and the countermanifesto of non-Fascist intellectuals see E. Papa, *Storia di due manifesti*.

24. G. Turi, "Il progetto dell'Enciclopedia Italiana," *Studi storici* 1 (1972): 141, cited in Amato et al., *Scuola nel regime fascista*, p. 124. Gentile's activities while director of the *Enciclopedia Italiana*, and the non-Fascist character of that publication, are discussed in Quazza et al., *Fascismo e società italiana*, pp. 214–17.

25. It is still not totally clear who was responsible for Gentile's murder, though most scholars agree that the assassination was the work of anti-Fascist partisans. See Minio-Paluello, *Education in Fascist Italy*, p. xi; Tannenbaum, *Fascist Experience*, pp. 286, 320; and Ricuperati, "Scuola e politica," p. 93. The most recent article on the subject indicates that the assassination was carried out by a group of Florentine *gappisti* working without the approval of the CLN (Comitato de Liberazione Nazionale). See Mughini, "Venne un ordine," pp. 100–104.

26. Quoted in Delzell, *Mediterranean Fascism*, p. 12.

27. De Felice, *Mussolini il fascista*, 1:762. On early PNF pronouncements on education see Ricuperati, "Scuola e politica," pp. 77–110; and M. Bellucci and Ciliberto, *Scuola e la pedagogia*, pp. 198–200.

28. Perhaps the best discussion of the social aspects of Gentile's thought in English is Harris's *Social Philosophy of Giovanni Gentile*. Borghi, *Educazione e autorità*, pp. 157–96, treats the ideas of Croce and Gentile and the applica-

tion of those ideas to education. On the thought of Gentile see also E. Gentile,
Origini dell' ideologia fascista, pp. 343–68; and Ostenc, *Education en Italie*,
pp. 21–36.

29. These ideas are expressed in Gentile's works *Che cosa è il fascismo?*
and *Origini e dottrina del fascismo* and in the 1932 article on fascism in the
Enciclopedia Italiana, pt. 1, "Dottrina-idee fondamentali."

30. G. Gentile, *Problema scolastico del dopoguerra*, pp. 35–36.

31. G. Gentile, *Che cosa è il fascismo?* pp. 83–91.

32. G. Gentile, *Fascismo e cultura*, p. 47.

33. G. Gentile, *Fascismo al governo della scuola*, p. 143.

34. G. Gentile, *Che cosa è il fascismo?* p. 38.

35. Gentile's educational theories are presented in the following works of
his: *Sommario di pedagogia*; *Riforma dell'educazione*; *Guerra e fede*; *Fascismo al governo della scuola*; *Problema scolastico del dopoguerra*; *Problemi attuali della politica scolastica*; *Nuova scuola media*; *Che cosa è il fascismo?*
and *Fascismo e cultura*.

36. Natale, Colucci, and Natoli, *Scuola in Italia*, p. 130. For a discussion
of neo-idealist educational theory, and its failures during the Fascist period, see Benito Incatasciato, "Leggere, scrivere, far di conto: Per una storia
della didattica nella scuola elementare," in Tomasi et al., *Istruzione di base*,
pp. 115–57.

37. Quoted in Borghi, *Educazione e autorità*, p. 194.

38. A great deal has been written on Gentile's educational theories, much of
it contentious and contradictory. I. L. Kandel edited the *Educational Yearbook
of the International Institute of Teachers College, Columbia University*, to
which Ernesto Codignola contributed articles in the late 1920s and 1930s. The
first English-speaking scholar to make use of the original Italian sources was
Howard R. Marraro, but his work is marred by an uncritical acceptance of the
Fascist line. His works include *New Education* and *Nationalism in Italian Education*. Another early study of Gentile's educational theories was Thompson,
Educational Philosophy of Giovanni Gentile. In 1944 Kandel commissioned a
piece on the problems of postwar educational reconstruction; the work was
later published by Borghi as *Educazione e autorità*. A valuable early study in
English of Italian education under fascism was commissioned by the Royal Institute of International Affairs in London and published there in 1946: Minio-Paluello's *Education in Fascist Italy*. A well-documented English study of Gentile's thought is Harris's *Social Philosophy of Giovanni Gentile*. A detailed
survey of all developments in education during the Fascist period is available in
the volume published by the Sotto-Commissione dell'Educazione, *Politica e la
legislazione scolastica*, which is documentary and dry as dust, but a gold mine
of information.

39. G. Gentile, *Problema scolastico del dopoguerra*, pp. 78–79, 104.

40. Ibid., p. 8. On Gentile's view of women see Macciocchi, *Donna
"nera,"* pp. 124–26.

41. Natale, Colucci, and Natoli, *Scuola in Italia*, p. 125.

42. The law on school attendance is the Royal Decree of 31 December 1923
(no. 3126).

43. Quoted in Tomasi et al., *Istruzione di base*, p. 22. The basic law on ele-

mentary education is reproduced in Marraro, *Nationalism in Italian Education*, pp. 108–13. On elementary education in the Gentile reform see Ostenc, *Education en Italie*, pp. 87–113.

44. Quoted in Canestri and Ricuperati, *Scuola in Italia*, p. 141. On the *scuola complementare* see also Sotto-Commissione dell'Educazione, *Politica e la legislazione scolastica*, pp. 80–82; and Borghi, *Educazione e autorità*, p. 251.

45. The laws on secondary education were the Royal Decrees of 6 May 1923 (no. 1054), 30 September 1923 (no. 2102), 31 October 1923 (no. 2410), 31 December 1923 (no. 3106), and 31 December 1923 (no. 3126). For a brief outline of the structural organization of the Gentile school system see Tomasi, *Idealismo e fascismo*, p. 42; Natale, Colucci, and Natoli, *Scuola in Italia*, pp. 127–34; and Goad and Catalano, *Education in Italy*, pp. 32–41.

46. Goad and Catalano, *Education in Italy*, pp. 37–39.

47. The case for and against the state examination is debated in Borghi, *Educazione e autorità*, pp. 249–50; Sotto-Commissione dell'Educazione, *Politica e la legislazione scolastica*, pp. 86–88; Ricuperati, *Scuola italiana*, p. 7; Guzzetti, *Movimento cattolico*, pp. 339–40; and Binchy, *Church and State*, p. 470. The state examination was safeguarded by article 35 of the Concordat.

48. Salvatorelli et al., *Stato e chiesa*, p. 154.

49. Administrative reforms were codified in the Royal Decrees of 8 February 1923 (no. 374), 11 March 1923 (no. 635), 27 May 1923 (no. 1209), 7 June 1923 (no. 1539), 16 July 1923 (no. 1753), 7 October 1923 (no. 2132), 3 November 1923 (no. 2453), and 31 December 1923 (no. 2996).

50. Gentile's views on administrative centralization are quoted in Tomasi, *Idealismo e fascismo*, p. 60 (n. 33). On administrative reforms under Gentile see Ostenc, *Education en Italie*, pp. 43–53.

51. Ricuperati, "Scuola e politica," p. 88.

52. Law of 26 April 1928 (no. 1297).

53. In fact, the number increased from seventeen to twenty-one while Gentile was minister. See Goad and Catalano, *Education in Italy*, pp. 47–51. On the reorganization of the universities see Sotto-Commissione dell'Educazione, *Politica e la legislazione scolastica*, pp. 96–106; Marraro, *Nationalism in Italian Education*, pp. 64–67; and Ostenc, *Education en Italie*, pp. 55–58.

54. Borghi, *Educazione e autorità*, pp. 247–48.

55. The text of this law is reproduced in Marraro, *Nationalism in Italian Education*, pp. 109–10. See also G. Gentile, *Fascismo al governo della scuola*, p. 249. This formula was repeated in article 36 of the 1929 Concordat and in the programs for elementary schools in 1945 and 1955. On religion in the Gentile reforms see Ostenc, *Education en Italie*, pp. 115–27; and Salvatorelli et al., *Stato e chiesa*, pp. 140–59.

56. The law of 5 June 1930 (no. 824) and the Royal Decree of 10 July 1930 (no. 1015) extended religious instruction to the secondary schools.

57. G. Gentile, *Fascismo al governo della scuola*, p. 38. See also Woolf, "Catholicism, Fascism and Italian Education," pp. 3–26.

58. Binchy, *Church and State*, pp. 442–46.

59. Quoted in Marraro, *New Education*, p. 57. For Catholic reaction to this

reform see "L'insegnamento religioso nella scuola: Propositi del Governo e spropositi dei liberali," in *Civiltà cattolica*, 8 February 1923, cited in Guzzetti, *Movimento cattolico*, p. 339.

60. Borghi, *Educazione e autorità*, p. 255.

61. Statistics indicate that whereas there had been 147,584 students enrolled in the *scuole tecniche* in 1922, the number had fallen to some 83,000 in the *scuole complementari* by 1923–24 and to 64,590 by 1925. See Natale, Colucci, and Natoli, *Scuola in Italia*, p. 132. The *scuole complementari* were replaced by the *scuole di avviamento al lavoro* in 1929 and then by the *scuole di avviamento professionale*, following the Royal Decree of 6 October 1930 (no. 1379).

62. Quoted in Tomasi, *Idealismo e fascismo*, pp. 59, 44. For a discussion of the effects of the Gentile reform on female school attendance see Barbagli, *Disoccupazione intellettuale*, pp. 211–68.

63. Quoted in Tomasi, *Idealismo e fascismo*, pp. 76, 56.

64. *La Stampa*, 1 May 1923; "La riforma della scuola e la politica scolastica del governo fascista," *Voce repubblicana*, 25 October 1923, cited in Tomasi, *Idealismo e fascismo*, pp. 62–63 (n. 38). On opposition to the Gentile reform, especially at the universities, see Giuntella, "Autonomia e autogoverno," pp. 239–52. On the question of the relationship between the Gentile reforms and the Italian labor market see Barbagli, "Sistema scolastico," pp. 456–92.

65. Piero Gobetti, "I miei conti con l'idealismo attuale," *Rivoluzione liberale*, 1 January 1923, quoted in Tomasi, *Idealismo e fascismo*, pp. 63–64.

66. Filippo Turati, *La più fascista delle riforme: Il pensiero socialista sulla riforma del filosofo del manganello* (Rome: Ufficio stampa del Partito socialista, 1924), cited in Tomasi, *Idealismo e fascismo*, p. 65.

67. Gramsci, *Intellettuali e l'organizzazione della cultura*, pp. 107–9. For a short overview of postwar evaluations of Gentile's work see Tomasi, *Idealismo e fascismo*, pp. 178–80. On criticisms of the Gentile reform see Ostenc, *Education en Italie*, pp. 309–13.

68. Quoted in Tomasi, *Idealismo e fascismo*, p. 85.

69. B. Mussolini, *Autobiography*, p. 148.

70. On Fedele see Ostenc, "Tappa della fascistizzazione," pp. 481–83, and *Education en Italie*, pp. 129–59.

71. Quoted in Tomasi, *Idealismo e fascismo*, pp. 84–85.

72. Pompei, "Educazione virile."

73. ACS, PCM, Gabinetto, Atti (1931–33), busta 678, fasc. 3–5/4023, session of 18 March 1931.

74. Finer, *Mussolini's Italy*, pp. 471–72.

75. Guido De Ruggiero, "Italy under Fascism," *The Yearbook of Education, 1948* (London: University of London, Institute of Education, 1948), p. 571. See also Ascoli, "Education in Fascist Italy," pp. 338–46.

76. Quoted in Canestri and Ricuperati, *Scuola in Italia*, p. 136.

77. ACS, SPD, Ris., busta 1, fasc. 7/R, sottofasc. 6, letter dated 4 August 1927.

78. Ernesto Codignola, "Gentile contro Fedele," *La nuova italiana*, 29 March 1925, cited in Tomasi, *Idealismo e fascismo*, p. 75.

79. Quoted in De Felice, *Mussolini il duce*, 1:188.

1. For criticism of the Gentilian vision see Corra, *Intellettuali creatori*, pp. 57–62; and Marinetti, *Futurismo e fascismo*, pp. 150–51.

2. For a summary of these discussions see Mazzatosta, *Regime fascista*, pp. 17–20.

3. For a text of this speech see Delzell, *Mediterranean Fascism*, pp. 57–61.

4. Law of 24 December 1925 (no. 2263). On this and other exceptional decrees see ibid., pp. 62–74; and Basso, "Dal delitto Matteotti," pp. 69–86, 101–26.

5. Royal Decree Law of 6 November 1926 (no. 1848); Decree Law of 25 November 1926 (no. 2008).

6. B. Mussolini, *Fascism*, pp. 183–94; Royal Decree of 2 September 1928 (no. 1993).

7. Law of 9 December 1928 (no. 2693), revised by the law of 19 December 1929 (no. 2099). On the consolidation of the Fascist state after 1925 see Aquarone, *Organizzazione dello Stato totalitario*, pp. 47–110; and Trentin, *Dieci anni*, pp. 4–88. The most exhaustive study of the period of consolidation is De Felice, *Mussolini il fascista*, vol. 2.

8. For a more detailed discussion of the role of Farinacci see Fornari, *Mussolini's Gadfly Roberto Farinacci*; Lyttelton, *Seizure of Power*, pp. 271–91; and De Felice, *Mussolini il fascista*, 2:168–77.

9. De Felice, *Mussolini il duce*, 1:200. Mack Smith, *Mussolini*, p. 165, referred to Turati as "the most effective party secretary of the whole Fascist period." His dismissal came in part because of the exaggerated rumors circulated by his enemies Farinacci and Starace, who claimed that he was guilty of sadomasochism, incest, homosexuality, and drug addiction. Turati's personal life was indeed the subject of much gossip, but it is also true that he made enemies in the leadership because of his campaign against corruption. His ouster as party secretary was attributed by one biographer of Mussolini to the influence of Arnaldo Mussolini (implicated in Turati's investigations), who claimed that he was a "flagellant and cocaine addict." See Collier, *Duce!*, p. 104.

10. See Lyttelton, "Fascism in Italy," pp. 75–100.

11. For Turati's view of the party see Turati, *Partito e i suoi compiti*.

12. PNF, *Gran Consiglio*, p. 257. This decision was reached in a meeting of the Grand Council on 6 January 1927 and stayed in effect until the tenth anniversary of the regime in October 1932.

13. For a text of the 1926 and 1929 statutes see Aquarone, *Organizzazione dello Stato totalitario*, pp. 386–92, 506–17.

14. On Giuriati see De Felice, *Mussolini il duce*, 1:209–16; and Aquarone, *Organizzazione dello Stato totalitario*, pp. 177–88.

15. De Vito, *Fascismo, antifascismo e resistenza*, p. 87.

16. Italy, Parlamento, Camera dei fasci e delle corporazioni, *La legislazione fascista, 1929–1934*, 2:1344, law of 12 September 1929 (no. 1661). On Mussolini's desire to emphasize *educazione* see ACS, PCM, Gabinetto, Atti (1931–33), busta 678, fasc. 3–5/4023, Mussolini to Balbino Giuliano, 18 September 1929.

17. MEN, *Annuario 1935*, p. 19.

18. Lupi, *Riforma Gentile*, pp. 271–92, 409–14.

19. Segre, "Scuola durante il periodo fascista," pp. 322–27; C. Hamilton, *Modern Italy*, p. 29.

20. Finer, *Mussolini's Italy*, p. 473.

21. Quoted in Cantarella, "Situation of the Learned Class," p. 48.

22. Marciano, *Concetto fascista*, p. 39.

23. On the intellectuals under fascism see Mangoni, *Interventismo della cultura*; A. Hamilton, *Appeal of Fascism*; Garin, *Intellettuali italiani*; Carpanetto Firpo, "Intellettuali e mass-media," pp. 356–76; Vita-Finzi, "Italian Fascism and the Intellectuals," pp. 226–44; Tannenbaum, *Fascist Experience*, pp. 279–302; Manacorda, *Letteratura e cultura*; and Bordoni, *Cultura e propaganda*.

24. For Borgese's view of fascism see Borgese, *Goliath*.

25. On these early exiles see Garosci, *Storia dei fuorusciti*; and Schiavetti, "Fuoruscitismo," pp. 363–67.

26. Ostenc, "Tappa della fascistizzazione," p. 488.

27. Antonicelli, "Professore antifascista," pp. 87–90.

28. Lyttelton, *Seizure of Power*, p. 408; ACS, PCM, Gabinetto, Atti (1931–33), fasc. 5/5–6829.

29. Natale, Colucci, and Natoli, *Scuola in Italia*, p. 138.

30. Royal Decree of 1 June 1933 (no. 641).

31. Salvatorelli and Mira, *Storia d'Italia*, 2:745.

32. MEN, *Bollettino dell'Opera Nazionale Balilla*, 15 November 1934.

33. Salvatorelli and Mira, *Storia d'Italia*, 1:519; PNF, *Foglio d'ordini*, 27 March 1930.

34. ACS, PNF, DN, busta 339; PNF, *Foglio di disposizioni*, 11 and 13 October 1933.

35. The text is reprinted in Delzell, *Mediterranean Fascism*, p. 147, and Marraro, *New Education in Italy*, p. 72. The oath was article 18 of the Law of 28 August 1931 (no. 1227).

36. The pope's defense of the oath appeared in the *Osservatore romano* on 4 December 1931. See Binchy, *Church and State*, pp. 464–65; and Borghi, *Educazione e autorità*, pp. 247–49.

37. All sources agree that these university professors refused to swear the oath and were removed: at the University of Milan, Giuseppe Antonio Borgese (professor of aesthetics) and Piero Martinetti (philosophy); in Turin, Mario Carrara (criminal anthropology), Senator Francesco Ruffini (church law), Lionello Venturi (history of art); in Rome, Ernesto Buonaiuti (history of Christianity), Gaetano De Sanctis (ancient history), Giorgio Levi della Vida (Semitic languages); in Pavia, Giorgio Errera (chemistry); in Bologna, Bortolo Negrisoli (surgery); and in Perugia, Edoardo Ruffini-Avondo (history of law). Some sources also add Michele Giua, professor of chemistry at the University of Turin. In addition, two professors asked for retirement: Vittorio Emanuele Orlando, professor of constitutional law in Rome, and Antonio De Viti De Marco, professor of financial science in Rome. Guido De Ruggiero refused to sign the oath but apparently kept his position. See Zangrandi, *Lungo viaggio*, p. 356; De Felice, *Mussolini il duce*, 1:109; Borghi, *Educazione e autorità*, p. 295; Friends of Italian Freedom, "Oath of the University Professors,"

and "Controversy Concerning the Oath"; and Salvemini, "Teachers' Oath," pp. 523–37.

38. Editorial in *La Tribuna*, 2 December 1932, quoted in Trentin, *Dieci anni*, p. 96.

39. Giovanni Gentile, "Contro demagogie e demagogi," in G. Gentile, *Fascismo al governo della scuola*, pp. 83–84, 128–29, circular to *provveditori* dated 23 April 1923.

40. For a more detailed history of these various organizations see *Almanacco Scolastico Nazionale*, pp. 185–88; Codignola, "Italy," in *Educational Yearbook, 1935*, pp. 351–67; Borghi, *Educazione e autorità*, pp. 106–18; and Ostenc, *Education en Italie*, pp. 160–76.

41. According to party statistics the number of teachers enrolled in the ANIF in 1927 was 72,000 (out of 95,000) and in 1928, 85,500. From 1933 to 1942 enrollments increased as follows:

1933–34	130,904	1938–39	170,573
1934–35	141,133	1939–40	179,971
1935–36	144,950	1940–41	182,683
1936–37	148,475	1941–42	189,615
1937–38	160,316		

Figures taken from ICS, *Compendio statistico*, 1933–42.

42. PNF, *Foglio di disposizioni*, no. 124, 6 June 1933. The Istituto Nazionale Fascista di Cultura was established by the Royal Decree of 6 August 1926 (no. 1408); the Royal Decree of 14 September 1939 (no. 1482) changed the name to the Istituto Nazionale di Cultura Fascista.

43. ACS, MCP, Atti, busta 84, fasc. 3, "Istituto Nazionale di Cultura Fascista," sottofasc. "Varie." On the INCF see also ACS, PNF, DN, busta 143, "Sovvenzioni del Partito alle federazioni ed alle organizzazioni dipendenti"; and PNF, *Foglio di disposizioni*, no. 1389, 15 August 1939.

44. "Il problema della scuola," *Critica fascista*, 15 April 1935, quoted in De Felice, *Mussolini il duce*, 1:192–93.

45. De Vecchi di Val Cismon, *Bonifica fascista della cultura*, p. 35. On De Vecchi see Ostenc, *Education en Italie*, pp. 332–42.

46. De Vecchi di Val Cismon, *Educazione nazionale*, p. 28.

47. Royal Decree Law of 17 June 1928 (no. 1314).

48. Borghi, *Educazione e autorità*, p. 295.

49. On these changes see Royal Decree Laws of 13 June 1935 (no. 1100), 20 June 1935 (nos. 1070 and 1071), 26 November 1935 (no. 1845), 28 November 1935 (no. 2044), and 10 April 1936 (no. 634); and law of 9 March 1936 (no. 400). See also Bascone, *Legislazione fascista*, pp. 9–12; Steiner, "De Vecchi Reform," pp. 140–44; and Codignola, "Italy," in *Educational Yearbook, 1937*, p. 332.

50. De Vecchi to the king, 12 November 1936, in ACS, SPD, Ris., fasc. D, "Vecchi di Val Cismon, Sen., Prof. Cesare Maria."

51. Quoted in Gentili, *Giuseppe Bottai*, p. 1.

52. ACS, MI, DGPS, DPP (1927–44), busta 164, fasc. M13, "Ministero Educazione Nazionale," reports dated 13 November 1936 from Genoa, 15 November 1936 from Florence, and 17 May, 18 and 27 July, and 15 November 1936 from Rome. See also reports for 29 October and 26 December 1935 and

15 and 22 April, 26 November, and 16 December 1936 from Rome, 21 November 1936 from Padua, and 21 November 1936 from Florence.

53. Ibid., report dated 14 November 1936 from Rome.

54. Jannelli Caravella, *Considerazioni sull' educazione fascista*, p. 12.

55. Ibid., pp. 24–25.

56. M. G. Reta, "Education in Fascist Italy," *World Education* 3 (September 1938): 161–63.

57. Umberto Renda, "Scuola e fascismo," p. 469.

58. Jannelli Caravella, *Considerazioni sull' educazione fascista*, p. 36. See also Marraro, *New Education in Italy*, pp. 64–66.

59. On these curriculum revisions see Mazzatosta, *Regime fascista*, pp. 20–21; Borghi, *Educazione e autorità*, pp. 295–96; Minio-Paluello, *Education in Fascist Italy*, pp. 167–76; and Ricuperati, *Scuola italiana*, pp. 23–24. See Isnenghi, *Educazione dell'Italiano*, pp. 32–49, for a list of books required in secondary school libraries; and Cannistraro, *Fabbrica del consenso*, pp. 427–34, and Ricuperati, *Scuola italiana*, pp. 226–46, for lists of authors forbidden in Italy.

60. Article 36 of the Concordat made religious instruction compulsory in the secondary schools. See Natale, Colucci, and Natoli, *Scuola in Italia*, pp. 134–35; and Canestri and Ricuperati, *Scuola in Italia*, p. 166.

61. M. Bellucci and Ciliberto, *Scuola e la pedagogia*, pp. 205–6; Minio-Paluello, *Education in Fascist Italy*, pp. 168–69.

62. Tannenbaum, *Fascist Experience*, p. 164.

63. Codignola, "Italy," in *Educational Yearbook, 1937*, pp. 335–36. See also Lyttelton, *Seizure of Power*, p. 412.

64. A. Giaccardi, "Le mummie della Facoltà di scienze politiche," *La Rivolta ideale*, 11 October 1925, cited in Giuntella, "Facoltà fascista di Scienze Politiche di Perugia," p. 298.

65. There were 96 students enrolled in Perugia in 1927–28 and 207 in 1928–29. By 1930 there were 806 students taking political science degrees in Italy, and by 1942–43 the number had risen to 3,996. See ICS, *Annuario statistico italiano* for the relevant years.

66. Law of 31 December 1934 (no. 2150). See also Schnapper, "Militarization," pp. 97–99; Canestri and Ricuperati, *Scuola in Italia*, pp. 164–69; and Ricuperati, *Scuola italiana*, pp. 170–82. The Royal Decree of 23 September 1937 (no. 1711) set out the program of the military culture courses in the secondary schools.

67. PNF, GIL, *Istruzione premilitare*, pp. 65–66.

68. Marraro, *Nationalism in Italian Education*, pp. 28, 40–44, 68, and *New Education in Italy*, pp. 67–69.

69. Law of 7 January 1929 (no. 5). For a draft of the law see Senato del Regno, Camera dei Deputati, *Bollettino Parlamentare*, 3 vols. (1929), 2:295.

70. Minio-Paluello, *Education in Fascist Italy*, p. 171.

71. ACS, PCM, Gabinetto, Atti (1931–33), busta 678, fasc. 3–5/4023.

72. Bottai, *Scritti*, p. 248.

73. For other studies of the state textbooks bearing on this discussion see Schneider and Clough, *Making Fascists*, pp. 94–100; and Finer, *Mussolini's Italy*, pp. 475–78. Texts used in the mid-thirties are discussed in Minio-Pa-

luello, *Education in Fascist Italy*, pp. 171–75; C. Hamilton, *Modern Italy*, pp. 2–25; Leeds, *Italy under Mussolini*, pp. 57–59; and Ricuperati, *Scuola italiana*, pp. 47–102. Two valuable articles on the same topic are Garofalo, "Veleno sui banchi," pp. 1430–38; and Abad, "Fascist Education," pp. 433–38. An indictment of the content and approach of these state texts can be found in Flora, *Appello al Re*, pp. 48–53.

74. Finer, *Mussolini's Italy*, pp. 183–84.

75. Gaiba and Oddi, *Libro della prima classe*. All of the state textbooks discussed in this section are available in the Collection of Constantine M. Panunzio, box 5, "School Books during the Fascist Regime," at the Hoover Institution, Stanford University, Special Collections. Gaiba and Oddi also wrote the post-Fascist text *Sillabario*. For a similar analysis of other Fascist textbooks see the Panunzio Collection.

76. Gaiba and Oddi, *Libro della prima classe*, pp. 133, 96.

77. The second-grade texts used were Petrucci and Bernardini, *Italiano nuovo*; Ballario and Angoletta, *Quartiere Corridoni*; and Belloni and Bernardini, *Libro per la seconda classe*. The text published after the fall of the regime was a combination of the last two volumes: Ballario and Angoletta, *Quartiere Nuovo*.

78. Petrucci and Bernardini, *Italiano nuovo*, pp. 141–44.

79. Ibid., pp. 57–59.

80. Ballario and Angoletta, *Quartiere Corridoni*, pp. 23–24.

81. Ibid., p. 160.

82. Belloni and Bernardini, *Libro per la seconda classe*, p. 22.

83. The state textbooks that were examined for the third grade were Zanetti and Zanetti, *Patria*; *Letture per la terza classe elementare*; *Libro della terza classe*; and *Sussidario della terza classe*.

84. Zanetti and Zanetti, *Patria*, pp. 122–28, 111–14.

85. Ibid., pp. 38–41.

86. Petrucci and Bernardini, *Italiano nuovo*, pp. 103–7.

87. The fourth-grade textbooks included in this sample were Bargellini and Della Torre, *Libro della quarta classe elementare*; *Libro della quarta classe elementare: Religione, grammatica, storia* (1942); *Libro della quarta classe elementare: Aritmetica, geografia, scienze*; *Libro della quarta classe elementare: Religione, grammatica, storia* (1944); and *Libro sussidario della quarta classe elementare*.

88. Bargellini and Della Torre, *Libro della quarta classe*, pp. 83–84, 171–74.

89. Forges Davanzati, *Balilla Vittorio*. The other fifth-grade texts examined in this sample are *Letture per la quinta classe*; *Libro della quinta classe elementare: Religione, grammatica, storia* (1941); *Libro della quinta classe elementare: Aritmetica, geografia, scienze* (1942); *Libro della quinta classe elementare: Aritmetica, geografia, scienze* (1944); *Libro della quinta classe elementare: Religione, grammatica, storia* (1944). On *Balilla Vittorio* see also Ricuperati, *Scuola italiana*, pp. 20, 40–41, 89–96.

90. Forges Davanzati, *Balilla Vittorio*, p. 55.

91. See, for example, *Libro della terza classe*, pp. 51–52, 60; *Libro della quarta classe elementare: Religione, grammatica, storia* (1942), pp. 121–22.

92. *Libro della terza classe*, pp. 238, 253.

93. *Libro della quarta classe elementare: Aritmetica, geografia, scienze*, p. 205.

94. Ibid., pp. 175, 180. In the 1944 version of this geography book, *Libro sussidario della quarta classe elementare*, Germany was portrayed as responsible for both world wars. In the 1944 book for the third grade the history section stopped at 1918 and there was no mention of fascism or Mussolini.

95. *Libro della quarta classe elementare: Aritmetica, geografia, scienze*, p. 141.

96. *Libro della terza classe*, pp. 69, 116, 118–21.

97. Ibid., pp. 188–93.

98. Campogrande, *Ordinamento dello stato italiano*, p. 6. See also Stanco, *Epitome di cultura fascista*. The contents of books used in the secondary schools and the volumes included in school libraries for students and teachers are listed in Isenghi, *Educazione dell'Italiano*, pp. 177–95, 247–323.

99. Biloni, *Cultura fascista*, p. 107. The other books used in these courses were Ferrari, *Italia fascista* (which was used in the *scuole medie e professionali*); and Pratesi, *Italia imperiale*.

100. Quoted in Berneri, *Mussolini*, pp. 40–41. This prayer was first printed in the Rome paper *La Tribuna* on 25 July 1927.

101. Bertone, *Figli d'Italia*, pp. 51–52. This book is a collection of classwork done in the village school in Canavesano, in the province of what is now Aosta. The town, not particularly zealous about the Fascist cause, then had about a thousand inhabitants, most of them farmers. In addition to excerpts from these school themes, Bertone also includes illustrations from state textbooks and poems and stories about Mussolini used in the schools.

102. Ibid., pp. 173, 208.

103. Vettori, *Duce & ducetti*, pp. 92–94.

104. "I Temi Ministeriali per gli esami di Stato," *Le Cronache scolastiche* 18 (November 1933): 69; 21 (November 1936): 87; 26 (November 1941): 23, quoted in Williams, "Political Indoctrination," pp. 313–14.

105. *Regime fascista*, 26 February 1939, quoted in Cantarella, "Situation of the Learned Class," p. 49.

106. Lyttelton, *Seizure of Power*, p. 411.

107. This is the view of many commentators. See Tannenbaum, *Fascist Experience*, p. 160; Minio-Paluello, *Education in Fascist Italy*, p. 165; Ostenc, "Tappa della fascistizzazione," p. 505; and Salvatorelli and Mira, *Storia d'Italia*, 1:400. A contrary view was advanced by Zangrandi, who in *Lungo viaggio*, pp. 354–56, maintained that the university was the most deeply fascistized level of the school system: "A too relevant part of them . . . bowed to fascism or were even fervently Fascist."

108. For an example of zealous Fascist teachers and school administrators in one classical *liceo* in Pistoia see Amato et al., *Scuola nel regime fascista*, pp. 32–40.

109. Testimony of Leone Bortone in Capitini, *Antifascismo tra i giovani*, pp. 291–92. See also the testimony of Francesco Arcangeli in Arbizzani and Caltabiano, *Storia dell'antifascismo italiano*, 1:120.

110. Testimony of Mario Pomilio in Albertoni, Antonini, and Palmieri, *Generazione degli anni difficili*, pp. 207–8.

111. Melis Bassu, "Fascismo come feticcio," p. 112.

1. M. De Simone, *Pagine eroiche della rivoluzione fascista* (Milan, 1925), cited in Nello, "Mussolini e Bottai," pp. 112–13.

2. Petersen, "Elettorato e base sociale del fascismo," pp. 663–64.

3. The number of students who served was 52,400, of whom 80 percent were officers. See De Negri, "Agitazioni e movimenti studenteschi," p. 734.

4. On fascism as a generational phenomenon see Treves, "Fascismo e il problema delle generazioni," pp. 119–46.

5. Balbo, *Diario, 1922*, pp. 5–6.

6. This was the case in, for example, Parma, Bologna, Pavia, Ferrara, Mantua, Bergamo, Cremona, Milan, Brescia, and Reggio Emilia. See ACS, MRF, busta 52; Nello, *Avanguardismo giovanile*, pp. 3–41; De Negri, "Agitazioni e movimenti studenteschi," pp. 736–42; Petersen, "Elettorato e base sociale del fascismo," pp. 660–61; and Lyttelton, *Seizure of Power*, pp. 56–62, 451 (n. 72). For a study of the *fascio* in Camerino see Santarelli, "Fascio universitario del 1919," pp. 93–113.

7. "Giovinezza" was composed by Giuseppe Blanc and Nino Oxilia in Turin in 1909; it was the official song of the *arditi* during the war. See PNF, *Panorami di realizzazioni del fascismo*, pp. 515–18. The early career of Giuseppe Bottai illustrates the appeal to the youth of futurism, *arditismo*, and fascism. See Guerri, *Giuseppe Bottai*, especially pp. 15–26.

8. On the Avanguardie see Giovanni Galli, *Avanguardismo rivoluzionario*; Gravelli, "Avanguardismo giovanile fascista," pp. 265–72; Caporilli, *Fascismo e i giovani*, pp. 61–67; and PNF, *Venti anni*, pp. 181–84. For examples of the pamphlets and propaganda of these early Avanguardie see Hoover Institution, Special Collections, Ts, P273; and ACS, MRF, buste 99–107, "Carteggio del Comitato Centrale dei Fasci."

9. Ferruccio Vecchi, *Arditismo civile* (Milan, 1920), pp. 78–79, cited in Nello, *Avanguardismo giovanile*, p. 82 (n. 20).

10. De Negri, "Agitazioni e movimenti studenteschi," pp. 747–48.

11. Petersen, "Elettorato e base sociale del fascismo," pp. 659–60.

12. Nello, *Avanguardismo giovanile*, pp. 117–18.

13. Caporilli, *Fascismo e i giovani*, pp. 59–63. At the time of the Rome Congress of the PNF (November 1921), the PNF had 151,644 members, 19,783 of them, or 13 percent, students. See Tasca, *Nascita e avvento del fascismo*, p. 257.

14. The statute of the Avanguardia Giovanile Fascista is reprinted in Nello, *Avanguardismo giovanile*, pp. 193–95, 203–5.

15. Gravelli, *Ai balilla*, pp. 12–13. The name "Balilla" had historic origins. It was chosen in memory of a half-legendary Genoese boy, Giovanni Battista Perasso (nicknamed Balilla), whose rock-hurling gesture of defiance led to a revolt against the Austrians in 1746. During the Risorgimento, patriotic poetry called on the sons of Italy to emulate the gesture of Balilla. See ibid., pp. 16–23; and Finer, *Mussolini's Italy*, pp. 437–38.

16. Nello, *Avanguardismo giovanile*, pp. 138–42.

17. Estimated enrollment in 1924 was about twenty-five thousand in the Avanguardie and about ten thousand in the Balilla. See PNF, *Gran Consiglio*,

pp. 127–29. Many of these early groups had their own newsletters or sections in the papers published by the local *fasci*. See Dominici, " 'Pagina dei giovani' dell' 'Assalto,' " pp. 297–311.

18. Marciano, *Concetto fascista*, pp. 67–68. The draft law was presented to the Chamber by Mussolini on 30 January 1926. The debates on the draft are included in Camera dei Deputati, *Legislazione fascista, 1922–1928*, 2:1298–1301. The text of the law and comments can be found in *Gazzetta Ufficiale*, no. 7, 11 January 1927; Senato del Regno, Camera dei Deputati, *Bollettino Parlamentare*, 3 vols. (1927), 2:283; MEN, *Opera Nazionale Balilla*. An English translation of the ONB law and commentary are available in B. Mussolini, *Fascism*, pp. 264–70. A collection of all the major provisions affecting the development of the ONB until 1937 can be found in ACS, PCM, Gabinetto, Atti (1931–33), fasc. 1.1.15, no. 3500, sottofasc. 1–11.

19. The structural skeleton proposed in the law of 3 April 1926 (no. 2247) was fleshed out by the Royal Decree of 9 January 1927 (no. 6). On these groups see also De Gaetano and Trizzino, *Libro dell' avanguardista*; Marzolo, *Opera Balilla, VIII Leva fascista*, and *Youth Movement*; Piccoli, *Organizzazioni giovanili*; and Giuliano, "Education nationale," pp. 172–83. For a recent study of the ONB see Ostenc, *Education en Italie*, pp. 233–69, 363–67.

20. The percentage of ONB chaplains who also served as MVSN officers was 20 in 1934, 23 in 1936, and 24 in 1937. See MEN, *Bollettino dell' Opera Nazionale Balilla*, 1 November 1934, 15 February and 15 October 1937.

21. Piccoli, *Youth Movement*, p. 23. On this religious instruction see Binchy, *Church and State*, pp. 423–39; and Giuntella, "Circoli cattolici," pp. 77–80.

22. The phrase was used by police agents in ACS, SPD, Ris., busta 45, fasc. 242/R, "Renato Ricci," sottofasc. 3, "Informazioni Pubblica Sicurezza."

23. Ibid., sottofasc. 1, "Varia."

24. ACS, PCM, Gabinetto, Atti (1937–39), fasc. 1.4.2, sottofasc. 4. On Ricci see also ACS, Fondo Renato Ricci, 166 (8 boxes); and Lasswell and Sereno, "Governmental and Party Leaders," pp. 914–29. For Ricci's comments on the ONB see his "Buts et activité de l'oeuvre des Balilla," pp. 147–56.

25. MPI, *Bollettino Ufficiale* (1928), p. 299, circular no. 63 dated 21 August 1928.

26. On the question of voluntary enrollment see Salvemini, *Under the Axe*, pp. 316–27; Abad, "Fascist Education," p. 436; and Togliatti, *Lezioni sul fascismo*, pp. 66–69.

27. Achille Starace, *Gioventù Italiana del Littorio* (Milan, 1939), quoted in Nello, "Mussolini e Bottai," pp. 361–62. See also Solmi, "Missione della donna," pp. 193–205; and Meldini, *Sposa e madre esemplare*, p. 68. For a Fascist view of the social role of women see Roberto Farinacci's speech opening the 1928–29 academic year at the Istituto femminile in Cremona, "La donna nella vita e nella storia," quoted in Isnenghi, *Educazione dell'Italiano*, pp. 200–207.

28. Royal Decree Law of 14 November 1929 (no. 1992).

29. Collino, "Le organizzazioni giovanili," p. 606. See also PNF, DN, *Programmi dei corsi affidati ai Fasci femminili*; and Caporilli, *Fascismo e i giovani*, pp. 167–69.

30. C. Hamilton, *Modern Italy*, pp. 35–40.

31. Starace, *Fasci giovanili*, pp. 72–73.

32. See the Royal Decree of 4 August 1924 (no. 1292) and the law of 29 December 1930 (no. 1759). See also Fabrizio, *Sport e fascismo*, pp. 102–5. The reaction of old army personnel to these innovations—and to the premilitary program in general—was often hostile. General Quirino Armellini, for example, claimed in his postwar memoirs (*Crisi dell'esercito*, p. 63) that the instruction given by the MVSN was "choreography" and not military training, and that the courses were designed to lull the nation into a false sense of security.

33. MEN, *Bollettino dell'Opera Nazionale Balilla*, 1 November 1934, 9 October 1938. In 1938 there were about thirty-five thousand instructors working in the program.

34. Tannenbaum, *Fascist Experience*, p. 125.

35. For example, see PNF, *Atti del PNF* 2 (1932–33): 387, Starace circular of 5 September 1933. See also ACS, PNF, DN, busta 310, for circulars and pamphlets on the various specialized training programs offered by the ONB.

36. "Fascismo e sport," *Popolo d'Italia*, 2 April 1924. See also Mario Patetta, "Sport elemento," p. 212.

37. PNF, ONB, *Obelisco Mussolini*; Marraro, *New Education*, pp. 190–91.

38. PNF, *Foglio d'ordini*, 4 December 1926.

39. Quoted in Fabrizio, *Sport e fascismo*, p. 116. On Mussolini and sports see Carli, *Mussolini e lo sport*.

40. Caporilli, *Fascismo e i giovani*, p. 103.

41. See Camera dei Deputati, *Legislazione fascista, 1922–1928*, 2:1295–98, for a text of the Royal Decree of 15 March 1923 (no. 684); and ACS, PCM, Gabinetto, Atti (1931–33), fasc. 1.1.15, no. 3500, sottofasc. 1–1. On the regime's physical training programs see Renda, "Scuola e fascismo," pp. 484–87; and L. Ferretti, "Fascismo e l'educazione sportiva," pp. 609–13.

42. The academy was established by the Royal Decree Law of 20 November 1927 (no. 2341).

43. Tannenbaum, *Fascist Experience*, p. 125; Fabrizio, *Sport e fascismo*, p. 34. For a Fascist view of these teachers see PNF, *Collegio Orvieto GIL*. Marraro, in *New Education*, pp. 190–93, claims that between 1929 and 1934 the academy awarded 350 diplomas, and that 500 young men and 200 young women attended these courses in 1934.

44. Marzolo, *Opera Balilla*, p. 9.

45. *Bollettino del Comando Generale della G.I.L.*, no. 24, 28 October 1938. In 1934, 1,851,716 ONB members took part in the Festa ginnastica; in 1935 the number was 2,048,536; in 1936 it was 2,071,575; and in 1937, 2,357,025. In 1935 boys and girls competed in 17,300 contests sponsored by the ONB; in 1936 the number had risen to 22,410. See MEN, *Bollettino dell'Opera Balilla*, 15 February and 15 October 1937. See also ACS, PNF, DN, busta 195, "G.I.L. Corrispondenza varia dal 1925 al 1943."

46. In 1934 the number of Avanguardisti attending the Campo Dux was 20,886; in 1936 some 25,000 young men participated; in 1937 the number was closer to 26,000. See MEN, *Bollettino Quindicinale dell'Opera Balilla*, 1 No-

vember 1934, 15 February 1937, 15 October 1937; ACS, MCP, busta 80, fasc. 1, "Campeggi della G.I.L.," sottofasc. 1.

47. ACS, MCP, busta 80, fasc. 11, sottofasc. 1.

48. PNF, GIL, *Regolamento delle colonie estive*, p. 29; PNF, Fasci italiani all'estero, *Figli degli Italiani all'estero*. See also PNF, *Atti del PNF* 4 (1934–35): 1127–54, for a long appendix on the organization of these camps. On government subsidies to the camps see PNF, DN, busta 143, "Sovvenzioni del Partito alle Federazioni ed alle organizzazioni dipendenti."

49. PNF, GIL, *Regolamento delle colonie estive*, p. 15.

50. See ACS, PNF, DN, busta 195, for detailed inspection reports of these camps in 1938. The organization of the camps was also the subject of the PNF's *Bollettino del Comando Generale della G.I.L.*, no. 18, 15 July 1940; and of Marpicati's "Azione educativa."

51. PNF, GIL, *Regolamento delle colonie estive*, p. 76.

52. Caporilli, *Educazione giovanile*, pp. 163–67. The Gentile law on rural schools was dated 31 October 1923 (no. 2410). See also Valitutti, "Elementary Education," pp. 792–93; and Codignola, "Italy," in *Educational Yearbook, 1937*, pp. 323–24.

53. Royal Decree of 17 March 1930 (no. 394).

54. Camera dei Deputati, *Legislazione fascista, 1929–1934*, 2:1451.

55. For a detailed discussion of this insurance fund see PNF, ONB, *Cassa mutua assistenza "Arnaldo Mussolini."*

56. In November 1934 Mussolini also organized the formations for boys and girls aged six to eight known as the Figli e Figlie della Lupa, or the "Sons and Daughters of the She-Wolf." See Piccoli, *Youth Movement*, p. 12.

57. ACS, SPD, Ris., busta 44, fasc. 242/R, "Giovanni Giuriati," circular dated 17 October 1930. See also ibid., busta 31, fasc. 242/R, sottofasc. 1, "Riunione del Direttorio, 3 giugno 1931 (IX)"; and Starace, *Fasci giovanili*, p. 14.

58. The class bias in the PNF groups is discussed in Tannenbaum, *Fascist Experience*, p. 240; Tomasi, *Idealismo e fascismo*, p. 142; and H. S. Hughes, *United States and Italy*, p. 70. See also G. Longo, "Organizzazioni giovanili"; Capaldo, "GUF e GIL"; Guizzardi, "Funzione della gioventù universitaria"; and Giovenale, "Fondamentale iniziativa."

59. PNF, *Gran Consiglio*, pp. 368–69.

60. On Scorza see ACS, SPD, Ris., busta 45, fasc. 242/R, "Carlo Scorza"; Deakin, *Brutal Friendship*, pp. 320–21; and Sforza, *Contemporary Italy*, p. 325.

61. On the *Leva fascista* see Caporilli, *Fascismo e i giovani*, p. 175; Marzolo, *Opera Nazionale Balilla*, and *VIII Leva fascista*; PNF, *Dottrina fascista per le reclute della IV Leva fascista*; and PNF, ONB, *XI Leva Fascista*, and *VII Leva Fascista*.

62. The status of the ONB during these years is still the subject of debate. Tannenbaum quotes (*Fascist Experience*, p. 143) a personal interview (July 1967) with Dr. Nicola Barattucci (in charge of personnel at the ONB during the 1930s), who insisted that the ONB, though legally part of the ministry, was never dependent on it.

63. For a text of Ricci's letter dated 30 May 1931 see ACS, SPD, Ris., busta 31, fasc. 212/R, "Riunione del Direttorio del PNF," sottofasc. 1, inserto B, "Lettere al Duce e all'On. Giuriati di Renato Ricci." Scorza's reply came in a letter to Mussolini dated 11 July 1931. See ibid., busta 31, fasc. 242/R, "Riunione del Direttorio del 14 luglio 1931," sottofasc. 2, inserto A, "Statistiche."

64. Ibid., busta 46, fasc. 242/R, "Achille Starace." There was also no love lost between De Vecchi and Ricci. See ACS, MI, DGPS, DPP (1927–44), busta 164, fasc. M13, "Ministero Educazione Nazionale," reports dated 17 June 1933 and 21 and 22 February 1935.

65. ACS, SPD, Ris., busta 46, fasc. 242/R, "Achille Starace," letters dated 19 March 1935 and 7 September 1937.

66. Police reports on Bottai during 1937–38 accused him of—among other things—being overly friendly to Jews and Masons, having a Jewish mother, and nepotism. See ACS, MI, DGPS, DPP (1927–44), busta 164, fasc. M13, "Ministero Educazione Nazionale," reports dated 10 March 1937 and 17 December 1938.

67. See ACS, SPD, Ris., busta 45, fasc. 242/R, "Renato Ricci," sottofasc. 3, "Informazioni Pubblica Sicurezza"; and ACS, MI, DGPS, DPP, busta 164, fasc. M13, "Ministero Educazione Nazionale."

68. For a collection of anonymous letters asking for Starace's ouster see ACS, SPD, Ris., busta 90, fasc. W/R, "Starace Achille," sottofasc. 1.

69. Tamaro, Venti anni, 2:456.

70. Ibid., pp. 216–17, 227.

71. Zangrandi, Lungo viaggio, p. 127. Mussolini was furious over Starace's order that all official correspondence end with Viva il Duce! He ordered the practice stopped and pointed out that Starace had "succeeded in making him look ridiculous to the whole of Italy." See Hibbert, Benito Mussolini, pp. 63–64; and ACS, PCM, Gabinetto, Atti (1937–39), fasc. 20/1/5668.

72. Quoted in Tannenbaum, Fascist Experience, p. 61.

73. De Felice, Mussolini il duce, 1:224.

74. On the 1932 statute see Aquarone, Organizzazione dello Stato totalitario, pp. 518–29. The 1938 PNF statute is reprinted in De Felice, Mussolini il duce, 1:826–37. The charismatic function of the Duce is discussed in Gambetti, Inchiesta, pp. 185–89.

75. PNF, Foglio di disposizioni, no. 71, 31 January 1933. See also PNF, Atti del PNF, 2 (1932–33): 212; and PNF, Foglio di disposizioni, no. 96, 2 April 1933.

76. PNF, Atti del PNF, 2 (1932–33): 260; PNF, Foglio di disposizioni, no. 170, 13 October 1933. See also PNF, Atti del PNF, 3 (1933–34): 438; and PNF, Foglio di disposizioni per le organizzazioni giovanili del PNF, no. 5, 28 July 1934.

77. For a discussion of the "anti-lei" campaign see Tamaro, Venti anni, 3:301–2. Several interesting articles on the subject of this Fascist "folklore" are included in the October 1952 issue of Il Ponte; see especially the editorial "Per la storia del costume fascista," pp. 1337–48; and Levi, "Snobismo del conformismo," pp. 1476–80.

78. This decision became law on 30 December 1935 (no. 2261). See ACS, SPD, Ris., busta 29.

79. PNF, *Foglio di disposizioni*, no. 1287, 14 March 1939. See also Starace, *Vademecum dello stile fascista*, p. 60. For autobiographical testimony concerning youthful resistance to the activities of the PNF groups see the testimony of Mario Pomilio in Albertoni, Antonini, and Palmieri, *Generazione degli anni difficili*, pp. 207–8.

80. G. Ciano, *Ciano's Hidden Diary, 1937–1938*, pp. 183–84, 203, 210. Starace was especially loathed by university students, who found his posturing laughable and his ignorance unsettling. A police agent reported, for example, that when during the ceremonies opening the academic year in 1937, the rector of the University in Milan read a message from Starace, "there was heard among the mass of students a loud expression of disapproval." See ACS, MI, DGPS, DAGR, cat. D9, "Agitazioni Studenti," busta 26/B, "Anno 1937," report dated 3 February 1937. For Starace's defense of his stewardship see ACS, SPD, Ris., busta 46, fasc. 242/R, "Starace Achille," sottofasc. 1. This forty-two-page letter to Ettore Muti (the new PNF secretary) and Mussolini was dated 8 December 1939.

81. On the removal of Starace see ACS, PCM, Gabinetto, Atti (1939), fasc. I.4.2, no. 8496, sottofasc. 1; G. Ciano, *Diario, 1939–1943*, p. 408, entry for 16 May 1941; and Collier, *Duce!* p. 166. Mack Smith, in *Mussolini*, pp. 175–81, claims that Starace's dossier also included charges of rape, pederasty, and peculation.

82. ACS, SPD, Ris., busta 31, fasc. 242/R, "Riunione del Direttorio del 14 luglio 1931," sottofasc. 2, inserto A, "Statistiche."

83. These monthly reports are collected in ACS, PNF, SPEP. The collection is incomplete, containing only material on cities beginning with the letters *G* through *Z*.

84. ACS, PNF, SPEP, busta 25, "Torino," letter dated 14 November 1931. See also ibid., letter dated January 1932; and ibid., busta 13, "Perugia," report of December 1931.

85. Ibid., busta 26, "Trento," letter of 27 April 1932. See also ibid., letters of 21 October 1930 and 15 November 1933; and ibid., busta 22, "La Spezia," letter of November 1930.

86. Ibid., busta 6, "Milano," letter of 24 June 1932; ibid., busta 21, "Siracusa," letter of 4 February 1934.

87. Ibid., busta 20, "Savona," letter of 8 January 1936.

88. Ibid., busta 25, "Torino," letter of 2 October 1937.

89. Ibid., busta 4, "Matera," letter dated 3 November 1933. See also ibid., letters of 25 November 1934 and 31 May 1935; ibid., busta 15, "Pola," dated 27 March 1934; and ibid., busta 28, "Vicenza," dated 30 December 1930.

90. Ibid., busta 21, "Siracusa," reports for May–June 1932. See also ibid., report for 4 February 1934; ACS, Fondo Renato Ricci, busta B7, fasc. 26, reports on groups in Trieste dated 12 March 1931; and ibid., fasc. 25, reports for Zara dated 2 January 1930 and 24 January 1935.

91. ACS, PNF, SPEP, busta 17, "Reggio Calabria," letter dated 28 March 1934. See also ibid., busta 9, "Napoli," dated 30 June 1934.

1. The following works are of interest on church-state relations under fascism: Jemolo, *Chiesa e stato*, and its English translation *Church and State*; Margiotta Broglio, *Italia e Santa Sede*; Martini, *Studi sulla questione romana*; Candeloro, *Movimento cattolico*; Guzzetti, *Movimento cattolico*; Binchy, *Church and State*; Halperin, *Separation of Church and State*; Miccoli, "Chiesa e il fascismo," pp. 183–208; Rogari, *Santa Sede e fascismo*; Scoppola, *Chiesa e il fascismo*; Scoppola and Traniello, *Cattolici tra fascismo e democrazia*; and Scoppola, "Chiesa e il fascismo durante il pontificato di Pio XI," pp. 195–232.

2. B. Mussolini, "L'uomo e la divinità," in *Opera omnia*, 33:12–21, 36.

3. Quoted in Megaro, *Mussolini in the Making*, p. 124. See also Kirkpatrick, *Mussolini*, p. 39; and De Felice, *Mussolini il rivoluzionario*, pp. 49–59.

4. Kirkpatrick, *Mussolini*, p. 42.

5. B. Mussolini, *Opera omnia*, 3:74; Megaro, *Mussolini in the Making*, pp. 210–14.

6. Binchy, *Church and State*, p. 105.

7. Delzell, *Mediterranean Fascism*, pp. 12–13, 15–17. See also De Felice, *Mussolini il rivoluzionario*, pp. 744–48.

8. Quoted in Delzell, *Mediterranean Fascism*, p. 24.

9. Quoted in Ludwig, *Colloqui con Mussolini*, p. 174.

10. B. Mussolini, *Opera omnia*, 26:399.

11. An interesting, if highly laudatory, character sketch of Pius XI can be found in Binchy, *Church and State*, pp. 71–99.

12. *Civiltà cattolica*, 7 November 1925, quoted in Rogari, *Santa Sede e fascismo*, p. 132.

13. Santarelli, *Storia del fascismo*, 2:164. On conflicts between the church and the regime over education see Ostenc, *Education en Italie*, pp. 271–83.

14. Quoted in Delzell, *Mediterranean Fascism*, p. 51.

15. Quoted in Guzzetti, *Movimento cattolico*, p. 329.

16. Ibid., p. 391; Rogari, *Santa Sede e fascismo*, pp. 51–52; Mack Smith, *Mussolini*, pp. 65, 159–61.

17. "L'insegnamento religioso nella scuola: Propositi del Governo e spropositi dei liberali," *Civiltà cattolica*, 8 February 1923, cited in Guzzetti, *Movimento cattolico*, pp. 338–39. See also Woolf, "Catholicism, Fascism and Italian Education," pp. 7–8.

18. On Gemelli and the Catholic University see Webster, *Cross and the Fasces*, pp. 153–61; and Binchy, *Church and State*, pp. 482–90.

19. Quoted in Scoppola, *Chiesa e il fascismo*, p. 65.

20. Law of 25 November 1926 (no. 2008). On the April congress and the PPI until 1926 see Giovanni Spadolini, introduction to Rogari, *Santa Sede e fascismo*, pp. 19–35; Jemolo, *Church and State*, pp. 194–228; Candeloro, *Movimento cattolico*, pp. 452–84; and Binchy, *Church and State*, pp. 131–95.

21. On the political activities and early history of Catholic Action see Candeloro, *Movimento cattolico*, pp. 484–95; Ferrari, *Azione cattolica*; Magri, *Azione cattolica*, vol. 1; and Binchy, *Church and State*, pp. 496–537.

22. Candeloro, *Movimento cattolico*, pp. 484–85; Delzell, *Mediterranean*

Fascism, p. 166, and *Mussolini's Enemies*, p. 102.

23. Binchy, *Church and State*, p. 509.

24. The distinction between the "substantially philo-Fascist" stance of the national leadership of Ca   lic Action and the activities of local groups is emphasized in Giuntella, "Circoli cattolici," pp. 31–92. The question of the relationship between Catholic Action and the regime elicited debate, especially in the immediate postwar period, with the establishment of the Democrazia Cristiana. In a letter to ex-PPI leader Stefano Jacini (probably dated 1944), Alcide De Gasperi was severe in his criticism of Catholic Action and its relations with the regime, which he termed a "miserable spectacle." De Gasperi claimed that many ex-Popolari and Catholic trade union leaders had left Catholic Action because of its pro-Fascist stance; he predicted that the organization would not provide the nucleus of a new Catholic movement in Italy because it had been too deeply compromised during the Fascist period. The letter is published in Maria Romana De Gasperi, ed., *De Gasperi scrive: Corrispondenza con capi di Stato, cardinali, uomini politici, giornalisti, diplomatici* (Brescia: 1974), 1:186–87, and excerpted in Scoppola and Traniello, *Cattolici tra fascismo e democrazia*, pp. 7–9.

25. The group was formally known as the Associazione Scoutista Cattolica Italiana. On its early history see Reineri, *Cattolici e fascismo*, pp. 37–39.

26. Binchy, *Church and State*, pp. 410–11.

27. Quoted in ibid., pp. 411–12.

28. On the 1926 violence against Catholic groups see Dominici, " 'Pagina dei giovani' dell' 'Assalto,' " pp. 308–11; Tramontin, *Cattolici, popolari e fascisti*, pp. 201–37; and Reineri, *Cattolici e fascismo*, pp. 111–26.

29. De Felice, *Mussolini il fascista*, 2:399–404.

30. Portions of this speech are reprinted in Scoppola, *Chiesa e il fascismo*, pp. 127–30; Rogari, *Santa Sede e fascismo*, p. 177; and De Felice, *Mussolini il fascista*, 2:402.

31. Royal Decree of 9 January 1927 (no. 6). By 1934 there were some two thousand ONB chaplains, and the number increased after the establishment of the GIL in 1937. On religious instruction in the Fascist youth groups see Binchy, *Church and State*, pp. 423–29; and E. Bellucci, "Educazione religiosa nell'ONB," pp. 105–12.

32. ACS, PCM, Gabinetto, Atti (1931–33), fasc. 1.1.15, no. 3500, sotto-fasc. 5.

33. Excerpts from the pope's letter are included in Guzzetti, *Movimento cattolico*, p. 396; and Rogari, *Santa Sede e fascismo*, p. 180.

34. ACS, MI, DGPS, DAGR (1920, 1923–45), cat. G1, busta 154, fasc. 102, "Anno 1929, Affari generali Opera Nazionale Balilla"; ibid., busta 8, fasc. 114, "Associazioni cattoliche 1927." This file also contains detailed reports from prefects on the activities of Catholic groups in 1927 and membership lists.

35. Ibid., busta 149, fasc. 60, "Corpo Nazionale dei Giovani esploratori cattolici," letter dated 1 October 1927. The bulk of these reports came from traditionally Catholic strongholds in the Veneto and from border areas (Pola, Fiume, Zara), though incidents were reported in other areas as well.

36. ACS, PCM, Gabinetto, Atti (1931–33), fasc. 1.1.15, no. 3500, sotto-fasc. 1–8, minister of the interior (Michele Bianchi) to all prefects, 19 April 1928 (no. 12257).

37. Quoted in Rogari, *Santa Sede e fascismo*, p. 237.

38. Quoted in Binchy, *Church and State*, p. 417.

39. Royal Decree of 9 April 1928 (no. 696). A memo to all prefects from Mussolini went out on 19 April 1928 with the same wording. ACS, PCM, Gabinetto, Atti (1931–33), fasc. 1.1.15, no. 3500, sottofasc. 1–8.

40. Tacchi-Venturi to Francesco Giunta dated 18 April 1928. See the series of letters exchanged between Tacchi-Venturi and Mussolini between 14 April and 4 May 1928 in ACS, PCM, Gabinetto, Atti (1931–33), fasc. 1.1.15, no. 3500, sottofasc. 1–8; and in ACS, SPD, Ris., busta 47, fasc. 404/R, "Tacchi-Venturi, Pietro," sottofasc. 1.

41. For the text of the circular (no. 15557) see ACS, MI, DGPS, DAGR (1920, 1923–45), cat. G1, busta 91, "Gioventù cattolica"; and ibid., busta 12, fasc. 144, "Circoli cattolici."

42. ACS, PCM, Gabinetto, Atti (1931–33), fasc. 1.1.15, no. 3500, sotto-fasc. 1–8. See also Rogari, *Santa Sede e fascismo*, p. 239; and De Felice, *Mussolini il fascista*, 2:412–13.

43. See reports dated 1 July 1928 to 31 December 1928 in ACS, MI, DGPS, DAGR (1920, 1923–45), cat. G1, busta 94, "Situazione della Pubblica Sicurezza dal lato politico nelle provincie del Regno e relazioni semestrali sull'attività dei partiti politici e riorganizzazione delle loro associazioni." Most activity was reported in Verona, Udine, Vicenza, Trent, Aosta, Turin, Bolzano, Treviso, and Gorizia.

44. Ibid., busta 91, "Gioventù cattolica: Affari generali, 1925–1942," especially reports from Treviso, Verona, Vicenza, Alessandria, and Sondrio. See also the report from Rome dated 20 November 1920 in ibid., busta 146, "Azione cattolica."

45. The provision on religious education in the secondary schools was written into the law of 5 June 1930 (no. 824) and the Royal Decree of 10 July 1930 (no. 1015). The terms of the treaty and Concordat are included in Delzell, *Mediterranean Fascism*, pp. 156–64; Senato del Regno, Camera dei Deputati, *Bollettino Parlamentare*, 3 vols. (1929), 1:29–64; and National Catholic Welfare Conference, *Treaty and Concordat*.

46. Quoted in Jemolo, *Church and State*, p. 323.

47. The role of local Catholic Action leaders in the plebiscite is discussed in Guasco, *Fascisti e cattolici*, pp. 65–67, 105–8. After the electoral reform of 1928, Italians voted on a single list of candidates in elections. An original list of 800 names nominated by Fascist labor syndicates and other organizations was pared down to 400 by the Fascist Grand Council. This list was then presented as a block to qualified voters—those who paid syndicate dues—who could vote "yes" or "no." The first election under this new system was held on 24 March 1929, a little over a month after the signature of the Lateran Accords. It resulted, not surprisingly, in a lopsided "yes" vote for the government list. For more information see Delzell, *Mediterranean Fascism*, pp. 69–70.

48. On the parliamentary deliberations see Jemolo, *Church and State*, pp. 238–50.

49. The text of this speech was published in Senato del Regno, Camera dei Deputati, *Bollettino Parlamentare* (1929), 2:3–55. Sections are included in B. Mussolini, *Opera omnia*, 24:75–76; and B. Mussolini, *Accordi del Laterano*, pp. 2–6.

50. See excerpts of the pope's speech in Candeloro, *Movimento cattolico*, pp. 509–10; and Guzzetti, *Movimento cattolico*, pp. 403–4.

51. B. Mussolini, *Accordi del Laterano*, p. 117.

52. Binchy, *Church and State*, p. 419.

53. On the FUCI see Webster, *Cross and the Fasces*, pp. 137–44; Giuntella, "Circoli cattolici," pp. 31–92; Moro, "Appunti sulla cultura religiosa," pp. 93–103; Lami, "Circolo della FUCI," pp. 429–34; Papini, "Fuci e le violenze fasciste," pp. 3–23; Moro, "Afascismo e antifascismo," pp. 733–99; Ballerio, "Federazione universitaria cattolica italiana," pp. 39–69; Giuntella, "Fatti del 1931," pp. 183–233; Pecoraro, *Chiesa, Azione cattolica e fascismo*, pp. 1061–1156; and Woolf, "Makings of Christian Democracy."

54. "La gioventù fascista e quella cattolica possono collaborare . . . ?" *Libro e moschetto*, 21 February 1929.

55. Julius Evola, "Per una educazione romana," *Vita nova*, September 1929, quoted in Giuntella, "Fatti del 1931," pp. 199–200.

56. The encyclical was published in Italian as *Rappresentanti in terra*; its English title was *On the Christian Education of Youth*. The text was published in Husslein, *Social Wellsprings*, 2:91–103.

57. De Felice, *Mussolini il duce*, 1:249.

58. ACS, MI, DGPS, DAGR (1920, 1923–45), cat. G1, busta 94, "Situazione della Pubblica Sicurezza dal lato politico nelle provincie." See reports for 1 January–30 March from Verona, Bolzano, Udine, Trent, and Vicenza; for 1 April–30 June from Bolzano and Vicenza; and for 1 July–30 September from Bolzano, Udine, Verona, Vicenza, Gorizia, Pola, Reggio Emilia, Pistoia, Trent, and Messina.

59. Ibid., reports for 1 October–31 December from Alessandria, Novara, Como, Padua, Udine, Verona, Vicenza, and Gorizia; ibid., busta 146, "Azione cattolica," report dated 25 March 1930 from Ancona.

60. ACS, PNF, SPEP, busta 28, "Vicenza," report for 23 September 1930. See also ibid., busta 26, "Trento," report for 21 October 1930; ibid., "Treviso," for 24 October 1930; and ibid., busta 28, "Vicenza," for 30 December 1930. Local studies also illustrate the development of these groups. See Guasco, *Fascisti e cattolici*, pp. 69–93; and Tramontin, *Cattolici, popolari e fascisti*, pp. 257–303. Both provide excerpts of reports on the activities of Catholic Action groups and detailed information on Fascist reprisals against these organizations. See also Palla, *Firenze nel regime fascista*, pp. 365–404.

61. Gherardo Casini, "Professionisti cattolici o cattolici di professione?" *Il Lavoro fascista*, 19 March 1931, and "Manovre cattoliche," ibid., 26 March 1931. These and other articles are discussed in De Felice, *Mussolini il duce*, 1:254–55.

62. ACS, MI, DGPS, DAGR (1920, 1923–45), cat. G1, busta 151, fasc. 77, "FUCI," sottofasc. 3, telegrams to the prefect of Ferrara on 29 March 1931 and to the prefects of Pavia, Viterbo, and Catania on 5–6 April 1931.

63. Excerpts of the letter are included in Tamaro, *Venti anni*, 2:444–45.

64. The message, no. 15379, is available in ACS, MI, DGPS, DAGR (1920, 1923–45), cat. G1, busta 146, "Azione cattolica." See also De Felice, *Mussolini il duce*, 1:257.

65. On the violence of 1931 see ACS, MI, DGPS, DPP (1927–44), busta 149, fasc. K112, "Attività sovversiva degli studenti (1929–1931)," letters dated 12 and 30 April and 10 May 1931 from Milan; ibid., busta 150, fasc. K114, "Incidenti fra cattolici e fascisti"; ACS, MI, DGPS, DAGR (1920, 1923–45), cat. G1, busta 146, "Azione cattolica"; ibid., busta 151, "FUCI"; and ibid., busta 131, "Roma, Associazioni giovanili cattoliche." The details were also presented in the *Osservatore romano*, 22–31 May 1931. See also Papini, "Fuci e le violenze fasciste," pp. 16–20; and O'Brien, "Italian Youth in Conflict," pp. 625–35.

66. ACS, MI, DGPS, DAGR (1920, 1923–45), cat. G1, busta 146, "Azione cattolica," executive order no. 15557, dated 27 May 1931.

67. Telegrams from prefects dated 30–31 May 1931 reported incidents in Aosta, Ivrea, Caltanisetta, Forlì, Trent, Como, Pesaro, Potenza, Milan, and Reggio Calabria. See ACS, SPD, Ris., busta 31, fasc. 242/R, "Riunioni del Direttorio del PNF," sottofasc. 1, "Riunione del 3 giugno 1931," inserto C, "Scioglimento dei gruppi giovanili cattolici."

68. ACS, PNF, SPEP, busta 25, "Torino," letters for 14–16 June and 20 July. See also ibid., busta 11, "Padova," for 25 February 1932; and ibid., busta 13, "Pavia," for 25 November 1931.

69. Tamaro, *Venti anni*, 2:446–47.

70. The encyclical's English title was *On Catholic Action*. For a complete text see Husslein, *Social Wellsprings*, 2:238–54.

71. Reaction to this mental reservation was outspoken in Fascist circles. See Tamaro, *Venti anni*, 2:448–49; and Salvemini and La Piana, *What to Do with Italy*, p. 87.

72. ACS, Fondo GUF, busta 976B, "Raccolta circolari." See letters exchanged between 5 February and 3 March 1930 in ACS, PCM, Gabinetto, Atti (1931–33), fasc. 1.1.15, no. 3500, sottofasc. 1–8. It is difficult to ascertain just how many PNF members resigned from Catholic Action (or vice versa) as a result of this decision. Reports from MVSN officers in July and August indicated that in Lombardy (Pavia and Bergamo) and the Veneto (Vicenza) many Giovani Fascisti left the PNF groups (the number cited for Verona, for example, was three hundred) rather than drop out of the Catholic groups. See ACS, PNF, SPEP, busta 13, "Pavia."

73. Quoted in Guzzetti, *Movimento cattolico*, p. 409. See also Tamaro, *Venti anni*, 2:451.

74. The *Tablet* editorial of 11 July 1931 is quoted in Husslein, *Social Wellsprings*, 2:237.

75. The order of the day was published in *Popolo d'Italia* on 15 July. The text of the message is included in Scoppola, *Chiesa e il fascismo*, pp. 274–76.

76. On these negotiations see Martini, *Studi sulla questione romana*, pp. 147–73.

77. ACS, PNF, SPEP, busta 19, "Roma."

78. Mussolini's summary of this meeting with the pope is included in De Felice, *Mussolini il duce*, 1:273–74.

79. ACS, MI, DGPS, DAGR (1930–31), Sezione I, busta 47, police report from Paris dated 5 September 1931, quoted in De Felice, *Mussolini il duce*, 1:270–71. For conflicting evaluations of this settlement see Binchy, *Church and State*, p. 432; Tannenbaum, *Fascist Experience*, pp. 202–3; and Tamaro, *Venti anni*, 2:454.

80. "Etiopia religiosa," *Civiltà cattolica*, 19 October 1935. On clerical support for the Ethiopian war see Boccetti, "Momenti di consenso," pp. 333–40.

81. See *Osservatore romano* for 14–15 September 1936, excerpted in Borghi, *Educazione e autorità*, p. 293.

82. ACS, PNF, SPEP, busta 11, "Padova," letter of 25 February 1932. See also ibid., busta 25, "Torino"; ibid., busta 6, "Milano"; and ACS, MI, DGPS, DPP (1927–44), busta 132, fasc. K11, "Attività sovversiva di studenti."

83. ACS, MI, DGPS, DPP (1927–44), busta 5, fasc. B46/22, "Milano, Attività cattolica e clero." This source also contains other files on Catholic activities in the post-1931 period: see busta 150, fasc. K114, "Incidenti fra cattolici e fascisti"; busta 205, fasc. 33/B, sottofasc. 26, "Corrispondenza del clero ed Azione cattolica"; and busta 149, fasc. K174, "Movimento cattolico antifascista."

84. ACS, PNF, SPEP, busta 15, "Pistoia," 8 May 1935; ibid., busta 26, "Trento," 21 June 1935. See also scattered reports in ibid.: busta 20, "Savona"; busta 11, "Padova"; and busta 6, "Milano," letter dated 15 July 1936.

85. ACS, MI, DGPS, DPP (1927–44), busta 218, cat. Q8, "Scuola, 1939–1943." See letters from Brescia (5 May 1939), Venice (13 March 1939), Rome (14 March 1939), and Padua (28 February 1939). Agents continued to report antiregime activity in Catholic groups throughout the war. See, for example, the report from the PNF federal secretary in Savona dated 4 December 1940 in ACS, PNF, SPEP, busta 20, "Savona." The clergy's correspondence was often censored, and police reports noted that many of the letters contained "defeatist propaganda." See ACS, MI, DGPS, DPP, busta 205, cat. 133/B, sottofasc. 26; ACS, MCP, busta 14, fasc. 193, "Stampa cattolica."

86. The racial laws are reproduced in De Felice, *Storia degli ebrei*, pp. 393–432. On the relationship between the Fascist regime and the Jews see Michaelis, *Mussolini and the Jews*.

87. De Felice, *Storia degli ebrei*, pp. 363–73. See the exchange of comments between the pope and Mussolini in Bernardini, "Origins and Development of Racial Anti-Semitism," pp. 447–48. On Mussolini's reactions to the pope's comments see G. Ciano, *Ciano's Diary, 1937–1938*, pp. 141, 146.

88. Giorgio Galli, *Storia della D.C.*, pp. 32–33. For the reminiscences of one young member of the Catholic Action groups during these years see Olivero, "Azione cattolica," pp. 178–81.

89. Cited in Giuntella, "Fatti del 1931," p. 216.

90. This realization and its repercussions are treated in Moro, "Afascismo e antifascismo," pp. 774–95.

91. ACS, MI, DGPS, DAGR (1920, 1923–45), cat. G1, busta 151, "FUCI," fasc. 77, sottofasc. 12, report of 4 September 1937. See also letters dated 28 April 1931 and 24 October 1942.

92. Ibid., busta 146, "Azione cattolica."

93. ACS, PNF, SPEP, busta 12, "Palermo," letter dated 6 March 1934.

94. Cited in Giuntella, "Organizzazione universitaria fascista," pp. 136–37.

95. ACS, MI, DGPS, DAGR (1920, 1923–45), cat. G1, busta 151, "FUCI," fasc. 77, sottofasc. 5.

96. Besides the Movimento Guelfo, the only other evidence of active antifascism in Catholic youth groups before the war was the manifesto of a Catholic Action youth organization in Rome led by Paolo Pecoraro. See Scoppola and Traniello, *Cattolici tra fascismo e democrazia*, pp. 16–17.

97. Amendola, *Intervista sull'antifascismo*, p. 130. See also Bocca, *Storia d'Italia*, pp. 441–43.

Chapter Six

1. "Very few figures," said Renzo De Felice (*Mussolini il duce*, 2:115), "had in the more than twenty-year history of fascism a role and an importance equal to that of Giuseppe Bottai. And no one—save obviously for Mussolini himself—had a greater."

2. Guerri, *Giuseppe Bottai*, pp. 15, 257–58; Zangrandi, *Lungo viaggio*, p. 103. See a critical letter dated 18 November 1936 from Ungaretti in ACS, MI, DGPS, DPP (1927–44), busta 164, "Ministero dell'Educazione Nazionale."

3. For Bottai's own reaction to this meeting and to Mussolini see Bottai, *Vent'anni e un giorno*, pp. 25–35, 85–100.

4. On Bottai's career and his revisionism see Guerri, *Giuseppe Bottai*; De Grand, "Giuseppe Bottai," pp. 697–731; Gentili, *Giuseppe Bottai*, pp. 1–7; Secchia, *Enciclopedia dell'antifascismo*, pp. 346–47; Mangoni, *Interventismo della cultura*, pp. 66–80; E. Gentile, *Origini dell'ideologia fascista*, pp. 295–315; and Nello, "Mussolini e Bottai." Bottai's *Diario, 1935–1944*, has recently been published but was not available during the research phase of this study.

5. Bottai, "Dichiarazioni di revisionismo," *Critica fascista*, 15 July 1924.

6. Quoted in E. Gentile, *Origini dell'ideologia fascista*, p. 301.

7. Bottai, "Polemica revisionistica." On Bottai's notion of the ruling class see De Felice, *Mussolini il fascista*, 2:342–52.

8. Bottai, "Giovani e più giovani." Elizabeth Wiskemann, in *Fascism in Italy*, p. 41, claimed that Bottai felt he had more "to contribute to the Fascism of the next generation than to that of his own."

9. Bottai, "Funzione della gioventù," and "Giovani nel partito."

10. See Bottai, "Giovani"; Lombrassa, "Prima studiare"; Granzotto, "Formazione di una classe dirigente"; and Pellizzi, "Educazione fascista." See also Nello, "Mussolini e Bottai," p. 338; and Guerri, *Giuseppe Bottai*, pp. 9–10.

11. Guerri, *Giuseppe Bottai*, p. 136.

12. Ibid., pp. 136–37.

13. Testimony of Ugoberto Alfassio Grimaldi in *Autobiografie di giovani*, p. 67.

14. Bottai, "Regno della noia," and "Esame di coscienza."

15. Cannistraro, *Fabbrica del consenso*, p. 161. See also Guerri, *Giuseppe Bottai*, pp. 179–95.

16. Figures are cited in Mazzatosta, *Regime fascista*, p. 80; and Minio-Paluello, *Education in Fascist Italy*, pp. 189–93.

17. On ENIM see Borghi, *Educazione e autorità*, pp. 305–6; Minio-Paluello, *Education in Fascist Italy*, pp. 191–92; and Guerri, *Giuseppe Bottai*, pp. 160–62. On Bottai as minister of national education see Ostenc, *Education en Italie*, pp. 344–54.

18. See the law of 27 October 1937 (no. 1839), which was approved in the Chamber on 7 December and in the Senate on 17 December. See Senato del Regno, Camera dei Deputati, *Bollettino Parlamentare*, 3 vols. (1937), 3:57–61; ACS, PCM, Gabinetto, Atti (1931–33), fasc. 1.1.15, no. 3500, sottofasc. 1–12. On the GIL see also PNF, GIL, *Gioventù sana e studiosa*; PNF, *Panorami di vita fascista: Gioventù Italiana del Littorio* (Milan: A. Mondadori, 1942); and PNF, *Venti anni*, pp. 202–3. For a recent study see Ostenc, *Education en Italie*, pp. 368–72.

19. The decision was published in PNF, *Bollettino del Comando Generale della G.I.L.*, no. 8, 15 February 1938. On the premilitary program see also PNF, GIL, *Istruzione premilitare*; Bozzoni, "Gioventù italiana," p. 428; Savarese, *Domani soldati!* and a memo sent by Starace in PNF, *Foglio d'ordini*, no. 198, 11 May 1938.

20. PNF, *Bollettino del Comando Generale della G.I.L.*, no. 24, 28 October 1938; ibid., no. 24, 28 October 1939.

21. ACS, PNF, SPEP, busta 14, "Piacenza," report dated 1 May 1940.

22. Feliciani, "Collegi della G.I.L.," p. 436. See also ACS, PNF, DN, buste 195, 197–201, 203; and PNF, *Panorami di vita fascista*, p. 47, law of 22 May 1939 (no. 866).

23. PNF, GIL, *Accademie e collegi della G.I.L.*; PNF, *Collegio Orvieto GIL*.

24. Royal Decree Law of 13 February 1939 (no. 310); ACS, PNF, DN, buste 195, 198.

25. PNF, *Bollettino del Comando Generale della G.I.L.*, no. 24, 28 October 1939; ibid., supplement to no. 20, 1 August 1939; ACS, PNF, DN, busta 183; PNF, GIL, *Conversazioni incontri e ludi*.

26. PNF, GIL, *Ludi Juveniles*, pp. 27, 41.

27. ACS, MCP, busta 81, fasc. 12, sottofasc. 7.

28. PNF, *Venti anni*, p. 212; PNF, *Gioventù Italiana del Littorio*, p. 65.

29. PNF, *Gioventù Italiana del Littorio*, p. 59. On these publications see ACS, PNF, DN, buste 231, 236, 239.

30. PNF, *Primo libro del fascista*, p. 95. Local GIL commands also published their own books, for example, PNF, GIL, *Via da seguire*. Older volumes still in use in the GIL in the later thirties included Cappi, *Parole ai giovani*; Negro, *Vola, Balilla!*; Perroni, *Duce ai Balilla*; and PNF, ONB, *Giovinezza eroica*.

31. PNF, *Primo libro del fascista*, pp. 10, 61, 39, 19, 77.

32. PNF, GIL, *Capo centuria*, p. 19. See also PNF, ONB, *Capo squadra Balilla*, pp. 1–12, for an earlier version.

33. Baciocchi de Peón, *Manuale del fascista*, pp. 61–62.

34. Meletti, *Libro fascista della Piccola Italiana*, pp. 85–88, 14–17, 103.

35. Ibid., p. 96.

36. De Gaetano and Trizzino, *Libro dell'avanguardista*, pp. 12–26, 71.

37. PNF, Comando federale della GIL Bologna, *Passeremo!* pp. 29–34, 44, 58–65, 80.

38. The text of the *Secondo libro del fascista* (1941 ed.) is reprinted in De Masi, *Libro e moschetto*, pp. 83–131 (quotations from pp. 88, 110). See also PNF, Comando federale della GIL Bologna, *Passeremo!* pp. 66–73.

39. Quoted in Binchy, *Church and State*, p. 410. For examples of such prayers see also Meletti, *Libro fascista della Piccola Italiana*, p. 120, and *Libro fascista del Balilla*, p. 11.

40. Meletti, *Libro fascista della Piccola Italiana*, pp. 29–30. See also Meletti, *Libro fascista del Balilla*, p. 40.

41. The first radio legislation passed in Italy was a law of 30 June 1910. In 1922 the only Italian transmitter, Radio Araldo in Rome, broadcast irregular programs still received by only a handful of listeners. On the radio in Italy see A. Papa, "Origini politiche della radio," pp. 45–66; Cannistraro, "Radio in Fascist Italy," pp. 127–54, and *Fabbrica del consenso*, pp. 225–71; Bordoni, *Cultura e propaganda*, pp. 87–93; Monteleone, *Radio italiana*; Monticone, *Fascismo al microfono*; A. Papa, *Storia politica della radio*; and Galante Garrone, "Aedo senza fili," pp. 1401–24. Studies from the Fascist period include Dal Piaz, *Radio nella scuola*; and Pinti, "Radio," pp. 71–78.

42. For comparative figures on radio subscribers see A. Papa, *Storia politica della radio*, 1:52, 90, 2:27, 36; Monticone, *Fascismo al microfono*, p. 43; and Cannistraro, *Fabbrica del consenso*, p. 386 (n. 16).

43. A. Papa, *Storia politica della radio*, 1:33.

44. SISERT was presided over by Marconi himself and organized by the Marchese Luigi Solari, both PNF members. The vicissitudes of the Marconi group in these early years have been traced by A. Papa in "Origini politiche della radio," pp. 45–49; Monteleone, *Radio italiana*, pp. 8–25; and Cannistraro, *Fabbrica del consenso*, pp. 225–28.

45. On these early broadcasts see Galante Garrone, "Aedo senza fili," p. 1403; Monteleone, *Radio italiana*, p. 15; and A. Papa, *Storia politica della radio*, 1:31. On Ciano's discussions of the radio with Mussolini see ACS, PCM, Gabinetto, Atti (1934–36), fasc. 13/1, no. 2057, sottofasc. 1.

46. On the URI see Monteleone, *Radio italiana*, pp. 25–26; Monticone, *Fascismo al microfono*, pp. ix–x, 1–9; and Cannistraro, "Radio in Fascist Italy," p. 227.

47. Morgagni began his career in journalism at the *Popolo d'Italia* in April 1915 and continued as director of the Agenzia Stefani until the fall of the regime, when he committed suicide. On the radio news see Ciano to Mussolini, 21 September 1926, in ACS, PCM, Gabinetto, Atti (1934–36), fasc. 13/1, no. 2057, sottofasc. 1.

48. Law of 17 November 1927 (no. 2207). See also Galante Garrone, "Aedo senza fili," pp. 1402–3; A. Papa, *Storia politica della radio*, 1:52–53; and Monticone, *Fascismo al microfono*, pp. 39–40.

49. Monticone, *Fascismo al microfono*, pp. 27–28; Cannistraro, *Fabbrica del consenso*, p. 234; Galante Garrone, "Aedo senza fili," pp. 1405–6; A.

Papa, *Storia politica della radio*, 1:62–63.

50. On "Condottieri e maestri" see Galante Garrone, "Aedo senza fili," p. 1407.

51. A. Papa, *Storia politica della radio*, 1:161; Monticone, *Fascismo al microfono*, chap. 4; Monteleone, *Radio italiana*, pp. 123–31.

52. For a text of one of these programs see Monticone, *Fascismo al microfono*, pp. 28–31. Other children's programs included "La palestra dei piccoli" in Genoa and Radio Torino's "Gaio radio giornalino."

53. Royal Decrees of 6 September 1934 (no. 1434), 24 June 1935 (no. 1009), and 27 May 1937 (no. 752). The Ministry of Popular Culture was managed until 1939 by Dino Alfieri and then by Alessandro Pavolini, who died with Mussolini in April 1945.

54. On the ERR see the law of 15 June 1933 (no. 791); Valitutti, "Elementary Education," pp. 790–810; and Cannistraro, "Radio in Fascist Italy," pp. 134–35. On control of the ERR see ACS, PCM, Gabinetto, Atti (1934–36), fasc. 13/1, no. 2057, sottofasc. 1; and ACS, SPD, Ris., busta 46, fasc. 242/R, sottofasc. 13, Starace to Mussolini, 16 February 1935. In late 1939, under the new PNF secretary Ettore Muti, the ERR was transferred to the control of the Ministry of Popular Culture, headed by Pavolini. In 1940 the ERR was officially suppressed and its activities taken over by the EIAR. See ACS, MCP, busta 79, fasc. 3, Muti to Mussolini, 8 November 1939.

55. Statistics vary. See, for example, Monticone, *Fascismo al microfono*, pp. 92–93; A. Papa, *Storia politica della radio*, 1:138–39; Monteleone, *Radio italiana*, p. 108; and Cannistraro, "Radio in Fascist Italy," p. 137.

56. Monteleone, *Radio italiana*, pp. 104–7.

57. *La radio rurale*, 25 February 1934, p. 7, quoted in Monticone, *Fascismo al microfono*, p. 390 (n. 28).

58. Data taken from the summary of programs transmitted in 1935–36 from *La radio rurale* for 25 September 1935, quoted in Monticone, *Fascismo al microfono*, p. 390 (n. 31). See also Galante Garrone, "Aedo senza fili," pp. 1411–13; and Mazzatosta, *Regime fascista*, pp. 174–76.

59. Isnenghi, *Educazione dell'Italiano*, pp. 111–15. On programs during the Spanish civil war see also A. Papa, *Storia politica della radio*, 2:60–71; and Monteleone, *Radio italiana*, pp. 169–96.

60. This speech was published in *Radiocorriere* for 27 February 1940; the text is also available in Monticone, *Fascismo al microfono*, pp. 114–17. Students were required to write themes on school broadcasts. See excerpts in Dal Piaz, *Radio nella scuola*, pp. 28–52.

61. Olschki, "Ricordi di scuola," p. 1492. See also MEN, *Ufficio per la radiofonia scolastica*, p. 14. The report said that the programs on literature aroused "more astonishment than interest" and that the lessons on the Italian language "left the students indifferent."

62. On the university GUF radio see ACS, PCM, Gabinetto, Atti (1931–33), fasc. 13/1; ibid., fasc. 14.3/4528; PNF, *Atti del PNF* 4 (1934), Circular 1-R for 30 October 1934; EIAR, *EIAR Anno XVII*, p. 37; A. Papa, *Storia politica della radio*, 2:60; and Monteleone, *Radio italiana*, pp. 115–17.

63. On "Radio scuola" see Bottai's circular to the *provveditori* dated Decem-

ber 1942, in ACS, SPD, Ord., fasc. 500009, sottofasc. 3; and Bottai to Mussolini, 16 January 1943, in the same file. See also Mazzatosta, *Regime fascista*,
pp. 177–80.

64. For texts of some of these programs see Monteleone, *Radio italiana*,
pp. 191–92, 217–18, 345–53; and A. Papa, *Storia politica della radio*, 2:109–
10.

65. Monteleone, *Radio italiana*, pp. 109–10.

66. Bottai's own comments on the School Charter can be found in his *Carta
della scuola*, *Nuova scuola media*, and *Scritti*, pp. 225–49. Many contemporary comments on the School Charter were published. See Carlini, *Verso la
nuova scuola*; Cavallaro, *Scuola in Italia*; MEN, *Dalla riforma Gentile alla
Carta della Scuola*; and Volpicelli, *Apologia della scuola media*, and *Commento alla Carta della Scuola*. On the presentation of the School Charter see
PNF, *Atti del PNF* 8 (1938–39): 61–82; and PNF, *Foglio d'ordini*, 16 February
1939. Recent studies of the charter include Gentili, *Giuseppe Bottai*; Guerri,
Giuseppe Bottai, pp. 154–60; Ostenc, *Education en Italie*, pp. 345–56; Canestri and Ricuperati, *Scuola in Italia*, pp. 176–89; Mazzatosta, *Regime fascista*, pp. 90–101; M. Bellucci and Ciliberto, *Scuola e la pedagogia*, pp. 348–
408; Ricuperati, "Scuola e politica," pp. 98–105; De Felice, *Mussolini il duce*,
2:120–25; and Tomasi, *Istruzione di base*, pp. 189–95, 230–32.

67. Bottai, *Carta della scuola*, pp. 155–56.

68. Quoted in Tomasi, *Idealismo e fascismo*, p. 158.

69. Bottai, *Carta della scuola*, pp. 28–34.

70. The text is included in Delzell, *Mediterranean Fascism*, pp. 148–55;
and in Gentili, *Giuseppe Bottai*, pp. 205–16.

71. Quoted in Mazzatosta, *Regime fascista*, p. 188.

72. Guerri, *Giuseppe Bottai*, pp. 176–78; Minio-Paluello, *Education in Fascist Italy*, p. 193.

73. *Calabria fascista*, 4 March 1939, quoted in De Felice, *Mussolini il
duce*, 2:119.

74. On the subject of work in the School Charter see Aliotta and Feola,
Scuola del lavoro; Rivadossi, *Scuola del lavoro*; Mazzetti, *Lavoro e la scuola*;
R. Università di Roma, Istituto di Pedagogia della Facoltà di Magistero, *Il
lavoro produttivo nella Carta della scuola* (Messina: Casa Editrice G. D'Anna,
1940); and Bottai, *Scritti*, pp. 234–40. For more recent comments see Mazzatosta, *Regime fascista*, pp. 102–37; and Ricuperati, *Scuola italiana*, pp. 183–
87. On the regime's evaluation of scholastic work service see the report by the
Ministry of National Education: "Esperimento di lavoro nella scuola fascista
nell'anno scolastico 1939–40," in Ricuperati, *Scuola italiana*, pp. 185–98; and
comments on the program in Morandi, "Attuazione del servizio del lavoro."

75. G. Gentile, "Carta della scuola." On reactions to the charter see also
Mazzatosta, *Regime fascista*, pp. 98–102; and Tomasi, *Idealismo e fascismo*,
pp. 174–80.

76. ACS, SPD, Ris., fasc. 242/R, "Bottai on. prof. Giuseppe." This per-
plexity was echoed by reports collected in ACS, MI, DGPS, DPP (1927–44),
busta 218, cat. Q8, "Scuola (1939–1941)." See reports dated 30 April 1940
from Florence, 18 March 1939 from Padua, and 20 February 1939 from Rome.

Also see reports in ibid., busta 164, fasc. M13, "Ministero Educazione Nazionale."

77. ACS, MI, DGPS, DPP (1927–44), busta 218, reports dated 5 February 1940 and 16 November 1939 from Padua, 5 June 1939 from Trent, and 30 March 1939 from Milan.

78. Ibid., reports dated 5 March 1939 from Genoa and 7 December and 30 April 1940 and 27 February 1941 from Florence.

79. Ibid., reports dated 19 February and 8 August 1939 and 18 October 1940 from Rome, 8 August 1939 from Milan, and 25 September and 23 October 1939 and 7 December 1940 from Florence.

80. Quoted in Ludwig, *Colloqui con Mussolini*, p. 75. According to the census of 1938 there were 10,173 foreign Jews resident in Italy and 47,252 Italian Jews (roughly 1.4 per 1,000). For these statistics see De Felice, *Storia degli ebrei*, pp. 25–36; Buffarini Guidi, *Vera verità*; and Secchia, *Enciclopedia dell'antifascismo*, 1:94–98.

81. There were some 750 Jews in the PNF in 1922, about 2,500 in 1928, and over 7,300 in 1933. See Ledeen, *Universal Fascism*, p. 137.

82. De Felice, *Storia degli ebrei*, pp. 147–61. The historic lack of anti-Semitism is also discussed in Leto, *OVRA*, pp. 190–91; and in Tamaro, *Venti anni*, 3:304–6. On the regime's anti-Semitic campaign see Acerbo, *Fondamenti della dottrina fascista della razza*; Sottochiesa, *Razza e razzismo*; Capasso, *Idee chiare sul razzismo*; Elmo, *Condizione giuridica degli ebrei*; and Leone Franzi, *Fase attuale del razzismo tedesco* (Rome: Istituto Nazionale di Cultura Fascista, 1939).

83. De Felice, *Storia degli ebrei*, p. 286. The importance of the German alliance in the Italian decision to pass anti-Semitic laws is stressed in Fermi, *Mussolini*, p. 365; Wiskemann, *Rome-Berlin Axis*, pp. 140–42; and De Felice, *Mussolini il duce*, 2:312–18. The colonial influence on this new racial policy is discussed by Pellizzi, *Italy*, pp. 192–93. Two valuable recent studies of the subject are Bernardini, "Origins and Development of Racial Anti-Semitism"; and Michaelis, *Mussolini and the Jews*.

84. The text of this manifesto appeared in most Italian papers on 15 July 1938. It is reprinted in De Felice, *Storia degli ebrei*, pp. 611–12; and in Delzell, *Mediterranean Fascism*, pp. 174–76.

85. For explanations of Bottai's motives see Guerri, *Giuseppe Bottai*, pp. 154–78; Tannenbaum, *Fascist Experience*, pp. 79–80; De Felice, *Storia degli ebrei*, pp. 284–85; and Michaelis, *Mussolini and the Jews*, pp. 178, 188.

86. Bottai, *Carta della scuola*, pp. 209–10.

87. See Tomasi, *Idealismo e fascismo*, p. 164, for a long list of anti-Semitic articles.

88. For a text of this Royal Decree Law of 5 September 1938 (no. 1390) see Federazione Giovanile Ebraica d'Italia, *Ebrei in Italia*, pp. 103–6. See also the 1938 laws of 23 September (no. 1630) and 17 November (no. 1728). For a discussion of all the anti-Semitic laws on the schools see Ricuperati, *Scuola italiana*, pp. 159–65; and Ostenc, *Education en Italie*, pp. 356–61.

89. Law of 15 November 1938 (no. 1779). On this legislation see also Gentili, *Giuseppe Bottai*, pp. 148–50; Borghi, *Educazione e autorità*, pp. 305–6;

Tomasi, *Idealismo e fascismo*, pp. 161–65; Guerri, *Giuseppe Bottai*, pp. 166–74; and Canestri and Ricuperati, *Scuola in Italia*, pp. 176–80.

90. See Ricuperati, *Scuola italiana*, pp. 161–64, for the effect of anti-Semitic legislation in the universities.

91. For a discussion of the racist competitions at these Littoriali see Spinetti, *Difesa di una generazione*, pp. 158–64; Zangrandi, *Lungo viaggio*, pp. 538–39; and testimony of Ugoberto Alfassio Grimaldi (who won third place in 1940) in Albertoni, Antonini, and Palmieri, *Generazione degli anni difficili*, pp. 45–54.

92. For these statistics see Secchia, *Enciclopedia dell'antifascismo*, 1:96–97; and Minio-Paluello, *Education in Fascist Italy*, pp. 193–94. Among Fermi's colleagues was Bruno Rossi, Eugenio Curiel's mentor at the University of Padua.

93. See an interesting article on the subject by B. Ricci, "Rapporti tra scuola e G.I.L."

94. ACS, PNF, SPEP, busta 19, "Roma," dated 26 October 1939.

95. The text of this lengthy circular can be found in ACS, SPD, Ord., busta 6, fasc. 500.108.

96. Malfi, *Scuola e G.I.L.*, p. 6. On relations between the GIL and the school see also Calendoli, "Carta della scuola," pp. 109–12.

97. Enrollment statistics for the various localities are available in monthly reports collected in ACS, PNF, SPEP. See also Giovenale, "GIL."

98. For information on the enrollment tactics of the local school authorities (in this case in Gubbio) see Giuntella, "Circoli cattolici," pp. 71–75.

99. The groups for older females accounted in Pescara for some 21 percent of the total and in Sassari for almost 18 percent. See also statistics for Padua, Mantua, Perugia, Parma, Rovigo, Pavia, Trent, Spezia, Pistoia, Rieti, Rome, Rodi, Pola, Pesaro, and Macerata in ACS, PNF, SPEP, buste 4, 9, 11–15, 19–20, 25.

100. See PNF, *Bollettino del Comando Generale della G.I.L.*, no. 20, 15 August 1939, no. 23, 1 October 1939.

Chapter Seven

1. Tannenbaum, *Fascist Experience*, p. 131.

2. B. Mussolini, *Opera omnia*, 20:130.

3. The phrase is Salvatore Gatto's, in PNF, *Gruppi dei fascisti universitari*, p. 13. On the GUF see also D. Fabbri, "Gruppi fascisti universitari," pp. 441–45; Gravelli, "Avanguardismo giovanile fascista," pp. 265–72; PNF, *Venti anni*, pp. 181–91; PNF, *Gruppo dei fascisti universitari dell'Urbe*; PNF, *Regolamento del servizio sanitario*; PNF, GUF, *Gruppi universitari fascisti*; PNF, Gruppo dei Fascisti Universitari "Amos Maramotti" Torino, *Tre anni XIV–XV–XVI*; PNF, GUF, *Vita dei GUF*; and PNF, Gruppo dei Fascisti Universitari dell'Urbe, *Che cosa è il G.U.F.* Recent studies include De Negri, "Agitazioni e movimenti studenteschi," pp. 733–63; Nello, *Avanguardismo giovanile*; Giuntella, "Gruppi universitari fascisti," and "Circoli cattolici"; and Ostenc, *Education en Italie*, pp. 374–78.

4. University groups were established before the *fasci* in Bologna, Pavia, Brescia, and Camerino, for example. On Camerino see Santarelli, "Fascio universitario del 1919," pp. 93–112. For other material on the early *fasci* see ACS, MRF, buste 99–107, "Carteggio del Comitato centrale dei fasci"; Mezzasoma, *Essenza dei GUF*; and ACS, MI, DGPS, DAGR (1920, 1923–45), cat. G1, busta 77, fasc. "Fascio universitario."

5. On these non-Fascist university organizations see Giuntella, "Gruppi universitari fascisti," pp. 6–7.

6. For the minutes of this meeting and the statute of the FNUF see ACS, MRF, busta 16, "Statuto regolamento della Federazione nazionale universitaria fascista," fasc. 94, "Federazione universitaria fascista." See also Nello, *Avanguardismo giovanile*, pp. 138–42, 196–98; De Negri, "Agitazioni e movimenti studenteschi," pp. 749–50; and Giuntella, "Gruppi universitari fascisti," p. 10.

7. On these early contrasts see De Negri, "Agitazioni e movimenti studenteschi," pp. 758–63.

8. Levi's letters to the officials in Pavia, Turin, and Milan are included in ACS, MRF, busta 16, fasc. 94.

9. Quoted in Giuntella, "Gruppi universitari fascisti," p. 16.

10. Basso, "Dal delitto Matteotti," pp. 69–86.

11. See E. Papa, *Storia di due manifesti*, p. 101. On Del Vecchio see Zangrandi, *Lungo viaggio*, p. 292.

12. On these struggles see Giuntella, "Gruppi universitari fascisti," pp. 20–30; and Andreis, "Antifascismo torinese," pp. 127–31.

13. Giuntella, "Gruppi universitari fascisti," p. 18.

14. Quoted in ibid., p. 30.

15. ACS, Fondo GUF, busta 965.

16. Information on the organization and structure of the GUF can be found in ACS, PNF, DN, busta 335, circular from Giuriati to all GUF secretaries dated 15 November 1930.

17. PNF, *Gruppi dei fascisti universitari*, pp. 50–51.

18. ACS, Fondo GUF, busta 8.

19. On the university militia see PNF, *Gruppi dei fascisti universitari*, pp. 153–76; and ACS, PNF, DN, buste 175–76, 253.

20. ACS, PNF, DN, buste 176, 253; PNF, *Gruppi dei fascisti universitari*, pp. 115–23; Royal Decrees of 28 August 1931 (no. 1227) and 31 August 1933 (no. 1592).

21. ACS, PNF, DN, busta 253, Marinelli to Bottai, 5 March 1938.

22. ACS, Fondo GUF, busta 980A; ACS, PNF, DN, buste 88, 176–77, 337, "Circolari Segretaria GUF 1940," especially the circular dated 8 October 1940, no. 8/528. On these international student exchanges see also PNF, Centro Studenti Stranieri dei GUF, *Convegno universitario Italo-Nipponico*.

23. On the Teatro sperimentale see especially ACS, PNF, DN, buste 178–82.

24. Leprohon, *Italian Cinema*, p. 64.

25. Ibid., p. 74. On the activities of the Cineguf see also Sacchi, "Stampa e il cinema," pp. 327–34.

26. ACS, Fondo GUF, busta 2, "Raccolta Circolari," circulars dated 24 January, 6 February, 25 March, and 18 June 1930; ibid., busta 964A, "Varie."

27. PNF, *Atti del PNF* 3 (1933–34): 79–80; PNF, *Foglio di disposizioni*, no. 356, 9 February 1935; ACS, PNF, DN, buste 183, 321, fasc. 132; Tripodi, "Centro nazionale di preparazione politica per i giovani," pp. 465–70. For the regulations of these courses see PNF, *Atti del PNF* 4 (1934–35): 249–56; and ACS, PNF, DN, buste 202, 321.

28. Gianni Granzotto argued the classless character of the program in "Classe dirigente." There were eight required texts for these political preparation courses, all published by the Libreria dello Stato in 1936. Their titles indicate the general tone of the courses: *La cultura fascista*, *La dottrina del fascismo*, *L'Italia nel Mediterraneo*, *L'ordinamento dello stato fascista*, *Il cittadino soldato*, *L'economia fascista*, *Il partito nazionale fascista*, *La politica sociale del fascismo*. Copies are available at the Hoover Institution, Stanford University.

29. The curriculum of the center was published in PNF, *Bollettino Quindicinale della GIL*, no. 20, 15 August 1939; PNF, *Bollettino del Comando Generale della G.I.L.*, no. 6, 15 January 1940; and PNF, *Gruppi dei fascisti universitari*, pp. 147–54.

30. For PNF views on the center see Mezzasoma, "Centro di preparazione politica per i giovani," pp. 3–5; Granzotto, "Formazione di una classe dirigente"; and Capaldo, "Classe dirigente." See also Lyttelton, *Seizure of Power*, p. 509 (n. 72), for his comments on the failure of these special schools to produce a Fascist ruling elite.

31. Mussolini's speech was published in the *Popolo d'Italia* on 1 December 1931. On Arnaldo and the Scuola di Mistica Fascista see Marchesini, *Scuola dei gerarchi*, and "Episodio della politica culturale," pp. 90–122. For official records see ACS, PNF, DN, busta 202, "Scuole del Partito"; ACS, MCP, busta 84, fasc. 1; and PNF, Scuola di Mistica Fascista "Sandro Italico Mussolini," *Corso di dottrina del fascismo*, pp. 11–15.

32. ACS, SPD, Ord., busta 509017, fasc. "Consegna del Duce alla Scuola di Mistica Fascista." See also ibid., fasc. "Scuola di Mistica Fascista, Varia."

33. Marchesini, "Episodio della politica culturale," p. 97.

34. Guizzardi, "Dalla 'ragione' alla 'fede,'" pp. 195–98; Giani, "Perche siamo dei mistici," p. 113. See also Giani, "La mistica come dottrina del fascismo," *Dottrina fascista* (September 1937). On the *mistici* see also Meldini, *Reazionaria*, pp. 155–56; and Santarelli, *Storia del movimento*, 2:344–46.

35. ACS, PNF, DN, busta 202, "Scuole del Partito," fasc. "Resoconto dell'attività svolta nell'anno XVII."

36. ACS, MCP, busta 83, fasc. 1; ibid., busta 84, fasc. 1, "Scuola di Mistica Fascista." See also Marchesini, *Scuola dei gerarchi*, pp. 162–63, 207–8.

37. Letter dated 21 February 1940 in ACS, MCP, busta 84, fasc. 1, "Atti vari." On this first national meeting see also Marchesini, *Scuola dei gerarchi*, pp. 164–87, and "Episodio della politica culturale," pp. 107–21, the latter of which also includes a list of themes and participants.

38. Zangrandi, *Lungo viaggio*, pp. 377–78.

39. Marchesini, "Episodio della politica culturale," p. 105.

40. Pellizzi, "Educazione fascista."

41. ACS, MI, DGPS, DAGR (1927–33), cat. C2, "Movimento sovversivo antifascista," busta 1, fasc. "Movimento studentesco antifascista," letter dated 30 May 1931.

42. ACS, SPD, Ris., busta 31, fasc. 242/R, "Riunione del Direttorio 14 luglio 1931," sottofasc. 2, "Inserto A-Statistiche," letter from Scorza dated 11 July 1931.

43. Quoted in Albertoni, Antonini, and Palmieri, *Generazione degli anni difficili*, p. 280.

44. Bottai, "Littoriali anno XVI."

45. Gastone Silvano Spinetti, *Fascismo universale* (Rome: La Sapienza, 1930), p. 25. On Spinetti see Ledeen, *Universal Fascism*, pp. 39–55, and "Italian Fascism and Youth," pp. 143–50; and Tannenbaum, *Fascist Experience*, pp. 131, 299. Spinetti wrote two books defending his generation for their belief that fascism could be reformed from within: *Difesa di una generazione* and *Vent'anni dopo*. Some university students during the 1930s were influenced by the ideas of leftist Fascists such as Ugo Spirito and the theory of "integral corporatism" espoused at the congress of corporate studies held in Ferrara in May 1932. Spirito and others called for the gradual fusion of capital and labor in all large enterprises and the formation of a *corporazione proprietaria* owned by all who worked in the enterprise. Fascist hierarchs were not happy with what they saw as Spirito's Bolshevik position, but the idea elicited a positive response among many students interested in reviving the radical social rhetoric of 1919. On Spirito's influence on the university students see Tannenbaum, "Goals of Italian Fascism," pp. 1203–4; and Zangrandi, *Lungo viaggio*, pp. 442–45.

46. *L'Universale* was published from 1931 to 1935 and *Il Saggiatore* from 1930 to 1933. On *L'Universale* see Folin and Quaranta, *Riviste giovanili*, pp. 33–44, 88–112; Tannenbaum, *Fascist Experience*, pp. 298–99; and Ledeen, *Universal Fascism*, pp. 56–60, and "Italian Fascism and Youth," pp. 148–53.

47. Quoted in Tannenbaum, *Fascist Experience*, p. 299, from *Rivoluzione* for 28 June 1940.

48. Zangrandi, *Lungo viaggio*, pp. 454–55.

49. On Zangrandi's book see Alatri, "Recenti studi sul fascismo," pp. 827–33, and "Lungo viaggio," pp. 472–76; Zangrandi, "Generazione dei Littoriali," pp. 14–15; Togliatti, "Battaglia delle idee," p. 37; and Capitini, "Nota sul libro di Ruggero Zangrandi," pp. 226–32. The book was originally published in 1947 and reissued in an enlarged edition in 1962.

50. Folin and Quaranta, *Riviste giovanili*, pp. 16–18, 224–63; Zangrandi, *Lungo viaggio*, p. 21.

51. For a list of contributors to these journals see Zangrandi, *Lungo viaggio*, pp. 433–35. Ledeen, in *Universal Fascism*, p. 38, discusses the possibility that the presence of Vittorio on the editorial board was a way of exposing anti-Fascists. On these journals see also Addis Saba, *Gioventù italiana del littorio*, pp. 36, 79–80. Copies of the journals themselves are available at the Biblioteca Alessandrina at the University of Rome.

52. Zangrandi, *Lungo viaggio*, p. 15.

53. Ibid., pp. 24, 29. On the Novist movement see also Ledeen, *Universal Fascism*, pp. 37–39, and "Italian Fascism and Youth," p. 143; and Santarelli, *Storia del movimento*, 2:74–75, 280–82.

54. ACS, MI, DGPS, DPP (1927–44), busta 142, fasc. K96, "Movimento Novista," reports dated 19 and 26 June and 24 October 1933 and 6 April 1935. See also ibid., busta 132, fasc. K11, "Attività sovversiva di studenti," report dated 26 April 1932, on activities at the Liceo Tasso.

55. Zangrandi, *Lungo viaggio*, pp. 32–33.

56. On the activities of the PSR see ibid., pp. 198–217, 241–51, 508–9; and Addis Saba, *Gioventù italiana del littorio*, pp. 79–82.

57. Preti, *Giovinezza, giovinezza*, pp. 27–32; PNF, *Gruppi dei fascisti universitari*, pp. 85–92; ACS, Fondo GUF, busta 980A, "Circolari." For official records on the Littoriali dello sport see ACS, PNF, DN, buste 184, 186–87, 192–93; and PNF, *Atti del PNF* 3 (1933–34): 59.

58. A. Fabbri, *Giovinezza, giovinezza*, p. 25.

59. PNF, DN, *Littoriali maschili del lavoro*, and *Littoriali femminili del lavoro*. See also ACS, PNF, DN, buste 183, 185, 188–91, 194; and PNF, GUF, *Littoriali maschili e femminili del lavoro*.

60. ACS, PNF, DN, buste 183, 185, 188, 193; Lazzari, *Littoriali*, p. 15. Guerri, in *Giuseppe Bottai*, p. 143, claims that Bottai suggested these competitions, but Lazzari, in *Littoriali*, p. 18, claims that they were inspired by a suggestion from Pavolini. On the role of Bottai in the Littoriali see ibid., pp. 62–70.

61. For a list of all *littori* from 1934–40 see Tripodi, *Italia fascista in piedi!* pp. 227–36.

62. ACS, PNF, DN, busta 183. On themes for 1935 see Finer, *Mussolini's Italy*, pp. 394–96. PNF, *Foglio di disposizioni*, no. 29, 23 December 1940, and ACS, PNF, DN, busta 194, contain programs for 1940. See also PNF, Istituto Nazionale di Cultura Fascista, *Littoriali dell'Anno XVI*; PNF, GUF, *Littoriali della cultura e dell'arte*; PNF, *Gruppi dei fascisti universitari*, pp. 79–85; and PNF, *Programma Littoriali della cultura e dell'arte*.

63. Testimony of Rosario Assunto in Zangrandi, *Lungo viaggio*, p. 495.

64. Trombadori, "Giaime Pintor," p. 332.

65. Testimony of Pietro Ingrao in Caputo, "Scuola e antifascismo," p. 402. See also Lazzari, *Littoriali*, p. 100; Ostenc, *Education en Italie*, pp. 374–78; and Spriano, *Storia del Partito comunista italiano*, 3:194–95.

66. Togliatti, *Lezioni sul fascismo*, p. 72; Alatri, *Antifascismo italiano*, 1:45–46; Tannenbaum, *Fascist Experience*, pp. 129–30. See also Addis Saba, *Gioventù italiana del littorio*, pp. 74–79; and Amendola, *Intervista sull'antifascismo*, pp. 104–5.

67. Testimony of Ugoberto Alfassio Grimaldi in *Autobiografie di giovani*, pp. 50, 56–57. See also Bonsanti, "Cultura degli anni trenta," p. 206. For official views of the Littoriali see Gaslini, "Cultura in funzione politica," pp. 772–74; and Ballarati and Buonassisi, "Convegno di dottrina del fascismo."

68. Lazzari, *Littoriali*, pp. 22–23. On police reports from the Florence meetings see ACS, MI, DGPS, DPP (1927–44), busta 132, fasc. K11, "Attività sovversiva di studenti."

69. Zangrandi, *Lungo viaggio*, p. 103; Lazzari, *Littoriali*, p. 209. See also Tamaro, *Venti anni*, 3:320; and PNF, *Atti del PNF* 5 (1935–36): 83–109. Zangrandi includes a list of all the participants in the Littoriali in *Lungo viaggio*, pp. 538–89.

70. On these meetings see Gambetti, *Anni che scottano*, pp. 274–75; Zangrandi, *Lungo viaggio*, pp. 138–42; de Antonellis, *Sud durante il fascismo*, pp. 204–7; R. Rossi, "Come si formò nei littoriali una opposizione giovanile," pp. 24–28; and Spano, "Nostri giovani."

71. Testimony of Mario Alicata in Albertoni, Antonini, and Palmieri, *Generazione degli anni difficili*, pp. 61–62. On the activities of Antonio Amendola after 1936 see Caputo, "Opposizione antifascista," pp. 35–37.

72. R. Rossi, "Come si formò nei littoriali una opposizione giovanile," p. 27.

73. Ugo Mursia to Zangrandi, 4 April 1946, in Zangrandi, *Lungo viaggio*, pp. 138, 466–67, 497–98. See also Lazzari, *Littoriali*, p. 37.

74. Testimony of Zevi in Capitini, *Antifascismo tra i giovani*, pp. 301–2; Bocca, *Storia d'Italia*, pp. 89–90; Gambetti, *Anni che scottano*, p. 293; Franchi, *Nuove generazioni*, pp. 38–40; Caputo, "Opposizione antifascista," pp. 62–72.

75. Caputo, "Opposizione antifascista," pp. 66–67. Interestingly enough, Alicata received eighth place in this competition, and Franco Lattes Fortini, a young Jewish student from Florence, won third place.

76. Curiel, "Littoriali a porte chiuse"; R. Rossi, "Come si formò nei littoriali una opposizione giovanile," pp. 23–28.

77. Caputo, "Opposizione antifascista," p. 68; Nasti, "Orientamenti dei giovani"; Gambetti, *Anni che scottano*, p. 336, and *Inchiesta*, pp. 219–20.

78. Tripodi, *Italia fascista in piedi!* pp. 20–25. Tripodi was *littore* of Fascist doctrine at the 1938 competitions in Palermo.

79. Capitini, *Antifascismo tra i giovani*, pp. 107–8, 227. See also Tannenbaum, *Fascist Experience*, pp. 338–39, for the views of Guido Calogero.

80. Bocca, *Storia d'Italia*, p. 88.

81. Personal correspondence with the author dated 5 December 1975.

82. R. Rossi, "Come si formò nei littoriali una opposizione giovanile," p. 27.

83. ACS, Fondo GUF, busta 2, "Raccolta circolari."

84. G. Ciano, *Diario, 1939–1943*, p. 423, entry for 11 June 1941 (quoted from the translation, p. 366).

85. For examples of some of these local pages see ACS, Fondo GUF, busta 968B, "Ritagli stampa"; ACS, MCP, busta 79, fasc. "Varie"; ACS, PNF, DN, busta 326, "GUF, Appunti vari"; and ACS, SPD, Ord., busta 102D, fasc. 545.711.

86. For a discussion of the general tone of these GUF papers see Melis Bassu, "Giovani vogliono restare soli?" p. 3; Pigliaru, "Considerazioni sulle riviste dei GUF," p. 74; Gambetti, *Anni che scottano*, pp. 280–81; Spinetti, *Vent'anni dopo*, pp. 72–85; Santarelli, *Storia del fascismo*, 2:279–84, 3:168–69; Zangrandi, *Lungo viaggio*, pp. 456–58; and Luti, *Cronache letterarie*, pp. 201–11.

87. Negarville, "Per un movimento giovanile," p. 468.

88. ACS, PNF, DN, busta 340, circular dated 5 January 1937; ibid., busta 220, "Gestione periodici."

89. Gambetti, *Inchiesta*, p. 194. For a discussion of most of these papers see PNF, GUF, *Vita dei GUF*, pp. 72–81; Folin and Quaranta, *Riviste giovanili*; and Paccagnella, "Stampa di fronda," pp. 83–110.

90. Quoted in Addis Saba, *Gioventù italiana del littorio*, p. 99.

91. "Questo è il signore 'travestito' da fascista," *Vent'anni*, 15 February 1941. See other articles in the issues for 3 February and 6 January 1940, 6 April, 20 July, 30 August, and 23 November 1941.

92. See issues for 7 September 1940 and 7 June and 30 August 1941.

93. "Commenti," *Il Campano*, April 1940. See also "Commenti," ibid., February 1941; "Lavorare in profondità," ibid., July 1941; Alberto Mario Cirese, "I valori dello spirito nella riorganizzazione europea," ibid., November–December 1941; and "Retorica del nostro tempo," ibid., May–June 1940.

94. *Il Barco*, May 1942 and December 1941.

95. "Invito al commando," *Il Barco*, November 1941; F. Rusconi, "La guerra come giustizia," ibid., October 1941. See also A. Gatto, "Non si tratta di un nastrino," ibid., September 1941.

96. Giuseppe Melis Bassu, personal correspondence with the author, 5 December 1975. Collections (though not complete ones) of these papers are available at the Biblioteca Alessandrina. Quite a bit has been written on *L'Intervento*: Pigliaru, "Fecero anche politica"; Kubelik, "Giornale universitario del deprecato ventennio"; Melis Bassu, "*Intervento* giornale del ventennio"; Addis Saba, *Gioventù italiana del littorio*, pp. 126–45, 214–23.

97. On *Architrave* see Folin and Quaranta, *Riviste giovanili*, pp. 25–26, 315–37; and Pini and Susmel, *Mussolini*, 4:109.

98. Renzi, "Rapporto di un ex-balilla," p. 116.

99. "Meridiani rivoluzionari," *Architrave*, 1 February 1941.

100. Bignardi, "Noi, giovani."

101. Guizzardi, "Fede in Mussolini." Guizzardi joined the Antonio Labriola group, an organization of Marxist intellectuals, at the end of 1942 just before he went to the front. He was killed in Sicily in the summer of 1943 "without knowing exactly why," as Zangrandi said in *Lungo viaggio*, pp. 187–88.

102. Renzi, "Rapporto di un ex-balilla," pp. 105–7.

103. Facchini, "Parlar chiaro"; Nazario Sauro Onofri, *I giornali bolognesi nel ventennio fascista* (Bologna: Editrice Moderna, 1972), pp. 211–12.

104. The particularly offensive articles in these issues were Chesi, "Responsabilità"; Gardini, "Il coraggio della verità"; and G. Rossi, "Fede in una libertà."

105. Testimony of Chesi in Onofri, *Giornali bolognesi*, pp. 220–21.

106. Rendina, "Motivo ideale." See also Bassoli, "Fiducia nella Patria."

107. Onofri, *Giornali bolognesi*, p. 225; Gambetti, *Inchiesta*, p. 220.

108. Folin and Quaranta, *Riviste giovanili*, pp. 18–21, 285–314; Paccagnella, "Stampa di fronda." On the University of Padua as an anti-Fascist center see Bobbio, "Concetto Marchesi," pp. 311–13.

109. "La figura giuridica del Segretario del partito," *Il Bò*, 1 October 1937.

110. Enzo Modica, "La vita e l'opera di Eugenio Curiel," introduction to Curiel, *Classi e generazioni*, p. v.

111. Mieli, "Eugenio Curiel," pp. 187–88, and "Eugenio Curiel puo dire che sono i comunisti"; Spriano, *Storia del Partito comunista italiano*, 3:197–99.

112. Modica, "Vita e opera di Eugenio Curiel," p. xxii. For collections of Curiel's writings see his *Classi e generazioni*; *Scritti*; and *Dall'antifascismo*. On Curiel see Garin, "Eugenio Curiel," pp. 3–24; Enzo Modica, "Curiel e la prospettiva unitaria," pp. 159–72; Agosti, "Eugenio Curiel," pp. 63–73; Delle Piane, "Alla ricerca di un'Italia civile," pp. 975–87; Longo, "Battaglia delle idee," pp. 514–16; Catalano, *Generazione degli anni '40*, pp. 49–98; Panzanelli, "Attività politica di Eugenio Curiel," pp. 253–96; and Giancarlo Pajetta, "La soppressione della libertà di stampa e la stampa clandestina antifascista," in Arbizzani and Caltabiano, *Storia dell'antifascismo italiano*, 1:83–90. For Curiel's letters to the leaders of the PSI see Merli, *Documenti inediti*.

113. All of his articles appear in Curiel, *Scritti*, pp. 27–200.

114. Spriano, *Storia del Partito comunista italiano*, 3:199. See also Modica's introduction to *Classi e generazioni*, p. xxxiv.

115. On these meetings see Amendola, *Intervista sull'antifascismo*, pp. 139–40; Modica, introduction to *Classi e generazioni*, p. xxxvii; and Ettore Luccini, "Operai e universitari," *Il Bò*, 31 August 1937. Curiel reported on this activity in "Relazione sull'attività svolta," in his *Scritti*, pp. 46–60. Examples of Curiel's syndical articles in *Il Bò* include "La rappresaglia sindacale," 20 August 1938; "Le corporazioni e l'accertamento dei costi di produzione," 2 April 1938; "L'organizzazione del lavoro ed il contributo della classe operaia," 5 March 1938; "Giustizia sociale e potenziamento del sindacato," 1 January 1938; "Educazione operaia e mentalità borghese," 19 February 1938; "Compiti dei sindacati: Assistenza legale," 1 October 1937; "Che cosa significa il 'largo ai giovani,'" 1 August 1937; and "Fine o potenziamento del sindacato?" 4 December 1937.

116. On the Fronte della gioventù see De Lazzari, *Storia della Fronte della gioventù*; Alatri, *Antifascismo italiano*, 2:957–58; Rosengarten, *Italian Anti-Fascist Press*, pp. 150–51; and Franchi, *Nuove generazioni*, pp. 43–60.

117. On Curiel's death see Vittorini, "Eugenio Curiel," pp. 149–52; Mieli, "Eugenio Curiel," and "Eugenio Curiel puo dire che sono i comunisti"; Banfi, "24 febbraio."

118. Melis Bassu, "*Intervento* giornale del ventennio," p. 3.

Chapter Eight

1. Quoted in Melograni, "Cult of the Duce," p. 231.

2. Amendola, *Intervista sull'antifascismo*, p. 139.

3. On the makeup of the party inner circle see Lasswell and Sereno, "Governmental and Party Leaders," pp. 914–29; Germino, *Italian Fascist Party*, pp. 47–50; and Lyttelton, *Seizure of Power*, p. 305.

4. Barbagli, *Disoccupazione intellettuale*, pp. 299–300.

5. For an expression of these ideas see the following articles: Bottai, "Regime dei giovani," "Avviamento alle responsabilità," "Giovani nel partito," and "Giovani e più giovani"; Secreti, "Giovani e il partito"; and Nasti, "Giovani, meno giovani, giovanissimi." For the outlines of this debate and Bottai's views see Mangoni, *Interventismo della cultura*, pp. 197–207, 284 (n. 1); Guerri, *Giuseppe Bottai*, pp. 138–40; and Nello, "Mussolini e Bottai," pp. 365–66.

6. Bottai, "Regno della noia"; Pompei, "Elezionismo nella vita del Partito."

7. Quoted in De Felice, *Mussolini il duce*, 1:237, from *L'Universale*, November 1931.

8. Nasti, "Avvenimenti e idee."

9. Lombrassa, "Indifferenza male di moda"; Bilenchi, "Indifferenza dei giovani"; Nasti, "Giovani e il regime"; Bottai, "Funzione della gioventù." See also Montalto, "Avvenire."

10. Giorgio Radetti, "Svecchiare," quoted in Germani, "Socializzazione politica dei giovani," p. 36.

11. ACS, MI, DGPS, DAGR (1930–31), sezione I, busta 1, letter dated 19 May 1931; ibid., DPP (1927–44), busta 149, fasc. K112, "Attività sovversiva degli studenti (1929–1931)," letters dated 12 and 30 April 1931 from Milan, 6 May 1931 from Turin, and 20 April 1931 from Naples.

12. ACS, MI, DGPS, DPP (1927–44), busta 132, fasc. K11, "Attività sovversiva degli studenti," letters dated 26 July and 4 June 1934 from Milan and 22 February 1934 from Rome.

13. Pellizzi's articles in *Selvaggio* were "Lettera con vari ragionamenti," 30 October 1931; "Seconda lettera sopra gli stessi argomenti della prima," 30 December 1931; "Terza lettera," 31 March 1932; and "Postilla alle lettere: Il fascismo come libertà," 1 May 1932. See also the response of Maccari in the same journal, "Risposta a volta di corriere," 30 December 1931. These letters are discussed in De Felice, *Mussolini il duce*, 1:239–41; and Mangoni, *Interventismo della cultura*, pp. 197–207.

14. Mussolini's article, "Punti fermi sui giovani," was published first in PNF, *Foglio d'ordini*, no. 64, 20 January 1930, and then in *Critica fascista*, 1 February 1930.

15. Cornelio Di Marzio, "Giovani e più giovani: Comando e moralità," *Critica fascista*, 15 January 1930. See also Nello, "Mussolini e Bottai," pp. 340–42.

16. Quoted in De Felice, *Mussolini il duce*, 1:117.

17. Emilio Lussu, "La nascita di Giustizia e Libertà," in Antonicelli, *Trent'anni di storia*, pp. 173–77. On Rosselli's influence on the young see Catalano, *Generazione degli anni '40*, pp. 7–31.

18. Alberto Tarchiani, "Il volo di Bassanesi su Milano e il processo di Lugano," in Antonicelli, *Trent'anni di storia*, p. 167. On Rosselli see Garosci, *Vita di Carlo Rosselli*; and Calogero, *Difesa del liberalsocialismo*, especially pp. 123–26, 231–36.

19. Mila, "Attività clandestina di Giustizia e Libertà"; Garosci, "F. De Rosa, R. Giua e C. Rosselli"; Fancello, "Un'azione fallita di Giustizia e Libertà." On police investigations of Giustizia e Libertà see ACS, MI, DGPS, DAGR (1920, 1923–45), cat. C2AG, busta 2/J, "Anno 1935 Movimento studentesco antifascista Giustizia e Libertà"; ibid., busta 3, "Anno 1934 Giovane Italia,

Giustizia e Libertà"; ibid., buste 21, 47; and ibid., DPP (1927–44), cat. 1, busta 141. On the activities of the Giellisti during the Resistance see *Giustizia e Libertà*.

20. Tarchiani, "Volo di Bassanesi su Milano," pp. 167–70; De Felice, *Mussolini il duce*, 1:122.

21. Testimony of Mario Pomilio in Albertoni, Antonini, and Palmieri, *Generazione degli anni difficili*, pp. 210–11. On the Scuola Normale Superiore see also Natta, "Scuola di antifascismo," pp. 11–16; Addis Saba, *Gioventù italiana del littorio*, pp. 61–62; and Zangrandi, *Lungo viaggio*, pp. 463–65. On the growth of antifascism see also Capitini, *Antifascismo tra i giovani*, pp. 170–95.

22. Capitini, *Antifascismo tra i giovani*, pp. 30–31. On the *liberalsocialisti* see also Rosengarten, *Italian Anti-Fascist Press*, pp. 72–74; Zangrandi, *Lungo viaggio*, pp. 481–84; and Borghi, *Educazione e autorità*, pp. 316–25. An especially important collection of essays on *liberalsocialismo* by one of its founders is Calogero, *Difesa del liberalsocialismo*; on Capitini see especially pp. 113–22, 311–31.

23. Capitini was arrested in Perugia in February 1942, and arrests followed in other important centers later that year. On these groups and their activities see Spriano, *Storia del Partito comunista italiano*, 4:80; Chabod, *Italia contemporanea*, pp. 91–92; and Tannenbaum, *Fascist Experience*, pp. 186, 318–19. For writings by the participants see Delle Piane, "Alla ricerca di un Italia civile," pp. 975–87; Capitini, "Esperienza religiosa," pp. 60–64; Capitini, Lombardi, and Mila, "Mia opposizione al fascismo," pp. 32–43; and Calamandrei, Renzi, and Aristarco, *Processo s'agapò*.

24. ACS, MI, DGPS, DPP (1927–44), cat. 1, busta 141. See also ibid., busta 133, fasc. K23/1, "Movimento Giovane Italia"; ibid., cat. K151, busta 147, "Movimento della gioventù italiana"; ibid., cat. K29, busta 102, fasc. 15, "Giovane Italia"; MI, DGPS, DAGR (1920, 1923–45), cat. G1, busta 3, "Anno 1934, Giovane Italia, Giustizia e Libertà"; and ibid., busta 21, fasc. 228–1, 228–2, "Giovane Italia."

25. De Felice, *Mussolini il duce*, 1:119. For information on some Catholic anti-Fascist activities see Olivero, "Azione cattolica," pp. 178–81; and Rosengarten, *Italian Anti-Fascist Press*, pp. 55–59.

26. Trentin, *Dieci anni*, p. 196.

27. De Bosis, *Story of My Death*, pp. 9–10.

28. Ibid., pp. 11–12. For De Bosis's reaction to fascism and the tale of his participation in the Alleanza Nazionale see ibid., passim. On De Bosis and the Alleanza Nazionale see Salomone, *Italy*, pp. 416–19; Salvatorelli and Mira, *Storia d'Italia*, 2:74–92; Salvadori, "Sacrificio di Lauro De Bosis," pp. 715–25; Trentin, *Dieci anni*, pp. 196–204; Dal Pont, Leonetti, and Massara, *Giornali fuori legge*, pp. 201–7; Gavagnin, *Vent'anni*, pp. 318–25; Vinciguerra, "Alleanza nazionale," pp. 170–73; "The Case of Vinciguerra and Rendi," *Italy To-Day*, May 1931; and "Lauro De Bosis," ibid., November–December 1931. Official information on De Bosis can be found in ACS, MCP, busta 164, fasc. 19, "Lauro De Bosis."

29. Copies of these leaflets are included in De Bosis, *Story of My Death*; and in "Lauro De Bosis," *Italy To-Day*. The authorities also had copies: ACS,

MI, DGPS, DAGR (1930), cat. F1, busta 169, "Alleanza nazionale per la libertà."

30. De Felice, *Mussolini il duce*, 1:119. Rosengarten, in *Italian Anti-Fascist Press*, p. 55, claims that Rendi died in prison.

31. De Bosis, *Story of My Death*, p. 16.

32. Salvadori, "Sacrificio di Lauro De Bosis," p. 716.

33. Quoted in Salomone, *Italy*, p. 420. A chair of Italian civilization, first occupied by his former mentor Gaetano Salvemini, was established in De Bosis's name at Harvard.

34. Zangrandi, *Lungo viaggio*, pp. 484–86; Garosci, "Ricomposizione del partito socialista," pp. 230–36.

35. Quoted in De Felice, *Fascismo e i partiti politici*, p. 12.

36. Amendola, *Comunismo, antifascismo e resistenza*, p. 30. See also Franchi, *Nuove generazioni*, p. 86; and Giorgio Amendola, introduction to Curiel, *Scritti*.

37. Palmiro Togliatti, "Contro l'opportunismo nel lavoro per la conquista dei giovani," *Lo Stato operaio* 6 (1934), quoted in Franchi, *Nuove generazioni*, pp. 28–29; italics in the original. See also Togliatti, *Lezioni sul fascismo*, pp. 69–72.

38. Quoted in Delzell, *Mussolini's Enemies*, p. 39. See also Spriano, *Storia del Partito comunista italiano*, 2:416–19, 3:18–39.

39. Amendola, *Comunismo, antifascismo e resistenza*, p. 31. See also Amendola, *Intervista sull' antifascismo*, pp. 103–4. On the PCI line and the youth see Negarville, "Per un movimento giovanile," pp. 468–75; Longo, "Lotta per la conquista della gioventù"; and Spano, "Nostri giovani."

40. Pajetta, "Carceri fasciste," p. 207.

41. Eugenio Curiel, "Tendenze e aspirazioni della gioventù intellettuale," *Lo Stato operaio* 12, no. 21 (December 1938), reprinted in *Scritti*, 2:219–24.

42. Spriano, *Storia del Partito comunista italiano*, 3:194–98.

43. Caputo, "Opposizione antifascista," and "Scuola e antifascismo"; Zangrandi, *Lungo viaggio*, pp. 486–93, 505–7; Spriano, *Storia del Partito comunista italiano*, 3:181–206.

44. The autobiographical literature on youth and fascism is a key source for any work on this topic. The most important and frequently cited books are those by Zangrandi (*Lungo viaggio*), Spinetti (*Difesa di una generazione* and *Vent' anni dopo*), Capitini (*Antifascismo tra i giovani*), Lajolo (*Classe 1912*), and Gambetti (*Anni che scottano*), as well as the collections of remembrances *Generazione degli anni difficili*, ed. Albertoni, Antonini, and Palmieri; and *Autobiografie di giovani*. In addition, see the following: Lajolo, *Voltagabbana*; Pellizzi, *Rivoluzione mancata*; Gambetti, *Né vivi né morti*; Tripodi, *Italia fascista in piedi!* (for a defense of the regime); Casucci, "Generazione del littorio," pp. 36–38; Renzi, "Rapporto di un ex-balilla," pp. 102–37; Chilanti, *Colpevole*; Pintor, *Sangue d'Europa*; Signoretti, *Come diventai fascista*; Magnani and Cucchi, *Crisi di una generazione*; Preti, *Giovinezza, giovinezza*; and Capitini, Lombardi, and Mila, "Mia opposizione al fascismo."

45. Zangrandi, "Giovani e il fascismo," p. 209. See also the testimony of F. Compagna in Albertoni, Antonini, and Palmieri, *Generazione degli anni difficili*, p. 94.

46. Testimony of Mario Pomilio in Albertoni, Antonini, and Palmieri, *Generazione degli anni difficili*, p. 207; testimony of Ezio Antonini in ibid., p. 8. See also, in ibid., the testimony of Franco [Lattes] Fortini, pp. 145–46, Giuseppe Melis Bassu, pp. 180–81, and Luciano Della Mea, pp. 118–19. See also Russo, "I giovani nel venticinquennio fascista," pp. 7–17.

47. See especially Zangrandi, *Lungo viaggio*, pp. 347–63. For this view of the "conspiracy of silence" among the older generations see Addis Saba, *Gioventù italiana del littorio*, pp. 51–55; Spinetti, *Difesa di una generazione*, pp. 23–25; and Salvemini and La Piana, *What to Do with Italy*, pp. 80–81.

48. Testimony of Mario Pomilio in Albertoni, Antonini, and Palmieri, *Generazione degli anni difficili*, pp. 208–9. On support from the church see Magnani and Cucchi, *Crisi di una generazione*, pp. 7–8.

49. Ugoberto Alfassio Grimaldi, in Albertoni, Antonini, and Palmieri, *Generazione degli anni difficili*, p. 50. See also Treves, "Fascismo e il problema delle generazioni," pp. 126–28; and Zevi, "Presentando i *Quaderni*," pp. 967–72.

50. Davide Lajolo, in Albertoni, Antonini, and Palmieri, *Generazione degli anni difficili*, p. 170.

51. Testimony of Bertolo Pento in Zangrandi, *Lungo viaggio*, p. 478.

52. Lajolo, *Classe 1912*, p. 13. See also Spinetti, *Difesa di una generazione*, pp. 18–20; testimony of Ugoberto Alfassio Grimaldi in *Autobiografie di giovani*, pp. 57–59; testimony of Zangrandi in Albertoni, Antonini, and Palmieri, *Generazione degli anni difficili*, p. 277; and Signoretti, *Come diventai fascista*, pp. 93–94.

53. Casucci, "Generazione del littorio," p. 37. On the same theme see Zangrandi, "Giovani e il fascismo," pp. 209–13.

54. Letter from Melis Bassu to the author dated 5 December 1975.

55. Zangrandi, *Lungo viaggio*, pp. 34, 53–57. See also Matthews, *Fruits of Fascism*, p. 220.

56. ACS, MI, DGPS, DAGR (1929), busta 49, Sezione II, cat. D9, "Agitazioni studenti," reports for 22–23 November 1928; ibid., cat. G1, busta 21, fasc. 228–1, letter from Milan dated 24 May 1928. Reports were also included in MI, DGPS, DPP (1927–44), busta 149, fasc. K112, "Attività sovversiva degli studenti (1929–1931)," letters from Milan dated 10 and 27 May 1931. A report in ibid. dated 23 April 1931 noted that Giustizia e Libertà had distributed a pamphlet at the University of Turin addressed "To Young Italians." Files on the same organization indicated that the Giellisti had enrolled some two thousand adherents (almost certainly an exaggeration) among university students in Milan in 1932. See ibid., busta 132, fasc. K11; and ibid., busta 215, "Giovane Italia." These same files also contain scattered reports on student activities in Bologna, Naples, Genoa, and Pavia. Other reports from 1935 indicated that police had infiltrated many student groups and that the mail of suspected anti-Fascist professors was being opened routinely.

57. ACS, MI, DGPS, DPP (1927–44), busta 132, fasc. K11, reports dated 26 April 1932 from Lugano, 2 June 1933 and 5 May and 16 June 1934 from Rome, 29 March 1934 from Zurich, 29 March and 27 June 1934 from Geneva, 28 March 1933 from Berne, and 21 December 1935 from Genoa.

58. Preti, *Miti dell'impero*, p. 34; De Felice, *Mussolini il duce*, 1:29–34;

Salvatorelli and Mira, *Storia d'Italia*, 2:296–98; Magnani and Cucchi, *Crisi di una generazione*, pp. 17–19. For the Italian reaction to the events of the late 1930s see Longanesi, *In piedi e seduti*.

59. On the propaganda aspects of the Ethiopian war see Mack Smith, *Mussolini's Roman Empire*, pp. 59–98, and *Mussolini*, pp. 196–203; and Tannenbaum, *Fascist Experience*, pp. 172–73.

60. Testimony of Ugoberto Alfassio Grimaldi in *Autobiografie di giovani*, p. 54.

61. Zangrandi received a copy of the book from Vittorio, who inscribed it: "To dear Ruggero, this book that I should not have written." Zangrandi, *Lungo viaggio*, p. 23.

62. Quoted in Binchy, *Church and State*, p. 651. On the church and the war see also De Felice, *Mussolini il duce*, 1:761–62; and Jemolo, *Chiesa e stato*, p. 260.

63. *Lo Stato operaio*, June 1936, quoted in De Felice, *Mussolini il duce*, 1:771. Leto, in *OVRA*, pp. 134–39, claimed that antifascism was not "an appreciable phenomenon" before the African war. See also Pesenti, "Avventura d'Etiopia," pp. 374–80; "Lettera da Roma: Borghesia, piccola borghesia ed intellettuali di fronte alla guerra," *Lo Stato operaio* 10, no. 2 (February 1936), quoted in Spriano, *Storia del Partito comunista italiano*, 3:44–45.

64. Santarelli, *Storia del fascismo*, 3:12.

65. Mack Smith, *Mussolini*, p. 202. Mack Smith claimed that Italy lost five thousand troops, mostly colonial forces. The necessary replacement of lost war matériel he calculated as equivalent to the entire military budget for three years.

66. Tamaro, *Venti anni*, 3:222. The connection between the myth of the Duce and the myth of the new civilization is discussed in De Felice, *Mussolini il duce*, 2:254–330.

67. Quoted in De Felice, *Mussolini il duce*, 2:255, 272.

68. Bottai, *Vent'anni e un giorno*, pp. 28, 85–86, 95–96; Bastianini, *Uomini, cose, fatti*, pp. 38–40, 48–52; Tamaro, *Venti anni*, 2:230; De Felice, *Mussolini il duce*, 1:798–808.

69. Testimony of G. C. in *Autobiografie di giovani*, pp. 14–15, 8–9. See also Capitini, *Antifascismo tra i giovani*, p. 64; and Borghi, *Educazione e autorità*, pp. 288–99.

70. Testimony of Rosario Assunto, quoted in Zangrandi, *Lungo viaggio*, p. 495; Zangrandi, ibid., p. 57.

71. On the general economic situation during this period see De Felice, *Mussolini il duce*, 2:169–215; Spriano, *Storia del Partito comunista italiano*, 3:192–93; and Coverdale, *Italian Intervention*, pp. 19–20.

72. Coverdale, *Italian Intervention*, pp. 19–24.

73. Amendola, *Intervista sull'antifascismo*, pp. 154–55. See also Valiani, "Intervento in Spagna," pp. 213–35; Garosci, "F. De Rosa, R. Giua e C. Rosselli," pp. 247–53; Spriano, *Storia del Partito comunista italiano*, 3:68–94; testimony of Lucio Lombardo-Radice in Capitini, *Antifascismo tra i giovani*, pp. 288–90; Franchi, *Nuove generazioni*, pp. 33–35; Preti, *Miti dell'impero*, pp. 44–48; and Franco Fortini in Zangrandi, *Lungo viaggio*, pp. 498–500.

74. Zangrandi, *Lungo viaggio*, p. 276. See also Elio Vittorini, "Il popolo spagnolo attende la liberazione," *Il Politecnico* 1 (29 September 1945): 1, quoted in Spriano, *Storia del Partito comunista italiano*, 3:90–91.

75. On the clandestine monitoring of foreign broadcasts see Coverdale, *Italian Intervention*, pp. 88–89; Zangrandi, *Lungo viaggio*, pp. 276–77; and Spriano, *Storia del Partito comunista italiano*, 3:183–87.

76. Mack Smith, *Mussolini*, pp. 211–12; Guerri, *Galeazzo Ciano*, p. 249; S. Hughes, *Fall and Rise*, pp. 176–88. Hughes claims that the Rossellis were murdered by French *cagoulards* in the pay of the Italian government. On Italian public opinion during the war see Aquarone, "Guerra in Spagna," pp. 121–26.

77. De Felice, *Mussolini il duce*, 2:880–92, "Le ripercussioni dello scoppio della guerra civile spagnola sulla popolazione italiana viste dai prefetti e dall'OVRA."

78. Coverdale, "Primi volontari italiani," pp. 545–54.

79. Quoted in De Felice, *Mussolini il duce*, 2:237.

80. Leto, *OVRA*, pp. 165–66.

81. De Felice, *Mussolini il duce*, 2:46–47. On the Special Tribunal and youth see also Spriano, *Storia del Partito comunista italiano*, 4:78–79, 279–85.

82. Zangrandi, *Lungo viaggio*, p. 507.

83. Quoted in Spriano, *Storia del Partito comunista italiano*, 3:200.

84. ACS, MI, DGPS, DPP (1927–44), busta 132, fasc. K11, letters dated 13 June 1937 from Genoa and 10 March 1937 from Zurich.

85. Ibid., letters dated 4 April 1937 and 17 September, 24 April, and 29 July 1936 from the chief of police, 8 July 1937 from Milan, and 30 March 1938 from Lausanne.

86. Ibid., letters dated 12 January and 8 April 1938 from Milan. See also MI, DGPS, DAGR, cat. D9, busta 10, "Agitazioni studenti," sottofasc. 48, "Milano," dated 27 January 1938.

87. Ibid., the prefect of Pavia to the minister of the interior, 1 March 1938. See also ibid., the prefect of Milan to the minister, 11 March 1938.

88. ACS, MI, DGPS, DPP, busta 132, fasc. K11, "Attività sovversiva dei studenti," letters dated 9 April and 18 May 1938 from Milan; ibid., busta 218, cat. Q8, "Scuola 1939–1941," letter dated 17 April 1939 from Rome. Student opposition was reported as especially strong in Milan, Padua, Venice, Turin, Genoa, Bologna, Florence, Rome, and Naples. See reports in ACS, MI, DGPS, DPP (1927–44), busta 132, fasc. K11, "Attività sovversiva dei studenti," letters dated 1 April, 31 May, and 3 September 1938 from Milan and 7 April 1938 from Rome. See also ACS, PNF, SPEP, busta 1, "Genova," dated 18 January 1940. On the general state of public opinion see ACS, DGPS, DPP (1927–44), buste 228–39.

89. Quoted in Barzini, *Italians*, p. 81.

90. Tamaro, *Venti anni*, 3:304, 309–11. On opposition to these laws see Supino, "Italiani di fronte al razzismo," pp. 155–63; Leto, *OVRA*, pp. 191–92; De Felice, *Storia degli ebrei*, pp. 353–73, 432–56; Gavagnin, *Vent'anni*, pp. 377–82; Mack Smith, *Mussolini*, pp. 220–23; Bocca, *Storia d'Italia*,

p. 21; and Matthews, *Fruits of Fascism*, p. 243. On the origins, motivations, and history of Fascist anti-Semitism see Bernardini, "Origins and Development of Racial Anti-Semitism"; and Michaelis, *Mussolini and the Jews*.

91. On the pope's speech on 30 July 1938 and Farinacci's attacks on the church see De Felice, *Storia degli ebrei*, pp. 364–73, 434–36. On Fermi see Zangrandi, *Lungo viaggio*, p. 181.

92. Testimony of Rosario Assunto in Zangrandi, *Lungo viaggio*, p. 495. In September 1938 Starace gave the order for every GUF to set up a Demography and Race section. Often, especially in some of the smaller locales, these sections took an active role in the anti-Semitic campaign; De Felice, in *Storia degli ebrei*, pp. 319, 355, 449–50, points to the sections at Campobasso, Trieste, Taranto, Perugia, and Catanzaro as particularly active. For others, however, the story was different: "Many other young people of those same GUF at that very time took the leap and rapidly became anti-Fascists." See also De Felice, *Mussolini il duce*, 2:250–53.

93. Levi, "Deportazione e sterminio," pp. 168–75, and *Survival in Auschwitz*.

94. Spriano, *Storia del Partito comunista italiano*, 3:276; Caputo, "Opposizione antifascista," pp. 65–67; testimony of Ugoberto Alfassio Grimaldi in *Autobiografie di giovani*, pp. 60–61.

95. Zangrandi, *Lungo viaggio*, p. 395.

96. Senise, *Quando ero capo della polizia*, pp. 44–45; Lyttelton, *Seizure of Power*, p. 302. See also Tamaro, *Venti anni*, 3:277.

97. G. Ciano, *Diario, 1939–1943*, p. 609 (quoted from the translation, p. 535).

98. Mack Smith, *Mussolini*, pp. 128–29. See also Senise, *Quando ero capo della polizia*, p. 21; and Tamaro, *Venti anni*, 3:230.

99. Senise, *Quando ero capo della polizia*, p. 154; E. Ciano, *Mia testimonianza*, pp. 182–85.

100. Quoted in Mack Smith, *Mussolini*, p. 286.

101. Leto, *OVRA*, pp. 22, 70; Bastianini, *Uomini, cose, fatti*, p. 235.

102. Leto, *OVRA*, p. 185.

103. Corrado Alvaro, *Quasi una vita: Giornale di un scrittore* (Milan, 1951), quoted in A. Hamilton, *Appeal of Fascism*, p. 70.

104. Tamaro, *Venti anni*, 3:219–20.

105. Mack Smith, *Mussolini*, pp. 281–82; Pini and Susmel, *Mussolini*, 4:156–57.

106. G. Ciano, *Diario, 1939–1943*, pp. 489, 504, 518, entries for 27 December 1941 and 24 January and 22 February 1942 (quoted from the translation, pp. 426–27, 439, 451). See also entries for 26 February and 7 August 1942.

107. Quoted in Tamaro, *Venti anni*, 3:468.

108. Togliatti, *Discorsi agli italiani*, p. 367, dated 7 May 1943.

109. Leto, *OVRA*, p. 243. See also Senise, *Quando ero capo della polizia*, p. 173; Bocca, *Storia d'Italia*, pp. 554–55; and Mack Smith, *Mussolini*, p. 289.

110. The text of this letter is available in ACS, SPD, Ris., busta 45, fasc.

242/R, "Carlo Scorza." See also a letter dated 23 June 1943 in ibid., busta 32, fasc. 242/R, "Riunioni del Direttorio."

111. Senise, *Quando ero capo della polizia*, pp. 96, 115–16, 120–23; Bottai, *Vent'anni e un giorno*, p. 230; Mack Smith, *Mussolini*, pp. 128–29, 277–86; Leto, *OVRA*, pp. 23, 146; Bastianini, *Uomini, cose, fatti*, pp. 39, 52; Kirkpatrick, *Mussolini*, p. 191.

112. G. Ciano, *Diario, 1939–1943*, pp. 412–13, entry for 26 May 1941 (quoted from the translation, p. 357).

113. Bocca, *Storia d'Italia*, p. 437; Bastianini, *Uomini, cose, fatti*, p. 56; Santarelli, *Storia del fascismo*, 3:9–11.

114. Quoted in G. Ciano, *Diario, 1939–1943*, p. 457, entry for 21 October 1941 (quoted from the translation, p. 395).

115. Quoted in Guerri, *Giuseppe Bottai*, p. 207.

116. Bastianini, *Uomini, cose, fatti*, p. 34; Guerri, *Rapporto al Duce*, p. 84.

117. Kirkpatrick, *Mussolini*, p. 193. See also Matthews, *Fruits of Fascism*, pp. 333–34.

118. Mack Smith, *Mussolini*, p. 290; De Felice, *Mussolini il duce*, 2:215–18, 261–65.

119. Mack Smith, *Mussolini*, p. 288. See also Dinale, *Quarant'anni*, pp. 183–86, 248; and Kirkpatrick, *Mussolini*, p. 193.

120. Bottai, *Vent'anni e un giorno*, p. 261. See also Mack Smith, *Mussolini's Roman Empire*, pp. 246–49.

121. Matthews, *Fruits of Fascism*, p. 332. See also Senise, *Quando ero capo della polizia*, pp. 135–38; Leto, *OVRA*, pp. 240–43; and Togliatti, *Discorsi agli italiani*, p. 366.

122. Nolte, *Three Faces of Fascism*, p. 235.

123. Dinale, *Quarant'anni*, p. 181. See also Salvatorelli and Mira, *Storia d'Italia*, 2:459; Matthews, *Fruits of Fascism*, pp. 253, 262; Zangrandi, *Lungo viaggio*, pp. 142–43; and Sarti, *Ax Within*, pp. 209–10.

124. G. Ciano, *Diario, 1939–1943*, pp. 101–2, 104, entries for 29 April and 2 May 1939 (quoted from the translation, pp. 74, 76). See also the entries for 10 and 18 September, 16 October, and 31 December 1939 and 10 January, 7 April, and 28–29 May 1940. On this same theme of military unpreparedness see Bottai, *Vent'anni e un giorno*, pp. 156, 178, 196, entries for 23 January, 25 June, and 13 December 1940.

125. Senise, *Quando ero capo della polizia*, p. 35. See also Alberto Aquarone, "Lo spirito pubblico in Italia alla vigilia della seconda guerra mondiale," *Nord e sud* 11 (January 1964): 117–25, reprinted in Sarti, *Ax Within*, pp. 212–20; Salvatorelli and Mira, *Storia d'Italia*, 2:458–59; Spriano, *Storia del Partito comunista italiano*, 3:274–75; and Bottai, *Vent'anni e un giorno*, p. 132, entry for 31 August 1939.

126. G. Ciano, *Diario, 1939–1943*, p. 185, entry for 13 September 1939 (quoted from the translation, p. 143).

127. Zangrandi, *Lungo viaggio*, pp. 183, 185.

128. Ibid., p. 184.

129. Roatta, *Otto milioni di baionette*, pp. 44–48.

130. Matthews, *Fruits of Fascism*, pp. 308–9.

131. ACS, MI, DGPS, DPP (1927–44), cat. Q8, busta 218, "Scuola 1939–1941," letter dated 23 February 1941 from Milan. See also Senise, *Quando ero capo della polizia*, pp. 137–38; and ACS, PNF, SPEP, busta 11, "Padova," dated 2 October 1940.

132. ACS, MI, DGPS, DPP (1927–44), cat. Q8, busta 218, letter dated 2 April 1941 from Padua. See also ibid., letters dated 5 March 1941 from Treviso, 2 March 1941 from Bolzano, 24 February, 4 and 6 March, 4 April, and 5 May 1941 from Rome, and 9 March 1941 from Florence.

133. Ibid., busta 132, fasc. K11, "Attività sovversiva di studenti," reports dated 24 February and 7 March 1941 from Rome. See also ibid., busta 218, cat. Q8, letters dated 7 May 1941 from Vicenza, 5 May 1941 from Trieste, 24 February 1941 from Rome, and 23 February 1941 from Milan.

134. Ibid., letters dated 11 May 1941 from Rome, 11 May 1941 from Milan, 13 May 1941 from Genoa, and 14 May 1941 from Florence.

135. Ibid., reports dated 13, 15, and 18 May 1941 from Rome.

136. On the *beffa delle stelle filante*—the distribution of antiregime streamers—at the University of Rome in May 1941 see Zangrandi, *Lungo viaggio*, pp. 510–11.

137. ACS, MI, DGPS, DPP (1927–44), cat. Q8, busta 218, reports dated 20 May 1941 from Forlì, 23 May 1941 from Parma, and 26 May 1941 from Bologna.

138. Quoted in G. Ciano, *Diario, 1939–1943*, pp. 317–18, 380, 525, entries for 21 June and 23 December 1940 and 9 March 1942 (quoted from the translation, pp. 267, 326–27, 458).

139. Melis Bassu, "Natale 1940."

140. Testimony of Cimino and Fortini in Zangrandi, *Lungo viaggio*, pp. 495–500. See also Spriano, *Storia del Partito comunista italiano*, 4:238–39.

141. Sereni, "Antifascismo nelle trincee," pp. 281–84. See also Zangrandi, *Lungo viaggio*, pp. 472–76.

142. Bottai, *Vent' anni e un giorno*, p. 222, entry of 10 April 1942. See also Gambetti, *Inchiesta*, p. 277.

143. Testimony of Davide Lajolo in Zangrandi, *Lungo viaggio*, pp. 517–19. See also Lajolo, *Classe 1912*, p. 12. On memories of the war see also Albertoni, Antonini, and Palmieri, *Generazione degli anni difficili*, pp. 51, 188; and Signoretti, *Come diventai fascista*, p. 179.

144. The story of Falco Marin is told in Zangrandi, *Lungo viaggio*, pp. 521–22.

145. Testimony of G. C. in *Autobiografie di giovani*, pp. 16–17.

146. B. Mussolini, *Opera omnia*, 32:178.

Collections from the
Archivio Centrale dello Stato, Rome

Carte Di Marzio.
Fondo GUF.
Fondo Renato Ricci.
Ministero della Cultura Popolare.
Ministero dell'Interno. Direzione Generale Pubblica Sicurezza. Divisione
 Affari Generali e Riservati. Categoria C2AG (1920, 1923–45). Categoria
 D9, "Agitazioni studenti." Categoria G1 (1920, 1923–45).
―――. Divisione Polizia Politica (1927–44).
Mostra della Rivoluzione Fascista.
Partito Nazionale Fascista. Direttorio Nazionale.
―――. Situazione Politica ed Economica delle Provincie.
Presidenza del Consiglio dei Ministri. Gabinetto. Atti. (1931–33, 1934–36,
 1937–39, 1940–42).
Segretaria Particolare del Duce. Carteggio Ordinario.
―――. Carteggio Riservato.

Published Sources

Abad, C. H. "Fascist Education in Italy." *Current History* 32 (July 1932):
 433–38.
Acerbo, Giacomo. *I fondamenti della dottrina fascista della razza*. Rome:
 Ministero della Cultura Popolare, 1940.
Addis Saba, Marina. *Il dibattito sul fascismo*. Milan: Longanesi, 1976.
―――. *Gioventù italiana del littorio: La stampa dei giovani nella guerra fa-
 scista*. Milan: Feltrinelli, 1973.
Agnesi, Giovanni. *Tappe fasciste*. Milan: Casa Editrice Alpes, 1930.
Agosti, Aldo. "Eugenio Curiel tra 'lavoro legale' e azione clandestina." *Italia
 contemporanea* 26 (April–June 1974): 63–73.
Alatri, Paolo. "Lungo viaggio attraverso il fascismo." *Belfagor* 17 (31 July
 1962): 470–77.
―――. "Recenti studi sul fascismo." *Studi storici* 3 (October–December
 1962): 757–836.
―――, ed. *L'antifascismo italiano*. 2 vols. Rome: Editori Riuniti, 1973.
Albertoni, Ettore A.; Antonini, Ezio; and Palmieri, Renato, eds. *La generazione degli anni difficili*. Bari: Laterza, 1962.
Alfassio Grimaldi, Ugoberto. "La generazione sedotta e abbandonata." *Tempo
 presente* 8 (January 1963): 59–66.

Aliotta, Antonio, and Feola, Pietro. *Scuola del lavoro e ordinamento corporativo*. Rome: Società Editrice Perrella, 1940.

Almanacco Scolastico Nazionale. Rome: Libreria del Littorio, 1929.

Amato, Maria Pia; Cellai, Mario Paolo; Gai, Monica; Vannacci, Andrea; Zinanni, Maria; and Perugi, Giampaolo. *La scuola nel regime fascista: Il caso del Liceo classico di Pistoia*. Pistoia: Amministrazione Comunale di Pistoia, 1977.

Amendola, Giorgio. *Comunismo, antifascismo, e resistenza*. Rome: Editori Riuniti, 1967.

————. *Intervista sull'antifascismo*. Edited by Piero Melograni. Bari: Laterza, 1976.

Amicucci, Ermanno. "Giornalismo nel regime fascista." In *La civiltà fascista*, edited by Giuseppe Luigi Pomba, pp. 493–510. Turin: Editrice Torinese, 1928.

Andreis, Mario. "L'antifascismo torinese nei primi anni del regime." In *Trent'anni di storia italiana, 1915–1945*, edited by Franco Antonicelli, pp. 127–31. Turin: Einaudi, 1961.

Antonicelli, Franco. "Un professore antifascista: Umberto Cosmo." In *Trent'anni di storia italiana, 1915–1945*, edited by Franco Antonicelli, pp. 87–90. Turin: Einaudi, 1961.

————, ed. *Trent'anni di storia italiana, 1915–1945*. Turin: Einaudi, 1961.

Aquarone, Alberto. "La guerra in Spagna e l'opinione pubblica italiana." In *1922–1945: Sintesi storica e documenti del fascismo e dell'antifascismo italiano*, edited by Francesco Chicco and Gigi Livio, pp. 121–26. Turin: Paravia, 1970.

————. *L'organizzazione dello Stato totalitario*. Turin: Einaudi, 1965.

————, and Vernassa, Maurizio, eds. *Il regime fascista*. Bologna: Il Mulino, 1974.

Arbizzani, Luigi, and Onofri, Nazario Sauro. *I giornali bolognesi della resistenza*. Bologna: Edizioni A.N.P.I., 1966.

————, and Caltabiano, Alberto, eds. *Storia dell'antifascismo italiano*. 2 vols. Rome: Editori Riuniti, 1964.

Argento, Elmiro. "Continuity and Change in Italian Education, 1859–1923." *Historical Papers* (London), 1978, pp. 94–105.

Armellini, Quirino. *La crisi dell'esercito*. Rome: Casa Editrice Priscilla, 1945.

Ascoli, Max. "Education in Fascist Italy." *Social Research* 4 (September 1937): 338–46.

Autobiografie di giovani del tempo fascista. Brescia: Morcelliana, 1947.

Baciocchi de Peón, M. *Manuale del fascista: Regolamento spirituale di disciplina*. Florence: R. Bemporad, 1923.

Balbo, Italo. *Diario, 1922*. Milan: Mondadori, 1932.

Ballarati, Giancarlo, and Buonassisi, Vincenzo. "Il convegno di dottrina del fascismo." *Critica fascista*, 1 May 1937.

Ballario, Pina, and Angoletta, Bruno. *Quartiere Corridoni: Letture per la seconda classe dei centri urbani*. Rome: Libreria dello Stato, 1942.

————. *Quartiere Nuovo: Letture per la seconda classe urbana e rurale*. Rome: Ministero della Pubblica Istruzione, 1944.

Ballerio, Carlo. "La Federazione universitaria cattolica italiana, 1925–1939." *Italia contemporanea* 27 (January–March 1975): 39–69.

Banfi, Antonio. "24 febbraio: oggi commemoriamo Eugenio Curiel." *L'Unità*, 24 February 1946.

Barbagli, Marzio. *Disoccupazione intellettuale e sistema scolastico in Italia (1859–1973)*. Bologna: Il Mulino, 1974.

———. "Sistema scolastico e mercato del lavoro: La riforma Gentile." *Rivista di storia contemporanea* 4 (1973): 456–92.

Bargellini, Piero, and Della Torre, A. *Il libro della quarta classe elementare: Letture*. Rome: Libreria dello Stato, 1942.

Bartoli, Domenico. "A diciotto anni anch'io credevo in lui." *Epoca*, 28 March 1965.

Barzini, Luigi. *The Italians*. New York: Atheneum Publishers, 1964.

Bascone, Francesco. *La legislazione fascista per la scuola elementare*. Bologna: La Diana Scolastica, n.d.

Basso, Lelio. "Dal delitto Matteotti alle leggi eccezionali del 1925." Pts. 1 and 2. In *Trent'anni di storia italiana, 1915–1945*, edited by Franco Antonicelli, pp. 69–86, 101–26. Turin: Einaudi, 1961.

Bassoli, Vincenzo. "Fiducia nella Patria." *Architrave*, 30 June 1943.

Bastianini, Giuseppe. *Uomini, cose, fatti: Memorie di un ambasciatore*. Milan: Vitagliano, 1959.

Belloni, Eros, and Bernardini, Piero. *Il libro per la seconda classe dei centri rurali*. Rome: Libreria dello Stato, 1942.

Bellucci, Emanuela. "L'educazione religiosa nell'ONB." In *Cattolici e fascisti in Umbria (1922–1945)*, edited by Alberto Monticone, pp. 105–12. Bologna: Il Mulino, 1978.

Bellucci, Maria, and Ciliberto, Michele. *La scuola e la pedagogia del fascismo*. Turin: Loescher, 1978.

Bernardini, Gene. "The Origins and Development of Racial Anti-Semitism in Fascist Italy." *Journal of Modern History* 49 (September 1977): 431–53.

Berneri, Camillo. *Mussolini: Psicologia di un dittatore*. Milan: Edizioni Azione Comune, 1966.

Berto, Giuseppe. *Guerra in camicia nera*. Milan: Garzanti, 1955.

Bertone, Gianni. *I figli d'Italia si chiaman balilla*. Rimini: Guaraldi, 1975.

Bertoni Jovine, D., and Malatesta, F. *Breve storia della scuola italiana*. Rome: Editori Riuniti, 1961.

Bignardi, Agostino. "Noi, giovani." *Architrave*, 1 March 1941.

Bilenchi, Romano. "Indifferenza dei giovani." *Critica fascista*, 15 April 1933.

Biloni, Vincenzo. *Cultura fascista*. Brescia: Giulio Vannini, 1930.

Binchy, D. A. *Church and State in Fascist Italy*. London: Oxford University Press, 1941.

Biondi, Dino. *La fabbrica del Duce*. Florence: Vallecchi, 1973.

Bobbio, Norberto. "Concetto Marchesi e la resistenza all'università di Padova." In *Trent'anni di storia italiana, 1915–1945*, edited by Franco Antonicelli, pp. 311–13. Turin: Einaudi, 1961.

Bocca, Giorgio. *Storia d'Italia nella guerra fascista, 1940–1943*. Bari: Laterza, 1969.

Boccetti, Erminio. "Momenti di consenso del clero al regime: l'impresa d'Etiopia." In *Cattolici e fascisti in Umbria (1922–1945)*, edited by Alberto Monticone, pp. 333–40. Bologna: Il Mulino, 1978.

Bonsanti, Alessandro. "La cultura degli anni trenta: Dai Littoriali all'antifascismo." In *Terzo Programma: Quaderni trimestrali*, 4:183–219. Turin: Edizioni della RAI, 1963.

Bordoni, Carlo. *Cultura e propaganda nell'Italia fascista.* Messina: Casa Editrice G. D'Anna, 1974.

Borgese, G. A. *Goliath: The March of Fascism.* New York: Viking Press, 1938.

Borghi, Lamberto. *Educazione e autorità nell'Italia moderna.* Florence: La Nuova Italia, 1951.

_____. "Italy." In *Educational Yearbook of the International Institute of Teachers College, Columbia University, 1944*, edited by I. L. Kandel, pp. 173–217. New York: Teachers College, Columbia University, 1944.

Bottai, Giuseppe. "Avviamento alle responsabilità." *Critica fascista*, 1 February 1930.

_____. *La Carta della scuola.* Milan: Mondadori, 1939.

_____. *Diario, 1935–1944.* Edited by Giordano Bruno Guerri. Milan: Rizzoli, 1982.

_____. "Dichiarazioni di revisionismo." *Critica fascista*, 15 July 1924.

_____. "Esame di coscienza." *Critica fascista*, 1 October 1923.

_____. "Funzione della gioventù." *Critica fascista*, 1 March 1933.

_____. "I giovani." *Critica fascista*, 1 May 1931.

_____. "Giovani e più giovani." *Critica fascista*, 1 January 1930.

_____. "I giovani nel partito." *Critica fascista*, 15 October 1930.

_____. "Littoriali anno XVI." *Critica fascista*, 1 May 1938.

_____. *La nuova scuola media.* Florence: G. C. Sansoni, 1941.

_____. "La polemica revisionistica." *Critica fascista*, 15 May 1924.

_____. "Un regime dei giovani." *Critica fascista*, 1 June 1928.

_____. "Il regno della noia." *Critica fascista*, 15 August 1928.

_____. *Scritti.* Edited by Roberto Bartolozzi and Riccardo Del Giudice. Bologna: Cappelli, 1965.

_____. *Vent'anni e un giorno.* Milan: Garzanti, 1949.

Bozzoni, Aurelio. "Gioventù italiana del littorio." In Partito Nazionale Fascista, *Panorami di realizzazioni del fascismo*, vol. 3, *Dai fasci al Partito nazionale fascista*, pp. 423–31. Rome, n.d.

Buffarini Guidi, Glauco. *La vera verità.* Milan: Sugar, 1970.

Buonassisi, Vincenzo. "Il bilancio dei Littoriali." *Critica fascista*, 15 May 1938.

Calamandrei, P.; Renzi, R.; and Aristarco, G. *Il processo s'agapò: Dall'Arcadia a Peschiera.* Bari: Laterza, 1954.

Calendoli, Giovanni. "La Carta della scuola e le organizzazioni giovanili." *Gerarchia* 19 (February 1940): 109–12.

Calogero, Guido. *Difesa del liberalsocialismo ed altri saggi.* Milan: Marzorati, 1972.

Cammarata, Angelo. *Pedagogia di Mussolini.* Palermo: Trimarchi, 1932.

_____. *La scuola del fascismo*. Palermo: Trimarchi, 1938.

Campogrande, Valerio. *L'ordinamento dello stato italiano fascista*. Turin: S. Lattes, 1928.

Candeloro, Giorgio. *Il movimento cattolico in Italia*. Rome: Editori Riuniti, 1961.

Canestri, Giorgio, and Ricupèrati, Giuseppe. *La scuola in Italia dalla legge Casati a oggi*. Turin: Loescher, 1976.

Cannistraro, Philip V. "Burocrazia e politica culturale nello Stato fascista: Il Ministero della cultura popolare." *Storia contemporanea* 1 (June 1970): 273–98.

_____. *La fabbrica del consenso: Fascismo e mass media*. Rome: Laterza, 1975.

_____. "Mussolini's Cultural Revolution: Fascist or Nationalist?" *Journal of Contemporary History* 7 (1972): 115–39.

_____. "The Radio in Fascist Italy." *Journal of European Studies* 2 (June 1972): 127–54.

Cantalupo, Roberto. "La classe dirigente e il suo duce." *Gerarchia* 5 (January 1926): 3–13.

Cantarella, Michele. "The Situation of the Learned Class under the Fascist Regime." In *Schoolmen's Week Proceedings, 1939*, pp. 36–50. Philadelphia: University of Pennsylvania, 1939.

Capaldo, Enzo. "Classe dirigente e corsi di preparazione politica." *Critica fascista*, 15 September 1937.

_____. "GUF e GIL." *Critica fascista*, 1 November 1938.

Capasso, Aldo. *Idee chiare sul razzismo*. Rome: Edizioni Augustea, 1942.

Capitini, Aldo. *Antifascismo tra i giovani*. 1947. Enlarged ed. Trapani: Edizioni Célèbes, 1966.

_____. "Un esperienza religiosa dell'antifascismo." *Il movimento di liberazione in Italia* 33 (November 1954): 60–64.

_____. "Nota sul libro di Ruggero Zangrandi." In Aldo Capitini, *Antifascismo tra i giovani*, pp. 226–32. Trapani: Edizioni Célèbes, 1966.

_____; Lombardi, R.; and Mila, M. "La mia opposizione al fascismo." *Il Ponte* 16 (January 1960): 32–43.

Caporilli, Pietro. *L'educazione giovanile nello stato fascista*. Rome: Edizioni Sapientia, 1930.

_____. *Il fascismo e i giovani*. Rome: Angelo Signorelli, 1939.

Cappi, Ferruccio. *Parole ai giovani*. Rome: Fratelli Palombi, n.d.

Caputo, Giorgio. "L'opposizione antifascista degli studenti romani alla vigilia della seconda guerra." *Mondo operaio* 23 (March 1970): 34–41; (April–May 1970): 62–72.

_____. "Scuola e antifascismo a Roma negli anni 1936–38: Contributo allo studio dell'evoluzione politica della gioventù sotto il fascismo." *Palatino* 12 (October–December 1968): 398–410.

Carabba, Claudio. *Il fascismo a fumetti*. Rimini: Guaraldi, 1973.

Carli, Francesco. *Mussolini e lo sport*. Mantua: Paladino, 1928.

Carlini, Armando. *Filosofia e religione nel pensiero di Mussolini*. Rome: Istituto Nazionale Fascista di Cultura, 1934.

————. *Verso la nuova scuola*. Florence: G. C. Sansoni, 1941.

Carpanetto Firpo, Raffaella. "Intellettuali e mass-media nell'Italia fascista." *Rivista di storia contemporanea* 3 (July 1974): 356–76.

Casucci, Costanzo. "La generazione del littorio." *Lo Spettatore italiano* 9 (January 1956): 36–38.

Catalano, Franco. *La generazione degli anni '40*. Milan: Contemporanea Edizioni, 1975.

Cavallaro, Angela. *La scuola in Italia*. Catania: Studio Editoriale Moderno, 1939.

Cesari, Maurizio. *La censura nel periodo fascista*. Naples: Liguori, 1978.

Chabod, Federico. *L'Italia contemporanea, 1918–1948*. Turin: Einaudi, 1961.

Chesi, Vittorio. "Responsabilità." *Architrave*, 31 July 1942.

Chicco, Francesco, and Livio, Gigi. *1922–1945: Sintesi storica e documenti del fascismo e dell'antifascismo italiano*. Turin: Paravia, 1970.

Chilanti, Felice. *Il colpevole*. Milan: All'Insegna del Pesce d'Oro, 1967.

Ciani, Plinio. *Graffiti del ventennio*. Milan: Sugar, 1975.

Ciano, Edda. *La mia testimonianza*. Milan: Rusconi, 1975.

Ciano, Galeazzo. *Diario, 1939–1943*. Milan: Rizzoli, 1971. Translated under the title *The Ciano Diaries, 1939–43*. Edited by Hugh Gibson. Garden City, N.Y.: Doubleday & Co., 1946.

————. *Ciano's Diary, 1937–1938*. Translated by Andreas Mayor. London: Methuen & Co., 1952.

————. *Ciano's Hidden Diary, 1937–1938*. New York: E. P. Dutton & Co., 1953.

Codignola, Ernesto. "Italy." In *Educational Yearbook of the International Institute, Teachers College, Columbia University, 1930*, edited by I. L. Kandel, pp. 343–86. New York: Teachers College, Columbia University, 1931.

————. "Italy." In *Educational Yearbook of the International Institute, Teachers College, Columbia University, 1932*, edited by I. L. Kandel, pp. 295–315. New York: Teachers College, Columbia University, 1933.

————. "Italy." In *Educational Yearbook of the International Institute, Teachers College, Columbia University, 1935*, edited by I. L. Kandel, pp. 351–67. New York: Teachers College, Columbia University, 1936.

————. "Italy." In *Educational Yearbook of the International Institute, Teachers College, Columbia University, 1937*, edited by I. L. Kandel, pp. 319–35. New York: Teachers College, Columbia University, 1937.

————. "The Philosophy Underlying the National System of Education in Italy." In *Educational Yearbook of the International Institute, Teachers College, Columbia University, 1929*, edited by I. L. Kandel, pp. 317–427. New York: Teachers College, Columbia University, 1930.

————. *Il problema dell'educazione*. Florence: Vallecchi, 1930.

————. *Il rinnovamento spirituale dei giovani*. Milan: Mondadori, 1938.

Collier, Richard. *Duce!* New York: Viking Press, 1971.

Collino, Luigi. "Le organizzazioni giovanili." In *La civiltà fascista*, edited by Giuseppe Luigi Pomba, pp. 597–609. Turin: Editrice Torinese, 1928.

Corra, Bruno. *Gli intellettuali creatori e la mentalità fascista*. Milan: Sonzogna, 1923.

Cortelazzo, Michele A. "Mussolini socialista e gli antecedenti della retorica fascista." In *La lingua italiana e il fascismo*, edited by Erasmo Leso, Michele A. Cortelazzo, Ivano Paccagnella, and Fabio Foresti, pp. 63–82. Bologna: Consorzio Provinciale Pubblica Lettura, 1978.

Coverdale, John F. *Italian Intervention in the Spanish Civil War*. Princeton, N.J.: Princeton University Press, 1975.

————. "I primi volontari italiani nell'esercito di Franco." *Storia contemporanea* 2 (September 1977): 545–54.

Curiel, Eugenio. "Cina e Giappone." *Il Bò*, 31 August 1937.

————. *Classi e generazioni nel secondo Risorgimento*. Rome: Edizioni di Cultura Sociale, 1955.

————. *Dall'antifascismo alla democrazia progressiva*. Edited by Mario Quaranta and Elio Franzin. Padua: Marsilio, 1970.

————. "Futuro di un problema." *Il Bò*, 23 April 1938.

————. "Littoriali a porte chiuse." *Il Bò*, 23 April 1938.

————. *Scritti, 1935–1945*. 2 vols. Rome: Editori Riuniti, 1973.

Dal Piaz, Riccardo. *La radio nella scuola*. Rome: Angelo Signorelli, 1939.

Dal Pont, Adriano; Leonetti, Alfonso; and Massara, Massimo. *Giornali fuori legge: La stampa clandestina antifascista, 1922–1943*. Rome: Associazione Perseguitati Politici Italiani Antifascisti, 1964.

Deakin, F. W. *The Brutal Friendship: Mussolini, Hitler and the Fall of Italian Fascism*. New York: Harper & Row, 1962.

De Antonellis, Giacomo. *Il sud durante il fascismo*. N.p.: Lacaita Editore, 1977.

De Bosis, Lauro. *The Story of My Death*. New York: Oxford University Press, 1933.

De Felice, Renzo. *Il fascismo e i partiti politici*. Bologna: Cappelli, 1966.

————. *Le interpretazioni del fascismo*. Bari: Laterza, 1974.

————. *Intervista sul fascismo*. Edited by Michael A. Ledeen. Rome: Laterza, 1975.

————. *Mussolini il duce*. Vol. 1, *Gli anni del consenso, 1929–1936*. Vol. 2, *Lo Stato totalitario, 1936–1940*. Turin: Einaudi, 1974, 1981.

————. *Mussolini il fascista*. Vol. 1, *La conquista del potere, 1921–1925*. Vol. 2, *L'organizzazione dello Stato fascista, 1925–1929*. Turin: Einaudi, 1966, 1968.

————. *Mussolini il rivoluzionario, 1883–1920*. Turin: Einaudi, 1965.

————. *Storia degli ebrei italiani sotto il fascismo*. Turin: Einaudi, 1961.

De Gaetano, V., and Trizzino, G. *Il libro dell'avanguardista*. Catania: Società Editrice Siciliana, 1927.

De Grand, Alexander. "Giuseppe Bottai e il fallimento del fascismo revisionista." *Storia contemporanea* 6 (December 1975): 697–731.

————. "Women under Italian Fascism." *Historical Journal* 19 (1976): 947–68.

De Grazia, Victoria. *The Culture of Consent*. Cambridge: Cambridge University Press, 1981.

De Lazzari, Primo. *Storia del Fronte della gioventù nella resistenza*. Rome: Editori Riuniti, 1972.

Del Buono, Oreste, ed. *Eia, eia, eia, Alalà!* Milan: Feltrinelli, 1971.

Del Giudice, Riccardo. *La Carta della scuola*. Rome, 1942.

――――. Delle Piane, Mario. "Alla ricerca di un Italia civile." *Il Ponte* 12 (June 1956): 975–87.

Delzell, Charles F. *Mediterranean Fascism, 1919–1945*. New York: Harper & Row, 1970.

――――. *Mussolini's Enemies: The Italian Anti-Fascist Resistance*. Princeton, N.J.: Princeton University Press, 1961.

De Masi, Domenico. *Libro e moschetto: Come il fascismo educava alla violenza*. Rome: La Nuova Frontiera, 1972.

De Negri, Felicita. "Agitazioni e movimenti studenteschi nel primo dopoguerra in Italia." *Studi storici* 16 (July–September 1975): 733–63.

De Vecchi di Val Cismon, Cesare Maria. *Bonifica fascista della cultura*. Verona: Mondadori, 1937.

――――. *Educazione nazionale*. Rome: Tipografia Italo-Orientale della Badia Greca, 1935.

De Vito, Pier Vincenzo. *Fascismo, antifascismo, e resistenza*. Udine: Arti Grafiche Friulane, 1973.

Dinale, Ottavio. *Quarant'anni di colloqui . . . con lui*. Milan: Editrice Ciarrocca, 1962.

Dominici, Stefania. "La 'Pagina dei giovani' dell' 'Assalto' (1926–1928)." In *Cattolici e fascisti in Umbria (1922–1945)*, edited by Alberto Monticone, pp. 297–311. Bologna: Il Mulino, 1978.

Elmo, Luciano. *La condizione giuridica degli ebrei in Italia*. Milan: Baldini & Castoldi, 1939.

Ente Italiano Audizioni Radiofoniche. *L'attività dell'Eiar nell'esercizio 1939 XVII–XVIII*. Turin: Società Editrice Torinese, 1940.

――――. *EIAR anno XVII*. Turin: Società Editrice Torinese, 1938.

Fabbri, A. Mario. *Giovinezza, giovinezza. . . .* Milan: Mondadori, 1964.

Fabbri, Domenico. "Gruppi fascisti universitari." In Partito Nazionale Fascista, *Panorami di realizzazioni del fascismo*, vol. 3, *Dai fasci al Partito nazionale fascista*, pp. 441–45. Rome, n.d.

Fabrizio, Felice. *Sport e fascismo: La politica sportiva del regime, 1924–1936*. Rimini: Guaraldi, 1976.

Facchini, Eugenio. "Parlar chiaro." *Architrave*, 1 April 1941.

Fancello, Francesco. "Un'azione fallita di Giustizia e Libertà." In *Trent'anni di storia italiana, 1915–1945*, edited by Franco Antonicelli, pp. 177–78. Turin: Einaudi, 1961.

Fascismo e antifascismo: Lezioni e testimonianze. 2 vols. Milan: Feltrinelli, 1962.

Federazione Giovanile Ebraica d'Italia. *Gli ebrei in Italia durante il fascismo*. Turin, 1961.

Feliciani, Fernando. "Collegi della G.I.L." In Partito Nazionale Fascista, *Panorami di realizzazioni del fascismo*, vol. 3, *Dai fasci al Partito nazionale fascista*, pp. 435–38. Rome, n.d.

Fermi, Laura. *Mussolini*. Chicago: University of Chicago Press, 1961.

Ferrari, Francesco Luigi. *L'Azione cattolica e il regime*. Florence: Parenti, 1957.

Ferrari, Santo. *L'Italia fascista*. Turin: Libraria Italiana, 1942.

Ferrarotto, Marinella. *L'Accademia d'Italia: Intellettuali e potere durante il fascismo*. Naples: Liguori, 1977.

Ferretti, Giovanni. "Clima scolastico." *Il Ponte* 8 (October 1952): 1439–43.

Ferretti, Lando. "Il fascismo e l'educazione sportiva della nazione." In *La civiltà fascista*, edited by Giuseppe Luigi Pomba, pp. 609–13. Turin: Editrice Torinese, 1928.

Ferri, Franco, ed. *Lo Stato operaio, 1927–1939*. 2 vols. Rome: Editori Riuniti, 1964.

Finer, Herman. *Mussolini's Italy*. New York: Henry Holt & Co., 1935.

Flora, Francesco. *Appello al Re*. Bologna: Edizioni Bologna, 1965.

————. *Stampa dell' era fascista: Note di servizio*. Rome: Mondadori, 1945.

Folin, Alberto, and Quaranta, Mario, eds. *Le riviste giovanili del periodo fascista*. Treviso: Canova, 1977.

Foresti, Fabio. "Proposte interpretive e di ricerca su lingua e fascismo: la 'politica linguistica.' " In *La lingua italiana e il fascismo*, edited by Erasmo Leso, Michele A. Cortelazzo, Ivano Paccagnella, and Fabio Foresti, pp. 111–33. Bologna: Consorzio Provinciale Pubblica Lettura, 1978.

Forges Davanzati, Roberto. *Il Balilla Vittorio*. Rome: Libreria dello Stato, 1930.

Fornaca, Remo. "Scuola e politica nell'Italia liberale." In *Scuola e politica dall' Unità ad oggi*, edited by Guido Quazza, pp. 31–76. Turin: Edizioni Stampatori, 1977.

Fornari, Harry. *Mussolini's Gadfly Roberto Farinacci*. Nashville, Tenn.: Vanderbilt University Press, 1971.

Franchi, Paolo. *Nuove generazioni democrazia socialismo*. Rome: Editori Riuniti, 1977.

Friends of Italian Freedom. "The Case of Vinciguerra and Rendi." *Italy To-Day* 2 (May 1931).

————. "A Controversy Concerning the Oath of the University Professors." *Italy To-Day* 3 (March–April 1932).

————. "Lauro De Bosis." *Italy To-Day* 2 (November–December 1931).

————. "The Oath of the University Professors." *Italy To-Day* 3 (February 1932).

Gaiba, Vera Cottarelli, and Oddi, Nerina. *Il libro della prima classe*. Rome: Libreria dello Stato, 1942.

————. *Sillabario: Il libro della prima classe*. Rome: Ministero della Pubblica Istruzione, 1944.

Galante Garrone, Alessandro. "L'aedo senza fili." *Il Ponte* 8 (October 1952): 1401–24.

Galli, Giorgio. *Storia della D.C.* Rome: Laterza, 1978.

Galli, Giovanni. *Avanguardismo rivoluzionario*. Rome: Edizioni Arte della Stampa, 1934.

Gambetti, Fidia. *Gli anni che scottano*. Milan: U. Mursia, 1967.

————. *Inchiesta sul fascismo, 1919–1945*. Milan: Mastellone, 1953.

————. *Né vivi né morti*. Milan: U. Mursia, 1972.

Gardini, Nino. "Il coraggio della verità." *Architrave*, 31 July 1942.

Garin, Eugenio. "Eugenio Curiel nella storia dell'antifascismo." *Studi storici* 6 (January–March 1965): 3–24.

_____. *Intellettuali italiani del XX secolo*. Rome: Editori Riuniti, 1974.

Garofalo, Anna. "Veleno sui banchi di scuola." *Il Ponte* 8 (October 1952): 1430–38.

Garosci, Aldo. "F. De Rosa, R. Giua e C. Rosselli." In *Trent'anni di storia italiana, 1915–1945*, edited by Franco Antonicelli, pp. 247–53. Turin: Einaudi, 1961.

_____. "La ricomposizione del partito socialista." *Storia e politica* 14 (1955): 230–36.

_____. *Storia dei fuorusciti*. Bari: Laterza, 1953.

_____. *Vita di Carlo Rosselli*. 2 vols. Florence: Vallecchi, 1973.

Gaslini, Pier Franco. "La cultura in funzione politica." *Gerarchia* 14 (September 1934): 772–74.

Gavagnin, Armando. *Vent'anni di resistenza al fascismo*. Turin: Einaudi, 1957.

Gentile, Emilio. *Le origini dell'ideologia fascista (1918–1925)*. Rome: Laterza, 1975.

Gentile, Giovanni. "La Carta della scuola." *Corriere della sera*, 22 March 1940.

_____. *Che cosa è il fascismo?* Florence: Vallecchi, 1925.

_____. *Il fascismo al governo della scuola*. Palermo: Sandron, 1924.

_____. *Fascismo e cultura*. Milan: Treves, 1928.

_____. *Guerra e fede*. Naples: Riccardo Ricciardi, 1919.

_____. *La nuova scuola media*. Florence: Vallecchi, 1925.

_____. *Origini e dottrina del fascismo*. Rome: Istituto Nazionale Fascista di Cultura, 1929.

_____. *Il problema scolastico del dopoguerra*. Naples: Riccardo Ricciardi, 1919.

_____. *I problemi attuali della politica scolastica*. Rome: Tipografia del Senato, 1930.

_____. *La riforma dell'educazione*. Bari: Laterza, 1920.

_____. *Sommario di pedagogia come scienza filosofica*. Bari: Laterza, 1925.

Gentili, Rino. *Giuseppe Bottai e la riforma fascista della scuola*. Florence: La Nuova Italia, 1979.

Germani, Gino. "La socializzazione politica dei giovani nei regimi fascisti: Italia e Spagna." *Quaderni di sociologia* 18 (January–June 1969): 11–58.

Germino, Dante L. *The Italian Fascist Party in Power*. Minneapolis: University of Minnesota Press, 1959.

Giani, Nicolò. "Perche siamo dei mistici." *Gerarchia* 19 (February 1940): 113–14.

Giovenale, Bernardo. "Una fondamentale iniziativa." *Critica fascista*, 15 February 1942.

_____. "La GIL: Compiti e problemi." *Critica fascista*, 15 October 1937.

Giuliano, Balbino. "L'éducation nationale et l'Oeuvre Nationale Balilla." In *L'Etat Mussolinien*, edited by Tomaso Sillani, pp. 172–83. Paris: Librarie Plon, 1931.

Giuntella, Maria Cristina. "Autonomia e autogoverno nell'opposizione anti-fascista alla riforma Gentile." In *L'opera e l'eredità di Carlo Cattaneo*, edited by Carlo G. Lacaita, 2:239–52. Bologna: Il Mulino, 1976.

————. "Circoli cattolici e organizzazioni giovanili fasciste in Umbria." In *Cattolici e fascisti in Umbria (1922–1945)*, edited by Alberto Monticone, pp. 31–92. Bologna: Il Mulino, 1978.

————. "La facoltà fascista di Scienze Politiche di Perugia e la formazione della classe dirigente fascista." In *Politica e società in Italia dal fascismo alla Resistenza*, edited by Giacomina Nenci, pp. 293–317. Bologna: Il Mulino, 1978.

————. "I fatti del 1931 e la formazione della 'seconda generazione.' " In *I cattolici tra fascismo e democrazia*, edited by Pietro Scoppola and Francesco Traniello, pp. 183–233. Bologna: Il Mulino, 1975.

————. "I gruppi universitari fascisti nel primo decennio del regime." *Il movimento di liberazione in Italia* 24 (April–June 1972): 3–39.

————. "L'organizzazione universitaria fascista e la federazione universitaria cattolica in una relazione del segretario del Guf di Viterbo." *Rivista di storia della chiesa in Italia* 26 (1972): 130–39.

Giustizia e libertà nella lotta antifascista: Attualità dei fratelli Rosselli a quaranta anni dal loro sacrificio. Florence: La Nuova Italia, 1978.

Goad, Harold, and Catalano, Michele. *Education in Italy*. Rome: Laboremus, 1939.

Gramsci, Antonio. *Gli intellettuali e l'organizzazione della cultura*. Turin: Einaudi, 1949.

Granzotto, Gianni. "Classe dirigente." *Critica fascista*, 15 May 1935.

————. "La formazione di una classe dirigente." *Critica fascista*, 15 May 1937.

Gravelli, Asvero. *Ai balilla delle nuove generazioni*. Milan: Alba, 1927.

————. "Avanguardismo giovanile fascista." In Partito Nazionale Fascista, *Panorami di realizzazioni del fascismo*, vol. 3, *Dai fasci al Partito nazionale fascista*, pp. 265–72. Rome, n.d.

————. *Uno e molti*. Rome: Nuova Europa, 1938.

Gregor, A. James. *Italian Fascism and Developmental Dictatorship*. Princeton, N.J.: Princeton University Press, 1979.

Guaitini, Grazietta, and Seppilli, Tullio. "L'organizzazione del consenso nel regime fascista: Quadro generale." In *Politica e società in Italia dal fascismo alla Resistenza*, edited by Giacomina Nenci, pp. 145–82. Bologna: Il Mulino, 1978.

Guasco, Maurilio. *Fascisti e cattolici in una città rossa: I cattolici alessandrini di fronte al fascismo, 1919–1939*. Milan: Franco Angeli, 1978.

Guerri, Giordano Bruno. *Galeazzo Ciano: Una Vita, 1903–1944*. Milan: Valentino Bompiani, 1979.

————. *Giuseppe Bottai: Un fascista critico*. Milan: Feltrinelli, 1976.

————, ed. *Rapporto al duce*. Milan: Bompiani, 1978.

Guizzardi, Gianni. "Dalla 'ragione' alla 'fede.' " *Gerarchia* 19 (April 1940): 195–98.

————. "Fede in Mussolini." *Architrave*, 1 April 1941.

————. "Funzione della gioventù universitaria e propaganda operaia." *Critica fascista*, 15 December 1939.

Guzzetti, G. B. *Il movimento cattolico italiano dall'unità ad oggi*. Naples: Edizioni Dehoniane, 1980.

Halperin, S. William. *The Separation of Church and State in Italian Thought from Cavour to Mussolini*. Chicago: University of Chicago Press, 1937.

Hamilton, Alastair. *The Appeal of Fascism: A Study of Intellectuals and Fascism, 1919–1945*. London: Anthony Blond, 1971.

Hamilton, Cicely. *Modern Italy as Seen by an Englishwoman*. London: J. M. Dent & Sons, 1932.

"Hanno assassinato Eugenio Curiel." *L'Unità*, 20 March 1945.

Harris, H. S. *The Social Philosophy of Giovanni Gentile*. Urbana: University of Illinois Press, 1966.

Hibbert, Christopher. *Benito Mussolini*. London: Longmans, 1962.

Hughes, H. Stuart. *Consciousness and Society*. New York: Random House, Vintage Books, 1958.

———. *The United States and Italy*. Cambridge: Harvard University Press, 1965.

Hughes, Serge. *The Fall and Rise of Modern Italy*. New York: Macmillan, 1967.

Husslein, Joseph. *Social Wellsprings*. Vol. 2, *Eighteen Encyclicals of Social Reconstruction by Pope Pius XI*. Milwaukee: Bruce Publishing, 1942.

Isenghi, Mario. *L'educazione dell'Italiano: Il fascismo e l'organizzazione della cultura*. Bologna: Cappelli, 1979.

Italy. Istituto Centrale di Statistica. *Annuario statistico italiano*. Rome, 1933–43.

———. *Compendio statistico*. Rome, 1930–42.

———. *VIII Censimento generale della popolazione 21 Aprile 1936–XIV*. Rome, 1938.

———. *VII Censimento della popolazione 21 Aprile 1931–IX*. Rome, 1933.

———. *Sommario di statistiche storiche italiane, 1861–1955*. Rome, 1958.

Italy. Ministero dell'Educazione Nazionale. *Annuario 1935*. Rome: Provveditorato Generale dello Stato, 1936.

———. *Dalla riforma Gentile alla Carta della Scuola*. Rome, 1941.

———. *Opera Nazionale Balilla per l'assistenza e l'educazione fisica e morale della gioventù*. Rome, 1932.

———. *Ufficio per la radiofonia scolastica: Relazione finale per l'anno XVIII*. Rome, 1940.

Italy. Parlamento. Camera dei Deputati. *Atti Parlamentari: Discussioni Legislatura XXVI, 1921–1923*. 12 vols. Rome, 1922–23.

———. *Atti Parlamentari: Discussioni Legislatura XXVII, 1924–1929*. 9 vols. Rome, 1929.

———. *Atti Parlamentari: Discussioni Legislatura XXVIII, 1929–1934*. 8 vols. Rome, 1934.

———. *Atti Parlamentari: Discussioni Legislatura XXIX, 1934–1937*. 4 vols. Rome, 1937.

———. *La legislazione fascista, 1922–1928*. 2 vols. Rome, 1929.

———. *La legislazione fascista, 1929–1934*. 2 vols. Rome, 1935.

Italy. Parlamento. Senato. *Atti Parlamentari: Discussioni Legislatura XXVI,*

1921–1923. 5 vols. Rome, 1923.

———. *Atti Parlamentari: Discussioni Legislatura XXVII, 1924–1929*. 10 vols. Rome, 1929.

———. *Atti Parlamentari: Discussioni Legislatura XXVIII, 1929–1934*. 6 vols. Rome, 1934.

Italy. Parlamento. Senato del Regno. Camera dei Deputati. *Bollettino Parlamentare*. Rome, 1927–38.

Jacobitti, Edmund E. "Hegemony before Gramsci: The Case of Benedetto Croce." *Journal of Modern History* 52 (March 1980): 66–84.

Jannelli Caravella, Rosa. *Considerazioni sull'educazione fascista nella scuola elementare*. Trani, 1938.

Jemolo, Arturo Carlo. *Chiesa e stato in Italia negli ultimi cento anni*. Turin: Einaudi, 1948. Translated by David Moore, under the title *Church and State in Italy, 1850–1950*. Oxford: Basil Blackwell, 1960.

Joll, James. *Three Intellectuals in Politics*. New York: Harper & Row, 1960.

Kandel, I. L., ed. *Educational Yearbook of the International Institute of Teachers College, Columbia University*. New York: Teachers College, Columbia University, 1924, 1929–30, 1932, 1935, 1937, 1941, 1944.

Keene, Frances, ed. *Neither Liberty nor Bread*. New York: Harper & Bros., 1940.

Kirkpatrick, Ivone. *Mussolini: A Study in Power*. New York: Hawthorn Books, 1964.

Kubelik. "Un giornale universitario del deprecato ventennio." *La nuova Sardegna* 62 (2 March 1952): 3.

Lajolo, Davide. *Classe 1912*. Rome: Edizioni di Cultura Sociale, 1953.

———. *Il voltagabbana*. Milan: Il Saggiatore, 1963.

Lami, Cesare. "Il circolo della FUCI di Perugia." In *Cattolici e fascisti in Umbria (1922–1945)*, edited by Alberto Monticone, pp. 429–34. Bologna: Il Mulino, 1978.

Lasswell, Harold D., and Sereno, Renato. "Governmental and Party Leaders in Fascist Italy." *American Political Science Review* 31 (October 1931): 914–29.

Lazzari, Giovanni. *I Littoriali della cultura e dell'arte: Intellettuali e potere durante il fascismo*. Naples: Liguori, 1979.

Le Bon, Gustave. *The Crowd: A Study of the Popular Mind*. London: T. Fisher Unwin, 1910.

Ledeen, Michael A. "Italian Fascism and Youth." *Journal of Contemporary History* 4 (July 1969): 137–55.

———. "The Radio in Fascist Italy." *Journal of European Studies* 2 (June 1972): 127–54.

———. *Universal Fascism: The Theory and Practice of the Fascist International, 1928–1936*. New York: Howard Fertig, 1972.

Leeds, Christopher. *Italy under Mussolini*. London: Wayland, 1972.

Leprohon, Pierre. *The Italian Cinema*. New York: Praeger Publishers, 1972.

Leso, Erasmo; Cortelazzo, Michele A.; Paccagnella, Ivano; and Foresti, Fabio. *La lingua italiana e il fascismo*. Bologna: Consorzio Provinciale Pubblica Lettura, 1978.

Leto, Guido. *OVRA: Fascismo, antifascismo*. Bologna: Cappelli, 1951.

318

Letture per la quinta classe dei centri urbani e rurali. Rome: Ministero della Pubblica Istruzione, 1944.

Letture per la terza classe elementare. Rome: Ministero della Pubblica Istruzione, 1944.

Levi, Carlo. "Lo snobismo del conformismo." *Il Ponte* 8 (October 1952): 1476–80.

Levi, Primo. "Deportazione e sterminio di ebrei." In *Storia dell'antifascismo italiano*, edited by Luigi Arbizzani and Alberto Caltabiano, 1:168–75. Rome: Editori Riuniti, 1964.

———. *Survival in Auschwitz: The Nazi Assault on Humanity.* New York: Collier, n.d.

Il libro della quarta classe elementare: Aritmetica, geografia, scienze. Rome: Libreria dello Stato, 1942.

Il libro della quarta classe elementare: Religione, grammatica, storia. Rome: Libreria dello Stato, 1942. New ed. Rome: Società Editrice Dante Alighieri, 1944.

Il libro della quinta classe elementare: Aritmetica, geografia, scienze. Rome: Libreria dello Stato, 1942. New ed. Rome: Società Editrice Dante Alighieri, 1944.

Il libro della quinta classe elementare: Religione, grammatica, storia. Rome: Libreria dello Stato, 1941. New ed. Rome: Società Editrice Dante Alighieri, 1944.

Il libro della terza classe: Religione, grammatica, storia, geografia, aritmetica. Rome: Libreria dello Stato, 1942.

Libro sussidario della quarta classe elementare: Aritmetica, geografia, scienze. Palermo, 1944.

"Littoriali anno XVI." *Critica fascista*, 1 May 1938.

"Littoriali dell'anno XVII." *Critica fascista*, 15 April 1939.

Lombrassa, Giuseppe. "L'indifferenza male di moda." *Critica fascista*, 15 January 1930.

———. "Prima studiare, poi discutere." *Critica fascista*, 15 February 1931.

Longanesi, Leo. *In piedi e seduti (1919–1943).* Milan: Longanesi, 1948.

Longo, G. "Le organizzazioni giovanili e l'ordinamento sindacale." *Critica fascista*, 1 June 1937.

———. "Perfezionare i Littoriali." *Critica fascista*, 15 April 1939.

Longo, Luigi. "La battaglia delle idee: L'insegnamento di Curiel." *Rinascita* 12 (July–August 1955): 514–16.

———. "La lotta per la conquista della gioventù." In *Lo Stato operaio, 1927–1939*, edited by Franco Ferri, 1:88–98. Rome: Editori Riuniti, 1964.

Ludwig, Emilio. *Colloqui con Mussolini.* Verona: Mondadori, 1932.

Lupi, Dario. *La riforma Gentile e la nuova anima della scuola.* Milan: Mondadori, 1924.

Luti, Giorgio. *Cronache letterarie tra le due guerre, 1920–1940.* Bari: Laterza, 1966.

Lyttelton, Adrian. "Fascism in Italy: The Second Wave." *Journal of Contemporary History* 1 (1966): 75–100.

———. *The Seizure of Power: Fascism in Italy, 1919–1929.* New York:

Charles Scribner's Sons, 1973.

Macciocchi, Maria Antonietta. *La donna "nera": "Consenso" femminile e fascismo*. Milan: Feltrinelli, 1976.

Mack Smith, Denis. *Mussolini*. New York: Alfred A. Knopf, 1982.

———. "Mussolini, Artist in Propaganda: The Downfall of Fascism." *History Today* 9 (April 1959): 223–32.

———. *Mussolini's Roman Empire*. New York: Viking Press, 1976.

Magnani, Valdo, and Cucchi, Aldo. *Crisi di una generazione*. Florence: La Nuova Italia, 1952.

Magri, Francesco. *L'Azione cattolica in Italia*. Vol. 1, *1775–1939*. Milan: Editrice La Fiaccola, 1953.

Malfi, Erasmo. *Scuola e G.I.L.* Rome: Coppitelli & Palazzotti, 1939.

Manacorda, Giuliano. *Letteratura e cultura del periodo fascista*. Milan: Principato Editore, 1974.

Mangoni, Luisa. *L'interventismo della cultura: Intellettuali e riviste del fascismo*. Rome: Laterza, 1974.

Marchello, Giuseppe. *La morale eroica del fascismo*. Turin: Paravia, 1934.

Marchesini, Daniele. "Un episodio della politica culturale del regime: la scuola di mistica fascista." *Rivista di storia contemporanea* 1 (January 1974): 90–122.

———. *La scuola dei gerarchi: Mistica fascista: storia, problemi, istituzioni*. Milan: Feltrinelli, 1976.

Marciano, Luigi. *Il concetto fascista dello Stato e l'educazione*. Teramo: Editrice La Fiorita, 1933.

Margiotta Broglio, Francesco. *Italia e Santa Sede dalla grande guerra alla conciliazione*. Bari: Laterza, 1966.

Marinetti, F. T. *Futurismo e fascismo*. Foligno: Franco Campitelli, 1924.

Marpicati, Arturo. "Azione educativa dello Stato fascista." *Il Popolo d'Italia*, 28 October 1932.

Marraro, Howard R. *Nationalism in Italian Education*. New York: Italian Digest and News Service, 1927.

———. *The New Education in Italy*. New York: S. F. Vanni, 1936.

Martini, Angelo. *Studi sulla questione romana e la conciliazione*. Rome: Edizioni Cinque Lune, 1963.

Marziali, G. B. *I giovani di Mussolini*. Palermo: Trimarchi, 1935.

Marzolo, Renato. *VIII Leva fascista: Opera Balilla*. Milan: Pizzi & Pizio, 1934.

———. *L'Opera Balilla e la leva fascista*. Rome: Reale Accademia Nazionale dei Lincei, 1937.

———. *The Youth Movement in Italy*. Rome: Novissima, 1939.

Matteini, Claudio. *Ordini alla stampa*. Rome: Editrice Polilibraria Italiana, 1945.

Matthews, Herbert L. *The Fruits of Fascism*. New York: Harcourt, Brace, & Co., 1943.

Mazzatosta, Teresa Maria. *Il regime fascista tra educazione e propaganda, 1935–1943*. Bologna: Cappelli, 1978.

Mazzetti, Roberto. *Il lavoro e la scuola*. Modena: Società Tipografia Modenese, 1939.

Megaro, Gaudens. *Mussolini in the Making*. Boston: Houghton Mifflin Co., 1938.

Meldini, Piero, ed. *Reazionaria: Antologia della cultura di destra in Italia, 1900–1973*. Florence: Guaraldi, 1973.

———. *Sposa e madre esemplare*. Rimini: Guaraldi, 1975.

Meletti, Vincenzo. *Il libro fascista del Balilla*. Florence: La Nuova Italia, 1936.

———. *Il libro fascista della Piccola Italiana*. Florence: La Nuova Italia, n.d.

Melis Bassu, Giuseppe. "Il fascismo come feticcio." *Ichnusa* 56 (1964): 109–32.

———. "I giovani vogliono restare soli?" *La nuova Sardegna*, 20 April 1951.

———. "*Intervento* giornale del ventennio." *La nuova Sardegna*, 9 March 1952.

———. "Natale 1940." *La nuova Sardegna*, 22 December 1960.

———. Personal correspondence. Sassari, Sardinia, 5 December 1975.

Melograni, Piero. "The Cult of the Duce in Mussolini's Italy." *Journal of Contemporary History* 11 (1976): 221–37.

Merli, Stefano, ed. *Documenti inediti dell'archivio Angelo Tasca*. Milan: Istituto Giangiacomo Feltrinelli, 1963.

Mezzasoma, Fernando. "Il centro di preparazione politica per i giovani." *Gerarchia* 19 (January 1940): 3–5.

———. *Essenza dei GUF*. Genoa: S. A. D'Arte Poligrafiche, 1937.

Miccoli, Giovanni. "La chiesa e il fascismo." In *Fascismo e società italiana*, edited by Guido Quazza, Valerio Castronovo, Giorgio Rochat, Guido Neppi Modona, Giovanni Miccoli, and Norberto Bobbio, pp. 183–208. Turin: Einaudi, 1973.

Michaelis, Meir. *Mussolini and the Jews*. Oxford: Clarendon Press, 1978.

Mieli, Renato. "Eugenio Curiel." *Quaderni di Rinascita: Trenta anni di vita e lotta del P.C.I.* 2 (n.d.): 187–88.

———. "Eugenio Curiel puo dire che sono i comunisti." *L'Unità*, 23 February 1946.

Mila, Massimo. "Attività clandestina di Giustizia e Libertà." In *Trent'anni di storia italiana, 1915–1945*, edited by Franco Antonicelli, pp. 203–6. Turin: Einaudi, 1961.

Miller, E. A. "Il Fascismo, Italian Education, and the Church." *School Review* 38 (September 1930): 510–24.

Minio-Paluello, Luigi. *Education in Fascist Italy*. London: Oxford University Press, 1946.

Modica, Enzo. "Curiel e la prospettiva unitaria del 'partito nuovo.'" *Critica marxista* 7 (November–December 1969): 159–72.

———. "Nella vita e nell'azione di Curiel le esperienze di una generazione." *L'Unità*, 20 February 1965.

Monelli, Paolo. *Mussolini piccolo borghese*. Milan: Garzanti, 1966.

Montalto, Domenico. "L'avvenire." *Critica fascista*, 15 February 1930.

Monteleone, Franco. *La radio italiana nel periodo fascista: Studio e documenti, 1922–1945*. Venice: Marsilio, 1976.

Montgomery, Roselle Mercier. "Mussolini, the Idol of Italy." *Current History* 24 (August 1926): 740–43.

Monticone, Alberto, ed. *Cattolici e fascisti in Umbria (1922–1945)*. Bologna: Il Mulino, 1978.

———. *Il fascismo al microfono: Radio e politica in Italia (1924–1945)*. Rome: Studium, 1978.

Morandi, M. "Attuazione del servizio del lavoro." *Critica fascista*, 15 June 1942.

Moro, Renato. "Afascismo e antifascismo nei movimenti intellettuali di Azione Cattolica dopo il '31." *Storia contemporanea* 6 (December 1975): 733–99.

———. "Appunti sulla cultura religiosa nella FUCI e nel Movimenti Laureati degli anni '30." In *Cattolici e fascisti in Umbria (1922–1945)*, edited by Alberto Monticone, pp. 93–103. Bologna: Il Mulino, 1978.

Mosse, George L. *The Nationalization of the Masses*. New York: Howard Fertig, 1975.

Mughini, Giampiero. "Venne un ordine: uccidete il filosofo." *Panorama*, 18 May 1981.

Mussolini, Arnaldo. *Ammonimenti ai giovani e al popolo*. Rome: Libreria del Littorio, 1931.

———. *Coscienza e dovere*. Rome: Gioventù Fascista, 1932.

Mussolini, Benito. *Gli accordi del Laterano*. Rome: Libreria del Littorio, 1929.

———. *Diuturna: Scritti scelti ed annotati per la gioventù*. Milan: Alpes, 1929.

———. *Fascism: Doctrine and Institutions*. Rome: Ardita, 1935.

———. *My Autobiography*. London: Paternoster, 1928.

———. *Opera omnia*. Edited by Edoardo Susmel and Duilio Susmel. 36 vols. Florence: La Fenice, 1954–63.

———. "The Political and Social Doctrine of Fascism." *International Conciliation* 306 (January 1935): 5–17.

Nasti, Agostino. "Avvenimenti e idee." *Critica fascista*, 1 February 1931.

———. "I giovani e il regime." *Critica fascista*, 1 August 1933.

———. "Giovani, meno giovani, giovanissimi." *Critica fascista*, 15 December 1930.

———. "Orientamenti dei giovani." *Critica fascista*, 15 April 1939.

Natale, Giuseppe; Colucci, Francesco Paolo; and Natoli, Antonino. *La scuola in Italia: Dalla legge Casati del 1859 ai decreti delegati*. Milan: Gabriele Mazzotta Editore, 1975.

National Catholic Welfare Conference. *Treaty and Concordat between the Holy See and Italy: Official Documents*. Washington, D.C., 1929.

Natta, Alessandro. "Una scuola di antifascismo." *Incontri oggi* (February 1955): 11–16.

Negarville, Celeste. "Per un movimento giovanile italiano." In *Lo Stato operaio, 1927–1939*, edited by Franco Ferri, 2:468–75. Rome: Editori Riuniti, 1964. Originally published in *Lo Stato operaio*, October 1936, pp. 687–93.

Negro, Piero. *Vola, Balilla!* Turin: Paravia, 1928.

Nello, Paolo. *L'avanguardismo giovanile alle origini del fascismo.* Rome: Laterza, 1978.

————. "Mussolini e Bottai: Due modi diversi di concepire l'educazione fascista della gioventù." *Storia contemporanea* 8 (June 1977): 335–66.

Nenci, Giacomina, ed. *Politica e società in Italia dal fascismo alla Resistenza.* Bologna: Il Mulino, 1978.

Nolte, Ernst. *Three Faces of Fascism.* New York: Holt, Rinehart, & Winston, 1966.

Nozzoli, Guido. *I ras del regime.* Milan: Bompiani, 1972.

O'Brien, Albert C. "Italian Youth in Conflict: Catholic Action and Fascist Italy, 1929–1931." *Catholic Historical Review* 68 (October 1982): 625–35.

Olivero, Giuseppe. "L'Azione cattolica e il fascismo." In *Trent'anni di storia italiana, 1915–1945,* edited by Franco Antonicelli, pp. 178–81. Turin: Einaudi, 1961.

Olschki, Marcella. "Ricordi di scuola." *Il Ponte* 8 (October 1952): 1492–99.

Orano, Paolo. *Mussolini al fronte della storia.* Rome: Pinciana, 1941.

————. *Mussolini da vicino.* Rome: Pinciana, 1928.

————. *Mussolini fondatore dell'impero.* Rome: Pinciana, 1936.

Ostenc, Michel. *L'éducation en Italie pendant le fascisme.* Paris: Publications de la Sorbonne, 1980.

————. "Una tappa della fascistizzazione: La scuola e la politica dal 1925 al 1928." *Storia contemporanea* 4 (September 1973): 481–505.

Paccagnella, Ivano. "Stampa di fronda: 'Il Bò' tra Guf e Curiel." In *La lingua italiana e il fascismo,* edited by Erasmo Leso, Michele A. Cortelazzo, Ivano Paccagnella, and Fabio Foresti, pp. 83–110. Bologna: Consorzio Provinciale Pubblica Lettura, 1978.

Padellaro, Nazareno. *Fascismo educatore.* Rome: Cremonese Libraio Editore, 1938.

Pajetta, Giancarlo. "Carceri fasciste: Scuola di antifascismo." In *Trent'anni di storia italiana, 1915–1945,* edited by Franco Antonicelli, pp. 206–8. Turin: Einaudi, 1961.

Palla, Marco. *Firenze nel regime fascista (1929–1934).* Turin: Leo S. Olschki, 1978.

Pallotta, Guido. "Questo è il signore 'travestito' da fascista." *Vent'anni,* 15 February 1941.

Panzanelli, Marino. "L'attività politica di Eugenio Curiel (1932–1943)." *Storia contemporanea* 10 (April 1979): 253–96.

Papa, Antonio. "Le origini politiche della radio in Italia (1924–1926)." *Belfagor* 30 (January 1975): 45–66.

————. *Storia politica della radio in Italia.* 2 vols. Naples: Guida Editore, 1978.

Papa, Emilio R. *Storia di due manifesti: Il fascismo e la cultura italiana.* Milan: Feltrinelli, 1958.

Papini, Massimo. "La Fuci e le violenze fasciste (1921–1931)." *Civitas* 26 (June 1975): 3–23.

Pareto, Vilfredo. *The Rise and Fall of Elites.* Totowa, N.J.: Bedminister, 1968.

Partito Nazionale Fascista. *Atti del PNF*. 1932–36, 1938–40.
———. *Bollettino del Comando Generale della G.I.L.* Rome, 1937–43.
———. *Il cittadino soldato*. Rome: Libreria dello Stato, 1936.
———. *Collegio Orvieto GIL*. Rome, 1940.
———. *La cultura fascista*. Rome: Libreria dello Stato, 1936.
———. *La dottrina del fascismo*. Rome: Libreria dello Stato, 1936.
———. *La dottrina fascista per le reclute della IV Leva fascista*. Rome:
    Libreria del Littorio, 1930.
———. *L'economia fascista*. Rome: Libreria dello Stato, 1936.
———. *Foglio di disposizioni*. 1926–43.
———. *Foglio d'ordini*. 1926–43.
———. *Gioventù Italiana del Littorio*. Milan: A. Mondadori, 1942.
———. *Il Gran Consiglio nei primi dieci anni dell'era fascista*. Rome: Nuova
    Europa, 1933.
———. *I Gruppi dei fascisti universitari*. Rome: Centro Studenti Stranieri dei
    GUF, 1941.
———. *Gruppo dei fascisti universitari dell'Urbe*. Rome, 1941.
———. *L'Italia nel Mediterraneo*. Rome: Libreria dello Stato, 1936.
———. *L'ordinamento dello stato fascista*. Rome: Libreria dello Stato, 1936.
———. *Panorami di realizzazioni del fascismo*. Vol. 3, *Dai fasci al Partito
    nazionale fascista*. Rome, n.d.
———. *Il Partito nazionale fascista*. Rome: Libreria dello Stato, 1936.
———. *La politica sociale del fascismo*. Rome: Libreria dello Stato, 1936.
———. *Il primo libro del fascista*. Rome, 1940.
———. *Programma Littoriali della cultura e dell'arte*. Bologna, 1940.
———. *Regolamento del servizio sanitario dei Gruppi universitari fascisti*.
    Bologna: Il Resto del Carlino, 1940.
———. *Venti anni*. Rome, 1942.
Partito Nazionale Fascista. Centro Studenti Stranieri dei GUF. *Convegno
    universitario Italo-Nipponico: Atti del Convegno*. Rome, 1943.
Partito Nazionale Fascista. Comando federale della GIL Bologna. *Passeremo!*
    Bologna: Cooperativa Tipografia Azzoguidi, 1939.
Partito Nazionale Fascista. Direttorio Nazionale. *Littoriali femminili del lavoro
    anno XIX*. Rome, 1941.
———. *Littoriali maschili del lavoro anno XIX*. Rome, 1941.
———. *Programmi dei corsi affidati ai Fasci femminili e all'Ente opere
    assistenziali*. Rome: Arti Grafiche Fratelli Palombi, 1936.
Partito Nazionale Fascista. Fasci italiani all'estero. *I figli degli italiani al-
    l'estero in patria nell'anno XII*. Rome: Istituto Poligrafico dello Stato,
    1934.
Partito Nazionale Fascista. Federazione fascista dell'Urbe. *Libro e moschetto*.
    Rome: Libreria del Littorio, 1928.
Partito Nazionale Fascista. Gioventù Italiana del Littorio. *Accademie e collegi
    della G.I.L.: Ammissioni anno XX–XXI*. Rome: Vallecchi, 1942.
———. *Il capo centuria*. Rome: Pizzi & Pizio, 1938.
———. *Conversazioni incontri e ludi*. Rome, 1942.
———. *Gioventù sana e studiosa*. Rome: Enrico Ricci, n.d.
———. *Istruzione premilitare*. Rome: Ruggero Cecconi, 1938.

————. *Ludi Juveniles della cultura e dell'arte*. Rome: Novissima, 1941.

————. *Regolamento delle colonie estive*. Rome: Unione Editoriale d'Italia, 1938.

————. *La via da seguire*. Bolzano: 1942.

Partito Nazionale Fascista. Gruppi Universitari Fascisti. *Gruppi universitari fascisti*. Bologna: Edizioni Nuova Guardia, 1936.

————. *I Littoriali della cultura e dell'arte dell'anno XV*. Naples, 1937.

————. *Littoriali maschili e femminili del lavoro*. Rome, 1941.

————. *Vita dei GUF negli anni XVI–XVII*. Rome: Segretaria dei GUF, 1940.

Partito Nazionale Fascista. Gruppo dei fascisti universitari "Amos Maramotti" Torino. *Tre anni XIV–XV–XVI*. Turin, 1938.

Partito Nazionale Fascista. Gruppo dei Fascisti Universitari dell'Urbe. *Che cosa è il G.U.F.* Rome, 1940.

Partito Nazionale Fascista. Istituto Nazionale di Cultura Fascista. *I Littoriali dell'anno XVI*. Rome, 1938.

Partito Nazionale Fascista. Opera Nazionale Balilla. *Il capo squadra Balilla*. Rome: Bemporad, 1936.

————. *La cassa mutua assistenza "Arnaldo Mussolini" nell'anno XIV*. Rome, 1936.

————. *XI Leva fascista*. Rome, 1937.

————. *Giovinezza eroica*. Rome, 1932.

————. *L'obelisco Mussolini*. Rome, 1934.

————. *VII Leva fascista: Lista generale*. Rome, 1933.

Partito Nazionale Fascista. Scuola di Mistica Fascista "Sandro Italico Mussolini." *Corsi di dottrina del fascismo anno XX*. Milan: Officine Grafiche Littorio, 1941.

Patetta, Mario. "Lo sport elemento della politica fascista." In Partito Nazionale Fascista, Federazione Provinciale Gruppo Universitario Fascista Novarese, *Dieci conferenze*, pp. 200–214. Novara: E. Cattaneo, 1931.

Pecoraro, Paolo, ed. *Chiesa, Azione cattolica e fascismo nell' Italia settentrionale durante il pontificato di Pio XI (1922–1939)*. Milan: Università Cattolica del Sacro Cuore, 1979.

Pellizzi, Camillo. "Educazione fascista e classe politica." *Critica fascista*, 1 July 1937; 1 August 1937.

————. *Italy*. London: Longmans, Green, 1939.

————. *Il partito educatore*. Rome: Istituto Nazionale di Cultura Fascista, 1941.

————. *Una rivoluzione mancata*. Milan: Longanesi, 1949.

"Per la storia del costume fascista." *Il Ponte* 8 (October 1952): 1337–48.

Perroni, Vito. *Il Duce ai Balilla*. Rome: Libreria del Littorio, 1930.

Pesenti, Antonio. "L'avventura d'Etiopia." In *Fascismo e antifascismo: Lezioni e testimonianze*, pp. 374–80. Milan: Feltrinelli, 1962.

Petersen, Jens. "Elettorato e base sociale del fascismo negli anni venti." *Studi storici* 16 (July–September 1975): 627–69.

Petrucci, Alfredo, and Bernardini, Piero. *L'Italiano nuovo: Letture della seconda classe elementare*. Rome: Libreria dello Stato, 1938.

Piccoli, D. S. *Le organizzazioni giovanili in Italia*. Rome: Novissima, 1936.

_____. *The Youth Movement in Italy*. Rome: Novissima, 1936.

Pigliaru, Antonio. "Considerazioni sulle riviste dei GUF." *Società nuova* 3–4 (October–December 1956/January–March 1957): 68–76.

_____. "Fecero anche politica." *La nuova Sardegna*, 9 March 1952.

Pini, Giorgio. *Filo diretto con Palazzo Venezia*. Bologna: Cappelli, 1950.

_____, and Susmel, Duilio. *Mussolini: L'uomo e l'opera*. 4 vols. Florence: Le Monnier, 1953–55.

Pinti, Luigi. "La radio." In *La scuola fascista*, edited by Mario Alla and Giulio L. Argan, pp. 71–78. Tivoli: Aldo Chicca, 1938.

Pintor, Giaime. *Il sangue d'Europa, 1939–1943*. Turin: Einaudi, 1950.

Pomba, Giuseppe Luigi, ed. *La civiltà fascista*. Turin: Editrice Torinese, 1928.

Pompei, Manlio. "Educazione virile." *Critica fascista*, 15 April 1932.

_____. "L'elezionismo nella vita del partito." *Critica fascista*, 15 August 1928.

Pratesi, Luigi. *L'Italia imperiale*. Leghorn: Raffaello Giusti, 1937.

Preti, Luigi. *Giovinezza, giovinezza. . . .* Milan: Mursia, 1964.

_____. *I miti dell'impero e della razza nell'Italia degli anni '30*. Rome: Opere Nuove, 1965.

Quazza, Guido, ed. *Scuola e politica dall'Unità ad oggi*. Turin: Edizioni Stampatori, 1977.

_____; Castronovo, Valerio; Rochat, Giorgio; Neppi Modona, Guido; Miccoli, Giovanni; and Bobbio, Norberto. *Fascismo e società italiana*. Turin: Einaudi, 1973.

Reale Università di Roma. *Il lavoro produttivo nella Carta della Scuola*. Messina: Casa Editrice D'Anna, 1940.

Reineri, Mariangiola. *Cattolica e fascismo a Torino, 1925–1943*. Milan: Feltrinelli, 1978.

Renda, Umberto. *Realizzazioni del fascismo*. Turin: Paravia, 1937.

_____. "Scuola e fascismo." In *La civiltà fascista*, edited by Giuseppe Luigi Pomba, pp. 463–93. Turin: Editrice Torinese, 1928.

Rendina, Massimo. "Motivo ideale." *Architrave*, 31 January 1943.

Renzi, Renzo. "Rapporto di un ex-balilla." In *Il processo s'agapò: Dall'Arcadia a Peschiera*, edited by P. Calamandrei, R. Renzi, and G. Aristarco, pp. 99–139. Bari: Laterza, 1954.

Ricci, Berto. "Rapporti tra scuola e G.I.L." *Critica fascista*, 1 April 1939.

Ricci, Renato. "Buts et activité de l'oeuvre des Balilla." In Centre Internationale d'Etudes sur le Fascisme, *Annuaire 1929*, pp. 147–56. Lausanne, 1929.

Ricuperati, Giuseppe. "Scuola e politica nel periodo fascista." In *Scuola e politica dall'Unità ad oggi*, edited by Guido Quazza, pp. 77–110. Turin: Edizioni Stampatori, 1977.

_____. *La scuola italiana e il fascismo*. Bologna: Consorzio Provinciale Pubblica Lettura, 1977.

Rivadossi, Cesare. *La scuola del lavoro*. Vercelli: Edizioni S.A.V.I.T., 1940.

Roatta, Mario. *Otto milioni di baionette: L'esercito italiano in guerra dal 1940 al 1944*. Verona: A. Mondadori, 1946.

Roberts, David D. *The Syndicalist Tradition and Italian Fascism*. Chapel Hill:

326

Bibliography

University of North Carolina Press, 1979.

Rocca, Massimo. *Come il fascismo divenne una dittatura*. Milan: Edizioni Librarie Italiane, 1952.

Rocco, Alfredo. "The Political Doctrine of Fascism." *International Conciliation* 223 (1926): 389–448.

Rogari, Sandro. *Sante Sede e fascismo: Dall'Aventino ai Patti Lateranensi*. N.p.: Arnaldo Forni, 1977.

Rosengarten, Frank. *The Italian Anti-Fascist Press (1919–1945)*. Cleveland: Case Western Reserve University Press, 1968.

Rossi, Guido. "Fede in una libertà." *Architrave*, 30 September 1942.

Rossi, Roi. "Come si formò nei littoriali una opposizione giovanile al regime." *Incontri oggi* (January–February 1954): 24–28.

Roth, Jack J. *The Cult of Violence*. Berkeley and Los Angeles: University of California Press, 1980.

————. "The Roots of Italian Fascism: Sorel and Sorelismo." *Journal of Modern History* 39 (March 1967): 30–45.

Russo, Luigi. "I giovani nel venticinquennio fascista (1919–44)." *Belfagor* 1 (15 January 1946): 7–17.

Sacchi, Filippo. "La stampa e il cinema nel ventennio." In *Fascismo e antifascismo: Lezioni e testimonianze*, pp. 327–34. Milan: Feltrinelli, 1962.

Salomone, A. William. *Italy from the Risorgimento to Fascism*. New York: Doubleday & Co., 1970.

Salvadori, Massimo. "Il sacrificio di Lauro De Bosis." In *L'antifascismo italiano*, edited by Paolo Alatri, 2:715–25. Rome: Editori Riuniti, 1973.

Salvatorelli, Luigi; Pettazzoni, Raffaele; Barile, Paolo; Falconi, Carlo; and Borghi, Lamberto. *Stato e chiesa*. Bari: Laterza, 1957.

————, and Mira, Giovanni. *Storia d'Italia nel periodo fascista*. 2 vols. Milan: A. Mondadori, 1969.

Salvemini, Gaetano. "The Teachers' Oath in Italy." *Harvard Educational Review* 7 (October 1937): 523–37.

————. *Under the Axe of Fascism*. New York: Viking Press, 1936.

————, and La Piana, George. *What to Do with Italy*. New York: Duell, Sloan, & Pearce, 1943.

Sammartano, Nino. *La funzione della scuola media in Italia dalla Marcia su Roma*. Rome: Istituto Nazionale Fascista di Cultura, 1935.

Santarelli, Enzo. "Un fascio universitario del 1919." In Enzo Santarelli, *Fascismo e neofascismo*, pp. 93–112. Rome: Editori Riuniti, 1974.

————. *Storia del fascismo*. 3 vols. Rome: Editori Riuniti, 1973.

————. *Storia del movimento e del regime fascista*. 2 vols. Rome: Editori Riuniti, 1967.

Santoni Rugiu, Antonio. "Scuola e politica ieri e oggi." In *Scuola e politica dall'Unità ad oggi*, edited by Guido Quazza, pp. 9–29. Turin: Edizioni Stampatori, 1977.

Sarfatti, Margherita. *DUX*. Verona: Mondadori, 1926. Translated by Frederic Whyte, under the title *The Life of Benito Mussolini*. New York: Frederick A. Stokes, 1926.

Sarti, Roland, ed. *The Ax Within*. New York: New Viewpoints, 1974.

Savarese, Roberto. . . . *Domani soldati!* Rome: Carlo Colombo, 1939.

Schiavetti, Fernando. "Il fuoruscitismo." In *Fascismo e antifascismo: Lezioni e testimonianze*, pp. 363–67. Milan: Feltrinelli, 1962.

Schnapper, M. B. "Militarization in the Fascist School." *School and Society* 43 (18 January 1936): 97–99.

Schneider, Herbert W., and Clough, Shepard B. *Making Fascists*. Chicago: University of Chicago Press, 1929.

———. *Making the Fascist State*. New York: Oxford University Press, 1928.

Scoppola, Pietro. *La chiesa e il fascismo: Documenti e interpretazioni*. Bari: Laterza, 1971.

———. "La chiesa e il fascismo durante il pontificato di Pio XI." In *Il regime fascista*, edited by Alberto Aquarone and Maurizio Vernassa, pp. 195–232. Bologna: Il Mulino, 1974.

———, and Traniello, Francesco, eds. *I cattolici tra fascismo e democrazia*. Bologna: Il Mulino, 1975.

Scotti, Francesco. "La guerra di Spagna." In *Fascismo e antifascismo: Lezioni e testimonianze*, pp. 380–90. Milan: Feltrinelli, 1962.

Secchia, Pietro, ed. *Enciclopedia dell'antifascismo e della resistenza*. 2 vols. Vol. 1, *A–C*. Vol. 2, *D–G*. Milan: La Pietra, 1968, 1971.

Secreti, G. "I giovani e il partito." *Critica fascista*, 1 August 1928.

Segre, Umberto. "La scuola durante il periodo fascista." In *Fascismo e antifascismo: Lezioni e testimonianze*, 1:322–27. Milan: Feltrinelli, 1962.

Senise, Carmine. *Quando ero capo della polizia, 1940–1943: Memorie di colui che seppe tutto*. Rome: Ruffolo, 1946.

Sereni, Emilio. "Antifascismo nelle trincee." In *Trent'anni di storia italiana, 1915–1945*, edited by Franco Antonicelli, pp. 281–84. Turin: Einaudi, 1961.

Sforza, Carlo. *Contemporary Italy*. New York: E. P. Dutton & Co., 1944.

Signoretti, Alfredo. *Come diventai fascista*. Rome: Volpe, 1967.

Silva, Umberto. *Ideologia e arte del fascismo*. Milan: Gabriele Mazzotta, 1973.

Simonini, Augusto. *Il linguaggio di Mussolini*. Milan: Bompiani, 1978.

Solmi, Arrigo. "La missione della donna nell'Italia fascista." *Educazione fascista* 11 (March 1933): 193–205.

Sorel, Georges. *Reflections on Violence*. New York: Collier, 1961.

Sottochiesa, Gino. *Razza e razzismo nell'Italia fascista*. Turin: G. B. Paravia, 1939.

Sotto-Commissione dell'Educazione della Commissione Alleata in Italia. *La politica e la legislazione scolastica in Italia dal 1922 al 1943*. Rome: Garzanti, 1946.

Spano, Velio. "I nostri giovani." *L'Unità*, 1 August 1944.

Spinetti, Gastone Silvano. *Difesa di una generazione*. Rome: Edizioni Polilibraria, 1948.

———. *Vent'anni dopo: Ricominciare da zero*. Rome: Edizioni di Solidarismo, 1964.

Spriano, Paolo. *Storia del Partito comunista italiano*. Vol. 2, *Gli anni della clandestinità*. Vol. 3, *I fronti popolari, Stalin, la guerra*. Vol. 4, *La fine del fascismo: Dalla riscossa operaia alla lotta armata*. Turin: Giulio Einaudi, 1969, 1970, 1973.

Stanco, Francesco. *Epitome di cultura fascista.* Turin: Società Editrice Internazionale, 1938.

Starace, Achille. *Fasci giovanili di combattimento.* Verona: A. Mondadori, 1933.

―――. *Vademecum dello stile fascista.* Rome: Nuova Europa, 1927.

Steiner, H. Arthur. "The De Vecchi Reform of Higher Education in Italy." *Journal of Higher Education* 8 (March 1937): 140–44.

Sulis, Edgardo. *Imitazione di Mussolini.* Milan: Casa Editrice Novecentesca, 1934.

Supino, Giulio. "Gli italiani di fronte al razzismo." In *Storia dell'antifascismo italiano,* edited by Luigi Arbizzani and Alberto Caltabiano, 1:155–63. Rome: Editori Riuniti, 1964.

Sussidario della terza classe: Religione, grammatica, storia, geografia, aritmetica, geometria. Rome: Ministero della Pubblica Istruzione, 1944.

Tamaro, Attilio. *Venti anni di storia, 1922–1943.* 3 vols. Rome: Editrice Tiber, 1953.

Tannenbaum, Edward R. "Education." In *Modern Italy,* edited by Edward R. Tannenbaum and Emiliana P. Noether, pp. 231–53. New York: New York University Press, 1974.

―――. *The Fascist Experience.* New York: Basic Books, 1972.

―――. "The Goals of Italian Fascism." *American Historical Review* 74 (April 1969): 1183–1204.

―――, and Noether, Emiliana P. *Modern Italy.* New York: New York University Press, 1974.

Tasca, Angelo [A. Rossi]. *Nascita e avvento del fascismo.* 2 vols. Florence: La Nuova Italia, 1950.

―――. *The Rise of Italian Fascism, 1918–1922.* London: Methuen & Co., 1938.

Thompson, Merritt Moore. *The Educational Philosophy of Giovanni Gentile.* Los Angeles: University of Southern California Press, 1934.

Togliatti, Palmiro. "La battaglia delle idee." *Rinascita* 5 (January 1948): 37.

―――. *Discorsi agli italiani.* Rome: Società Editrice L'Unità, 1945.

―――. *Lezioni sul fascismo.* Rome: Editori Riuniti, 1974.

Tomasi, Tina. *Idealismo e fascismo nella scuola italiana.* Florence: La Nuova Italia, 1969.

―――; Genovesi, Giovanni; Trancredi Torelli, Maria Pia; Incatasciato, Benito; Ulivieri, Simonetta; and Catarsi, Enzo. *L'istruzione di base in Italia (1859–1977).* Florence: Vallecchi, 1978.

Trabalza, Ciro, and Allodoli, Ettore. *Grammatica degli Italiani.* Florence: Le Monnier, 1934.

Tramontin, Silvio. *Cattolici, popolari e fascisti nel Veneto.* Rome: Edizioni Cinque Lune, 1975.

Tranfaglia, Nicola; Murialdi, Paolo; and Legnani, Massimo. *La stampa italiana nell'età fascista.* Rome: Laterza, 1980.

Trentin, Silvio. *Dieci anni di fascismo, 1926–1936.* Rome: Editori Riuniti, 1975.

Treves, Renato. "Il fascismo e il problema delle generazioni." *Quaderni di sociologia* 8 (April–June 1964): 119–46.

Tripodi, Nino. "Centro nazionale di preparazione politica per i giovani e i corsi proviciali." In Partito Nazionale Fascista, *Panorami di realizzazioni del fascismo*, vol. 3, *Dai fasci al Partito nazionale fascista*, pp. 465–70. Rome, n.d.

———. *Italia fascista in piedi! Memorie di un littore.* Milan: Edizioni del Borghese, 1960.

Trombadori, Antonello. "Giaime Pintor e la crisi di una generazione." In *Trent'anni di storia italiana, 1915–1945*, edited by Franco Antonicelli, pp. 332–36. Turin: Einaudi, 1961.

Turati, Augusto. *Il partito e i suoi compiti.* Rome: Libreria del Littorio, 1928.

Ulivieri, Simonetta. "I maestri." In *L'istruzione di base in Italia (1859–1977)*, edited by Tina Tomasi, Giovanni Genovesi, Maria Pia Trancredi Torelli, Benito Incatasciato, Simonetta Ulivieri, and Enzo Catarsi, pp. 163–211. Florence: Vallecchi, 1978.

Valiani, Leo. "L'intervento in Spagna." In *Trent'anni di storia italiana, 1915–1945*, edited by Franco Antonicelli, pp. 213–35. Turin: Einaudi, 1961.

Valitutti, Salvatore. "Elementary Education in Italy." In *The Yearbook of Education, 1937*, pp. 790–801. London: University of London Institute of Education, 1937.

Venturi, Franco. "Il regime fascista." In *Trent'anni di storia italiana, 1915–1945*, edited by Franco Antonicelli, pp. 176–95. Turin: Einaudi, 1961.

Vettori, Giuseppe, ed. *Duce & ducetti.* Rome: Newton Compton, 1975.

Vinciguerra, Mario. "L'Alleanza nazionale e Lauro De Bosis." In *Trent'anni di storia italiana, 1915–1945*, edited by Franco Antonicelli, pp. 170–73. Turin: Einaudi, 1961.

Vita-Finzi, P. "Italian Fascism and the Intellectuals." In *The Nature of Fascism*, edited by S. J. Woolf, pp. 226–44. New York: Random House, 1968.

Vittori, Giuliano, ed. *C'era una volta il duce: Il regime in cartolina.* Rome: Savelli, 1975.

Vittorini, Elio. "Eugenio Curiel." *Mercurio* 2 (December 1945): 149–52.

———. *Il garofano rosso.* Verona: A. Mondadori, 1948. Translated by Anthony Bower, under the title *The Red Carnation.* Garden City, N.Y.: New Directions, 1952.

Volpicelli, Luigi. *Apologia della scuola media.* Rome: Istituto Nazionale di Cultura Fascista, 1941.

———. *Commento alla Carta della Scuola.* Rome: Istituto Nazionale di Cultura Fascista, 1940.

Webster, Richard A. *The Cross and the Fasces: Christian Democracy and Fascism in Italy.* Stanford, Calif.: Stanford University Press, 1960.

Widener, Alice. *Gustave Le Bon: The Man and His Works.* Indianapolis: Liberty Press, 1979.

Williams, George L. "Political Indoctrination of Secondary School Students in Fascist Italy." *School and Society* 100 (Summer 1972): 312–18.

Wiskemann, Elizabeth. *Fascism in Italy: Its Development and Influence.* London: Macmillan, 1969.

———. *The Rome-Berlin Axis.* London: Collins, 1966.

Woolf, Richard J. "Catholicism, Fascism and Italian Education from the Riforma Gentile to the Carta della Scuola 1922–1939." *History of Education Quarterly* 20 (Spring 1980): 3–26.

———. "The Makings of Christian Democracy: The Federazione Universitaria Cattolica between Church and State, 1925–1943." Ph.D. dissertation, Columbia University, 1979.

Zanetti, Adele, and Zanetti, Maria, eds. *Patria: Il libro di lettura per la terza classe dei centri urbani*. Rome: Libreria dello Stato, 1940.

Zangrandi, Ruggero. "La generazione dei Littoriali." *Il Punto* 1 (1 December 1956): 14–15.

———. "I giovani e il fascismo." In *Fascismo e antifascismo: Lezioni e testimonianze*, 1:209–16. Milan: Feltrinelli, 1962.

———. *Il lungo viaggio attraverso il fascismo: Contributo alla storia di una generazione*. Milan: Garzanti, 1971.

Zevi, Bruno. "Presentando i *Quaderni*." In *L'antifascismo italiano*, edited by Paolo Alatri, 2:967–72. Rome: Editori Riuniti, 1973.

Zincone, Vittorio. "Funzione dei Littoriali: Cinque anni di esperienze." *Critica fascista*, 1 May 1938.

187–88; and the Ethiopian war, 235–36

Natoli, Aldo, 230, 231

Nazi Germany, xix, 31, 234, 241; alliance with, 116, 168, 230, 236, 240; and Italian racial laws, 139, 140; and propaganda organizations, 159; influence on education, 166; attacks on by students, 206

Negarville, Celeste, 209, 231

Negrisoli, Bortolo, 67, 265 (n. 37)

Neo-idealism: in education, 33, 40–41, 45, 47–48, 60, 250; and fascism, 41–42; and Gentile, 44–47. *See also* Actual idealism; Ethical state; Gentile, Giovanni

"New Fascist Man," xvii, 34, 42, 46, 95, 116, 199, 246, 251

"New Imperial Climate," 143–83 passim

Nietzsche, Friedrich, 3, 17

Nitti, Fausto, 224

Non mollare, 64, 223

Nostra lotta, La, 215, 229

Nuclei Universitari Fascisti, 188

Ojetti, Ugo, 18

Olivelli, Teresio, 249

Olschki, Marcella, 162

Opera Nazionale Balilla (ONB), xviii, 38, 47, 63, 65, 75, 90, 91, 149, 152, 171, 189, 227, 237, 239, 250, 272 (n. 45); and rural schools, 55, 103–5, 148; chaplains in, 94, 137, 138, 271 (n. 20), 277 (n. 31); organization of, 94–95, 106; religious instruction in, 94, 124–25; pressure to belong, 95–96; activities for females, 96–98; and social assistance programs, 96, 102–4; and military training, 98–99; and sports training, 100–101; scholarship program, 104; conflicts over the status of, 108–9, 273 (n. 62); police reports on, 114; and Catholic Action groups, 123–25, 132; statistics on, 172–83 passim. *See also* Youth groups

Opera Universitaria, 190

Orano, Paolo, 17, 74

Ordine Nuovo, 185

Orlando, Vittorio Emanuele, 73, 265 (n. 37)

Osservatore romano, 123, 124, 130, 133, 134, 135

OVRA, 239

Pajetta, Giancarlo, 230

Pallotta, Guido, 193, 196, 210

Panunzio, Sergio, 74

Pareto, Vilfredo, 4, 6, 7, 74

Partito Comunista Italiano (PCI), 202, 204, 206, 214, 215; and *lavoro legale*, 229–30; and work among the young, 230–31, 248–49; and Spanish civil war, 239. *See also* Antifascism; Communists

Partito Nazionale Fascista (PNF), xix, 13, 14, 17, 20, 27, 31, 32, 41, 42, 43, 50, 54, 59, 66, 71, 72, 84, 264 (n. 12), 270 (n. 13); and cult of the leader, 13, 111; and education, 44; changes in leadership, 61–62; depoliticization of, 61–62, 109–11, 242; and youth groups, 87, 89, 90–91, 93–94, 106, 185–87; and the state, 90–91, 106–8, 170–72; and sports federations, 99; under Starace, 110–11; conflict with the church over education, 115, 131, 280 (n. 72); anticlericalism in, 118, 129, 134; views on Catholic Action, 130–31, 135–36, 141; Jews in, 168; on relations between youth groups and the school, 170–71; ties to the GUF, 188; and leadership schools, 192, 194; and the GUF press, 212–13; bankruptcy of, 242–46. *See also* Mussolini, Benito; Youth groups

Partito Socialista Italiano (PSI), 204, 229. *See also* Antifascism; Socialists

Partito Socialista Italiano di Unità Proletaria (PSIUP), 229